AN INTRODUCTION TO
COUNSELLING AND PSYCHOTHERAPY

Companion Website

As a purchaser of *An Introduction to Counselling and Psychotherapy* you can access a Companion Website featuring a wealth of chapter-by-chapter resources to be used alongside the book. From extended case studies through to web resources, links and PowerPoint presentations, these extra resources will help aid and enhance your learning and understanding.

Prompts for you to refer to these extra resources are indicated in the text by the icon:

When you see this icon, visit www.sagepub.co.uk/reeves to view the relevant material.

AN INTRODUCTION TO
COUNSELLING AND PSYCHOTHERAPY

FROM THEORY TO PRACTICE

ANDREW REEVES

Los Angeles | London | New Delhi
Singapore | Washington DC

Los Angeles | London | New Delhi
Singapore | Washington DC

SAGE Publications Ltd
1 Oliver's Yard
55 City Road
London EC1Y 1SP

SAGE Publications Inc.
2455 Teller Road
Thousand Oaks, California 91320

SAGE Publications India Pvt Ltd
B 1/I 1 Mohan Cooperative Industrial Area
Mathura Road
New Delhi 110 044

SAGE Publications Asia-Pacific Pte Ltd
3 Church Street
#10-04 Samsung Hub
Singapore 049483

Editor: Alice Oven
Assistant editor: Kate Wharton
Production editor: Rachel Burrows
Copyeditor: Elaine Leek
Proofreader: Anna Gilding
Indexer: David Rudeforth
Marketing manager: Tamara Navaratnam
Cover design: Lisa Harper
Typeset by: C&M Digitals (P) Ltd, Chennai, India
Printed by: MPG Books Group, Bodmin, Cornwall

Library of Congress Control Number: 2012937675

British Library Cataloguing in Publication data

A catalogue record for this book is available from
the British Library

MIX
Paper from
responsible sources
FSC® C018575

ISBN 978-0-85702-054-3
ISBN 978-0-85702-055-0 (pbk)

Contents

About the Author

Dr Andrew Reeves has worked as a counsellor and supervisor in various settings for over twenty years. Originally qualified as a social worker, he specialised in child protection and adult mental health before moving to working full-time as a counsellor at the University of Liverpool. Following the death by suicide of one of his clients early in his career, he undertook extensive research into ways in which counsellors and psychotherapists work with suicidal clients and he has written extensively about this since. His recent book with SAGE, *Counselling Suicidal Clients* (2010), has quickly become a popular title, as has *Key Issues for Counselling in Action* (second edition), which he co-edited with Professor Windy Dryden. His award-winning training DVD, *Tight Ropes and Safety Nets: Counselling Suicidal Clients* (with Jon Shears and Sue Wheeler) is now being used by many therapy training programmes throughout the UK.

His new book, *An Introduction to Counselling and Psychotherapy: From Theory to Practice* (2013) has several aims: to help provide prospective students of counselling and psychotherapy with information to support their training decisions; to help integrate theory into their early steps in working with clients on a practice placement; and to help bridge the move from qualification into practice as a therapist.

He has other new projects in the pipeline, including editing the new series Essential Issues for Counselling and Psychotherapy, in which he will be writing the new title *Working with Risk in Counselling and Psychotherapy*, as well as working with Windy Dryden on the sixth edition of the bestselling SAGE text, *The Handbook of Individual Therapy*.

Preface

The idea for this book was brought to me while I sat on a couch in a London hotel during the celebrations for the 25th Anniversary of the Counselling in Action series of books. The idea was for an introductory text for counsellors and psychotherapists, but the nature and scope of the book was for me to consider. It was an exciting opportunity but also a daunting one too: I had only to look around the room to see some of the key writers and theorists of the last two and a half decades, who had produced such beautifully written and invaluable texts. I was aware of the rich depth and breadth of textbooks available to counsellors and psychotherapists, including some seminal introductory texts, books on different aspects of practice, on theory, on ethics, on training, and so on; where on earth would I begin?

As is the case for so much of counselling and psychotherapy, I had to begin with some self-reflection and consider my role in the process. The book simply wasn't going to appear, but was rather to be shaped and crafted by me. I had to begin with where my heart is, and that is in the room with people who come for therapy. I enjoy theory but I am not a theorist; I am engaged by learning but don't work full-time as a trainer; I respect academe but am not an academic; I am fascinated by practice and I am a practitioner. That is fundamentally who I am, regardless of the other things I do; they are all informed by the work I do as a counsellor. Of the thousands of people I have worked with over the years, no single relationship has ever been the same: each person's story has always been different, and the process of therapy and the nature of our relationship has always been defined by those differences. I therefore needed to write a text that spoke of those differences and spoke of practice. So that is at the heart of this book: a book about practice, by a practitioner.

But what to include? There are many books about practice, each focusing on particular aspects or nuances and shedding their own, particular light on the detail of our work. Beginning to write this book coincided with me starting to work with a new supervision group of trainees as they began their placement. As we talked in the early group meetings of the work they were about to embark on – seeing real clients and starting to put into practice ideas, concepts and theories they had been exploring in the first stages of their training – it occurred to me that there weren't so many books that brought together all the areas of practice we were now discussing. Certainly it was possible to collect quite a few resources together and begin to create a salient whole, but there were few books that held all that information in one volume. Most striking, however, was the expression they used, and one I have heard so many times over the years, which was about linking theory to practice. This was something they were very anxious about: how would they take those important theoretical concepts and apply them in real-world settings? How would they acquire the necessary information about particular situations and circumstances to be able to think through how they might respond, or what to say, or what to write, and so on? In many ways therefore, this book is a record of those sorts of supervisory conversations that take place throughout a placement experience, and in supervisory relationships with trainees everywhere.

The nature and scope of the book began to emerge: I wanted to write a book for new practitioners, from the position of a practitioner, that incorporated all of the things I could think of that might confuse, stimulate, encourage, facilitate or hinder new trainees as they began moving into their work as therapists. I wanted to include as much as I could and resolved that everything I had ever been asked about would be addressed and discussed. I conceptualised the process of becoming a counsellor or psychotherapist as a journey, and instead of picking up the journey simply from when a trainee commences a placement, I would pick it up right at the beginning: when we start to think about the type of training we might embark on, deliberately focusing on the thoughts and considerations we might have as we embark on our training, perhaps having just completed an introductory or skills course before taking our next steps. For this book the journey therefore begins as we think about training, through the training experience, into the placement, then on to the development of practice and experience, through to qualification, and then into the early stages of shaping a career as a therapist.

The other important consideration for me in writing this book was how I would position myself as a writer. I wanted to reflect the conversational experience from supervision and so have taken, deliberately, a fairly informal position in how I discuss concepts and ideas. I am saying it to you, from me, for you to reflect on, consider, accept or disregard as you see fit, much in the same way I would if we were sitting in a room together talking these things through. So, this is my introduction to counselling and psychotherapy, and it is one that aims to help link theory to practice. There is material on the accompanying website (www.sagepub. co.uk/reeves), which presents some of the material contained in these pages in different ways to help with learning.

So much has changed from when I started to write this book to now: the context in which counselling and psychotherapy are practised continues to evolve and shift; funding ebbs and flows; statutory regulation of the profession (in the UK) is no longer, well … statutory; and my trainee supervisees I referred to earlier are now all qualified and working as therapists in different settings. Yet, so much is the same also – the heart of counselling and psychotherapy still beats loudly and strongly, and the soul is still alive and vibrant. It is a profession that continues to be built, but one with strong foundations. I have tried to capture that sense in my writing and to the best of my ability.

Andrew Reeves
Liverpool

Acknowledgements

There are many people for me to thank in bringing this book to fruition, some known to me, and others not. Initially I am enormously grateful to the team at Sage Publications: Susannah Trefgarne, who originally approached me with the idea, and Alice Oven, Kate Wharton and Rachel Burrows, for their truly exceptional support, encouragement, wisdom and faith, and also for food in the sky and a chocolate bunny in a shoebox.

I am enormously grateful to the following people: Kirsten Amis, Tim Bond, Mick Cooper, Angela Couchman, Windy Dryden, Colin Feltham, Jules Howdin, Nancy Rowland, Clare Symons, Sue Wheeler and Sally Evans – in very different ways you have all played an important part. I am grateful to all the anonymous peer reviewers, who read each chapter and the final text, for your sensible suggestions, expertise, time and a capacity to deliver praise and criticism with a fair hand.

It might sound like a cliché, but I really couldn't have written a word of this book without all the counsellors, psychotherapists, supervisors, supervisees, trainees and trainers I have worked with over the years, and most importantly every person I have ever worked with in therapy: each one of you is represented here in the words and meaning – thank you.

I would like to dedicate this book to Diane, Adam, Katie and Emily for their unconditional care, love, time, encouragement and belief – it has been so important and is never, ever taken for granted.

Finally to Snowdonia – so often she thought I was coming to play but had to sit patiently while I worked. Perhaps it is playtime again …

Guided Tour of the Book

The book is structured over three parts; Setting the Context, The Therapeutic Relationship and The Professional Self. Throughout all of these parts, you'll come across the following features to help you navigate the book, as well as critically engage with and reflect on what you have learned.

CHAPTER OVERVIEW

A clear outline of the aims, objective and content of each chapter.

SECTION OUTLINE

Places the chapter in the context of the previous chapter, and the book as a whole.

DISCUSSION QUESTIONS

Encourages critical engagement with core content and key issues.

PAUSE FOR REFLECTION

Prompts reflection on learning and consideration of the key aspects of each chapter.

CASE STUDY

To help illustrate particular key points and issues, as well as show how theory translates into actual real-life practice.

WEBSITES

Links to key textual, audio or video resources.

FURTHER READING

Suggested books and journals that will take you to the next step.

1

Introduction to Counselling and Psychotherapy: From Theory to Practice

1.1 INTRODUCTION

CHAPTER OVERVIEW

Counselling and psychotherapy, following their initial emergence, have moved from the periphery into the mainstream. This chapter considers key definitions of counselling and psychotherapy and outlines the debate on the relationship (in terms of differences and similarities) between the two. In addition, the position of counselling and psychotherapy within wider helping professional roles is explored. The chapter also offers an outline of the overall structure of the book.

So much change in so little time

It is difficult to imagine when thinking of counselling and psychotherapy in today's context that, not too long ago, it was quite different. The proliferation of therapy across a range of settings and the subsequent embedding of therapy as viable choices for proportions of the population would be almost unheard of just a few decades ago. Indeed, I recall clearly in the mid- to late 1980s when I began my training that finding placements proved to be a significant challenge. Not, as is the case today, because of the number of people chasing the same opportunities, but rather because it was difficult to find counselling and psychotherapy in many settings at all outside of independent practice or specialist environments. Therapy in primary and secondary care was very limited, with opportunities existing mostly in the third sector.

A number of factors have led to change in the intervening years. They include: work by a number of professional bodies to communicate the benefits of counselling and psychotherapy; increasing acknowledgement of the importance of mental health and the link between mental and physical wellbeing; a slow move away from a medication culture, with a population more willing perhaps to question the treatment they receive; an increasing evidence base demonstrating the efficacy of the psychological therapies across a range of difficulties; a challenge (led by mental health charities) to the stigma of mental health distress and the promotion of help-seeking; a higher profile of counselling and psychotherapy in the media; and a change in policy, particularly around mental health, towards a greater involvement of service users and the increasing potency of the client/patient voice.

When I qualified as a social worker and began working in adult mental health secondary care settings, psychiatry was still a very dominant force: the psychiatrist was rarely questioned and intervention for people experiencing acute and chronic mental health distress typically consisted of medication or in- and out-patient care. Over the intervening years the dominance of psychiatry has waned: the psychiatrist remains an important figure, but one who is now part of a mental health team. Nursing, social work, advocacy and psychology have become more prominent and hospital admission is seen very much as a last alternative. Advances in medication have given medical personnel greater treatment options and people experiencing difficulties have demanded alternatives to medication and hospitalisation. Counselling and psychotherapy have increasingly come to be seen as a viable and beneficial alternative or addition to other forms of support. Therapy has moved from the periphery into the mainstream. In the process, it has further embedded itself into mainstream culture, such as in films, music, literature, art and television and, in doing so, has entered the public consciousness.

This change has brought challenges. Counsellors and psychotherapists need to be equipped by their training to work in a wider variety of contexts and to acquire skills and knowledge to meet a wide range of presenting issues. Each working context demands its own level of competence, with therapists trained on generic courses needing to undertake further training to equip them for their role. With this proliferation too comes the need to ensure that practice remains ethically and legally pertinent, offering high levels of care and integrity to those accessing help. With a greater demand for innovative and effective treatments comes a necessity to demonstrate efficacy in the face of falling budgets and closing services. Counsellors and psychotherapists need to develop competency as researcher-practitioners, or at least as competent critical consumers of research. The imperative is for counselling and psychotherapy to clearly and unequivocally demonstrate a sound evidence base for practice. We cannot just assume that what we do works: we need to demonstrate it in the language of commissioners, budget holders and policy developers. The development and implementation of benchmarking tools and outcome measures demand that therapists find ways of integrating such tools into their day-to-day work with clients.

The rapid development of technology too has made its inroads into the provision of therapy. This has occurred not only in terms of record keeping, databases and tracking client demographic information, but also in the actual delivery of therapy, moving away from face-to-face contact and transporting therapy into a virtual world of email, synchronous chat and message boards. Clients now, quite rightly, demand up-to-date information not just about the types of therapy on offer, but also the form and nature of the delivery of the therapy they will receive. They have become informed consumers, requesting specific therapies and particular interventions.

Counselling and psychotherapy: from theory to practice

There is so much for new trainees to discover that it is quite impossible for courses, however hard they try, to cover all that is needed. The place of supervision is important here in helping new practitioners to make the link from theory to practice in both contextualising and understanding the lessons from direct work with clients. The responsibility for self-direction in personal and professional development is key too.

When beginning to think about this book, I reflected on what was already available and where the gaps were between existing resources. There are a number of excellent introductory texts that help draw on research and academic learning to inspire new therapists. There are also some great texts that explore the acquisition and development of skills. As a practitioner I have sought to write something that could accompany you from your earliest steps at the beginning of your training, into the practice placement, then on to the process of reflecting on how you begin direct work with clients. I have aimed too for the book, as your competence and experience develops, to help link practice learning and theory and to explore the possibility of employment and, finally, qualified practice. That is, I have wanted to produce a book that would accompany you every step of the way – a book written by a practitioner for new practitioners. I have tried to include everything in here – including the kitchen sink! I have sought to include all those aspects of practice that we consider, think about and reflect on. Though in the end I haven't actually been able to include the sink, I hope that the book proves to be useful and thought-provoking and that it prompts further questions and discovery.

The book as a whole: what's in store

Here I want to offer a pen picture of each chapter so you can quickly see how the book is structured, 'signposting' you to sections most relevant for your stage on the journey into practice. The book is structured over three parts: Setting the Context (in which we will look at training, theories, settings, law and ethics); The Therapeutic Relationship (in which we will consider the types of problems we may work with in sessions with clients and the management of the therapeutic relationship); and The Professional Self (in which we will consider key aspects of, and beyond, contact with clients that help determine accountable and professional practice).

Chapter 1: Introduction to Counselling and Psychotherapy

Well, you're here already! This first chapter outlines definitions of counselling and psychotherapy and how they are different and similar (and, trust me, that is no easy task!), before moving on to an overview of their development. The process of tracing this emergence provides a helpful overview in locating today's practice in a wider historical context. It is important to view the current situation in the context of its history and development – the past so often helps us make sense of the present.

Part One: Setting the Context

Chapter 2: Becoming a Counsellor or Psychotherapist: The Training Journey

The next chapter examines all the factors that inform, shape, support and challenge the process of becoming a counsellor or psychotherapist, starting right at the very beginning of training. While it is, without doubt, a fascinating and life-changing process, it can also bring difficult challenges that you need to consider before you begin. Likewise, knowing what sort of training you are looking for, the context you might wish to work in when you qualify, as well as the multitude of practical considerations, all require commensurate thought.

Chapter 3: Principal Counselling and Psychotherapy Approaches and Skills

Here I provide an overview of the main theories and models that inform contemporary counselling and psychotherapy. The chapter does not seek to provide an exhaustive list (given the estimated 450 models of therapy available!): instead, it focuses on the key models and provides a checklist for each of the principal ideas and philosophical assumptions. Models include cognitive-behavioural approaches, the psychodynamic approaches, as well as the humanistic models. Additionally, the chapter considers current developments in counselling and psychotherapy thinking, including the emergence of models such as mindfulness-based cognitive-behavioural therapy and working pluralistically.

Chapter 4: Professional Settings and Organisations

The sheer scope of working contexts and settings in which counselling and psychotherapy are found can be overwhelming. This chapter considers why and how the setting in which counselling and psychotherapy take place is so important in shaping the form and nature of the therapy on offer, as well as how counselling and psychotherapy 'sit' within a procedural and political frame and the importance of your having an understanding of the policies that have particular influence on their setting and practice, including independent practice.

Chapter 5: Law, Policy, Values and Ethics

Counselling and psychotherapy operate within a legal framework and are informed by policy, yet are fundamentally rooted in strong values and ethics. This chapter looks at how law and policy define what we do, but also how our values and ethics as counsellors and psychotherapists shape and structure our thinking and approach to practice. Here we will consider how the soul of the therapeutic relationship is enlivened by our core beliefs.

Part Two: The Therapeutic Relationship

Chapter 6: Clients and Presenting Issues

Clients present with a wide range of problems in counselling and psychotherapy, from struggles with worry and wellbeing, through to complex and long-standing mental health problems. Some clients will have a formal diagnosis of mental health distress, while others will not. Before we can critically reflect on diagnostic structures and labels (or reject them) we need to understand how they work so that we can see problems in context. The problems explored in greater detail will include: anxiety and panic attacks; depression; post-traumatic stress; eating disorders; loss and bereavement; suicide and self-harm; sexual problems; psychosis; and personality disorders.

Chapter 7: Managing Aspects of the Therapeutic Relationship

Counselling and psychotherapy are about beginning, structuring, contracting, maintaining and ending, and managing all aspects in between; the therapeutic process begins before the client ever enters the room. Here we will outline and explore all these factors so that you can support your learning and offer your clients a safe, respectful and appropriate space for them to explore their difficulties.

Chapter 8: Challenges in the Therapeutic Relationship

There are a number of important areas integral to the therapeutic process that can also present particular challenges to it, including: transference and countertransference;

dependency; missed appointments and cancellations; clients who are resistant to therapy; self-disclosure; and getting 'stuck'. While the chapter won't be able to offer a blueprint response applicable to all situations all of the time, having the confidence to understand them as part of the therapeutic process, as opposed to outside of it, can help us work more effectively with them.

Chapter 9: Working with Diversity and Difference

It is important that we acknowledge the diversity in human experience and how that will be presented in counselling and psychotherapy sessions, including through sexual orientation, gender, faith and spirituality, culture and disability. We must challenge the idea that there is a 'one size fits all' approach to therapy and reflect on and adapt our practice in accordance with our clients' needs. This will involve questioning our own underlying assumptions and stereotypes.

Part Three: The Professional Self

Chapter 10: Managing Professional Responsibilities

There are a number of important skills and boundaries for us to consider that not only facilitate the therapeutic relationship, but can also be important aspects of it. How we communicate with clients outside of sessions, keep our relationships appropriate and manage dual relationships (where we may have contact with clients in other settings or roles) all demand commensurate skill. Likewise, whether or how to use touch as part of our work, how to check we continue to work within the boundaries of competency and, finally, how we take care of ourselves all demand time and consideration.

Chapter 11: Supervision and Consultation

Supervision is an integral part of what we do as counsellors and psychotherapists and, in the UK, is an ethical requirement of practice. Here we will look at what is meant by the term, offering definitions that help explore the different components of a successful supervisory relationship. The process begins with finding the right supervisor, and then includes how to contract, review and, eventually, end a supervisory relationship: all these aspects are considered fully.

Chapter 12: Counselling, Psychotherapy and Research

We have already highlighted how, in moving from the periphery to the mainstream, counselling and psychotherapy need to demonstrate their efficacy not only to funders and commissioners, but also (and most importantly perhaps) to those accessing help at times of distress. We need to become at least a research-aware profession, if not a research-active one. Here we will consider some of the main skills required in critically evaluating research, as well as theories and ideas that might help us take the first steps to becoming researchers.

Chapter 13: Endings and the Next Steps

Like all journeys, this one has an ending. This chapter will aim to prompt reflection to help you consider the process you have been through and look forward to what may be next. When we finish our training we step out into the world as qualified practitioners and are tasked with making important decisions about our personal and professional future. The journey from placement to practice is the point at which theory becomes alive, speculations become reality and the immense satisfaction that can be gained in meeting with another to help them find their way through difficulty and disturbance becomes realised. I hope that you enjoy your journey as much as I am enjoying mine and that you will find this book of benefit to you along the way. On the companion website I have made a short video talking through the structure of the book, which you may want to watch.

So, let's begin ...

1.2 DEFINING COUNSELLING AND PSYCHOTHERAPY

SECTION OUTLINE

There is much debate over the differences and similarities between 'counselling' and 'psychotherapy' and this has vexed theorists, academics, practitioners and researchers for some considerable time. This section explores the question of whether counselling and psychotherapy are discrete disciplines or, in contrast, whether the overlap is sufficient to render distinction irrelevant.

There are always challenges in trying to define 'counselling' and 'psychotherapy' as it inevitably and immediately leads into contentious territory about similarities and differences. If one writes about 'counselling', the risk is that those psychotherapists who see their role as different from counselling will disengage. Likewise, writing about 'psychotherapy' runs the risk of leaving a proportion of counsellors out in the cold. To write about 'counselling and psychotherapy', however, runs the risk of presuming they are two, distinct activities, while to use 'psychological therapies' as a 'catch-all' phrase runs the risk of leaving everyone out in the cold.

These dilemmas present problems not only for textbook authors: imagine the implications for delivery of services, regulation and accreditation, training and, most importantly, the confusion potential clients might experience when considering what services to access. Should they see a counsellor or a psychotherapist, and (they may ask) what's the difference between the two anyway?

Kanellakis and D'Aubyn (2010) undertook a study of the public's perception of the titles of counsellor and psychotherapist. Four hundred and fifty members of the UK public were interviewed by researchers and asked their thoughts about the terms 'counsellor', 'psychotherapist' and 'psychological therapist': 30% thought the terms 'counsellor' and 'psychotherapist' were almost identical, while 64% thought them significantly different. Only 24% thought the terms 'psychotherapist' and 'psychological therapist' were significantly different, while 66% thought them almost identical. In this study the public's perception was that 'psychotherapist' was much closer to 'psychological therapist' than to 'counsellor'. Perhaps there is as much confusion in the public perception as there is within the professional field between the different terms.

Definitions

The British Association for Counselling and Psychotherapy (BACP, 2012) defines counselling and psychotherapy as:

> umbrella terms that cover a range of talking therapies. They are delivered by trained practitioners who work with people over a short or long term to help them bring about effective change or enhance their wellbeing.

The American Counseling Association (ACA, 2005, p. 4) says that counselling

> encourage[s] client growth and development in ways that foster the interest and welfare of clients and promote formation of healthy relationships. Counselors actively attempt to understand the diverse cultural backgrounds of the clients they serve. Counselors also explore their own cultural identities and how these affect their values and beliefs about the counseling process.

Feltham (2012, p. 3) says of counselling and psychotherapy that they are:

> mainly, though not exclusively, listening-and-talking based methods of addressing psychological and psychosomatic problems and change, including deep and prolonged human suffering, situational dilemmas, crises and developmental needs, and aspirations towards the realisation of human potential. In contrast to biomedical approaches, the psychological therapies operate largely without medication or other physical interventions and may be concerned not only with mental health but with spiritual, philosophical, social and other aspects of living. Professional forms of counselling and psychotherapy are based on formal training which encompasses attention to pertinent theory, clinical and/or micro-skills development, the personal development/theory of the trainee, and supervised practice.

According to the United Kingdom Council of Psychotherapy (UKCP, 2012) psychotherapy

> aims to help clients gain insight into their difficulties or distress, establish a greater understanding of their motivation, and enable them to find more appropriate ways of coping or bring about changes in their thinking and behaviour. Psychotherapy involves exploring feelings, beliefs, thoughts and relevant events, sometimes from childhood and personal history, in a structured way with someone trained to help you do it safely. Depending on the nature of [the] problem, therapy can be short or long term. Sessions can be provided for adults, adolescents and children on a one-to-one basis, or for couples, families and within groups whose members share similar problems.

The British Psychological Society (BPS, 2005, pp. 1-2) states that counselling psychology

> draws upon and seeks to develop phenomenological models of practice and enquiry in addition to that of traditional scientific psychology. It continues to develop models of practice and research, which marry the scientific demand for rigorous empirical enquiry with a firm value base grounded in the primacy of the counselling or psychotherapeutic relationship. These models seek:
>
> 1   to engage with subjectivity and intersubjectivity, values and beliefs;
> 2   to know empathically and to respect first person accounts as valid in their own terms; to elucidate, interpret and negotiate between perceptions and world views but not to assume the automatic superiority of any one way of experiencing, feeling, valuing and knowing;
> 3   to be practice led, with a research base grounded in professional practice values as well as professional artistry;
> 4   to recognise social contexts and discrimination and to work always in ways that empower rather than control and also demonstrate the high standards of anti-discriminatory practice appropriate to the pluralistic nature of society today.

In distinguishing the terms 'counselling' and 'psychotherapy' it is helpful to explore a number of themes in more detail. For example:

1   The nature of the activity: the extent to which it is seen as (a) medical or (b) social
2   The typical duration of the intervention – the extent to which it is likely to be short or long term
3   The depth of intervention
4   The type of training required.

Below, we explore each of these themes in turn. You may also want to look at the companion website for a **PowerPoint presentation** of the definitions of counselling and psychotherapy.

The nature of the activity: medical or social?

The Oxford English Dictionary (OED, 2012) states that counselling is 'the provision of professional assistance and guidance in resolving personal or psychological problems', while psychotherapy is 'the treatment of mental disorder by psychological rather than medical means'. Even though they are the simplest, perhaps the OED definitions are also the most helpful in beginning to tease out some of the points of differentiation that some claim to exist between counselling and psychotherapy. The emphasis placed on counselling is that of offering assistance and guidance in an attempt to resolve problems. The emphasis in psychotherapy is on the treatment of mental disorder without using medical means. Here we see an implication that counselling assists and guides, while psychotherapy treats. Also, the use of the term 'medical' in the psychotherapy definition strikes at the heart of a philosophical differentiation, according to commentators who claim that psychotherapy is more allied to medicine, while counselling is more allied to a psychosocial model of help.

However, the suggestion that psychotherapy is more akin to a medical model, while counselling is more akin to a social model, does not resolve the problem of differentiation. For example, person-centred therapy has been a predominant model of choice for training for several years in the UK. Rejecting a medicalising or pathologising view of the human condition, this approach is based instead on a philosophical standpoint of equality, acceptance, and empathy. In most modalities the therapist does not take the 'expert' role and certainly does not explicitly intend to offer a 'treatment'. Yet it is possible to train either as a person-centred counsellor or a person-centred psychotherapist. Both retain their non-medical position yet use different titles. Some argue this anomaly strengthens the view that there is more commonality than difference between counselling and psychotherapy.

Counselling and Psychotherapy in Scotland (COSCA, 2011a), Scotland's counselling and psychotherapy professional body, additionally suggest that differentiation might be found in the traditions of each discipline, with psychotherapy developing with the emergence of psychoanalysis in the 1920s, while counselling developed somewhat later, in the 1950s.

Duration of intervention: short or long term

Another point of differentiation often made is that counselling typically offers shorter-term or brief interventions, while psychotherapy offers longer-term interventions. Psychotherapy has often been linked with longer-term approaches, and while this may be true historically, over recent years, and with funding restrictions hitting therapy services hard, many therapy providers now offer time-limited interventions, delivered by both counsellors and psychotherapists. Likewise, there are agencies who offer longer-term counselling and, in independent practice where practitioners are freely able to determine their own length of contract, open-ended or longer-term work is offered by both counsellors and psychotherapists. The distinction between the length of contract offered as a means of differentiating between the two titles is less pertinent in today's financially demanding world.

Depth of intervention

According to McLeod, some have argued that 'although there is a certain amount of overlap between the theories and methods of counsellors and psychotherapists, and the types of clients they see, there is nevertheless a fundamental difference between the two, with psychotherapy representing a deeper, more fundamental level of work over a longer period, usually with more disturbed clients' (McLeod, 2009, p. 10). Psychoanalysis is probably the first approach that comes to mind when people think about psychotherapy. The stereotype of a couch, the therapist (very probably with a goatee beard and an Austrian accent) sitting out of sight encouraging free association and interpreting the results represents many people's image of 'in-depth' therapy. Certainly in my own setting new clients often comment on the fact that I don't have a couch (or an Austrian accent) with a mixture of relief and disappointment. Of course, the premise of this approach is not just a stereotype: psychoanalytic therapy is alive and well – albeit out of the reach of many clients given its long-term nature (typically it lasts many years), frequency (typically several sessions per week) and cost.

Beyond psychoanalysis, however, the depth and extent of work offered by psychotherapists becomes harder to differentiate from that of counsellors. Again in my own setting (namely, higher education), I work in a team, some members of which are trained as psychotherapists, and others as counsellors. The nature of the work is the same: the complexity of work is not differentiated between the two titles and the extent of work (i.e., the duration and frequency) is identical too. In supervising across a range of contexts over the years, including primary and secondary care settings, education, third-sector and independent practice, this seems generally true. However, there are settings where the desired qualification is in psychotherapy rather than counselling. These tend to be specialist settings, such as therapeutic communities for people with personality disorders, or eating disorders. Interestingly, the commonality between such settings where psychotherapy is preferred is that they are often allied to a medical intervention, such as psychiatry. Related to this, some psychiatrists will undertake additional therapy training and will describe themselves as consultant psychiatrist psychotherapists. I have yet to come across a consultant psychiatrist counsellor (though they may exist).

Training

Perhaps the clearest point of distinction between counsellor and psychotherapist has been the structure of training. Although in the UK therapy training is in a process of change following a debate on the possibility of statutory regulation, psycho-therapy training is often structured differently to that of counsellor training. These differences are discussed in more detail in Chapter 2. In summary, we may say here that psychotherapy training is often structured over four years, part-time, leading to a postgraduate diploma in psychotherapy (and registration with UKCP). It is not uncommon for psychotherapy training to require a 20–25 day psychiatric observa-tion placement, and that the trainee be in personal therapy for the duration of their training. In contrast, counsellor training is typically structured over a three-year, part-time course, without a psychiatric placement (although there is often a special-ist module on mental health), with the personal therapy requirement ranging from none, through to 40 hours or thereabouts. Exit awards during counsellor training tend to include a certificate in skills. The qualifying award for counsellor training was, for many years, a diploma (or postgraduate diploma). Both counsellor and psychotherapy training have, however, increasingly moved towards a Masters-level qualifying award over recent years, with more courses including a requirement that their students undertake research.

UKCP emphasise training as a key difference for them between counselling and psychotherapy. They state:

> Different people use the words counselling and psychotherapy in different ways, so there is no commonly agreed definition. There is a general understanding that a psychotherapist can work with a wider range of clients or patients and can offer more in-depth work where appropriate. UKCP believes the difference lies in the length and depth of training involved and in the quality of the relationship between the client and their therapist. UKCP-registered psychotherapists are trained to Masters level. UKCP registers psychotherapists and psychotherapeutic counsellors. Psychotherapeutic counsellors are counsellors who have received more in-depth training than that undertaken by most counsellors. UKCP's train-ing standards for both qualifications seek to ensure that UKCP registrants are competent to practise to the highest standards. (UKCP, 2012)

During fierce debate in early stages of the (now-defunct) plan to introduce statutory regulation in the UK, the differentiation in training was brought into focus with a consultation document that placed psychotherapists as having a higher level of training than counsellors, citing a greater degree of research competence and emphasising the specialist treatment of mental disorder. This provoked much debate (which was never fully resolved) and the principle was rejected by some leading therapy organisations.

Overall: what difference?

It remains very difficult, if not impossible, to bridge the two sides of the 'different vs. the same' debate. BACP's position is that counselling and psychotherapy describe the same activity; UKCP see a distinction between them. Spinelli (2006, p. 38) states: 'Some have suggested that the main distinction between psychotherapy and counselling is that while the former requires clients to recline on a couch, the latter only provides an armchair.' For each of the points outlined above, there will be several different perspectives. This has implications for clients, who have to make important decisions when seeking help.

For my own view, while I acknowledge differences in the structure and provision (and cost) of training, over the 20 years (plus) that I have been practising I have always worked with practitioners who, regardless of their title, have essentially undertaken the same work. I would define myself as a counsellor in virtue of my training, which was a 'counsellor' training. The title for me is defined simply by what my certificate says, rather than any substantive difference between what I do and the role of my psychotherapist colleagues.

Returning to my earlier authorial dilemma, for the purposes of this text I will use a variety of terms. Essentially I will refer to 'counsellors and psychotherapists' and 'counselling and psychotherapy' to acknowledge that, regardless of the actuality of the situation, people define themselves using these terms. I will also use terms like 'therapy', 'therapist' and 'practitioner' for example, simply to facilitate the flow of text – there is no other intent behind the use of these terms!

DISCUSSION QUESTIONS

1 How would you define counselling?
2 How would you define psychotherapy?
3 What do you consider to be the key similarities and differences between counselling and psychotherapy?
4 In what ways do you feel current debates around counselling and psychotherapy (a) help inform the development of the profession and (b) hinder it?

1.3 THE EMERGENCE OF COUNSELLING AND PSYCHOTHERAPY AS DISCIPLINES

SECTION OUTLINE

It is best to understand the nature and scope of counselling and psychotherapy as practised today by placing them within the context of their history. The historical development of counselling and psychotherapy has influenced the shape of current theories and ideas, as well as the contexts in which they operate. This section outlines key milestones of that development and provides the historical background required to contextualise counselling and psychotherapy in general and the particular facets of practice considered elsewhere in this book.

When we begin therapy with a new client it is important that, at some stage of the therapeutic process, we find out a little bit more about who they are, their context and where they have come from. Some modalities emphasise the importance of this more than others. Some therapists take very specific steps in taking a client history, while others allow the information to emerge during the course of therapy. However, there would be fewer therapists who would maintain that history isn't important at all. The more we can understand about the background to something, the more we are able to see its current presentation in a more informed context.

For the same reason, it would be unhelpful to launch into the other sections of this book without taking a moment to consider how counselling and psychotherapy came into being. Certainly, in my own work as a therapist I have, over a relatively short period of time (20 years), seen major changes. The proliferation of counselling and psychotherapy as it is practised today is very different to when I first came into the profession. When I speak with colleagues who have been working as therapists for longer than me, they report the same phenomenon. So, while it is perfectly possible to become a counsellor or psychotherapist without any understanding or insight into the history of our profession, it would be a bit like working with a client while having no knowledge or interest in anything about them beyond their immediate presentation; this option, though possible, is limited.

Many people assume that Sigmund Freud was the 'founder' of modern-day psychotherapy. While certainly his influence has been profound, and many of our current working practices can be traced back to his work, psychotherapy as an activity certainly existed before Freud began writing. It may be impossible to truly locate the origins of talking therapy given that the human propensity to communicate and be in relationships goes back many, many centuries. The process of counselling and psychotherapy, albeit not in a form that we might understand today, can be traced back to early religious and community rituals. In many ways we might argue that what we now call counselling and psychotherapy is merely a systematic form and type of communication with a specific purpose. One could, in addition, argue that all that has happened over the past 100 years, coinciding with the emergence and development of professions such as psychiatry and medicine, has been the application of scientific principles to the human art of discourse.

Medicalisation of distress

The way in which distress has been viewed has changed over the centuries. Ancient Greek and Roman perspectives on mental illness generally looked at causation, and cure, as both coming from the gods. During the 5th and 6th centuries BC the link between madness and the gods was challenged, partly informed by the work of Hippocrates. In the 4th century a tentative relationship between madness with physical imbalance began to be postulated. He proposed that mental illness was related to a physical imbalance in the bodily humours, namely blood, yellow bile, phlegm, and black bile. They corresponded to the four supposed basic qualities of matter, namely heat, cold, moisture and dryness. The treatment of distress thus came to focus more on the rebalancing of the physical self. This took many forms, but included the management of diet, bathing and purges, and the use of vapours.

Aristotle proposed the idea that the mind and body were divided, but that bile mediated channels between the two. One of the earliest recorded instances of terms that have some resonance with those used today comes from Galen, a Roman physician (130–200 AD). He described several syndromes, including dysthmymia, paranoia and hysteria, linked to anxiety and sexual tension. His premise, unlike that of Hippocrates, was that mental illness was more due to an imbalance between aspects of the soul as opposed to the body. According to Merkel (2003, p. 3), the soul was seen to have 'rational, irrational and lustful parts'.

During the Middle Ages the church reasserted its influence on how mental illness was seen. However, this influence began to decline once again in the 15th and 16th centuries with the emergence of science, with Descartes (1596–1650) arguing that the soul and mind were divided, with the soul having a spiritual dimension while the mind a mental one. However, he did believe there was interaction between the two. Merkel (2003) suggests that during this time the body was seen as primarily mechanical, materialistic and quantifiable, whereas the mind was seen as unlimited, nonmaterial, and situated in the realm of consciousness and thought.

The conception of the body as essentially mechanical began to gain further credibility in the 17th century with the increasing use of anatomical studies. In the 19th and 20th centuries there was acknowledgement of organic and environmental causes for mental illness. Psychiatry began to organise and categorise concepts of mental illness, thus heralding early examples of diagnostic structures in relation to mental illness (the term 'mental health' would have been a misnomer given theories were still predominantly driven by medical models of illness and insanity).

The organisation of ideas: the development of psychotherapy

With the categorisation of mental illness (the term itself evolved from 'insanity'), greater interest in treatments continued to develop. Here we can see the earliest emergence of psychotherapy as a systematic and organised form of response to disorder. Dendy, an English psychiatrist, in 1853 is credited with using the term 'psycho-therapeia' to describe a talking cure for psychological problems. Around the same time there was great interest in the use of hypnosis for both psychological and physiological problems. Hypnosis was seen to be able to calm and anaesthetise during medical procedures. McLeod (2009, p. 26) notes that 'hypnosis was helpful to patients (because) it gave access to an area of the mind that was not accessible during normal waking consciousness. In other words, the notion of the "unconscious" mind was part of the apparatus of 19th-century hypnotism.'

Freud, a psychiatrist working in the late 19th and early 20th centuries, began to move away from models of psychiatry and hypnosis predominant at the time and looked to develop a new approach to treatment. By developing psychoanalysis, Freud had a profound influence on the subsequent development of psychotherapy. Early analysis relied on the interpretation of dreams and the use of free association. Freud wrote about his experiences with patients extensively and these works are still read and have influence today (Freud, 2004, 2009, 2010). We should make reference too to some of Freud's collaborators who worked with him early on, but later split away to further develop their own ideas. Most notable of these were Carl Jung and also Alfred Adler, Sandor Ferenczi and Otto Rank. They continued to develop theories and ideas set within a psychodynamic tradition.

A shift in emphasis: the emergence of the 'person'

The work of Carl Rogers from the 1940s and 1950s onwards marked a dramatic shift in the progression of the talking therapies. Until this point, psychotherapy had been developed primarily by psychiatrists and psychologists and, while moving in different directions, retained an important 'nod' towards medicine. Rogers began developing client-centred therapy, drawing more on the existence and use of human qualities than scientific principles. It was his assertion that, given the right conditions, each individual had the propensity to move towards health. These conditions included acceptance, empathy and warmth. There was a philosophical shift away from conceptualising the therapist as expert and towards therapy as a collaborative process between the therapist and client.

The early influences on Rogers came from religion, but as he began his training to become a minister he decided instead to study psychology. His interest first centred on work with children and in 1939 he wrote *The Clinical Treatment of the Problem Child*. Then in 1942 he wrote *Counseling and Psychotherapy*, where he first proposed the ideas of client-centred therapy.

The development of counselling and psychotherapy was not informed only by the work of individuals, but also by the emergence of the institution of therapy. Table 1.1 outlines how the professionalism of counselling and psychotherapy was inextricably linked with the development of therapy institutions, together with other key events. For example, the early 1900s, around the time of Freud's early influence, saw the establishment of several key psychoanalytic organisations, such as the International Psychoanalytical Association in 1910 and the Institute of Psycho-analysis in 1919. Likewise, the emergence of client-centred therapy and the writing of Rogers in the late 1940s and early 1950s coincided with the development of counselling organisations drawing on humanistic principles. While the writing of key theorists and practitioners is often associated with the development of counselling and psychotherapy, the emergence of the profession is also located in the development of its organisation and institution.

Key historical developments

Table 1.1, extracted from Feltham and Horton's *Handbook of Counselling and Psychotherapy* (2012), outlines the key historical developments in counselling and psychotherapy from 1900 to the present day.

In summary, while early development was dominated by psychodynamic and psychoanalytic therapy, the emergence of humanistic approaches from the 1940s began to dramatically change the nature and shape of counselling and psychotherapy. Up until 1938, organisations had predominantly centred on psychoanalysis. The National Marriage Guidance Council marked the first instance of a non-psychoanalytic therapy organisation and also the development of a relationship between counselling and the voluntary sector. If psychotherapy was born out of medicine, counselling was perhaps born out of the voluntary movement and education. From the 1950s, with the establishment of the Samaritans and then later CRUSE, a bereavement charity, humanistic approaches became more prominent and the development of theory and practice grew apace. The British Association for Counselling (now the British Association for Counselling and Psychotherapy – BACP) was established in 1977. It is illustrative of the growth of counselling as a professional activity that BACP is now the second largest counselling organisation in the world, with membership of approximately 40,000.

Contemporary counselling and psychotherapy practice

As we have seen, there has been much debate over the similarities and differences between counselling and psychotherapy. A number of issues have been highlighted and, despite the best efforts of theorists and practitioners, there remains little consensus on the matter. Without historical context, it is hard to understand why such debates fuel passion and divergence. However, when viewed through a historical lens this becomes easier to understand: while there have been many commonalities over the years, essentially the disciplines were born from two different traditions.

Perhaps the debate has provoked such passion because counselling and psychotherapy 'speak' of very different ways of viewing the world and human experience. Indeed, much of the discussion around the difference between counselling and psychotherapy centres on whether human distress is located within a medical frame. Whatever the philosophical

TABLE 1.1　Key historical developments in counselling and psychotherapy since 1900

Year	Birth/growth of institutions and professional organisations	Significant events	Appearance of schools (approximate dates)
1900		Freud's *Interpretation of Dreams*	
1907	British Psychological Society Vienna Psychoanalytic Society		
1908		First (careers) counselling centre, Boston, USA (Frank Parsons)	
1910	International Psychoanalytical Association		
1913	National Vocational Guidance Association (USA)		Analytical psychology (Jung)
1919	London Psychoanalytic Society Institute of Psycho-analysis		Behavioural psychology
1920	Tavistock Clinic		Psychodrama
1921			
1924	British Psychoanalytic Society		
1926	London Clinic of Psychoanalysis Medico-Psychological Association (MPA; previously AMOAH I,　＼ originally 1841)		
1935	Alcoholics Anonymous		
1936	Society of Analytical Psychology		
1937		Death of Adler	
1938	National Marriage Guidance Council (now Relate)		
1939		Death of Freud	
1940			Client/person-centred approach
1948		British National Health Service T groups First student counselling service (University College Leicester)	
1950	International Association for Vocational and Educational Guidance (IAVEG)		Gestalt therapy
1951			Rogers's client-centred therapy
1952	Group Analytical Society American Association for Counseling and Development (AACD) American Counseling Association (ACA; originally NVCA)	*Diagnostic and Statistical Manual* (*DSM*) 1st edn	
1953	Samaritans		
1955			Rational emotive behaviour therapy (originally RT then RET) Personal construct therapy B
1957			Transactional analysis
1958			Behaviour therapy

Year	Birth/growth of institutions and professional organisations	Significant events	Appearance of schools (approximate dates)
1959	Cruse Scottish Pastoral Association		
1960		First fee-charging counsellor in private practice in UK Death of Melanie Klein	
1961		Death of Jung J.D. Frank's *Persuasion and Healing*	
1962			Cognitive therapy
1965		Halmos's *The Faith of the Counsellors*	
1966		Counselling training at Universities of Reading and Keele	
1969	Westminster Pastoral Foundation Association of Humanistic Psychology (USA 1962, UK 1969)		
1970	First Standing Conference for the Advancement of Counselling (annual) MPA becomes Royal College of Psychiatrists	Death of Perls and Berne	Primal therapy
1971		*Foster Report* on Scientology	
1975	National Association of Young People's Counselling and Advisory Services (later Youth Access)		Neuro-linguistic programming
1977	British Association for Counselling (BAC)		
1978		*Sieghart Report* on statutory regulation of psychotherapists	
1980	Association of Humanistic Psychology Practitioners (AHPP)	Smith et al. *The Benefits of Psychotherapy*	
1982		Rugby Psychotherapy Conference (set up by BAC)	
1983	Society for the Exploration of Psychotherapy Integration (SEPI)	First BAC accreditation scheme	Solution-focused therapy
1987		Death of Carl Rogers	
1989	United Kingdom Standing Conference on Psychotherapy (UKSCP)		
1990		Death of Bowlby	Cognitive analytic therapy
1991	British Confederation of Psychotherapists		
1992	European Association for Counselling	BPS Charter of Counselling Psychologists First UK Chair of Counselling (Windy Dryden)	
1993	United Kingdom Council for Psychotherapy (UKCP, originally UKSCP): advice, guidance, counselling and psychotherapy lead body		
1994	Independent Practitioners' Network UKCP Register of Psychotherapists	BPS Division of Counselling Psychology	
1995		BCP Register NHS Psychotherapy Services in England Review	

(Continued)

TABLE 1.1 *(Continued)*

Year	Birth/growth of institutions and professional organisations	Significant events	Appearance of schools (approximate dates)
1996	United Kingdom Register of Counsellors (UKRC) (individuals)	NHS Psychotherapy Services in England, Department of Health (DoH) Strategic Policy Review	
1998	World Council for Psychotherapy Association of Counsellors and Psychotherapists in Primary Care (CPC) UKRC (organizations)	Data Protection Act CORE introduced	
1999	National Institute for Health and Clinical Excellence (NICE)		
2000	BAC renamed British Association for Counselling and Psychotherapy (BACP) Universities Psychotherapy Association (UPA) adds 'Counselling' to its title, becoming UPCA	BACP's *Ethical Framework for Good Practice in Counselling and Psychotherapy*	
2001		Lord Alderdice's Psychotherapy Bill *Treatment Choice in Psychological Therapies and Counselling: Evidence-Based Clinical Practice Guidelines* (DoH) BACP's *Guidelines for Online Counselling and Psychotherapy*	
2002		Health Professions Council (HPC) is identified as the regulatory body for all health professions, including counselling and psychotherapy ('talking therapies')	
2003		UKCP establishes its Psychotherapeutic Counselling Section BACP Service Accreditation Scheme Telephone counselling (contractual) is accepted by BACP for accreditation hours	
2004	College of Psychoanalysts British Psychoanalytic Council	Graduate mental health workers in primary care British Confederation of Psychotherapists (BCP) renamed British Psychoanalytic Council (BPC)	
2006		Improving Access to Psychological Therapies	
2007		Death of Albert Ellis	
2008		BACP represented on HPC's Professional Liaison Group	
2009		HPC Register for Applied Psychologists opened	
2011		Statutory regulation plans abandoned	

differences, however, the application of counselling and psychotherapy (i.e., how it is delivered in practice to clients/patients) is harder to differentiate. As this chapter has argued, there is very little difference today between the work of many counsellors and psychotherapists, regardless of their working context.

It could be argued, therefore, that we are potentially witnessing a key historical shift: the merging of the two disciplines. Possibly, in time, the terms counselling and psychotherapy will cease to exist as distinct from each other and will be instead replaced with a more generic phrase such as 'psychological therapies'. An important influence on how counselling and psychotherapy further develop will be the application of research and the further emergence of an evidence base. As services close due to financial constraints, the imperative to demonstrate efficacy and success-ful outcome will perhaps be the dominant factor in determining which discipline(s) survive(s), and in what form. If you visit the companion website there is a list of web resources for key organisations in counselling and psychotherapy.

DISCUSSION QUESTIONS

1 What is your understanding of the history of the setting in which you work?
2 How is the setting in which you work influenced by its history?
3 What do you consider to be the main factors currently influencing counselling and psychotherapy?
4 In your working context, how do you see the services provided developing in the future?

PART ONE
SETTING THE CONTEXT

2

Becoming a Counsellor or Psychotherapist: The Training Journey

2.1 INTRODUCTION

CHAPTER OVERVIEW

There are many factors to be taken into account when beginning training in counselling or psychotherapy. The training journey will bring many challenges, opportunities and obstacles and will, hopefully, provide the structure for profound personal and professional development. This chapter will discuss the factors that might need to be taken into account when embarking on training so that the learning opportunities are maximised.

All journeys start with a beginning: the journey towards becoming a counsellor or psychotherapist is no different. Having made up your mind that this is the career for you, you will have thought about which training course to apply for. Depending on your geographical location, there may be many or few courses to choose from. It is at this point, however, that you may already have realised that the choice of the right counsellor or psychotherapy training programme was not necessarily as simple as the question of which one was most geographically accessible.

My own first training was in social work. Consequently, my choice of course was relatively simple. While I researched which courses had a 'good reputation', essentially my choice was informed by where in the country I wished to live. My personal circumstances to a large extent informed where I applied. At the time of my application, and still today, there were national UK benchmarks for social work training (Department of Health, 2002). Wherever I applied, though there may have been differences in ethos or emphasis, essentially the core of the curriculum was the same. One quickly realises that this is not the case for counsellor and psychotherapy training, and that choices will be informed and influenced by several different factors, many of which demand that you are somehow able to see into the future and 'know' what type of counsellor or psychotherapist you want to become.

While many counsellors and psychotherapists emerge from training satisfied with their choices and equipped to work in areas or with types of client groups they have developed a passion for, there are also many trainees who emerge thinking they would have made different choices and who struggle to find employment in the areas in which they wish to work – or who begin a whole new training to achieve what they want. I have heard many trainees over the years say something like, 'If I were to start again now I would have done x instead.' That is not to say that everyone who emerges from social work training, or teacher training, or nurse training, and so on is necessarily and inevitably happy with the choices they have made, but in counselling and psychotherapy training the variants, and thus the potential for ill-informed decisions, seem much greater. Thus the importance of a potential counsellor or psychotherapist carefully reflecting on their motivations, interests and ambitions, is high.

If you are reading this book it might be assumed you are already a trainee having embarked on training. However, it might also be that you have recently completed an introductory or skills course and are now ready to take on the commitment of a qualifying training programme. Or instead you might be considering the first steps in training and are undertaking early research, very aware of the financial commitments that come with education in today's market. At whatever early stage you find yourself, this chapter aims to provide you with an overview of what it is really like: the types of choices to be made; the costs, demands and expectations; as well as the benefits, opportunities for growth and development, and the learning that can be achieved. The aim here is not to guarantee that all choices will be 'right' ones – sometimes losing our way and navigating a new path can be enormously valuable – but rather to provide a framework for reflection and consideration.

The first section, Embarking on Training, provides a discussion of the differences between counsellor and psychotherapy training structures and levels and the curriculum expectations of these different types of programmes. It also outlines how courses are typically structured around a particular modality or theory (or perhaps an integration of theories) and, in addition, how courses are targeted at working with particular client groups or in practice settings.

This is followed by a section entitled The Challenges and Joys of Training, which looks more closely at the realities of training – those aspects that become important or demanding as the training progresses, but are not necessarily apparent on pre-course information. They include financial costs, time expectations, the demands on one's partner or family, and work commitments. Additionally, the challenges and joys of the training placement are considered – specifically, how to find one, finding the right one, ensuring that the opportunities for learning and development are maximised, as well as finding the right supervisor to help you through the process. Finally, the role and importance of personal therapy in training is considered. While not all courses demand that their trainees undergo personal therapy, many do. While training clearly facilitates professional development, the role and importance of personal development cannot be overstated. Knowing when to time this in the context of the wider demands of the course requires commensurate thought. Too many trainees begin personal therapy quickly to 'get it out of the way', or rather leave it to the end because of other time and financial commitments. Either way, timing personal therapy for the wrong reasons can make it a dissatisfying process that feels an unnecessary and undesired hindrance to the more 'important' things happening on a placement or in the training group.

2.2 EMBARKING ON TRAINING AND FINDING THE RIGHT COURSE

SECTION OUTLINE

This section provides information as to the choices available when embarking on training, and offers a number of reflective questions to help you structure and refine your thinking about what training might best equip you for your future role as a counsellor or psychotherapist.

Embarking on any training programme, not least one in counselling or psychotherapy, is a significant step for anyone. Knowing whether and when to take such a monumental step requires care and reflection. While there will certainly be many benefits, the personal investment of time, money, and intellectual and emotional energy will be profound. All education is arguably an intense journey in which the learner gains insight not only into the world around them, but also into themselves: their motives, desires, passions and philosophy; counselling and psychotherapy training demands much, but also offers much in return. Indeed, many speak of counselling and psychotherapy training as a turning point in their lives, a point at which they were able to change profoundly the direction in which their lives were heading.

Too many people though embark on a training course only to realise one or two years into it that it was not for them, or that the chosen course could not offer them what they had hoped – or that the modality of the training or particular specialisms covered would not equip them to work in the area they had intended. With such realisations, people can leave training frustrated at having wasted time and money – if also somewhat wiser.

The purpose of this section is to explore the key considerations for anyone considering their training journey. A summary list is also available on the companion website. It does not offer an exhaustive list – undoubtedly for some people and situations there will be additional considerations – and the intention here is not to promise that, having read what I have to say or reflected on the questions posed, all will necessarily become immediately clear. After all, sometimes the getting lost or taking the wrong turn can be as profound a learning experience as always knowing the way.

Personal and professional motivations

It is likely there will be a number of factors motivating a decision to undertake counselling or psychotherapy training. Of all the courses and possibilities, the question, 'Why counselling and psychotherapy?' lies at the heart of any purposeful reflection. It is certainly true that some fall into counselling and psychotherapy training through a happy (or occasionally unhappy) accident. I have supervised several people (who incidentally all turned into excellent therapists) who began their training by looking through an adult education prospectus and picking 'counselling' because the course times fitted with their availability – or perhaps because 'Advanced Digital Photography' was full.

Many others, however, decide to begin training to become a counsellor or psychotherapist for purposeful reasons. They include the following:

- Counselling or psychotherapy training offers the possibility of extending existing skills or work. This may apply in the case of social workers, teachers, nurses, or mental health workers, for example.
- The training offers the possibility of career change – perhaps the chance to do something completely different, something that is viewed as 'worthwhile'. Over the years I have met people who have opted for counselling or psychotherapy as a change from careers as various as legal worker, lorry driver, dressmaker, human resource manager and beautician.
- A positive (or negative) experience of having been a client of counselling or psychotherapy can often act as a motivator for training.

In addition, people sometimes embark on counselling or psychotherapy training as a means of having personal therapy (either misunderstanding the nature of training, or understanding it very well). Sometimes such people will leave courses when subjects such as ethics or case management arise, while others continue and become excellent therapists. There are still some people who hold the misguided view that undertaking a counselling or psychotherapy training will 'fast track' them to a professional status where employment will be easily found. As we will discuss in more detail later, this view is profoundly inaccurate. With these points in mind, it is worth reflecting on Adam, who is considering applying for a place on a psychotherapy training course (see Box 2.1).

CASE STUDY 2.1
Adam

Adam is a 32-year-old catering manager. He has had this career since leaving school and has become aware of his dissatisfaction with the routine of his work. Four years ago he experienced a period of depression and, on the recommendation of his GP, attended a number of sessions of counselling. He found these helpful and his depression improved. He has become fascinated by psychology and is an avid reader of self-help books. Many of his friends have told him that he is a good listener and always provides excellent advice. His partner, Allan, is unsure about Adam's choice to train as a psychotherapist. He believes that Adam is only doing it because of his own positive experiences and perhaps is looking for more therapy, rather than training to become a therapist.

1 What might be Adam's primary motives to apply for psychotherapy training?
2 What do you think of Allan's concerns, particularly around his suspicion that Adam is seeking more therapy rather than a psychotherapy training?
3 How should they each manage this situation?

There is no hierarchy of motivation, with one motive better than another. The many and varied reasons why people embark on such training all add to the diversity and breadth of experience that is likely to be encountered in any training group. The following questions might help structure your reflection:

1 Does counselling or psychotherapy training fit into your existing set of skills or employment?
2 If not, are counselling and psychotherapy skills likely to enhance your work? If so, how?
3 Have you ever been a client for counselling or psychotherapy? If so, was this a positive experience (and what was particularly helpful)?
4 Have you ever thought of seeking counselling or psychotherapy for yourself but decided against it? If so, why?

5   Is there a danger that you are considering counselling or psychotherapy training instead of actually going to receive counselling or psychotherapy yourself?

6   Do you know what counselling and psychotherapy is? Have you done some research to find out more?

7   Are you at a point in your life where you want or need a change in direction? Have you thought that being a counsellor or psychotherapist would be 'worthwhile'?

8   Have you looked into the career prospects for counsellors and psychotherapists?

9   Do you understand the different types of counselling and psychotherapy and have you thought about the ones that might interest you most?

Counselling, or psychotherapy?

As we discussed in the previous chapter, the question of whether and how to differentiate between the titles 'counsellor' and 'psychotherapist' has caused profession-wide controversy, with little sign of this being easily resolved. The reality is that in many settings counsellors and psychotherapists are employed alongside each other, often on the same contract of employment, job description and person specification. There will be no discernible difference between what they do and the complexity of clients they see. In a minority of settings, counsellors may be employed in preference to psychotherapists, or vice versa. Essentially though, it is hard to decipher difference in the typical application of job title.

As we have already discussed, training is perhaps the area of practice where the difference between the two activities is most apparent. Traditionally, the structure of counsellor and psychotherapist training programmes is quite different. However, the level at which such programmes are delivered has, over recent years, begun to reach parity. While traditionally, counsellor training programmes were non-graduate level and psychotherapist training programmes were graduate or postgraduate level, this differentiation is disappearing, with the majority of counsellor training programmes now at graduate level or higher. However, there remain important differences to keep in mind. A **PowerPoint summary** is available on the companion website that summarises key aspects of counsellor and psychotherapist training.

Training to become a counsellor

Counsellor training programmes can be based within further or higher education institutions. In addition, a significant number remain available in the private or voluntary sector and are typically part-time. There are very few full-time training programmes. Part-time training is usually structured across a day or evening per week, or weekends. The traditional diploma in counselling was structured across a 10-week introduction course, followed by an intermediate or skills-based course typically running for one academic year and then, finally, by a two-year qualifying diploma. This structure is slowly being superseded by three-year degree level programmes or, in some instances, Masters degree qualifying programmes. This represents a clear move towards the professionalisation of counselling as a graduate activity in response to the presumed imminence of regulation. Some regret this development, arguing that an academic-orientated counsellor training has the potential to exclude those people who, without any academic background or ambition, prove themselves to be skilful counsellors and contribute much to the profession. Additionally, it has been argued that by further introducing an academic culture to counselling, the human and relational quality at the core of counselling may be obscured or lost.

While all counsellor training programmes lead to a 'qualifying level', they are not necessarily equal in value. For example, a privately owned counsellor training programme that offers a 'diploma in counselling' not approved by a recognised awarding body is not necessarily to be equated to a programme whose 'diploma in counselling' is so approved. When courses are offered by privately owned organisations, it is important to research the validity of the awarding body to ensure that standards have been benchmarked at a nationally approved level, which will also indicate the qualifying level at which the programme is pitched. The same is true for training offered within further education institutions – the same caveats apply. Nevertheless, there are many excellent counsellor training programmes delivered within the private or voluntary sector, or further education settings, that are regarded highly and worthy of consideration.

It is important to understand that, for many courses, the qualification may have two components: an academic one and a professional accreditation. For example, when counsellor training is located within higher education, typically the institution itself will award an academic qualification (i.e., a diploma, postgraduate diploma, degree or Masters degree, awarded by the University of Wherever). Elsewhere the academic award will not necessarily be offered by a university, but instead an awarding body, such as the Counselling and Psychotherapy Central Awarding Body (CPCAB) – and ABC, for example. Awards from such bodies will be benchmarked against national qualification standards. It is certainly worth looking at the website of the training organisation to see who awards their qualifications to ensure they are mapped against agreed national standards.

WEBSITES

CPCAB: www.cpcab.co.uk
ABC: www.abcawards.co.uk

Many excellent courses will attract an academic award, with a professional award alongside. It is perhaps important to note here the existence of professional accreditation programmes. In the UK, professional bodies – e.g. BACP, COSCA, UKCP,

British Association for Behavioural and Cognitive Psychotherapy (BABCP), College of Sexual and Relationship Therapists (COSRT) etc. – often provide their own 'accreditation' schemes. Such schemes typically set out benchmarks for standards across the programme, including minimum teaching hours, curriculum content, requirements for placements, personal therapy and supervision. They then assess the course based on an application received from the course team and visits to the programme to talk to academic staff and students, before deciding on whether to grant the course 'accredited status'.

It does not necessarily follow that courses without professional accreditation are poor. Many courses that provide high-quality training with a nationally approved award are not accredited, perhaps because they have not had sufficient resources (in terms of time or finance) to submit an application. However, in a competitive market, a course accredited by a national and respected counselling organisation arguably provides certain benefits to its graduates. For example, employers often prefer therapists who have undertaken such an accredited course. In the UK the recent move has been away from a model of statutory regulation of counselling and psychotherapy in favour of a system of voluntary regulation managed by the Council for Healthcare Regulatory Excellence (CHRE), to become the Professional Standards Authority for Health and Social Care sometime in 2012. This is a changing field and it will be important to keep up to date with the latest guidelines from professional organisations. However, the integrity of an academic award and any professional accreditation it attracts will be a key factor in the emergence of voluntary registers and benchmarks for standards.

WEBSITE

CHRE: www.chre.org.uk

Almost all training courses in counselling require that the trainee undertake a practice placement, under supervision, where they build up a set number of counselling hours, i.e., face-to-face sessions with 'real' clients. Such placements may be located in a wide variety of settings, including health care, social care, education and voluntary sector. The number of required placement hours may vary from course to course, but can typically amount to a minimum of 100–150 hours over a specific period of time. Supervision is an ethical requirement for all counsellors practising in the UK, including trainees. The minimum amount of supervision is usually stipulated by the course, which may be informed by professional guidelines if the course is accredited. Many courses also have a requirement for trainees to undertake personal therapy, with a minimum number of hours required. Again, this can vary widely from course to course, ranging from 10 to 40 hours or longer. Over recent years the requirement for personal therapy has become increasingly a matter of preference rather than insistence, with other forms of personal development (e.g. other courses, reading, or involvement in groups) now being taken into account.

Training to become a psychotherapist

In the UK there are fewer psychotherapy training courses available, and while, as with counsellor training, they may provided by a variety of types of organisations (e.g. privately owned providers, further or higher education institutions), they will all be affiliated to a college of the United Kingdom Council for Psychotherapy. The UKCP colleges are:

- Council of Psychoanalysis and Jungian Analysis College
- Humanistic and Integrative Psychotherapy College
- College for Sexual and Relationship Therapists
- College for Family, Couple and Systemic Therapists
- College of Hypno-Psychotherapists
- College of Constructivist Psychotherapies
- Cognitive Psychotherapies College
- Psychotherapeutic Counselling and Intersubjective Psychotherapy College
- University Training College
- College of Medical Psychotherapists.

It is only possible to register with the UKCP as a psychotherapist if you have completed one of the member organisation's training programmes. It is vital that, if you decide to train as a psychotherapist rather than as a counsellor, careful consideration is given to the preferred modality of training, as organisations are grouped into colleges by modality.

Psychotherapy training programmes are also typically part-time. They are more often grouped across a number of weekends throughout the year. Training courses usually last four years, though it is not uncommon for training to last much longer, particularly if a component of the training is self-planned learning: a number of self-selected courses making up the final period of training. Trainees are required to undertake a supervised practice placement, along similar lines to those for counsellor training. The minimum number of hours may vary, but UKCP require a minimum of two years' practice under supervision seeing a minimum of four clients weekly to register. Supervision is a requirement of practice, and most psychotherapy training courses make it a requirement that trainees undergo personal therapy, consistent with the taught model, throughout the duration of the training. This is a significant cost consideration where weekly personal therapy is required for a minimum four-year duration. Additionally, many psychotherapy training courses will require trainees to undertake a specific psychiatric placement, where they can observe mental health care and understand diagnostic processes. This placement is usually for a minimum of 20 hours but can be much longer. See the website links in Box 2.2 for further information.

Prospective trainees' choices will be informed by the nature of work they are thinking of pursuing post-training or whether preferred work settings stipulate one form of training above another. Beyond these considerations, training preference will be informed by personal and professional motivation and such pragmatic factors as availability and affordability.

BOX 2.2   GUIDES TO TRAINING IN COUNSELLING AND PSYCHOTHERAPY

UKCP student pages: www.psychotherapy.org.uk/students_trainees.html
BACP student pages: www.bacp.co.uk/student/
BABCP training information: www.babcp.com/Training/Training.aspx
COSCA home page (with links to training): www.cosca.org.uk
BPS Counselling Psychology: www.bps.org.uk/

There are many other professional organisations. For information about training in specific areas see their websites.

FURTHER READING

Guides to UK universities

The Guardian UK University Guide: www.guardian.co.uk/education/universityguide
The Times UK Good University Guide: www.thetimes.co.uk/tto/education/good
    universityguide/

Where to study

As discussed previously, training can be offered by a variety of providers, which increases the possibility of finding the right course for you. While a university setting might initially be more attractive, it isn't necessarily the best place to study simply by virtue of being a university. Certainly, the larger the institution, the more likely there are to be additional resources – for example, a full academic library, access to online journals and reference databases, student support. Some would argue, however, that with size of institution comes a loss of intimacy and personal contact. Counselling and psychotherapy training courses, given the focus on personal and group development, typically have a much smaller cohort than many degree programmes in other subjects, but a smaller institution can in addition sometimes offer a greater sense of being 'held' and known than a larger one.

Pragmatics are, of course, extremely important in making a decision. The 'perfect' course might be identified, but if it is a three-hour train journey away then it is important to consider whether this is sustainable over the duration of a long and demanding training programme. Additionally, if you are interested in attending specialist training in transactional analysis, for example, but the course is three hours away, it is important to also consider whether you are in a position to access suitable and appropriate placements and to receive supervision locally and personal therapy (if required), without having to travel for them too.

REFLECTIVE TASK

Write two lists of 10 items each: first, what motivates you to undertake training in therapy; second, what practical factors you would need to take into account to manage the demands of training, (e.g. finances, time, etc.). Having completed these lists, consider the balance between 'costs' and 'benefits'.

Client group and working context

When thinking about becoming a counsellor or psychotherapist the pitfall of thinking generically, rather than specifically, is an easy one to fall into. Wanting to be a counsellor or psychotherapist is a good start, but what type of counsellor or psychotherapist you want to be, or what client group you might be interested in working with, are equally important considerations. That is not to say that considering such questions will necessarily provide clarity of answers. The point here isn't to suggest that all people considering counsellor or psychotherapist training will know how they imagine their professional futures – but reflecting on the detail can be enormously helpful, particularly if there is a specific ambition harboured.

Many counselling and psychotherapy services are generic adult services, i.e., they provide counselling and psychotherapy, often after assessment, to any adult (18 years onwards) who accesses the service. In practice this will mean that any adult, with any psychological difficulty, is able to access the service. If, following assessment or basic screening, the difficulties are deemed suitable for therapy, the person will become a client of the service. That might mean that 'longer term' or 'brief' therapy is offered. It is difficult to define 'longer term' and 'brief', given that services will define these terms differently. I have worked 'briefly' (as we say) in various services: such work has ranged from 10 sessions (of 50 minutes each) down to two sessions. I have also worked 'longer term', which in practice has meant anything from in excess of 10 sessions to several years. Some counsellors and psychotherapists, often depending on their modality, may work with a client for even longer than that.

Here we have two distinctions in the type of counsellor or psychotherapist one might wish to become – the distinction between working briefly or longer term, and that between working with adults or young people. On this latter point, it is worth noting that many counsellor and psychotherapy programmes do not offer qualifications in working with young people and children. In that case, practice placements will be with adult clients, and the particular skills required for working with young people or children will not be fully addressed. However, some courses specify their training is for work with young people or children: they gear their curriculum and qualification accordingly. If your interest is in working with young people and children, it is important that you ensure your training will equip you to do that work, or be prepared to undertake additional training once you qualify. I have met many trainees who clearly want to work with children but have later found that their generic adult training was insufficient or inappropriate, leaving them having to start a new course once they have finished the last. Some counsellors and psychotherapists with generic adult qualifications do find employment in young people's services, perhaps undertaking additional training while in employment. Latterly, however, there has been a trend towards such employers looking for practitioners with young-people-specific training. Thus, employment opportunities of this type without a specialist qualification are becoming hard to find.

There are other client groups where specific or additional training might be required. For example, working with people with learning difference demands particular expertise, perhaps with new communication skills or knowledge of different conditions and presentations. Working with people with severe and enduring mental illness requires detailed knowledge of psychopathology (whether or not you subscribe to the philosophical assumptions of 'mental illness') and mental health systems. Working with adult survivors of sexual abuse, or perhaps people diagnosed with post-traumatic stress disorder (PTSD) can also require additional knowledge and skills. For many such types of presentation, a generic adult training will be a good start: it is, however, worth undertaking research to see whether any of these courses offer additional specialisms in relevant areas.

In general terms, considerations of preferences concerning working contexts are likely to take a similar form. For example, latterly there has been a trend towards health service employers preferring people with qualifications in cognitive-behavioural therapy (CBT), particularly so since the development of Improving Access to Psychological Therapies (IAPT) provision. These services are generally structured around either 'low intensity' (e.g. self-help, bibliotherapy-type) or 'high intensity' (e.g. CBT) interventions on a stepped-care model of delivery. The message here is that a CBT qualification will generally make you more employable in health care settings than others. This is not a fixed rule – there are many person-centred or psychodynamic practitioners working in health care settings, for example – but the general principle is worth considering.

WEBSITE

IAPT: www.iapt.nhs.uk

Some organisations may expect a qualification in relationship or sexual therapy, while others may require particular skills and knowledge concerning trauma. Some organisations in the UK (e.g. the relationship counselling organisation, Relate) will offer their own training programme. If you have a particular interest or know the type of counselling or psychotherapy you will wish to provide, it is essential that you research what employers in the relevant areas expect or require.

Purism or pluralism

Perhaps one of the most difficult considerations is that of modality. For many decades counselling and psychotherapy has been structured around modality (as discussed in Chapter 1). While many key writers and theorists in the profession have argued against such 'tribalism' (Bond, 2003; Di Loreto, 2009), the situation remains. As we have already noted, it is only possible to register with the UKCP as a psychotherapist after completing training with a member organisation: these member organisations are structured around 'colleges' which, in turn, are structured around modality. While there is no such rigid structure for counsellor training, courses are still offered on the basis of modality (e.g. person-centred training or psychodynamic training).

Too many trainees begin one course and find after, say, the first year that they should have enrolled on another instead. Often trainees have told me they have realised they will have to find another course after they have qualified. There are no hard and fast rules as to what type of person is best suited to which course. Ogunfowora and Drapeau (2008) considered whether personality type could tell us anything about who might do what training. They concluded personality played some part in a preference for training in humanistic/existential, psychodynamic, cognitive-behavioural and feminist theoretical approaches in their sample groups.

Chapter 3, Principal Counselling and Psychotherapy Approaches and Skills, provides overviews of the principal counselling and psychotherapy approaches practised in the UK. Additionally, some excellent resources discuss modalities in more detail. They include Feltham and Horton's *The SAGE Handbook of Counselling and*

Psychotherapy (3rd edn, 2012), and Dryden's *Handbook of Individual Therapy* (Dryden, 2007). Such texts can provide a good 'overview' of key modalities and their theoretical principles. If you find yourself drawn to one theory rather than another, use the recommended further reading to help you delve more deeply. Making such explorations at an early stage may save you a great deal of time and money in the longer term.

PAUSE FOR REFLECTION

1 If you have had your own counselling or psychotherapy, what do you know of the approach the therapist used? Was it helpful or unhelpful? In what ways?
2 Are you drawn to working with adults, or children and young people? Why?
3 Is there a particular setting you are interested in working in? What is it about that setting that interests you?
4 Do you like concrete ideas and principles, applied to a particular problem?
5 Are you interested in approaches that might teach clients skills, knowledge and ideas?
6 Do you prefer uncertainty, a sense of 'inner' knowledge and wisdom, and self-direction?
7 Are you interested in approaches that draw on the knowledge of the person so that they can solve their own problems?
8 Are you interested in relationships and the influence of the past on the present?

It may be that no one particular modality interests you, or that you are drawn to several. There are a number of integrative courses available both in counselling and psychotherapy that bring together two or three key modalities and integrate them into a new approach (for example, by integrating person-centred and psychodynamic ideas). More recently in the UK there has been a growing interest in pluralistic approaches to counselling and psychotherapy (Cooper and McLeod, 2010), where therapists draw on the expertise of the client to direct therapy, developing further the ideas of integrative approaches.

One factor that often drives people to train in a particular model is positive experience of that approach as a client. A positive experience of an approach in which we felt respected, listened to, taken seriously and ultimately helped, will motivate us strongly towards replicating that approach in our own training. This is not a bad thing, and when done with awareness can be very positive. Nevertheless, the questions provided above remain worth considering to ensure that the commitment made, in terms of time, money and emotional energy, is directed in as informed a way as possible.

Conclusions

We can see that selecting a suitable counselling or psychotherapy course involves striking a careful balance between several important, and sometimes competing, factors. Your motivation for undertaking training in the first place; the course providers and the level and type of qualifications provided; whether it is counsellor or psychotherapist training specifically that interests you; the geographical location of the course; the context or setting you wish ultimately to work in and the type of client group you may wish to work with; and the modality that most interests you and reflects your personal and philosophical view of the world – all these factors, like spinning plates, have to be carefully balanced.

Overall, it is essential not to underestimate the commitment – both personally and professionally – that training requires of you, your partner, family, friends and workplace, should you decide to embark on a course. Unlike in some traditional areas of academic study, you will not only be learning a whole new set of theories and ideas that will need integration, you will also need to develop competence in a whole new range of skills. Indeed, it is the need to transfer theory to practice that can form the most significant challenge when the practice placement begins. In short, there are many joys to undertaking a counselling and psychotherapy training, but many challenges too. The next section explores these in more detail.

PAUSE FOR REFLECTION

1 Why are you interested in undertaking training to become a counsellor or psychotherapist?

2 What do you already know about therapeutic concepts and ideas? Which ones appeal to you, and why?

3 What do you know of the financial requirements of training, and are you prepared to meet them?

4 What do you know of the personal requirements of training, and are you prepared to meet them?

5 Have you talked through your thoughts regarding training with your partner, family or friends and explained the demands of training and how they might be impacted by them?

6 Do you have the time?

7 Do you have any ambitions to work with a particular client group or in a particular setting? If so, have you researched if there are any specific training requirements?

2.3 THE CHALLENGES AND JOYS OF TRAINING

SECTION OUTLINE

Training to become a counsellor or psychotherapist is unlikely to be a neutral experience for you. As well as the many exciting opportunities, there can be challenges along the way that can, at the time, test your commitment. This section explores these in more detail and considers ways of supporting ourselves.

Training to be a counsellor or psychotherapist is a not a neutral experience. If you come away from training feeling that the experience has had little impact on your life, then either you, or the course, has done something very wrong. Some have likened the experience to a fairground roller-coaster, with some slow, relentless uphill slogs, followed by exhilarating moments where it is almost impossible to catch your breath; the entire ride can form a profound but sometimes physically and emotionally draining experience. Whatever your personal experience of training, there will undoubtedly be highs and lows, all of which will need careful negotiation.

The purpose of this section is to flag some of those challenges and joys. The aim here isn't to help you avoid the difficult bits and only experience the good parts: both aspects ultimately contribute to the experience and have a valuable part to play. Instead, the hope is to help you begin training with some degree of awareness and preparation. Pre-course information is important in this regard and should be read carefully and fully. The application process, which often involves a group or individual interview, is another essential part of the awareness-raising process. It is important to prepare for the selection process carefully: ensure you understand the structure and time demands of the course; be clear as to the financial implications; and, most importantly, don't be afraid to ask questions of tutors during the selection process. They will hope and expect that you will be curious and inquisitive and will be willing to answer questions honestly and fully. All of these aspects will contribute to your engaging with your course of choice, and prepare you for the forthcoming years. On the companion website there is a summary list of practical issues you might want to consider when thinking about embarking on training.

The challenges

The personal journey

Arguably, all good-quality education provision should provide a space for personal growth and reflection, in addition to the acquisition of new knowledge and skills. You will expect to attend your course and be given information about key theories and theorists, as well as an opportunity to understand and practise key counselling and psychotherapy skills. While you may understand that personal growth will be a part of that process, it may not be immediately apparent that personal reflection will be an explicit aspect of the training process, as well as an implicit one too.

The case scenario of Suzanne, outlined in Box 2.3, is based on the accounts of a number of trainees I have worked with.

CASE STUDY 2.3
Suzanne

Suzanne is a 43-year-old counsellor trainee in the second year of her training. She is separated from her partner and is the main carer for her three young children. She works full-time and relies heavily on family and friends for child care and other support. She attends personal therapy once per fortnight, attends supervision twice per month, is on placement for half a day a week and attends her training course for four hours per evening once per week. She talks in personal therapy about the demands she is facing: she feels that she spends all her energy 'spinning plates' and 'trying to make the unbalanceable balance'. She is tearful, tired and increasingly irritable.

1   What are your thoughts in response to Suzanne's situation?
2   If you were her therapist, how might you respond?
3   How similar is Suzanne's situation to your own? How do you manage?

A trainee once said to me that the course team had explained early on that the process of training would be emotionally challenging, and potentially life changing. The group, in response, had said 'yeah, right' or something to that effect. She told me this story towards the end of her training, during which almost everything in her life that could have changed, had changed – mostly as a consequence of her training experience. She reflected on the profundity of the advice she had received from her tutors early on and wished she had had the wisdom to appreciate it at the time. Of course, it would have been impossible for her to fully grasp the scale of what it was she was embarking on, but her experience might resonate for many.

The early days of counsellor and psychotherapist training are often spent acquiring and practising new skills, alongside experiential teaching that first establishes a safe environment for learning, and then moves on to personal reflection. Trainees are openly encouraged, within the context of what they feel is safe and appropriate, to talk about their personal experiences with group members, and to use their own life experience in skills development, e.g. to talk in pairs about personal experiences while practising counselling skills such as reflection or paraphrasing. These first few months can be a powerful and intimate time, where members of the training group come together in a shared endeavour.

Alongside this process is the personal development group. This group of trainees, either the full training group or a fixed selection of it (depending on the size of the course), meet regularly – perhaps weekly or fortnightly – to talk about themselves: their lives, struggles, ambitions, hopes and hurts, for example. Payne (2004, p. 511) states that personal development groups, 'offer opportunities for reflection on inter-actions and other important learning of counsellor [therapist] skills and processes'. Usually facilitated by a member of the tutor team, this group resembles a therapy group, without actually being one – the important distinction being that the per-sonal development group is located within a training context, and is facilitated by a tutor who will also, very probably, have an assessment role. In some instances the personal development group process is separated from the assessment process, but not in all cases. There has been much research into the efficacy and experience of the personal development group (Donati and Watts, 2000; Johns, 1996; Lennie, 2007; Payne, 2004).

Personal development is a process that should underpin everything throughout your training. For some, it will be a painful process where many difficult avenues will be explored; for others it will be liberating and life changing, while for others again it will affirm already held knowledge about themselves. Elsewhere I have used potholing as a metaphor for the process of counselling and psychotherapy (Reeves, 2010a). The task of the therapist is to accompany the client into their underground caverns, exploring those known areas, sometimes coming across new cave systems, but ensuring that after the exploration both are able to exit safely and appropriately, knowing that the caves are still there for exploration another day. I would also apply this metaphor to personal development on training. The purpose is to help the trainee explore their own cave systems, accompanied by tutors or other training group members, so that they become familiar with their own experience. Where difficult caves are encountered, the trainee can go to personal therapy to explore them more fully. It can be difficult and sometimes claustrophobic, but also power-fully enlightening and fascinating.

Financial commitment

Generally courses try to be as transparent as possible about the financial commit-ment of counselling and psychotherapy training. Pre-course information should make clear the costs of each module (if based on a modular structure), as well as any other costs that will be incurred (e.g. for supervision, personal therapy and textbooks). Like all courses, the stated costs at the outset are likely to be exceeded. For counselling and psychotherapy training in the UK the full implications of costs might be difficult to comprehend when presented in paper form. For example, individual personal psychotherapy might be quoted as somewhere in the region of £40 per hour. Where the requirement is for weekly personal therapy for the duration of the course (which minimally might be a four-year training), the costs become extensive. For example, if we assume a trainee attends personal psychotherapy for 40 weeks of the year at an hourly rate of £40, for the duration of a four-year course the financial commitment for personal psychotherapy would be around £6,400. The sum of £40 per week might appear manageable, but £6,400 is a stark figure. These figures may alter in various parts of the UK with different prevailing rates, and are likely to increase over time. However, the point here is to illustrate the financial undertaking of training – and here we are only considering the personal therapy component. A costs calculator is available on the companion website to help you estimate costs.

Likewise, the commitment to supervision can also be significant. All courses in the UK should make a requirement for trainees to attend supervision, as it is an ethical expectation of almost all professional bodies and accrediting organisations. How supervision will be structured will vary considerably, ranging from individual-only through to group-only, with mixtures of the two somewhere in between. Take, for example, a BACP-accredited counsellor training programme that I am familiar with: the supervision expectation is one hour of individual supervision per month, plus two group meetings per month – a rough equivalent of two hours individual supervision per month. Assume a cost per hour of supervision of £30 (which in some parts of the UK would be very low) over a placement in which the required number of client hours is 150 and the trainee sees three clients per week; assume too that every client attends every week (though that never in fact happens): it will then take the trainee a minimum of 50 weeks to accrue the required hours (i.e., approximately 12 months). This approximates the supervision costs at around £720. It has to be stated that these estimates are for the very best scenario: in practice the costs are almost certain to be higher. Taken together, then, supervision and personal therapy alone are going to cost at the least well in excess of £7,000.

The average cost of a counselling or psychotherapy training is difficult to estimate – and would in any case provide a redundant figure, as costs vary greatly. Psychotherapy training is generally more expensive than counselling training, not least because of relative duration. It is not uncommon for training courses to cost at least £3,000 minimum, and they can range into the many thousands. Many courses and placement providers will require trainees to take out personal indemnity insurance. With the costs of textbooks (especially since smaller training institutions might not have adequate library provision) and travel, the financial implications of counselling and psychotherapy training are often in excess of £15,000. In the UK it must also be remembered that universities have introduced higher tuition fees from September 2012, which will also have a significant financial impact on you. Very little financial support is available for trainees and most courses in counselling and psychotherapy do not attract student loans or funding. Some universities do provide for financial difficulty, offering bursaries, and some courses, particularly in the private and voluntary sector, offer a lower cost training route: even then, however, costs are not insignificant. With the implementation of higher tuition fees in the UK it remains to be seen how or whether the cost structure of counselling and psychotherapy training will change.

While it is easy to become frightened by these numbers, the experience might not be quite as stark and difficult as the figures suggest: after all, people would never have children if they fully costed them beforehand! However, it is right that, before embarking on training, you fully understand the financial implications so that you can plan and prepare for the commitments effectively.

The demands of time

Training, supervision, placements and personal therapy make demands on time as well as finances. Many trainees struggle through not fully anticipating how time-demanding training can be. Course attendance is the most transparent call on time: it may be structured over a day or evening a week for each academic term, or perhaps instead over blocks of weekends throughout the academic year. In addition to basic attendance (which generally requires a minimum attendance rate of 80%), placement attendance can be particularly demanding: typically it will be for a minimum of three or four hours per week, often in the evenings. Personal therapy may demand one hour per week or fortnight (depending on course requirements) and supervision is likely to be structured similarly.

These are the basic 'givens' of attendance. The less specific, but often more taxing, demands on time will be generated through the preparation of course work and assignments. Courses will differ greatly on the level and extent of written work to be prepared, but will often include several formal academic assignments of around 3,000 words, together with personal development statements, placement logs and reports, and so on. Reading will be a requirement – not just for the preparation of assignments and course work, but for further professional and personal development, and to support direct work with clients.

It is important that, before embarking on a counselling and psychotherapy training course, you consider carefully your existing commitments and reflect on how you will be able to meet the additional time requirements of training. It may be that you already have the time, or that there are current commitments that you are able to suspend or end. It may possible to 'bolt on' counsellor or psychotherapy training to existing commitments without any mitigation, but the personal costs (e.g. exhaustion, ending up doing everything poorly) can be high. A **time calculator** is available on the companion website to help you estimate your time costs.

Relationships

Time commitments, financial requirements and personal development rarely impact in isolation. Unless you live in a bubble and have no contact with anyone else, counselling and psychotherapy training is likely to prove demanding for those around you. It is not uncommon for training to profoundly change the nature and form of personal relationships, and this needs to be carefully considered.

It is essential to consider how training might impact on those around you, particularly if you are in a relationship. The task of the trainee is to find a way of 'bridging' the training experience with their existing relationships so that one isn't held secretly, or so that a split occurs between the good ('the course') and the bad ('the existing relationship'). Neither is necessarily all good or all bad, but the process of training may shed light on aspects of the relationship that have previously been unseen, like sunlight shining through windows that haven't been washed for a while.

Likewise, friends and work colleagues may notice changes in you and how you view the world. You are likely to be profoundly affected by what you learn and the skills you begin to master. It is tempting to use these skills widely, and not uncommon to be told at some point by a frustrated friend, 'Stop counselling me!' The personal development aspects of the course provide an important opportunity to explore changes and how those around you experience them, so that you retain the integrity and authenticity of relationships that you value.

The training group and the tutors

It may be that the training group will gain profound significance for you, enabling you to explore relational dynamics and processes in a way that has previously been impossible. It is not uncommon for training groups to be experienced like a family, with all the support, love, respect, friction, splitting and rage that entails. For some people this newly constituted family will be a place of encouragement, for that will resonate with their early family experiences; for others it will be frightening, unfamiliar or exposing, particularly when early family experiences were fractured or traumatic.

Training groups provide an important opportunity to explore your own experience in groups, and notice how you behave and react with others. Many groups are female-dominated, given that still so few men enter counselling and psychotherapy training. This can sometimes limit the opportunities for exploring dynamics around gender, sexuality and power.

If training groups have the potential to act as newly constituted families, tutors may be positioned as the 'parents'. There will be potentially valuable insights to be had into how you relate to tutors, and how you experience their 'position' in the group and your experience of their power. This may shed light on your own early experiences of being parented, and how you resolved (or didn't) early dilemmas around power, control, love, attachment and abandonment, for example. Undoubtedly tutors can be a valuable source of support and encouragement, and it is important that you work hard to make the most of the relationship you have with them. Clearly they are likely to have an assessment role, and this may inhibit some aspects of the relationships, though skilful and experienced tutors are often able to handle the assessment aspect of their work with a lightness of touch that helps minimise any inhibitory factors.

Placements

Often the most stressful aspect of the practice placement is finding one: they remain scarce. Finding a placement at all is difficult, but finding one that provides the required scope and range of learning opportunities is even harder. Additionally, finding a placement that already has a counsellor or psychotherapist working within it, to undertake early assessments to ensure the appropriateness of early referrals, or to provide accessible advice and support, is harder still. Finding one that is accessible, relevant and meets your own time requirements is, as the saying goes, a bit like looking for hen's teeth.

They do exist, however, but resilience and determination in the search are necessary qualities to improve the chance of success. Some courses will have preferred placement providers, where formal links with agencies and services have already been established. It is important to ask your tutors whether such links have been made and, where they have, act quickly when given permission to arrange a placement. When there are no such links, as is the case in the majority of situations, you will be required to find and arrange your own placement.

It is important to contact potential placements, outlining clearly the nature of the placement you are seeking (for example, the number of clients, for what training) and sending an up-to-date copy of your curriculum vitae (CV). Many placements are inundated with requests and will interview prospective trainees. Some see this as overly complicated and unnecessary, but many placement providers, including my own place of work, see it as an equitable and fair way of allocating placements and of keeping in focus the wellbeing of clients using the service.

It will be important to ask questions of the placement to ensure that it will provide an appropriate and safe learning environment. The questions in Box 2.4 might help you consider these further.

BOX 2.4   QUESTIONS TO CONSIDER WHEN BEGINNING A PLACEMENT

1 Is this a busy service, i.e., do you have sufficient clients accessing counselling or psychotherapy to support a training placement? (You will need to ensure suitable clients are available for you to see to avoid the frustration of turning up on placement only to be told no clients are available.)

2 How are clients assessed for a trainee, or are they allocated without assessment? (Ideally all clients will be assessed by an experienced therapist prior to you seeing them to ensure you are able to work within your competence, and the client is aware beforehand they will be seeing a trainee.)

3 How many sessions can a trainee see a client for? Are trainees expected to work briefly and, if so, what does this mean? (It is important to be aware of placement expectations so as to ensure they are consistent with what is expected by the course.)

4 What are the hours of the placement? (It is essential that the placement is available on a day and at a time when you are able to attend and give it your full attention.)

5   Is the trainee expected to arrange their own external supervision, or does the placement provide supervision? If the latter, what are the costs and how is this paid? (If the placement offers supervision, it is important to ensure it is consistent with course expectations and that the placement supervisor is sufficiently qualified and able to offer supervision in line with the model of therapy being taught.)

6   What consultative support is available outside of formal supervision? (It is better if there is someone on placement who is able to offer consultative support in the event of uncertainty or concerns regarding risk.)

7   Is the trainee the only counsellor or psychotherapist in the service? (Consider the implications for working as a lone therapist while on placement, and discuss with the course tutor if this is the case and what additional support might be offered.)

8   How is the trainee supported when working with clients at risk? (Do policies exist within the placement to support and inform you, and what are you expected to do in the event of concern.)

9   Will the trainee be given all relevant policies and procedures at the beginning of the placement? (What form of induction will there be to ensure you are fully aware of all working protocols and expectations.)

10   Does the placement allow audio-recording of sessions (where this is a course requirement), with appropriate consent? (If you are required to make and present audio recordings of client work, ensure the placement understands this and is willing for this to take place.)

11   Will the placement be willing to contribute to the placement report, when it is required (if this is a course requirement)? (Courses may expect the placement to provide a report detailing progress on the placement in addition to a supervision report (if they are different people) – make sure the placement is aware of this and happy to do such a report if it is required).

12   Are there any additional training opportunities trainees can access while on placement? (Many placements make training available for their staff. Indicate your interest in participating as early as possible so you can be included, if appropriate.)

These questions do not constitute an exhaustive list: there may be others specific to your particular circumstances. However, questions such as these provide a useful structure for assessing the quality or appropriateness of a placement.

Supervision

Many courses will hold a list of 'approved' supervisors that they require trainees to work with. An 'approved' list is usually made up of established and experienced supervisors whom the course have confidence in, or who have supplied a CV detailing their qualifications and experience as a supervisor. There is still often the possibility of working with a supervisor not on an 'approved' list, but this will need authorisation from the tutor team beforehand.

Chapter 11, Supervision and Consultation, discusses in more detail the factors to consider when choosing a new supervisor and how to contract early on in supervision, as well as how to get the most out of supervision. Suffice it to say here that supervision is not only an ethical requirement for good practice, it is also likely to be an immeasurably important source of support and learning throughout the training process. A good supervisor will help you make sense of client work and develop your skills, will provide opportunities to consider ethical dilemmas and challenges, and help you to link the theory from your course to the practice of client work. However, this doesn't just happen automatically.

Unlike supervisors post-qualification, the supervisor you work with while in training will almost certainly have an additional assessment role. This can sometimes complicate the supervisory relationship if not managed carefully as it can inhibit a full and honest exploration of client work and of the trainee's areas for further development. You might silence yourself sometimes, or talk only about the work that you feel reflects best on your practice. If audio recording is a requirement of training, playing a recording of a session to a supervisor, while potentially a valuable learning experience, might also feel quite exposing.

Finally, it is important to negotiate carefully with the supervisor his or her relationship with the placement (if the supervisor works externally to the placement), and with the course. This is potentially a four-way relationship (trainee–supervisor–placement–training provider), and certainly a three-way relationship (trainee–supervisor–training provider) and so the boundaries and areas of responsibility need to be negotiated and clearly contracted to avoid problems arising.

Personal therapy

Some courses require you to have personal therapy, and will, as for supervisors, provide you with a list of 'approved' therapists. Where personal therapy is a requirement, the expectation usually is that you see a therapist whose modality is the same as that taught on the programme (e.g. the trainee must see a person-centred counsellor if undertaking person-centred training). Where there isn't a course stipulation for personal therapy (although such is generally the case for many psychotherapy training courses), many trainees will still chose to undertake some personal therapy to help them explore in more detail some of the issues emerging from their personal development on the course.

The challenge here is for any personal therapy, whether mandatory or not, to be integrated both (a) on a personal level and (b) back into the professional development. A danger can arise when personal therapy contradicts or comes into conflict with essential or important stages of the course. The task is for you to discuss with your therapist at the beginning of therapy how they (and you) see their relationship with the course, if any. Some courses will ask for personal therapists to confirm that trainees have attended the sessions they say they have, while more rarely some courses will ask for a report from the therapist.

The biggest challenge can be where personal therapy is a course requirement, but the trainee attends reluctantly or resentfully. Sadly I have met, far too often, trainees who have started their therapy with me with the words, 'I don't really need this; I'm only here because the course insists'. My heart sinks and the hope I have for the value of the therapy we are about to embark on quickly evaporates. I have been proved wrong: occasionally the therapy becomes an energetic and dynamic exchange of learning for both of us despite the early scepticism or resistance – but so rarely does this transition occur that I now refuse to see people who do not want to be there. Personal therapy has potentially enormous value for trainees, if only to provide an experience of having been a client. To participate reluctantly, or with resentment at having to be there, does not provide the best framework for beginning therapy (or perhaps to continue with training?).

The joys

As will be evident below, many of the joys of training stem from the same sources as the challenges identified above.

The personal journey

Few courses have as much potential to contribute to your personal development as counselling or psychotherapy training. Even in training in modalities where personal development is not a specific focus (as is the case with some CBT approaches), the process of learning about counselling and psychotherapy can open many doors and provide great insight into ourselves.

For most counselling and psychotherapy training, personal development – through group interaction, personal development groups and personal reflection, for example – forms an integral part of the learning process. While the delivery of theoretical concepts and ideas is key to understanding the work of counsellors and psychotherapists, and the acquisition of skills essential to the 'doing' of counselling and psychotherapy, many argue (and I would agree) that personal development is crucial to the 'being' of counselling and psychotherapy. It serves to integrate a personal philosophy, interpersonal and intrapersonal change, and our understanding of our own part in the process with a client. The insights into our own personal experience play a profoundly important role in creating an essential context for theory and skills development. Taken together, they provide for the best possibility of a trainee becoming a 'rounded' counsellor or psychotherapist, i.e., one that is able to be fully present in a therapeutic relationship, without having to resort to a role or stereotype. See the example of David in Box 2.5.

CASE STUDY 2.5
David

David is 32 years old. At 16 he was diagnosed with depression and referred to a Child and Adolescent Mental Health Service (CAMHS) to assess and manage his perceived suicide risk. He was given anti-depressants and more general support, but did not take up the option for therapy and soon fell into using alcohol and drugs as a way of coping. He later went to university to study for a degree in mathematics. He struggled emotionally at university and took three overdoses at times of crisis. He eventually agreed to go for counselling at the university counselling service. Sceptical initially, he developed a good relationship with his counsellor and made, by his own definition, 'life changing progress'. With the support of his GP he came off anti-depressants and was awarded an Upper Second (2:i) degree. Having worked for a time in insurance, he decided to re-train in counselling. The course, a COSCA-accredited programme at a local university, was demanding financially, emotionally and practically. However, David completed it successfully. He believes it was the toughest, but most empowering, experience of his life. He now works with a drugs agency in a city; he isn't paid as well as when working in insurance, but he believes he has found a career best suited to his ambitions.

Relationships

As understanding of the self develops, so can an understanding of the self in relation to others. Ultimately counselling and psychotherapy is a relational activity, one in which we work with others – either individually or in groups – to help address emotional or psychological distress. Our ability and capacity to connect with another is arguably the root of all successful counselling and psychotherapy. While I am drawing here on the professional implications of enhanced awareness of relational dynamics, the same is potentially true for our personal relationships with family and friends.

Simply thinking in relational terms can help provide different insights into what we do in relationships and how we respond to others closest to us. That is not to say that counsellors and psychotherapists are experts at relationships, and all personal and professional ones will be successful: sadly nothing could be further from the truth. Regardless of training, knowledge and a willingness to consider process as well as content of experience, counsellors and psychotherapists struggle as much as anyone else. However, there are opportunities to make use of our increased self-awareness to connect more fully with others and have dialogue about our part in any process.

The training group and the tutors

Above, I compared the training group and its tutors to a reconstituted family in which old and familiar dynamics may be enacted. This provides an opportunity for us to challenge and change how we see some of our previous experiences. We cannot rewrite history, but we can perhaps revisit it in the context of a training group, hopefully willing to support our own process of learning. Certainly on a day-to-day level the training group can be one of the most powerful vehicles for learning, in which we can try out ideas and new ways of 'being', while receiving feedback. This is specifically true for skills development, where working with other group members in pairs and triads (i.e., three people working together) can help develop and refine counselling and psychotherapy skills before we see 'real' people, that is, clients on placement.

Along with pairs and triads work, courses often create additional opportunities for group feedback, such as practice enhancement groups (courses may name these differently). These groups, sometimes containing all training group members or instead a selection of them (depending on the size of the course), meet to discuss skills development, providing a space to try out new skills in front of others, or play audio recordings of practice sessions previously undertaken. While this can be a little anxiety provoking, when facilitated well these sessions can be extremely helpful. See the story of Stacy in Box 2.6.

CASE STUDY 2.6
Stacy

Both Stacy's parents were killed when she was very young. Her paternal grandmother cared for Stacy for a while, but she reached a point when she could no longer cope. With no other family Stacy was looked after by the local social care agency. She lived in a number of foster homes, all of which were caring environments. Now with a partner of her own, Stacy feels generally settled, although feels that she missed out on important stability during her growing up. She found settling into the training group on her psychotherapy training course difficult, struggling to trust the quality or sustainability of the new relationships she was making. Over time she was encouraged to take emotional risks, disclosing some of her fears. While she did not get on as well with everyone in her group, the experience of being 'part of' was enormously liberating for Stacy and provided her with an opportunity to begin to address, initially in the group and later in personal therapy, some of the emotional problems she experienced, which she believed originated from her childhood.

Placements

Once the practical stresses of finding and organising a training placement have been successfully negotiated, their value can become apparent. Many trainees talk of their placements becoming the real focus of their learning, providing them with an invaluable and irreplaceable opportunity to see counselling in action. While skills development work prior to the placement beginning has typically focused on work with other course members, the placement is the opportunity to begin working with 'real' clients and 'real' problems.

While clearly all counselling and psychotherapy brings challenges and sometimes difficulties, many counsellors and psychotherapists, regardless of the number of years they have been in practice, talk of the passion they feel for direct work with clients. When combined with supportive, challenging and encouraging supervision, the practice placement can provide the trainee with apparently limitless opportunity for professional and personal development.

Supervision

Chapter 11 discusses how integral, and thus beneficial, good supervision can be for any counsellor or psychotherapist in practice. In short, the supervisor, if selected with care and the working contract negotiated carefully, can be pivotal to the trainee's capacity and willingness to bridge the space between their theoretical learning and the challenges of practice. Many trainees struggle with linking theory to practice, and the supervisor is well placed to contribute to an environment in which exploration and learning is both encouraged and facilitated.

Personal therapy

While for some trainees the prospect of personal therapy is, as discussed above, simply an unwelcome opportunity to spend more time and money on their training, for many it provides an opportunity to bring all aspects of their developing selves to a place where they can integrate and assimilate the separate parts, while also further exploring aspects of themselves that have, in many instances, been flagged or highlighted either during personal development on their course or during client work.

Many find that the opportunity to work closely alongside an experienced therapist, preferably practising in a way consistent with the core model of training for the trainee, provides a space to consider 'self' in depth. While supervision can consider the impact of personal struggles on client work, it does not itself constitute personal therapy and a good supervisor will hold this line carefully. Likewise, while a good course provides trainees with opportunities for personal reflection, it rarely provides the same level of space and safety for therapeutic engagement as can be achieved with another therapist.

Finally, one learns from seeing an experienced therapist 'in action': how they approach contracting; how they create, define and sustain a safe therapeutic environment; their careful management of confidentiality; their use and application of therapeutic skills; the ability to help focus, while also acknowledging client autonomy, and so on. These aspects, and others, become valuable learning opportunities, adding to the value of the counselling or psychotherapy in its own right.

Conclusions

Embarking on training in counselling or psychotherapy should not be undertaken lightly. There are many personal, professional, financial, time and emotional demands made of trainees. Many of these are clearly communicated by courses in pre-course literature and information, while others are only appreciated once immersed in the process of training itself. Any learning process ultimately involves a balancing of the costs and benefits. However, few training programmes demand as much of trainees as a counselling or psychotherapy course.

This is as it should be. Any person who leaves a training in counselling and psychotherapy feeling they haven't been challenged or moved, or who hasn't experienced the profundity of relational contact with another, or hasn't reconsidered themselves (or profoundly changed themselves) in some way, or hasn't acquired, developed and enhanced their ability to be with another, might carefully consider asking for their money back! Counselling and psychotherapy training should always involve more than regular attendance and a qualifying piece of paper: it should involve reflection on every aspect of the view en route to the top of the hill.

PAUSE FOR REFLECTION

1 What might be the particular challenges you face during counselling or psychotherapy training, e.g. time, financial, geographical?
2 How might you realistically address these challenges to minimise their adverse impact on you?
3 What excites you about counselling or psychotherapy training?
4 How might you incorporate course attendance, a placement, supervision and perhaps personal therapy into your existing routine?
5 What additional preparations might you need to support your training journey?

3

Principal Counselling and Psychotherapy Approaches and Skills

3.1 INTRODUCTION

CHAPTER OVERVIEW

The terms 'counselling' and 'psychotherapy' identify the nature of an activity – one involving a therapist and client (or clients, working with couples or groups). They do not, however, describe the process of that activity. It would be wrong to assume there is a generic approach to offering counselling and psychotherapy: rather, there are many different models and theories that inform and shape practice. The multitude of different approaches can be broadly (and loosely) categorised as follows: (1) psychodynamic; (2) humanistic-existential; (3) cognitive-behavioural; and (4) integrative and pluralistic. This chapter outlines the main theories within each category, including their key philosophical assumptions and ways of viewing the person. Additionally, the primary skills of counselling and psychotherapy are described and illustrated.

The terms 'counselling' and 'psychotherapy' are now embedded within mainstream culture. However, their general usage belies the complexity and distinctions that the terms entail. As we have seen in the previous chapter, the debate over the differences and similarities between the activity of 'counselling' and that of 'psychotherapy' is impassioned and ongoing. As we have noted, the differences may stem more from the historical development of these two approaches and from philosophical 'positioning' – in relation to ideas of collaboration, empowerment, treatment, wellbeing and disorder, for example – than the actuality of how and where therapy takes place.

This complexity, however, is simply the tip of the iceberg. If we were talking only about differences between counselling and psychotherapy, the debates and divisions would, perhaps, be easier to resolve. The real debate that rages in the profession is more about the relative efficacy and benefit of different types of counselling and psychotherapy. Many within the profession have charged it with 'tribalism' (Di Loreto, 2009), with 'my approach is better than yours' positions ultimately contributing more harm than good. However, Di Loreto (2009) also sees tribalism as a source of strength within the psychotherapies in facilitating academic robustness.

Writing about it now, I must confess to feeling a little ashamed. As I write I reflect that, over the years, it is an argument that I have also engaged in with colleagues and one that has become such a normal part of the professional way of being that it has seeped into one's day-to-day thinking, quietly contaminating it. It is only when someone makes a challenge to this thinking, or when it is written about and thus reflected on in a more deliberate and conscious way, that the ridiculousness of it becomes strikingly apparent. The sheer energy that is spent on trying to prove the superiority of one approach over another is staggering.

However, what is most concerning is that the debate is not simply a benign one; though neither is it a debate devoid of any benefit. In positive terms the debate about relative efficacy between theoretical approaches prompts enquiry and a questioning of all approaches. It helps us not to take what we do for granted or assume that, simply because we do it and have done so for some time, it must work. As we will discuss in Chapter 12, the imperative for a sound evidence base for counselling and psychotherapy pushes us, whether we like it or not, into asking questions in a systematic way. This is of enormous value to clients, who increasingly need to be reassured that the profession takes seriously the task it is entrusted to deliver. Essentially, if we engage with a discussion about whether approach A is more or less beneficial than approach B in working with someone with, for example, depression, we can hope that the process of refinement, critical reflection and evolution will contribute to the development of an approach (perhaps A, or B, or maybe C representing an integration of what worked best in A and B) that will be of most benefit to the client with depression. The benefits of this process are evident from the way that the various approaches have evolved over the years and from the way that different approaches have gained prominence for particular types of presentation.

Notwithstanding these positive outcomes, the debate between theoretical schools can also be tiresome and even destructive. An example of this is the current debate over the perceived dominance of cognitive-behavioural approaches. Cognitive-behavioural therapy (CBT) is now the treatment of choice for many of the primary client presentations, as defined in national treatment guidelines (for example, those issued by NICE, the National Institute for Health and Clinical Excellence, in the UK). It is used for clients with depression, anxiety, trauma, eating disorders and so on. The CBT schools have taken the initiative and developed a sound evidence base for its efficacy and many would agree that it can be of enormous benefit to clients with those presentations. The critics of CBT would argue that there is a sound evidence base for other approaches too, such as psychodynamic and humanistic ones, but that such evidence has been developed using less 'acceptable' research methodology. Whereas CBT has made extensive use of quantitative methods, including randomised controlled trials (RCTs), that represent the application of 'science' to evaluation, other approaches have made extensive use of qualitative methods: these may be less acceptable to policy makers and commissioners because they are less generalisable and are seen as using a 'softer' method.

Critics of CBT argue that the policy makers and commissioners of services are mostly CBT trained, producing an inherent bias in how different models of therapy are viewed and privileged. Whereas 20 years ago psychoanalysts held much of the power, there has been a slow process of shift towards the cognitive-behavioural models. In turn, the psychodynamic and humanistic schools have begun a shift towards creating new evidence: they begin to 'play the evidence game', using methodologies (such as commissioning large randomised trials) rooted in 'science' to demonstrate their efficacy – given that such methodologies are seen as the 'gold standard' for research (Cooper, 2011). Others argue, however, that whatever the nature of evidence used to demonstrate the efficacy of psychodynamic or humanistic approaches, if the 'lens' through which it will be viewed is a CBT-shaped one, they will always flounder.

These are real debates taking place right now. The difficulties here are perhaps less to do with the search for efficacious approaches to counselling and psychotherapy, but rather effectiveness at the expense of other approaches. For example, the position currently taken seems to be that if approach A is shown to work well with a particular problem, then approach A is preferred. This is as opposed to a view that says, yes approach A works well with a particular problem, but there may also be other approaches that work well too, or aspects of approaches B, C and D that seem effective. There seems to be a 'tunnel vision' perception of effectiveness, rather than a more expansive and inclusive view. The additional problem being that person A with depression might respond to a clear cognitive-behavioural focus, while person B with depression might respond to a relational-explorative approach. The 'science' mistakenly takes 'depression' as the lead factor (in much the same way it would with medicine, i.e., this particular infection responds most effectively to this particular type of antibiotic), rather than the person.

In more philosophical terms, the debate pushes people into taking positions rather than encouraging them to think in a more connected and collaborative way.

Instead of thinking on meeting person A, 'perhaps we might work together and consider how you think about your problem and how you then subsequently act', and on meeting person B saying, 'perhaps we might work together and reflect on how you are feeling about yourself and your world', we are instead pushed into tribalistic mechanisms where we are more inclined to think, 'I am a person-centred/cognitive-behavioural/psychodynamic counsellor/psychotherapist, and that is what I deliver'. Thus we become model-driven rather than person-centred (in the widest definition of the phrase).

It is an interesting anomaly about counselling and psychotherapy that there are modality divisions in training. It is hard to bring any other professional group to mind where this is the case: nursing; social work; teaching; psychology; law; dentistry; veterinary science; medicine – each of these (and others) begin with a core curriculum: everyone begins at the same point and receives the same grounding and only later has the option to specialise. It is important to consider your model in context: that is, in relation to other approaches to therapy. As we outlined in the previous chapter, you may have been attracted to a model because of a setting you are interested to work in, or a client group you are drawn to. Likewise, it is also important to reflect on your own values, beliefs and views of the world that have been instrumental in selecting your training.

It is estimated there are in excess of 450 different 'types' of counselling and psychotherapy. With the best intent in the world it would be impossible for me to adequately (or even poorly) address them all here. Neither is it possible to offer a comprehensive account of the detail of each main theory. Rather, I have taken the main four 'schools' of therapy – psychodynamic, humanistic, cognitive-behavioural, and integrative and pluralistic – and outlined the key models within each and the primary philosophical assumptions and interventions that inform that particular way of working. I begin with an overview of psychodynamic therapy, then move on to humanistic therapy and then cognitive-behavioural therapy, and finally integrative and pluralistic approaches. In this final section I will also briefly highlight some other training opportunities that you might consider at some point in your professional development.

The chapter finishes with a section on key counselling and psychotherapy skills – those skills that transcend models and facilitate a therapeutic relationship. The hope is that there is sufficient detail here to orientate you to the different approaches, with some recommended reading offered to enable you to go deeper into those that appeal. On the companion website there is a **PowerPoint presentation** summarising key points from the three main modalities considered in this chapter.

I acknowledge that in offering this flavour of some key approaches I will inevitably offer a reductionist overview of key principles – a flavour that will not be to everyone's palate. But my hope is to orientate you to other approaches and ideas and help you find resources to follow up those ideas in more detail.

3.2 PSYCHODYNAMIC APPROACHES

SECTION OUTLINE

Psychoanalytic theory and how it informed psychodynamic therapy have been pivotal in informing and influencing the nature of counselling and psychotherapy, as well as inspiring the development of a range of other models and schools of therapy. This section outlines the main principles of psychoanalytic and psychodynamic therapy, highlights a number of the key theorists who have contributed to its development, and indicates some of their principal ideas.

Introduction

With any discussion of psychodynamic therapy it is important to begin with psychoanalysis. Many of the key theories and principles of psychoanalysis still sit at the heart of contemporary psychodynamic practice but, as with all dynamic and changing theories, the practice of therapy within the psychodynamic frame has changed significantly over many years. Some might argue that any discussion of therapy per se must begin with psychoanalysis. As we will discover when we discuss the other key approaches to counselling and psychotherapy, psychoanalysis and some of its core theories have been central to the development of therapy in many forms. This has been either because other approaches have incorporated some key ideas (such as the use of ego states in transactional analysis) and developed them within a different frame, or because new approaches have emerged as a response against some of the philosophical ideas of analysis (such a person-centred therapy and the 'third force' of humanism in psychology). Either way, aspects of psychoanalysis can be found in much of what we do and how we conceptualise the process of therapy, regardless of orientation.

The development of psychoanalysis

Sigmund Freud (1856–1939), a neurologist working in Vienna in the 1880s onwards, began to develop an approach of treating his patients' psychological distress through the process of structured and systematic talking about early childhood memories and traumas. He did this primarily through the use of dreams, which Freud argued were the gateway to the unconscious, defined by the Oxford English Dictionary (OED) as, 'the part of the mind which is inaccessible to the conscious mind but which affects behaviour and emotions' (OED, 2012). Freud hypothesised that problems originated from a sexual source and concluded that sexual frustration was at the core of many difficulties. Not all of Freud's contemporaries agreed with his ideas and Freud experienced an early backlash. He was particularly interested in what was then termed 'hysterical illness' (illness without any apparent biological cause). The case of Anna O, a patient being treated by Josef Breur (1842-1925) with hypnosis, with whom Freud worked in Vienna, was an important landmark in the development of psychoanalysis. It was Anna O's ability to talk of past traumatic experiences while deep in hypnosis, resulting in some recovery from her symptoms, that led to the assertion that psychological distress (or hysterical illness) could be treated through the use of a 'talking cure'.

Freud and Breur worked together on these ideas, but Freud later moved away from the assertion that hypnosis was necessary to access repressed thoughts and emotions. The importance of the unconscious remained central to Freud's developing ideas and, in 1899, he published *The Interpretation of Dreams*, having first used the term 'psychoanalysis' in 1896. Later, in 1901, he published *The Psychopathology of Everyday Life* and developed further his theories of the personality. He suggested that psychological problems stemmed from conflicts between different aspects of personality, which he termed the id, ego and superego.

Id, ego and superego

The premise of different aspects of personality was important in developing ideas about the relationship between the conscious (what we are aware of) and unconscious (what we are unaware of) mind. The different aspects of 'selves' – id, ego and superego – were an important 'next step' in the development of psychoanalytic thinking in that Freud proposed that psychological problems originated from conflict between the different aspects of personality.

The id: primary instincts that drive biological need, including: food, warmth and sex, for example. The id is subdivided into two driving forces: *thanatos* (the instinct towards death) and *eros/libido* (the instinct towards life and sex). The desires of the id are either met immediately (the pleasure principle), or may be deferred, thus leading to fantasies of the desire (primary process thinking). The id is an unconscious process.

The ego: develops from the id and is the mechanism by which rational thought, based in the realities and part-conscious thinking, mediates and manages the impulses and drives of the id. The ego facilitates the needs of the id but through a more conscious process. For example, the ego enables the young infant to recognise that not all impulses and desires are met immediately, or met at all. Freud termed this the reality principle.

The superego: described as 'higher level functioning', the superego is the means by which moral and social standards are incorporated into the personality through learning from early caregivers and then, later, through the development of self. The superego operates at a conscious and unconscious level and is divided into two parts: the conscience (discriminating between good and bad thoughts and behaviours); and the ego ideal (what we wish to become).

In addition to these aspects of personality, another important component of Freud's work was based on his psychosexual stages of development, as outlined in Box 3.1.

BOX 3.1   FREUD'S PSYCHOSOCIAL STAGES OF DEVELOPMENT

Oral   Ages 0-2 (sucking, mouth fixation)
Anal   Ages 2-3 (retention and elimination of faeces)
Phallic   Ages 3-6 (focus on genitals and sexual arousal)
Latency   Ages 6-12 (receding of sexual fascination)
Genital   Ages 12- (sexual development and gratification)

While these stages are an important component of classical psychoanalytic therapy, it is not my intention to dwell on them here and more detail can be found in the recommended further reading section. They do not feature as core aspects in contemporary psychodynamic counselling and psychotherapy, but are important to highlight in their development of early psychoanalytic ideas. It is sufficient to note that Freud believed all stages needed to be negotiated successfully for the development of a healthy personality. Aspects of note from these stages include the Oedipus complex, Electra complex, and the development of what Freud termed neurotic anxiety.

More recent development in counselling and psychotherapy has, perhaps, centred on the work of Erik Erikson (1902–1994) and his psychosocial stages of personality development (1950). While Erikson subscribed to many of Freud's theories, including the importance of early experience in the development of the personality and the structures of the ego, he did not agree with the emphasis on infant sexuality. Rather, he asserted that social and environmental factors were significant in development. Erikson's psychosocial stages are outlined in Box 3.2.

BOX 3.2   ERIKSON'S PSYCHOSOCIAL STAGES OF DEVELOPMENT

Trust vs. Mistrust   Age 0-1
Autonomy vs. Shame and doubt   Age 2-3
Initiative vs. Guilt   Age 3-6

Industry vs. Inferiority	Age 7-12
Identity vs. Role confusion	Age 12-20
Intimacy vs. Isolation	Age 20-30
Generativity vs. Stagnation	Age 30-50
Integrity vs. Despair	Age 50+

Erikson argued that each stage is dependent on the development of the stage that went before it and each is based on the importance of social tasks and the management and negotiation of conflicts. Many view Erikson's stages to have wider application to those proposed by Freud and are easier to integrate into broader ideas of personality, distress and the nature of change.

The practice of psychoanalysis

The role of the therapist in the process of psychoanalysis is to bring unconscious material into awareness as a means of helping the client (or analysand) to resolve conflict. Without conflict resolution all that will be achieved is the treatment of symptoms, and if one symptom is treated then another will only replace it (symptom substitution).

The analyst will use a number of therapeutic strategies and skills to facilitate the exploration of unconscious material (Errington and Murdin, 2006, p. 252):

- Basic facilitative skills: empathy, other communication skills
- Interpretation: using Malan's (1979) triangle of defence (defence of the pain; the anxiety caused; and the defence against the anxiety), and the triangle of transference (past relationship; present relationship outside therapy; the relationship with the therapist), analysts will use interpretations to link two or more points of the triangle
- Boundaries: time, place and 'self' of the therapist
- Blank screen: self-disclosure will be minimal so as to avoid interfering with the exploration of unconscious and transferential material
- Careful attention: attention to the conscious material, but also to the potential for unconscious material (in what is not said)
- Depth and intensity: a great deal of time is required to explore unconscious material, so that analysis will typically take place over several years with a high level of frequency of sessions (minimally once per week)
- Free association: the opportunity for the client to talk about anything that comes to mind, including describing dreams (which will be viewed as an opportunity to explore unconscious material).

Criticisms of classic psychoanalytic theory

As outlined in the introduction to this section, psychoanalysis has been profoundly important in shaping not only the nature and development of contemporary psychodynamic counselling and psychotherapy, but also in shaping, either through the contribution of theory or the rejection of some of the theoretical and philosophical positions of psychoanalysis, many other important approaches. However, psychoanalysis has not been immune from criticism. Freud's theories, rooted in sexual repression, were revolutionary in that they were developed at a time when such ideas were not seen as acceptable. In challenging these societal boundaries many have claimed Freud to be a radical and innovative thinker who, in pushing accepted boundaries, prepared the ground for major philosophical, ideological and practice development. However, the application of psychoanalysis with clients takes many years, with frequent sessions. This makes accessing such therapy very limited; it is available only to those who can fund it, or for the very few referred through health care systems.

Critics have additionally claimed (and continue to do so) that psychoanalysis has no real evidence base and its principles can never be open to scientific scrutiny. It is argued that the principles of psychoanalysis are based in ideas, rather than measurable and quantifiable concepts. Fonagy (2002, p. 287) noted, 'There are no definitive studies which show psychoanalysis to be unequivocally effective relative to an active placebo or an alternative method of treatment.'

Contemporary psychodynamic therapy

Historical development

Contemporary psychodynamic therapy (as opposed to classical psychoanalytic therapy) continues to draw heavily on the early principles and ideas of psychoanalysis, although the early work of Freud has been significantly developed and much of current psychodynamic thinking draws on the work of other theorists, including Jung (1875–1961), Adler (1870–1937), Klein (1882–1960) and Bowlby (1907–1990).

Carl Jung and Freud were close friends and worked together on the development of psychoanalysis for some time. However, Jung did not subscribe to Freud's emphasis on infant sexuality and libido, instead believing there to be other influences on an individual and their experience of distress that worked across the life span (unlike Freud's psychosexual stages, which were early-age specific). Jung developed a number of important ideas integral to the understanding of personality, including developing the ideas of personality difference, including introvert (where a drive and focus rests with a sense of an internal world), and extrovert (where a drive and focus rests with a sense of an external world). Jung's writing on individuation (an integration of self through the resolution of conflicts: a move towards growth) is also important in shaping understanding of personality and change.

Alfred Adler's view was more focused on the individual's strive for power, in response to their early experience of powerlessness in childhood and as a means of avoiding feelings of inferiority, rejecting also Freud's focus on sexual drives.

He argued, through his development of individual psychology, that as a means of avoiding inferiority individuals set goals to achieve superiority. He located these ideas in a social context and recognised the important influencing factors of family, relationships and society. By becoming aware of those goals that become self-destructive, Adler believed individuals could make significant positive change.

Melanie Klein is perhaps most strongly associated with her development of the theory of object relations. This view is based on introjective and projective mechanisms, as opposed to Freud's focus on id control and management. Her theories were outlined in her work *The Psychoanalysis of Children*, published in 1932. In her work she described processes by which she believed young children introject (bring into self) facets of important carers or relationships which, in turn, become influential parts of a developing ego: this process then shapes how the individual relates to the environment and those within it. The concept of splitting refers to problems in ego development when the child has incorporated mixed or conflicting messages from key people (perhaps a loving, but also disconnected parent). The 'split' is experiencing someone or something as all good, or all bad (e.g. an ideal therapist who is experienced by a client as encouraging and facilitative can quickly become experienced as neglectful or disinterested in the event of difficulties or disagreements).

Alongside the work of Klein, psychodynamic theory and practice perhaps now draws most heavily on theories of attachment and how insecure attachments can lead to psychological problems. John Bowlby's work on attachment, later developed by Mary Ainsworth and colleagues (1978), is central to the development of attachment theory and its relevance to therapy. It is important to view attachment alongside the concept of dependency. Donald Winnicott (1965, p. 84) described three forms of dependency: the absolute dependence of early infancy; relative dependence; and 'toward independence'. How the process of dependency has been experienced will partly inform the experiences of attachment. Ainsworth outlined the following forms of attachment following child observations:

- Secure: confidence in the security of the relationship and presence of carer
- Insecure-ambivalent: child remains angry and distressed on the return of the carer
- Insecure-avoidant: child does not miss the carer and does not initiate contact on their return
- Insecure-disorientated: child becomes immobilised, or 'frozen' on separation.

Attachment is an important aspect of psychodynamic therapy in that it provides an important opportunity for the therapist to work with relational and transferential dynamics – working with early childhood experiences and patterns of behaviour that have formed as a consequence. However, attachment theory is not exclusively a psychodynamic model and has relevance for other approaches. Finally, Erikson, who we have already briefly discussed, offers important ideas and insights into psychodynamic therapy.

Key theoretical principles

Psychodynamic ideas work on the premise that much of human experience takes place unconsciously in the unconscious part of our thinking, containing thoughts, feelings, ideas and drives, and that early important relationships with caregivers are influential in the processing of emotional wellbeing; problems in those early relationships can lead to emotional difficulties later. However, while early psychoanalytic thinking was important in shaping ideas of personality, including the functions of the id, ego and superego, a much greater emphasis is now placed on a relational, social and environmental context of people.

The importance of the unconscious remains central in much of the thinking, but theories of attachment, object relations, and power and motivation are important also. While there remains disagreement about the particular focus or emphasis of psychodynamic theory (with different 'schools' holding different positions), there is much more common ground.

The nature of therapeutic change

The nature of change focuses on work with unconscious processes that are represented in a variety of ways, including drawing on theories of attachment and object relations. Clear assessment of problems is important at the outset to enable the therapist to understand how difficulties are experienced and presented. This can provide invaluable information in formulating ideas and early speculations. Such information will include taking a careful history of family formation, relationships and early experiences so as to give insight into possible patterns of behaviour or relating.

By setting clear boundaries of time, space and relationship, the therapist is able to work more effectively with transference and possible resistance dynamics as they present in the relationship, as well as exploring defence mechanisms. This requires commensurate skills given that anything the therapist brings to the relationship has the capacity to change and influence it. The careful management of therapeutic space and boundaries provides a better opportunity for therapist interpretation to help bring unconscious dynamics into conscious awareness, thus enabling the client to move towards change. Segal (2012, p. 273) states that the understanding of the therapist includes, 'the capacity to face unpleasant, destructive, shameful feelings as well as deeply loving ones, in themselves as well as the client'.

Working in context

Psychodynamic counselling or psychotherapy, unlike psychoanalytic therapy, is not necessarily long-term and is therefore much more accessible. Psychodynamic therapists can be found in a wide range of settings, including health and social care, education, third sector and in independent practice. Like other modalities there have been developments in brief models of psychodynamic work, which allows for its delivery in a wider range of settings. Models of delivery have been developed for working across the age span and with a range of client groups, and also with a range of presenting problems. Psychodynamic approaches are included in treatment guidelines for moderate to severe depression, as well as other mental health problems.

Research profile

Cooper (2008, p. 164) notes, 'Psychodynamic therapies are well-supported by the evidence on the importance of the therapeutic alliance, as well as research linking the use of interpretations to positive outcomes. However, frequent use of transference interpretations tends to be contraindicated by the research.' Abbas et al. (2006) notes that short-term psychodynamic therapy seems to be effective for a range of common problems with mild to moderate benefits lasting into the medium and longer term. Cooper (2008) outlines a number of other studies that demonstrate the effectiveness of psychodynamic therapy with a range of client problems.

3.3 HUMANISTIC APPROACHES

SECTION OUTLINE

The humanistic therapies are widely practised, particularly in the UK, with more than half of BACP's 40,000 membership identifying themselves as humanistic practitioners. This section considers some principal models, outlining key theories, philosophical assumptions, primary principles of practice and key skills associated with working from that orientation.

Introduction

As was outlined in Chapter 1, the humanistic movement began to gain prominence in the 1940s and 1950s in the United States. At that time the field was dominated by psychoanalytic approaches and behaviourism. Psychoanalysis was particularly strong following the early work of Freud and his associates. While these early psychotherapy developments represented a 'turn away' from mainstream psychiatry and medicine, they were still closely allied to it and worked on philosophical assumptions of disorder and treatment.

The humanistic approaches, in contrast, rejected a number of important philosophical parameters of psychoanalysis and behaviourism and, in doing so, opened a new approach to the psychological therapies. The humanistic approaches, for many, represented for the first time a very real alternative to existing ideas and beliefs. Informed by humanistic psychology, the philosophical principles were quite startling for that period. They gained further momentum in the 1960s and 1970s, perhaps reflecting (and some would argue, leading – in their field) social movements at the time.

Humanistic psychology evolved from phenomenological and existential thinking, with key writers such as Heidegger (1889–1976), Merleau-Ponty (1908–1961) and Sartre (1905–1980). It was in the 1950s that three psychologists, Carl Rogers (1902–1987), Abraham Maslow (1908–1970) and Clark Moustakas (b. 1923) met in Detroit in the United States to develop what was later called the 'third force' in psychology (the first being psychoanalysis, and the second behaviourism). Maslow's concept of self-actualisation was profoundly important in helping to shape wider ideas around humanistic psychology and then psychotherapy. His 'hierarchy of needs' is outlined in Figure 3.1.

Maslow (1968, p. 10) wrote, 'Human nature is not nearly as bad as it has been thought to be… It is as if Freud supplied us with the sick half of psychology and we must now fill it out with the healthy half.' This statement typifies the underpinning philosophy of humanistic thinking, that while, in the view of Maslow, psychoanalysis attended to the 'sick' half – disorder and treatment – humanistic psychology instead attended to the 'healthy' half – growth, potential and self-actualisation. It is the premise and assumption of growth, human potential and move towards self-actualisation on which humanistic therapies are based.

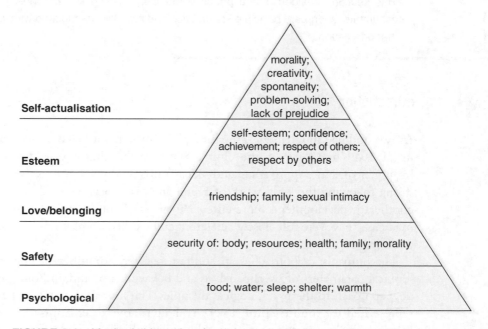

FIGURE 3.1   Maslow's hierarchy of needs

A number of key theories fall within the humanistic-existential school paradigm. I will briefly focus on three of the most widely practised:

1 Person-centred (Rogers)
2 Gestalt (Perls)
3 Transactional analysis (Berne).

Person-centred therapy

Historical overview

Zimring and Raskin (1992) (outlined in Tudor et al., 2004) suggest that the development of person-centred therapy can be viewed across four distinct periods. This development begins with a talk by Rogers in 1940 entitled 'Some newer concepts of psychotherapy at the University of Minnesota', during which he began to introduce some of the earliest ideas. During this period Zimring and Raskin note how Rogers began to focus on what were to become important therapist qualities: responding to feelings rather than focusing on content; and the therapist's acceptance of both positive and negative feelings. The second period, in the 1950s, saw the publication in 1951 of *Client-Centred Therapy* and further work by Rogers on the nature of therapeutic change and the development of the six 'necessary and sufficient conditions' for change to occur.

The third period, in the 1960s, saw Rogers publishing *On Becoming a Person*, in which he began to focus even more on the relational aspects of therapy and the importance of the nature of experiencing and being. Finally, the fourth period, from the 1970s and beyond, saw Rogers further developing core theoretical concepts with the steady emergence of 'person-centred therapy' as the dominant term for the approach.

The impetus for the development of person-centred practice for Rogers came from his own experience of having been a client, and his views of the predominant theories of the time, behaviourism and psychoanalysis. For Rogers, behaviourism represented a reductionist approach to human personality: individuals, in developing entrenched ways of being from experience, were essentially helpless and unable to make significant or meaningful change. Whereas psychoanalysis, he believed, constructed people as always driven by basic biological drives, never free from these primitive instincts and behaviours. Additionally, it was his view that psychoanalysis essentially focused on the negative aspects of human behaviour, always driven by destructive impulses. Whether his perceptions were accurate about those approaches at that time, Rogers instead focused on his view that individuals, given the right conditions, had the capacity to change and move towards a position of health and growth.

It is worth noting that many writers have criticised person-centred therapy for being very light on theory and suitable only for those with mild psychological problems. Kovel (1976, p. 116) wrote that 'Rogerian treatment works best where the person doesn't have to go very deep …'. However, others have refuted such charges, with Mearns and Thorne (2000, p. x) stating:

> We have concluded that such misconceptions are not always the outcome of ignorance but in some cases, at least, have much deeper roots. It would seem that our approach has the strange capacity to threaten practitioners from other orientations so that they seek refuge in wilful ignorance or in condemnatory dismissiveness.

Underlying assumptions

According to Casemore (2011), person-centred therapy draws on three primary philosophical beliefs: humanism, existentialism and phenomenology. Humanism is based on the belief that each individual has the potential for growth and development, with self-actualisation a fundamental human drive. That said, the move towards self-actualisation is more a process rather than an end-point, with individuals engaged in a search for meaning and importance, rooted in a belief of dignity and self-respect. Existentialism informs person-centred therapy through its assertion that we all possess free will and make choices based on our beliefs and experiences. Casemore (2011, p. 7) outlines six primary concepts that underpin existentialism:

- Humankind has free will
- Life is a series of choices, creating stress
- Few decisions are without any negative consequences
- Some things are irrational or absurd, without explanation
- If one makes a decision, he or she must follow through
- The only important meaning which can be attached to life is that which I give to it.

Essentially, with free choice comes responsibility: individuals are free to make their own choices, but with those choices come responsibility and consequence, which must be dealt with.

Phenomenology, developed by Husserl in the early 20th century, asserts there is no one, single reality but rather reality is constructed through our own individual experience. That is, my experience of an event or situation may be very different to another's, even if the situation was the same for both. We therefore must pay careful attention to an individual's account of their reality to begin to understand it fully. As Casemore (2011, p. 9) states, a phenomenological approach to therapy entails 'noticing all the events, feelings, experiences, behaviours, words, tones of voice and anything else that we see or hear, as they are in the moment and not interpreting them on the basis of our past experiences'. In person-centred terms this demands the therapist stays in the frame of reference of the client, as any interpretation of the client's experience would, undoubtedly and unavoidably (because of phenomenological assumptions), be framed within the therapist's own reality.

Key theoretical principles

Person-centred therapy is based on the assumption that human personality is positive, with the belief that all people are potentially fully functioning (i.e., someone with a positive self-concept, who is healthy and capable of development through new experiences and potential). Individuals experience conditions through their lives, which are informed by a judgement of what is worthy and what is not. People learn that their acceptability to others increasingly becomes conditional (e.g. I am only lovable if I am 'good'); conditions of worth shape an individual's view of themselves. Purton (2004, p. 4) describes conditions of worth where an individual 'denies or distorts their own felt needs so as to develop a self-concept which fits the "conditions of worth" of those around them'. The therapist's unconditionality in the relationship is therefore essential as a reparative factor.

Regardless of previous harm or the effects of conditions of worth, each individual retains the potential for growth and thus move towards their organismic (real) self. Within this frame it is believed that every individual retains the potential for change: each individual has an actualising tendency, a motivation for self-development and growth. Self-experience can only be healthily processed cognitively and emotionally by the individual whose experience it is (the principle of phenomenology). Organismic valuing recognises the potential for good for individuals to engage with and experience activities and behaviours they enjoy.

The nature of therapeutic change

The nature of the relationship is fundamental to the nature of change in person-centred therapy. The person and being of the therapist is essential here in creating the right conditions for change to take place. Person-centred theory asserts that the circumstances for change to take place need to be present. The core conditions of any relationship must not only be present, but must be communicated by the therapist so that the client experiences them. The therapist needs to empathically understand the client's experience from the client's frame of reference, and must communicate that empathic understanding. The therapist must experience unconditional positive regard for the client, in that they must be accepting and non-judgemental, and communicate unconditional positive regard; finally, the therapist must be congruent with the client, so that the client is able to experience the true self of the therapist in context of the therapeutic relationship. Person-centred therapists do not work from a professional façade of being, nor a position of expertise, but rather with a willingness and capacity to meet with the client where the client is, emotionally, experientially and psychologically.

Rogers (1959, p. 213) set out six 'necessary and sufficient conditions', within which the three 'core' conditions are embedded, for therapy:

1   That two persons are in contact
2   That the first person, whom we shall term the client, is in a state of incongruence, being vulnerable, or anxious
3   That the second person, whom we shall term the therapist, is congruent in the relationship
4   That the therapist is experiencing unconditional positive regard toward the client
5   That the therapist is experiencing an empathic understanding of the client's internal frame of reference
6   That the client perceives, at least to a minimal degree, conditions 4 and 5, the unconditional positive regard of the therapist for him, and the empathic understanding of the therapist.

Person-centred therapy is non-directive (its first, original name) in that, unlike many other therapies, the therapist does not set the goals, focus nor direction of therapy. Instead, the client's emerging experience in the moment is the driving focus of the work. As we have outlined previously, the therapist's role is not to interpret the experience of the client (for that would take them away from the client's frame of reference). With the communication of the core conditions, therapeutic change occurs during moments of self-acceptance and integration and the client's increasing awareness of conditions of worth that inhibit growth and the process of self-actualisation.

Working in context

Person-centred therapy is widely practised in the UK and in Europe, but has been less of an influence in the United States over recent years. In the UK, person-centred therapy can be found in a wide range of contexts, including health, social care, education, third sector and in independent practice. As will be discussed in more detail in Chapter 12, its presence in some health care settings is threatened with only a peripheral presence in the treatment guidelines for psychological therapies for depression, with CBT, interpersonal and psychodynamic approaches having greater prominence. However, the humanistic movement remains very strong and is important in continuing to challenge the increasing medicalisation of human experience and the ever-growing development of diagnostic categories of mental disorder.

Person-centred therapy remains a dominant force in training, with many and varied training programmes in person-centred therapy continuing to be very active and influential. The principles of person-centred therapy, and certainly the concept of the 'core conditions', have been widely accepted not only by other therapeutic modalities but by other disciplines, such as nursing, social work and mental health.

However, some have expressed concern by what they consider to be a misuse of the concepts and ideas of person-centred therapy. Merry (1996, p. 507) wrote, 'I am troubled by ... the way "person-centred" is becoming widely used to describe situations which do not do justice to the spirit or the original meaning of that term ...'.

Research profile

A study by Stiles et al. (2008) noted that person-centred therapy is as effective as psychodynamic therapy and CBT for a wide range of problems when analysing data from UK primary care settings. Additionally, there is evidence for efficacy of person-centred therapy for mild to moderate depression in adults and young people (King et al., 2000; Gibbard and Hanley, 2008). An increasing number of qualitative studies are being published that further demonstrate the value and benefit to clients of person-centred therapy.

FURTHER READING

Cooper, M., O'Hara, M., Schmid, P.F. and Wyatt, G. (eds) (2007) *The Handbook of Person Centred Psychotherapy and Counselling*. Basingstoke: Palgrave Macmillan.

Mearns, D. and Thorne, B. (2007) *Person-Centred Counselling in Action*. London: Sage.

Sanders, P. (2006) *The Person-Centred Counselling Primer: A Steps in Counselling Supplement*. Ross-on-Wye: PCCS Books.

Wilkins, P. (2003) *Person-Centred Therapy in Focus*. London: Sage.

Gestalt therapy

Historical development

Like person-centred therapy, gestalt therapy began to gain prominence in the 1950s with the emergence of the 'third force' of humanistic psychology in the United States. Developed by Frederick (Fritz) Perls (1893-1970), Laura Perls and Paul Goodman, gestalt therapy emerged as a new model with the publication of *Gestalt Therapy: Excitement and Growth in the Human Personality* in 1951, although Fritz Perls had previously published *Ego, Hunger and Aggression*, which outlined fundamental beliefs that were later to be incorporated into the therapeutic approach. Perls originally trained in medicine in Germany and qualified in 1921 before training as a psychoanalyst. Laura Perls worked with Kurt Goldstein and studied gestalt psychology, while Goodman was a philosopher.

For many years and, still for some today, gestalt therapy was associated with the particular unique style of its co-founder Fritz Perls who, in the 1960s, embarked on a number of large demonstrations of particular techniques. From that point gestalt has been synonymous with the use of particular therapeutic exercises, experiments and techniques (Mackewn, 1997). The 'empty chair' exercise (where the client is invited to engage in a dialogue with aspects of their 'self') remains strongly associated with a gestalt approach. While some may still use this particular technique, gestalt has evolved considerably over the last 30 years, adopting an increasingly relational focus, adapting to the changing needs of clients and services (Parlett and Hemming, 1996; Yontef, 1991).

'Gestalt' is a German word without a direct translation into English. The OED (2012) defines gestalt as 'an organized whole that is perceived as more than the sum of its parts', and gestalt is generally taken as meaning pattern, configuration or form. In the same way as person-centred counselling, gestalt and gestalt psychology may be said to draw on three primary aspects: phenomenology and existentialism; Eastern religion; and drama and movement (Ellis and Leary-Joyce, 2000). Phenomenology emphasises the importance of experience being seen as subjective, rather than an objective process, in that each individual experiences their own, unique view of their world. Existentialism, as was previously outlined in the section on person-centred therapy, highlights the importance of choices and individual responsibility. Eastern religions, such as Taoism and Zen, emphasise the importance of being and experiencing in the moment. Drama and movement was an important influence on Fritz Perls, who was interested in the work of Moreno's psychodrama approach.

Underlying assumptions

Gestalt is based on an assumption of holism, in that it is impossible to understand self through the interpretation or exploration of one part, given that the whole is greater than the sum of the individual parts. As such, the focus of therapy is about the configuration of the whole self and how it relates to its world/environment. We cannot be understood as separate from our environment (relationships, culture, family, class etc.) and must therefore be seen as in relationship with our environment through our means of being in contact with it. As per the humanist tradition, each individual retains the potential for growth and self-actualisation. Perls (1969, p. 31) wrote: 'Every individual, every plant, every animal has only one inborn goal – to actualise itself as it is.'

The core of gestalt is awareness, and helping to increase a client's awareness through the therapeutic process. Awareness in this instance would go beyond simply an intellectual awareness, but would also include an 'organismic experienced awareness' (Ellis and Leary-Joyce, 2000, p. 339). The 'here and now' experience of contact is essentially important, and gestalt therapists work to facilitate a client's 'here and now' experience and their contact with their environment. Growth occurs as we achieve contact with our environment, with different needs becoming 'figural' (everything in the environment that is the focus of attention) and returning to 'ground' (the environment surrounding the figure) as they become more or less important.

Gestalt therapy draws heavily on the work of Buber (philosopher) and his concepts of I–thou and I–It contact. I–thou (being as present as possible to another relationally) and I–It (where there is some goal or purpose to the meeting; that is, where the meeting moves beyond simply being in psychological and emotional contact). Human connection in therapy works toward an I–thou contact, although both I–thou and I–It are important for living in the world.

Key theoretical principles

Field theory is important in gestalt in working with awareness and how the client experiences their world and the meanings they attribute to it. Joyce and Sills (2001, p. 24) identify three important aspects of 'phenomenological investigation':

- The internal world of the client
- The external world or environment (including the therapist)
- The ever-changing relationship between them.

Taken as a whole they describe this as 'the field'. Field theory was first developed in psychology by Kurt Lewin (1952). He asserted that the relationship between the person and the environment was essential, and this is a key tenet of gestalt therapy. Clarkson (1999, p. 9) states that 'human beings can be understood only within the system of which they are a significant component part. A gestaltist would always work within the matrix of the person with needs in a sociocultural context'. Mackewn (1997, p. 49) offers a useful overview of field theory as it relates to gestalt therapy, summarised here:

- People cannot be understood in isolation but only as part of their sociocultural background.
- The field consists of all the 'interactive phenomena' of the individual and the environment.
- Human behaviour cannot be linked to any one cause but rather from the relationship between events in the field.
- Individuals constantly change their perspective of the field as they experience it differently.
- Some aspects of the field come into focus, while others move into the background.
- Individuals attribute their own meaning to events and experiences and by doing so contribute to creating their own experience (they 'co-create the field').
- Behaviour and experience happen in the present and can only be explained in relation to the present field.
- As all aspects of the field are 'interconnected', a change in one part will influence the whole field.

The gestalt cycle of experience (or formation and destruction cycle) is another key concept in gestalt, and a useful metaphorical means of illustrating contact and loss of contact with the environment. It assumes that healthy human experience is based on the formation of figure (needs) against the ground (environment) in a responsive and free-flowing way. However, problems occur when this process is disrupted. Early human relational experience is assumed to be important in setting patterns in this process. The cycle of awareness is illustrated in Figure 3.2.

The terms in brackets in Figure 3.2 represent what Perls called 'neurotic mechanisms' or 'contact boundary disturbances', which limit an individual's contact with their environment at all experiential levels. We can consider each of the ways in which contact with our environment can be disrupted:

Desensitisation is the way in which we can disconnect from both our environment and ourselves: not experiencing feeling, physical sensation, taste, sex etc. We do not experience a healthy sense of our sensitised experience of our world.

Deflection is the means through which we 'turn away' from positive contact with our environment.

Introjection is where ideas, beliefs, attitudes or other negative aspects from our environment are taken in ('swallowed') without question or assimilation.

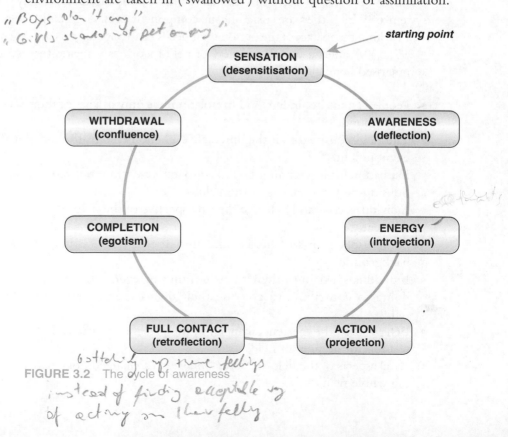

FIGURE 3.2   The cycle of awareness

Projection is the mechanism through which beliefs, attitudes, ideas or other negative aspects are attributed to others or other aspects of our environment.

Retroflection is the process of turning 'back in' on ourselves, thus to avoid full contact – avoiding expressing our experience for the risks it might bring.

Egotism is an excessive preoccupation with our own thoughts, feelings or behaviours (akin to an ongoing internal self-commentary).

Confluence is the loss of boundaries between self and environment, including other people.

The nature of therapeutic change

Gestalt therapy draws on a number of therapeutic strategies that aim to increase an individual's awareness. This includes awareness of the body and physical awareness, the language the client uses, and the nature and form of contact they have with their environment. The therapist may also encourage 'experiments' occasionally in which clients will be supported to try out new ways of being, different discourses, or ways of being with their environment, e.g. increasing sensation if the client is desensitised.

The therapist will pay particular attention to the client's way of being in the world, and in relationship with the therapist. In this way the nature and form of the therapeutic relationship will be extremely important in gestalt therapy, with the therapist working to be fully connected with the client in a meaningful and relational way. Gestalt therapy is based on the premise that change occurs with greater awareness. As Beisser (1970, p. 88) states: 'Change occurs when one becomes what he is, not when he tries to become what he is not'.

Working in context

Like person-centred therapy, gestalt therapy can be found in a wide range of contexts, including health and social care, education, third sector organisations and in independent practice. Again, consistent with other humanistic approaches to therapy, a dearth of scientifically accepted evidence means its position in health care settings is becoming more peripheral, with a move instead towards approaches such as CBT, with a strong, quantitative evidence base.

Research profile

As stated, research has not been a primary driver in the gestalt world for many decades, with only relatively recent moves towards developing an evidence base. A study by Strümpfel and Goldman (2002) demonstrated that gestalt was as effective as CBT and person-centred therapy when working with clients who were depressed, with some phobias and other problems.

FURTHER READING

Bar-Yosef, T.L. (2012) *Gestalt Therapy: Advances in Theory and Practice.* London: Routledge.

Clarkson, P. (2004) *Gestalt Counselling in Action.* London: Sage.

Joyce, P. and Sills, C. (2010) *Skills in Gestalt Counselling and Psychotherapy*, 2nd edn. London: Sage.

Sills, C., Fish, S. and Lapworth, P. (1997) *Gestalt Counselling (Helping People Change).* Milton Keynes: Speechmark Publishing.

Transactional analysis

Historical development

Transactional analysis (TA) was founded in the 1950s by Eric Berne (1910–1970), a psychiatrist with training in psychoanalysis. With roots in a psychoanalytic tradition, TA now has firm roots as a humanistic approach. Berne was influenced by the work of Paul Federn, his training analyst, whose ideas of a system of ego psychology was particularly important for Berne's later work. As well as Federn, Berne was also strongly influenced by the work of Erik Erikson, who introduced Berne to the concept of the social and developmental influences on personality.

A key point in the development of TA was the rejection of Berne's application for membership of the San Francisco Psychoanalytic Institute in 1956, which then prompted Berne to undertake further work on his own theories. By 1958 all the primary aspects of what was to become TA were published in various articles and papers. Initially developed through these various papers and ideas, TA assumed a more coherent form in 1961 when Berne published *Transactional Analysis in Psychotherapy*. It developed a more popular appeal with Berne's publication in 1964 of his mainstream text, *Games People Play*, which introduced some of the basic principles of TA to a wider population. TA is now an established model within counselling and psychotherapy and continues to develop.

Underlying assumptions

Similar to other humanistic approaches, TA assumes that all individuals have a basic drive for health and growth. It is assumed that each individual is able to think and take full responsibility for their own actions but that decisions people have made can be changed (through 're-decision' work) and people can be responsible for their own destiny. Such decisions may be conscious and in awareness, but may also be unconscious or out of direct awareness.

Autonomy is a goal for individuals – this does not necessarily mean individual and isolating autonomy, but one that includes and is dependent on others to achieve. Awareness is central to the work of TA, encouraging individuals to live in the moment and to perceive it without interruption through rumination and moving away from a here-and-now experience. Like person-centred and gestalt approaches, TA stresses the importance of spontaneity, the validity of individual experience and how people construct their own worlds, and personal autonomy and responsibility, believing that change is possible. Finally, Berne proposed a third 'instinct' – physis (creative instinct) – to build on the instincts proposed by Freud, namely thanatos (death instinct) and eros (sexual instinct).

Key theoretical principles

One of the central concepts of TA is that of the three ego states: parent, adult and child. Clarkson (1999, p. 222) defines ego states as 'the subjectively experienced reality of a person's mental and bodily ego with the original contents of the time period it represents'. The three ego states, as depicted by Berne, are detailed in Figure 3.3.

Here the parent (P) ego state contains two aspects: the nurturing parent and the controlling parent. The parent ego state represents past experiences in that it draws on the patterns of behaviour and parent style as experienced in childhood. The nurturing parent represents the parent that was unconditionally caring and supportive, while the controlling parent represents the disciplinarian and restricting parent. The child (C) ego contains two aspects: the free child and the adapted child. The free child is playful, happy, adventurous and explorative but is able to access sad and painful feelings too, while the adaptive child (often responding to the controlling

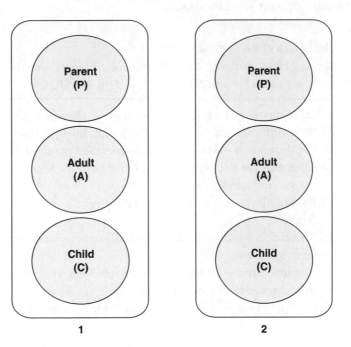

FIGURE 3.3 The three ego states (for details, see text)

parent) is managed, passive and overly focused on 'good' behaviour. The child ego state also draws on past experience, including feelings, thoughts and behaviours related to our own experience of childhood. The adult (A) ego state, represents adult virtues, such as autonomy, clear thinking and 'here and now' responses.

Transactions occur between individuals originating from particular ego states. In Figure 3.3, where 1 represents one person and the ego states in panel 2 represent another, we can draw lines between them to illustrate transactions. For example, we may find ourselves responding to another from a controlling parental position ('I wish you wouldn't do that, it is really irritating') that might trigger an adapted child response from another ('I'm sorry, I won't do it again'). Transactions can occur from any of the three primary ego states (and the two sub-divided ones) and trigger responses in another from particular ego states, depending on how the transaction, or communication, has been experienced by them. This constitutes a simple and helpful diagram to use in counselling and psychotherapy in that it quickly illustrates the co-defined process of communications and how our communications can be influential for another.

Other important aspects to TA theory are psychological games, which describe repeating patterns of behaviour leading to familiar self-deprecatory feelings. Such behaviours are energised by 'unfinished business', and such games reinforce an individual's 'scripts'. Scripts are unconscious life plans, usually set down in early childhood, which are formed in response to external influences and a subsequent sense of internal vulnerability.

The nature of therapeutic change

Berne (1966) outlined eight 'therapeutic operations' fundamental to TA. They are outlined in Tudor and Sills (2012, p. 338) as follows:

1 Interrogation or enquiry – inviting the client to talk about him/herself
2 Specification – categorising and highlighting certain relevant information
3 Confrontation – using previously specified material to point out inconsistencies; often this has the purpose and effect of disconcerting the client's Parent, Child or contaminated Adult
4 Explanation – explaining a situation with a view to strengthening the client's Adult
5 Illustration – using an anecdote, simile or comparison to reinforce a confrontation or explanation
6 Confirmation – using new confrontations to confirm the issues and patterns that emerge in the client's discourse
7 Interpretation – offering ways of understanding a client's underlying motives, designed to stabilise the client's Adult control and 'deconfuse' the Child
8 Crystallisation – making summary statements to help the client make autonomous choices.

Lister-Ford (2002) outlines several distinguishing characteristics of a TA therapist, which need to be present for therapeutic change to be facilitated:

- The pursuit of autonomy in self and others
- Respect for self and others – 'I'm OK, you're OK'
- Personal responsibility and self-knowledge
- A humanistic stance
- Open communications
- Avoiding psychological games
- Cooperative
- Emotionally literate
- Making clear contracts.

The process of therapeutic change in TA is outlined by Berne, and detailed by Tudor and Sills (2012, p. 338) as:

- Social control: the control of dysfunctional behaviours
- Symptomatic relief: the personal relief of subjectively experienced symptoms
- Transference cure: when the client can stay out of their script, as long as the therapist is around either literally or 'in their head'
- Script cure: by which the person's own Adult ego state takes over the previous role of the therapist and the person makes autonomous decisions.

Working in context

TA is a widely used approach in counselling and psychotherapy, albeit not in the same numbers as person-centred, and has continued to develop both in theory and practice. Traditional models of TA, drawing on the original theories and ideas of Berne, are increasingly supplemented by a relational TA, which focuses more attention on the nature of the relationship between therapist and client, as in many of the other humanistic traditions.

Again, like person-centred and gestalt, TA can be found in many of the mainstream contexts for counselling and psychotherapy, but is not generally cited as a treatment of choice in treatment guidelines for many of the primary mental health conditions, thus making its use in health care settings more peripheral to cognitive-behavioural and psychodynamic therapy.

Research profile

The research evidence for TA over the years has been patchy, with comparatively few empirical studies. The last decade has seen the emergence of a research culture within TA, with an increasing number of qualitative, case study and quantitative papers being published.

FURTHER READING

Fowlie, H. and Sills, C. (2011) *Relational Transactional Analysis: Principles in Practice.* London: Karnac Books.
Lapwood, P. and Sills, C. (2011) *An Introduction to Transactional Analysis: Helping People Change.* London: Sage.
Steward, I. (1996) *Developing Transactional Analysis Counselling.* London: Sage.
Widdowson, M. (2009) *Transactional Analysis: 100 Key Points and Techniques.* London: Routledge.

3.4 COGNITIVE-BEHAVIOURAL APPROACHES

SECTION OUTLINE

Cognitive behavioural approaches have become a dominant force in UK therapy provision, particularly within health care settings for the treatment of anxiety and depression. This section considers the development of cognitive-behavioural therapy, from an integration between behavioural and cognitive approaches, through to current practice.

Introduction

It is important to understand that what we now term as 'cognitive-behavioural therapy' (CBT) is an integration of several approaches to personality and the development of psychological difficulties. To understand that integration and to appreciate its current application in practice, it is helpful first to deconstruct the model and look a little more at its constituent parts: behaviourism and behaviour therapy, and cognitive theories and their application in therapeutic settings. Of course, CBT is not simply a bringing together of these two distinct parts, but drawing on the principles of the two that CBT has continued to evolve, through practice experience and empirical research, into the forms in which it is currently practised. It is also important to note that other developments in the UK, such as the Improving Access to Psychological Therapies (IAPT) programme, have furthered the approach to psychological difficulties and the delivery of treatments in primary care settings (Robinson et al., 2012). CBT is not a single model of therapy, applicable to all clients in all situations. This has been one of the criticisms incorrectly levelled at CBT, that its 'one size fits all' approach to the complex nature of human problems will, inevitably, fail to meet the needs of many, or (at best), simply focus on symptom reduction (House and Loewenthal, 2008). CBT is as much based on the development of a therapeutic alliance as it is in a psychodynamic or humanistic approach. The success of therapy will be, at least partly, informed by the nature of the therapeutic process, and not simply the application of particular theoretical ideas, as some suggest.

Behaviourism and classical conditioning

The birth of behaviourism can probably be traced back to the work of Ivan Pavlov (1849-1936), a Russian physiologist. He is credited with the development of theories of classical conditioning, one of the central tenets of behavioural explanations of psychology and, later, behaviour therapy (developed in the 1960s) and CBT. Classical conditioning describes a process whereby 'if a stimulus produces a response, it can be paired with another stimulus and the second stimulus will produce the same response' (Kinsella and Garland, 2008, p. 187). This was most clearly demonstrated in Pavlov's well-known experiment (Pavlov's Dog) in which dogs salivated in response to the presentation of food (unconditional stimulus = food; unconditional response − salivation). The food was paired with a bell (i.e., a bell was rung on the presentation of food), so that the dogs began to associate the bell with the likelihood of food; the bell alone then led to the dogs' salivating (conditioned stimulus = bell; conditioned response = salivation). This experiment demonstrated the process of learning (classical conditioning is an important concept in learning theory, alongside operant conditioning, habituation and modelling). Classical conditioning has particular relevance when applied to understanding the development of psychological problems, in that if the environmental stimulus is changed, problems can be treated. Classical conditioning can also help explain the development of phobias (conditioned stimulus = spiders, for example; conditioned response = fear and anxiety).

Operant conditioning

B.F. Skinner (1904-1990), developing the earlier work of American psychologist Edward Thorndike, used the term operant conditioning to describe a process whereby a 'response is altered as a result of its consequences … the consequence of the reward will increase the behaviour and that of punishment reduce it' (Kinsella and Garland, 2008, p. 187). Essentially, if a reward (positive reinforcer) is present every time a task is completed (behaviour), it is more likely the task (behaviour) will be repeated. If a punishment (negative reinforcer) is present, the task (behaviour) is less likely to be repeated. As Joseph (2010, p. 77) states, 'operant conditioning explains the persistence of the maladaptive behaviour and classical conditioning explains the formation of the behaviour in the first place'. Mowrer's (1947) two-factor theory of fear and avoidance is outlined thus by Joseph (2010, p. 77): 'fear is acquired through classical conditioning (first factor) and maintained through operant conditioning via negative reinforcement (second factor) as the person avoids his or her fear'.

Habituation

Habituation simply means that if someone is repeatedly exposed to a stimulus, the level and intensity of the response will reduce. We can probably think of many situations in our own lives where we might identify the process of habituation. If a house alarm goes off we may initially pay careful attention to it. If it goes off subsequently and repeatedly, however, our response will wane until we eventually ignore it, or do not hear it. The concept of habituation has been used in work with phobias, anxiety disorders and obsessive-compulsive disorder (OCD), for example, where a repeated exposure to the feared stimulus can lead to a reduced anxiety response.

Modelling

The concept of modelling (Bandura, 1969) refers to the increased likelihood of adopting a behavioural/emotional response having observed that response to a given stimulus in another person. We might consider, alongside the other concepts outlined, the importance of modelling in the development of phobias. If we assume we are not born with a fear of small house spiders, modelling might play an important role in the development of the fear in having witnessed the fear of spiders in others. Behaviour therapy, therefore, based on the concepts of learning theory and, in particular the role of classical and operant conditioning, aims to reduce and eradicate symptoms, to help the individual develop new behaviours as well as changing the experience of environmental reinforcers. One means by which this is achieved is through systematic desensitisation, which is associated with Joseph Wolpe (1915-1997), although Wolpe used the term systematic desensitisation to describe a process that had already been successfully used to treat children, outlined by Jones (1925). This can be described as a process of steady and managed exposure to a feared stimulus following a period of relaxation training. For example, once an individual is taught to increase their sense of relaxation, they are exposed to a low level of the feared stimulus (having first been enabled to identify situations or events that cause different levels of difficulty) in a controlled way until no response is experienced (through the process of habituation). This is then repeated with a higher level of the feared stimulus until no response is experienced, and continued until the stimulus does not trigger the response. Other techniques based on the principles of classical conditioning include flooding (exposure to high levels of the feared stimulus) until extinction of the response occurs, and aversion therapy, involving pairing an unpleasant consequence with an unwanted behaviour to reduce frequency.

Cognitive therapy

While behaviourism is clearly rooted in the process of learning, much of the research in the development of the concepts outlined was conducted in animal behaviour experiments. What may happen with animal behaviour may not always be extrapolated to human behaviour, as Kinsella and Garland (2008, p. 187) state with reference to the concept of operant conditioning: 'because of [human] cognitive abilities they are more likely to question the necessity of continuing the behaviour or the desirability of the reward'. The development of cognitive approaches to understanding human distress therefore aimed instead to look at thinking processes that might influence behaviour and emotional responses. The two principal writers in the development of cognitive therapy were Aaron T. Beck (b. 1921) and Albert Ellis (1913-2007).

Beck's cognitive therapy asserts that the processes of thinking influence, and are also influenced by, emotional difficulties. Therefore, if thinking processes can be changed through the process of therapy a reduction in the emotional difficulties may result. As outlined by Sanders and Wills (2005, p. 3), 'While clients may well come to therapy asking for help with their negative thoughts, more often they come because they are feeling bad. Despite its focus on thinking, cognitive therapy is actually all about reaching and working with emotion.'

The original model of cognitive therapy was outlined in two key publications, *Cognitive Therapy and the Emotional Disorders* (Beck, 1976) and *Cognitive Therapy of Depression* (Beck et al., 1979). If a person can be supported through therapy to change the way they think about a situation, they can influence the way they experience the situation and thus facilitate emotional change. For example, Beck suggested that people experiencing depression typically think about themselves in ways that accentuate the negatives, having developed such patterns of thinking when young. Essentially, Beck argued that underlying emotional difficulties were illogical thoughts and maladaptive ways of experiencing the world.

Cognitive therapy is essentially based on the assumption that, as humans, we interact with our environment through the process of thinking, interpretation and evaluation. In turn, these are linked to our feelings and behaviour (as well as our physical wellbeing, as has increasingly been acknowledged). Cognitions are available to us knowingly, that is, they are conscious (and thus cognitive therapy does not work with the unconscious in the way psychoanalysis would). Beck described three types of cognition: information processing, automatic thoughts and schema. Information processing describes how individuals constantly receive information from within themselves (body experiences), and their environment. Automatic thoughts represent an individual's internal dialogue that occurs in an unplanned way, while schema describes 'hypothetical cognitive structures which act as templates to filter incoming information' (Mytton, 2012, p. 287). Schemas are the core beliefs and views of the world an individual develops when young that help them to function in their life by filtering out unnecessary information and creating an internal 'map'. There are recent developments in schema therapy that try to help people re-structure fundamental, core beliefs through an integration of cognitive-behavioural therapy, object relations, gestalt and, most recently, mindfulness-based approaches (Rafaeli et al., 2010).

Beck outlined a number of illogical ways of thinking, some of which are described in Box 3.3.

BOX 3.3   ILLOGICAL WAYS OF THINKING

Arbitrary inference:	Reach conclusions about situations without evidence
Catastrophising:	Predicting an overly negative outcome without taking into account other possible outcomes
Overgeneralisation:	Sweeping negative beliefs about a situation
Magnification:	Emphasising problems and failures
Minimising:	Reducing the value of successes and achievements
Dichotomous thinking:	Using extreme terms in thinking, e.g. 'never'
Filtering:	Selecting negative aspects at the expense of a fuller picture

Cognitive therapy relies on a strong therapeutic alliance between therapist and client and emphasises the importance of relational dynamics as well as the behavioural and/or cognitive aspects of the client's presentation. Cognitive therapy begins with the therapist helping the client to understand the model of therapy (especially concerning the place and importance of cognitions in their distress). Clients are then facilitated to begin to identify problematic cognitive processes and are supported by their therapist to challenge and re-structure this thinking, trying new ways of being and experimenting with new thoughts and ideas in response to given situations.

> **FURTHER READING**
>
> Sanders, D. and Wills, F. (2005) *Cognitive Therapy: An Introduction*, 2nd edn. London: Sage.

Rational emotive behaviour therapy

Previously known as rational therapy, then rational emotive therapy, rational emotive behaviour therapy (REBT) now incorporates a behavioural and cognitive aspect to its approach. Albert Ellis, an American psychologist and psychotherapist, originally developed rational therapy in 1955. Like Beck, he was disillusioned with psychoanalysis and developed an approach that focused on a client's emotional and thinking disturbances. The key principles of REBT (adapted from Dryden, 2012) include that rational beliefs contribute to the core of psychological health. Conversely therefore, irrational beliefs are considered to be at the core of psychological distress and are represented as inconsistent with the individual's actual reality, rigid, extreme and self-defeating.

The four types of rational belief are: non-dogmatic preferences; non-awfulising beliefs; high frustration tolerance beliefs; and acceptance beliefs. The four types of irrational beliefs are: rigid demands; awfulising beliefs; low frustration tolerance beliefs; and depreciation beliefs. REBT works on an ABC approach to therapy (A = aspect of the situation the person focuses on; B = beliefs (rational or irrational); and C = consequences). If A represents irrational beliefs then psychological disturbance is likely. If A represents rational beliefs then psychological health is likely. Individuals are seen to have both rational and irrational beliefs and, with work, all have the capacity to identify, challenge and change irrational beliefs. Finally, many irrational beliefs are learnt from parental disturbed behaviour or other unhelpful experiences. Box 3.4 shows the examples offered by Dryden and Neenan (2006, p. 2–3) for the four types of rational and irrational beliefs.

BOX 3.4   RATIONAL AND IRRATIONAL BELIEFS, WITH EXAMPLES

Rational beliefs

1   Non-dogmatic preferences: 'I want to be approved of, but I don't have to be'
2   Non-awfulising beliefs: 'It is bad to be disapproved of, but it isn't the end of the world'
3   High frustration tolerance beliefs: 'It is difficult to face being disapproved of, but I can tolerate it'
4   Acceptance beliefs: 'I can accept myself if I am disapproved of'.

Irrational beliefs

1   Rigid demands: 'I must be approved of'
2   Awfulising beliefs: 'If I'm disapproved of it is the end of the world'
3   Low frustration tolerance beliefs: 'I can't tolerate being disapproved of'
4   Depreciation beliefs: 'I am worthless if I am disapproved of'.

REBT does not have a particular theoretical position on the nature and form of disturbance, but instead sees psychological distress as a consequence of an individual's views formed in response to events. The role of the REBT therapist is to help clients consider their own part in distress and consider ways in which they might begin to think about events differently. Given an assumption that, with insight, individuals are able to take control over their lives, the role of the therapist is to facilitate that process. This might involve periods of challenge. There is an acknowledgement that the qualities of the therapist (e.g. warmth, acceptance) are important: however these are not seen as integral to the process of change. The process would instead focus on identifying irrational beliefs, questioning and challenging irrational beliefs until the individual is able to see them as false and unhelpful (in contrast to their rational beliefs), and then working to integrate newly formed rational beliefs into their cognitive structure.

FURTHER READING

Dryden, W. (2001) *Reason to Change: A Rational Emotive Behaviour Therapy (REBT) Workbook.* London: Routledge.
Dryden, W. (2006) *Getting Started with REBT.* London: Routledge.

Cognitive-behavioural therapy

Gilbert has suggested there are at least 16 different approaches to CBT (Gilbert, 1996, cited in Kinsella and Garland, 2008), each placing a different emphasis on behavioural, cognitive and/or interpersonal factors to the provision of therapy. The truth is there are probably many more, given that how therapists integrate different aspects of behavioural and cognitive theories and approaches to therapy will vary greatly. Wills (2008) notes, however, that common to the different styles of CBT is the importance of the relationship, placing emphasis on empathy, warmth and genuineness (akin to the core conditions of empathy, congruence and unconditional positive regard in person–centred therapy).

The development of CBT has been heavily influenced by its application with particular problems and presenting issues, such as depression and anxiety. Practitioners have sought to place different emphasis on aspects of the approach depending on the type of difficulties experienced by clients, but also more specifically on the particular needs of individual clients as they present for therapy. In that sense, CBT can be seen as a particular bespoke approach to working with clients, with an emphasis on individual therapy plans targeted as specific problem areas, albeit within a wider behavioural and cognitive frame. For example, while the emphasis may vary, the ideological, philosophical and theoretical stance of CBT would not place great emphasis on an in–depth exploration of an individual's psychodynamic history, other than to identify sources of schematic problem and behavioural difficulty, nor would it seek to work with unconscious processes. Claringbull (2010) suggests some common concepts inherent within CBT, outlined in Box 3.5.

BOX 3.5   COMMON CBT CONCEPTS

- Events are not important in themselves, but rather the interpretation of those events.
- Learning theory is important in understanding the development of behaviour and maladaptive behaviour patterns.
- Behavioural emphasis is helpful with some problems, e.g. phobias and anxiety, while cognitive approaches are more so with depression.
- CBT represents a varied integration of behavioural and cognitive approaches to working with emotional problems.

- Our mental health is individually defined and we are each affected by where we are on our particular continuum.
- Priority for change will be defined by the immediacy of the problem as we experience it.
- Feelings, thoughts, behaviours and physical symptoms are all interrelated – change can occur through change in any one aspect.

Adapted from Claringbull, 2010, pp. 76–7

There are a number of particular developments of note within CBT. Acceptance and commitment therapy (ACT: Hayes et al., 1999) uses CBT techniques, mindfulness together with strategies for commitment for behaviour change. The aim is to facilitate a healthier experience of memories, thoughts, feelings and physical sensations through the use of experiential exercises, metaphor and paradox. The intervention stresses the importance of being in the moment and experiences thoughts and feelings as such.

Cognitive analytic therapy (CAT), developed by Ryle (1990), draws on cognitive and analytic theories and is time-limited. The shorter-term focus of CAT is achieved through the use of some cognitive therapy techniques, including setting of goals and Socratic questioning. Socratic questioning in CBT is an important approach that facilitates a deeper and particular type of thinking. Sanders and Wills (2005, p. 109), drawing on the work of Padesky (2004a, 2004b), outline four related stages of Socratic questioning:

1   Asking informational questions to uncover information beyond the client's current awareness
2   Accurate listening and empathic reflection
3   A summary of information discovered
4   Asking synthesising questions which help apply the new information discussed to the client's original thought or belief.

Other approaches include compassion focused therapy (CFT; see later in this chapter for a brief discussion of CFT) and dialectic behavioural therapy, amongst others.

Criticisms of CBT

Despite a strong evidence base for its efficacy across a wide range of difficulties, and its being recommended as the treatment of choice for many presenting problems in treatment guidelines, CBT has attracted a great deal of criticism during the last two decades, and particularly following Layard's (2003) 'wellbeing and happiness' agenda that led to the development of IAPT services and the implementation of adapted CBT approaches (Mytton, 2012). Some feel the research evidence is overstated in its claims (White, 2000), while others argue that the findings of CBT and its application in practice are overly simplistic (Smail, 1996). Joseph (2010) notes, however, that the increasing adaption of the medical discourse and psychiatric approaches to understanding and describing human distress, as seen in the American Psychiatric Association's *Diagnostic and Statistical Manual of Mental Disorders* (2000, currently in consultation for a 5th edition), have been important in the increasing acceptability of CBT to the scientific community.

DISCUSSION QUESTIONS

1 Why do you think CBT has evolved as a reaction against psychoanalysis?
2 What do you consider to be the relative strengths and weaknesses of (a) cognitive therapy and (b) behaviour therapy?
3 How might the principles of CBT inform your thinking as a therapist, regardless of orientation?
4 According to Dryden, 'cognitive-behaviour therapy ... attract[s] a greater number of practitioners, and is more academically respectable' than rational REBT. Why do you think this is the case?

3.5 INTEGRATIVE AND PLURALISTIC APPROACHES

SECTION OUTLINE

Integrative ways of working draw on a number of models to bring about a new integration of approaches. Typically, an 'integrative practitioner' will work with theoretical assumptions and principles of practice informed by several approaches. Working 'pluralistically' takes the idea of integration a stage further. This section considers the differences between integrative and pluralist ways of working and discusses the implications for practice.

While for many years the major counselling and psychotherapy approaches were adopted in a purist way (i.e., each delivered without being informed by another predominant model), there has over recent years been a move toward an integration of different ideas and principles. Such an approach has attracted several different terms, including eclecticism, integration, a synthesised approach and, most recently, pluralistic approaches (though the writing on pluralism differentiates it from integration, rather than simply offering a new name for the same concept). The critics of integrated approaches suggest that important perspectives on personality are lost, and that therapy becomes intervention-based rather than relational-driven.

In contrast, the proponents of integrative therapy argue that, when considering the sheer range of client problems that counsellors and psychotherapists can encounter in practice, it is never appropriate to take a 'one size fits all' approach to supporting people in distress: integration, they argue, offers a mechanism by which the most helpful aspects of theoretical approaches can be brought together to form a new model.

Definitions

The OED (2012) defines eclectic as, 'deriving ideas, style, or taste from a broad and diverse range of sources', while integrate is defined as, 'combine (one thing) with another to form a whole'. Synthesis is defined as, 'the combination of components or elements to form a connected whole'. From the definitions here we can see that integrative and synthesis essentially describe a similar process, even though they have been used in a differentiated way in the literature. More significant is the distinction between eclectic and integrative.

There are a number of reasons why an integrative approach may be preferred over a more purist one. Messina (2005, cited in Amis, 2011) offers the following:

1   The proliferation of therapies
2   The inadequacy of a single therapy relevant to all clients and problems
3   External socioeconomic realities (e.g. insurance protection)
4   The popularity of short-term, prescriptive, problem-focused therapies
5   The paucity of differential effectiveness among therapies
6   Recognition of therapeutic commonalities' major role in therapy outcomes
7   The development of professional societies aimed at integrating psychotherapies.

Norcross and Goldfried (2005, p.8) outline general 'routes' to integration as follows:

1   Common factors: some have suggested there are common factors across the counselling and psychotherapy models that contribute to their effectiveness. By drawing together these common factors there is potential to develop an effective integration, although some aspects may be theory dependent and thus diluted if used out of context.
2   Technical eclecticism: in which therapists use particular approaches or interventions in response to clients' problems and needs, without necessarily doing that in a coherent way.
3   Theoretical integration: where the hope is that the new whole will be better than the individual constituent parts. An example of theoretical integration would be cognitive analytic therapy (Ryle and Kerr, 2002), where psychodynamic theory, including object-relations theory, is integrated with a cognitive-behavioural approach.

4   Assimilative integration: works on the basis that any counsellor or psychotherapist will train in one particular approach and have a theoretical and practice grounding in it, but through practice and experience will begin to assimilate new or different approaches to complement existing skills and knowledge. However, an increasing number of integrative training courses do not rely on a 'base' model, but instead encourage trainees to develop an integrative approach as their core model.

Eclecticism vs. integration

A metaphor I have heard on several occasions (and sadly cannot attribute) is that of a therapeutic 'soup'. Each model of therapy represents individual ingredients or a set of ingredients. Each can be nourishing of itself and is not necessarily dependent on other ingredients being added. However, it is possible to take particular ingredients and put them together to make a new whole. Eclecticism might correspond to all the ingredients being put together in a pot; they still exist in their constituent parts and can easily be identified as such. While they do make a new 'whole', it is more to do with them being collected together rather than anything more. Integration would correspond to a careful selection of ingredients brought together and put through a liquidiser; all of the ingredients are still present, but they have been closely adapted into something new. Of course, great care has to be taken in the selection of ingredients, as some simply do not work together.

The challenge of integration is to make a careful and thoughtful selection of ideas, principles, philosophical assumptions and interventions that can work together in a new, integrated theory or approach. The critics of eclecticism argue that, unlike integration, eclecticism instead brings together different parts in a more ad hoc style; that is to say, without particular thought as to how they work together or how they might be held together in a new, cohesive whole. On this view, eclecticism might be thought of as like trying to fix a broken piece of furniture with a range of different screwdrivers and hammers, simply trying them all until one seems to work. Unlike broken furniture, of course, vulnerable and distressed clients attending counselling and psychotherapy take great personal risks in trusting the therapist and would hope their counsellor and psychotherapist wouldn't simply go through the toolbox until they find something that works. Doing so runs the risk of causing further harm along the way.

The 'ingredients' for integration go beyond the essential components of different counselling and psychotherapy models. In addition, the counsellor or psychotherapist's particular personal and professional experiences, working context, client presentations and expectations, and training, will inform the 'blend' of integration. Fundamentally, the philosophy behind integration is that no single approach has the answer for all clients and that, though two or more approaches have something to offer separately, they have even more to offer when combined.

McMahon (2000, p. 118) offers an outline of using integrative therapy with a client:

1   The counsellor or psychotherapist will, like all therapy, need to develop a sound working relationship with the client, 'building rapport and establishing core values' (p. 118).
2   During this early process the therapist will be looking out for client skills, strengths and also points of struggle or vulnerability.
3   An assessment will inform both the therapist and client as to the potential value and efficacy of therapy and, if deemed appropriate, a contract will be agreed.
4   Both therapist and client will keep an eye on agreed goals so that changes in emphasis can be monitored and responded to.
5   The integrative counsellor or psychotherapist has no predetermined approach or theoretical perspective through which to view the client's difficulties, but rather will allow themselves to be informed by the client's problems and place a different emphasis on their approach depending on this. A therapist working from a more purist frame may follow the similar steps, but will ultimately approach the 'tasks' of therapy from their preferred position, whether that be cognitive-behavioural, psychodynamic, person-centred, or so on.

As McMahon states: 'There is no set format for a typical session in integrative counselling, which will vary according to the needs of the client, the stage of therapy and the particular approach or techniques being employed by the counsellor' (2000, p. 121).

Pluralistic approaches

Cooper and McLeod (2010, p. 7–8) define pluralistic counselling and psychotherapy as based on 'the assumption that different clients are likely to benefit from different therapeutic methods at different points in time, and that therapists should work collaboratively with clients to help them identify what they want from therapy and how they might achieve it.'

Cooper and McLeod (2010, p. 9) argue that a pluralistic approach to counselling and psychotherapy differs from an integrative approach on the following grounds:

1   A pluralistic approach is not just a practice, but a way of viewing therapy as a whole
2   Pluralism is not one combination of methods or theories but has 'the potential to embrace an *infinite* variety of theories, practices and change mechanisms' (p. 9)
3   Places emphasis on 'tailoring' (p. 9) each session of therapy to the client

4   Dialogue around the goals, tasks and methods of therapy based within the formation of maintenance or a collaborative therapeutic relationship
5   There is no one set of factors that determine therapeutic change for all clients
6   Puts emphasis on the client as the agent of change
7   Introduces a framework for thinking about, researching and practising therapy.

We see here that integration is seen to be a more static entity, given that a counsellor or psychotherapist will integrate different models of therapy into a new approach embedded within their personal style. The needs of the client will bring a different focus or intervention, but it will still be in the context of the nature and form of the integration. Pluralism instead offers something that is perhaps more fluid and responsive to the client's needs; engages the client as an active and equal collaborator in their own therapy; is more responsive to the changing needs of the client; and forms a negotiated approach in which the client has an important investment. This may ring true for some purist approaches too, but again the therapist will still be coming to the work from a certain frame (as opposed to coming from where the client is at, emotionally and psychologically). Even though integrative approaches have been in place for some time, the new challenges of pluralism take those steps even further and task the therapist with giving away more of their power and expertise, in the tradition of humanistic psychology.

FURTHER READING

Cooper, M. and McLeod, J. (2010) *Pluralistic Counselling and Psychotherapy.* London: Sage.

Culley, S. and Bond, T. (2004) *Integrative Counselling Skills in Action*, 2nd edn. London: Sage.

Faris, A. and van Ooijen, E. (2011) *Integrative Counselling and Psychotherapy: A Relational Approach.* London: Sage.

Gilbert, M. and Orlans, V. (2011) *Integrative Therapy: 100 Key Points and Techniques.* Hove: Routledge.

DISCUSSION QUESTIONS

1   How well do the following terms describe your approach: (a) 'purist'; (b) 'eclectic'; (c) 'integrative'; and (d) 'pluralistic'?
2   Given your answer to (1) above, what motivates your position?
3   Which models of therapy are you most attracted to, and why?
4   How does your own personality and way of being influence your theoretical choices as a therapist?

3.6 OTHER MODELS OF THERAPY

SECTION OUTLINE

Beyond the four principal schools of counselling and psychotherapy lie a number of approaches and techniques, often allied to existing schools, but also drawing on alternative ideas and approaches. This section outlines a number of associated ways of working and considers their relevance for contemporary practice.

The four principal schools of counselling and psychotherapy – psychodynamic; humanistic–existential; cognitive-behavioural; and integrative and pluralistic – all hold within them particular theories and styles of therapy informed by both practice and philosophy. There are some other approaches to therapy increasingly used in mainstream counselling and psychotherapy services, some of which may be positioned within one of the four principal schools, while others sit slightly apart. Some of these therapies might not constitute a first training in counselling and psychotherapy (such as EMDR, for example), but rather might be followed up after a core training. In this section we briefly discuss the following in turn:

- Eye movement desensitisation and reprocessing (EMDR)
- Solution-focused therapy
- Mindfulness-based cognitive-behavioural therapy/mindfulness-based stress reduction (MBSR)
- Compassion-focused therapy
- The skilled helper model.

Eye movement desensitisation and reprocessing

Eye movement desensitisation and reprocessing (EMDR) was developed by Francine Shapiro in the late 1990s and early 2000s to help working with trauma. While it is used with other presenting problems, trauma remains its primary focus. The key principles of EMDR are outlined in Box 3.6.

BOX 3.6   KEY PRINCIPLES OF EYE MOVEMENT DESENSITISATION AND REPROCESSING

1. EMDR is a collaborative approach, primarily for clients experiencing trauma.
2. It draws on a number of principles from different therapeutic schools, including psychodynamic, humanistic-existential and cognitive and behavioural.

(Continued)

(Continued)

3   The therapist makes use of specific techniques, not used in any of the other primary therapies, to facilitate a reduction in the trauma response.
4   The primary intervention is bilateral stimulation (eye movements, tapping or tones).
5   EMDR is structured across an eight-phase treatment programme.
6   EMDR focuses on the processing of memory and enhances memory processing networks, thus leading to a reduction in trauma response symptoms, such as hyperarousal, flashbacks etc.
7   EMDR initiates neurological and physiological change that facilitates the processing of trauma memory.

Treatment is conducted over eight phases, and repeated as necessary. The phases of treatment are as follows.

Phase I: History and treatment planning

The therapist takes a client history and a treatment plan is discussed and outlined. Specifically, potential areas for EMDR are identified.

Phase II: Preparation

Clients are encouraged to identify a 'safe place' (i.e., image or memory with positive associations) to help with self-support during, or after, sessions.

Phase III: Assessment

A negative cognition is identified – a negative statement about the self usually triggered when thinking of the trauma – and a positive cognition – a positive self-statement – to counteract the negative one. Additionally, the client is encouraged to identify particular responses, such as emotions (e.g. anger) and other responses (e.g. cold hands, butterflies in the stomach).

Phase IV: Desensitisation

The client is asked to focus on the image they have previously been encouraged to bring to mind, the negative cognition and the distressing emotion or body sensation. The bilateral stimulation is undertaken (eye movements, tapping, tones, etc. – it is believed that bilateral movements help 're-wire' the processing of memories). The client is then asked to report briefly on what has come up for them, (e.g. a thought, feeling, or physical sensation). The client will usually be asked to focus on the thought, but may be asked instead to focus on the original target memory. The client is occasionally asked to report their current level of distress using the Subjective Units of Disturbance (SUDS) scale. The desensitisation phase usually ends with a SUDS score of 0 or 1.

Phase V: Installation
The client is asked about the positive cognition, if it is still valid, and build on it. Treatment continues and the client's position measured using a Validity of Cognition (VOC) scale until they reach the maximum score of 7 (ideally), or 5 or 6.

Phase VI: Body scan
The client is asked if they experience any physical pain, stress or discomfort when they think of the target memory. If so, further reprocessing will take place. If not, treatment can move on to the next phase.

Phase VII: Closure
This is used at the end of each treatment session to ensure the client is able to function safely and appropriately when they leave.

Phase VIII: Re-evaluation
This takes place at the beginning of each new session where the client is invited to review the previous week and discuss any new problems or experiences. The level of disturbance of previously targeted memory is assessed.

FURTHER READING

Shapiro, F. (2001) *Eye Movement Desensitization and Reprocessing: Basic Principles, Protocols, and Procedures*. London: Guilford Press.

Solution-focused therapy

Solution-focused therapy originated at the Brief Family Center in the United States in the 1980s. Originally located as part of family and systemic therapy, solution-focused therapy has been further developed for work with individuals. It focuses on clients' existing resources and strengths. Its key assumptions include the following (taken from O'Connell, 2012, p. 393):

- Clients have ideas about their preferred futures
- Clients are already carrying out constructive and helpful actions (otherwise things would be worse)
- Clients have many resources and competences, many of which go unacknowledged by themselves and by others
- It is usually more helpful to focus on the present and the future. The past can be useful as a source of evidence for prior successes and skills
- It can be useful to find explanations for problems, but it is not essential, and in some cases this quest can delay constructive change
- Constructing solutions is a separate process from problem exploration
- The 'truth' of a client's life is negotiable within a social context. Fixed objective 'truths' are unattainable. There are many truths about the client's life.

The role of the therapist is to facilitate change through the process of engagement with the current situation, resources and coping mechanisms. O'Connell (2012, p. 394) outlines a number of specific strategies, including:

- Pre-session change: clients are encouraged to notice what they have coped with and how they have managed between making initial contact for therapy and therapy commencing
- Problem-free talk: clients are encouraged to talk about themselves and their interests without focusing specifically on their 'problems', thus highlighting important information for therapy
- Listening to evidence of client's strengths, qualities and skills: the therapist pays careful attention to the client's strengths, qualities and skills, and brings these to the client's attention at suitable times during therapy
- Building on exceptions: clients are encouraged to focus and explore those times when they are coping more effectively, thus further highlighting coping strategies and existing strengths
- The 'miracle question': helping clients to consider life without the problem. The question, as originally outlined by de Shazer et al. (1988) was, 'Imagine one night when you are asleep, a miracle happens and the problems we've been discussing disappear. As you were asleep, you did not know that a miracle had happened. When you wake up what will be the first sign to you that a miracle has happened?'
- Scaling: the therapist asks the client to measure progress on a scale of 0-10 and consider what needs to happen (and how the client can influence) a move up the scale (the higher being more positive)

- Feedback: each session finishes with feedback to the client, including negotiating in-between session tasks
- Tasks: noticing what works and what doesn't, and continuing to do those things that help.

FURTHER READING

Winbolt, B. (2010) *Solution Focused Therapy for the Helping Professions.* London: Jessica Kingsley.

Mindfulness-based stress reduction/mindfulness-based cognitive-behavioural therapy

Mindfulness-based CBT (mCBT) was developed by Zindel Segal, Mark Williams and John Teasdale, based on the work by John Kabat-Zinn and mindfulness-based stress reduction (MBSR). Kabat-Zinn developed MBSR at the University of Massachusetts Medical School in the 1970s as support for patients with chronic pain, hypertension, cancer, depression, anxiety, gastrointestinal disorders and panic. The course runs for eight two-and-a-half-hour sessions, plus an all-day session, and draws heavily at a philosophical level on Buddhist teachings and meditation. However, MBSR is not Buddhist-based and thus is accessible to everyone, regardless of their spirituality or faith. MBSR teaches people moment-to-moment non-judgemental awareness of self in relation to environment, with evidence suggesting an increase in self-awareness and a significant reduction in anxiety, panic and depressive symptoms.

Segal, Williams and Teasdale developed mBCT specifically for the treatment of depression. Mindfulness-based CBT has been recommended by NICE for relapse prevention in depression and there is a growing evidence base as to its efficacy. Again, like MBSR, mCBT is structured around group work over eight two-and-a-half-hour sessions to help clients develop the capacity to respond to negative events rather than react to them.

FURTHER READING

Kabat-Zinn, J. (2001) *Full Catastrophe Living: How to Cope with Stress, Pain and Illness Using Mindfulness Meditation.* Essex: Piatkus Books.
Kabat-Zinn, J., Zindel V., Segal, J., Williams, M. and Teasdale, T. (2002) *Mindfulness-Based Cognitive Therapy for Depression: A New Approach to Preventing Relapse.* London: Guilford Press.

Compassion-focused therapy

Compassion-focused therapy (CFT) was developed by Paul Gilbert (2010), drawing on Buddhist principles of compassion and self-care. While all counselling and psychotherapy needs to be conducted compassionately, the distinctive aspect of CFT is that is uses compassion as a central tenet and encourages clients to become self-compassionate. CFT draws on a range of other modalities, including cognitive-behavioural therapy. It was developed for people with chronic, long-term, complex mental health problems where self-criticism and shame are deeply embedded, originating from abusive and harmful upbringings.

Gilbert et al. (2008) noted in a study that when participants experienced feelings of calmness, wellbeing, contentment and safety they experienced measurably lower levels of depression, anxiety and stress. Gilbert (2010) suggests there are different types of positive feelings: some higher-energy feelings that are related to excitement, success and achievement; and resting-energy feelings, such as calmness, peace and a sense of safety. CFT focuses on the calmer level feelings to help the client acquire and develop a capacity for self-compassion.

Gilbert (2010, pp. 5–6) states that as CFT is a 'multimodal' therapy, it uses a wide range of intervention styles, including:

- Socratic dialogues
- Guided discovery
- Psycho-education
- Thought, emotion, behaviour and 'body' monitoring
- Behavioural experiments
- Exposure
- Mindfulness
- Learning emotional tolerance
- Making commitments for effort and practice
- Expressive (letter) writing
- Learning to understand and cope with emotional complexities and conflicts.

FURTHER READING

Gilbert, P. (2010) *Compassion Focused Therapy.* Hove: Routledge.

The skilled helper model

The skilled helper model was originally developed by Gerard Egan (b. 1930) in the mid–1970s. Being positioned within a more integrative school of counselling and psychotherapy, the model allows for therapists to use a number of skills and interventions within a goal-centred structure of helping. The key principles of the skilled helper approach are outlined in Box 3.7.

BOX 3.7   KEY PRINCIPLES OF THE SKILLED HELPER MODEL

1   Problems are better dealt with proactively rather than reactively.
2   Dealing with problems provides people with additional opportunities to learn new skills.
3   The task of intervention is to facilitate individuals to manage their problems more effectively, additionally to become more of a self-resource in tackling future problems.
4   Therapy should be about individual empowerment.
5   All intervention should be informed by the client's position and point of view.
6   Individuals are seen not in terms of pathology, but rather as having deficits in coping and problem-solving skills.
7   Intervention is conducted over a number of stages.

Egan uses the mnemonic SOLAR to outline the five key skills helpers must demonstrate in working with clients:

- Sit facing the client squarely
- Maintain an Open posture
- Lean towards the client
- Maintain Appropriate eye contact with the client
- Be Relaxed, to facilitate the quality and comfort of the sessions.

The model is structured over a number of stages (problem definition, goal-setting and action planning) as follows:

Stage One: Explore the client's existing situation

Stage Two: Help the client establish aims and goals

Stage Three: Help the client develop strategies.

While the skilled helper approach is presented by Egan in a clearly delineated fashion, the actual implementation of the model with clients is likely to be much more fluid, with dialogue moving between and across the different stages depending on the focus of work, and allowing for a linking between different narratives and accounts of difficulties.

FURTHER READING

Egan, G. (2009) *The Skilled Helper: International Edition.* Belmont, CA: Wadsworth.

DISCUSSION QUESTIONS

1 What are the main features of the new therapies currently being developed?
2 How might you make yourself more aware of new therapies and their contribution to client need?
3 Of the therapies briefly described above, how do they (or how don't they) relate to your own way of working?
4 Which of the approaches discussed above do you think you would most benefit from studying further?

3.7 KEY COUNSELLING AND PSYCHOTHERAPY SKILLS

SECTION OUTLINE

There are a number of skills and interventions specific to different models of therapy. However, there are also some skills relevant to all types of approaches that help the counsellor and psychotherapist to engage clients and to develop and sustain relationships. Different approaches place slightly different emphases on the ways in which the skills are implemented (concerning their frequency, for example), but all approaches integrate these skills into their core theoretical model.

We have discussed in previous sections of this chapter how specific models of therapy adopt preferred interventions and skills. It would very unusual, for example, to find a psychodynamic practitioner (where the emphasis is on therapist abstinence to facilitate the transferential process) to set homework, whereas a cognitive-behavioural practitioner might. Likewise, interpreting a client's thoughts, comments or behaviour, as would happen in psychodynamic therapy, is very unlikely to take place in person-centred therapy (where the emphasis is on the client's frame of reference and understanding, not the therapist's). We may say that there are particular tools or approaches that are quite model-specific and not easily transferable because of philosophical incompatibilities.

There are, however, a number of micro-skills that cross the divisions of modality and are used by most therapists, most of the time. Each approach might place a different emphasis on particular skills (e.g. person-centred counsellors are less likely to use questioning than a cognitive-behavioural or psychodynamic counsellor), but the use of questions would not be prohibited by the model (despite the persistent myth that person-centred counsellors are 'not allowed' to use questions). Before we begin to consider some of these skills, however, we need to reflect further on what it is that makes an effective counsellor or psychotherapist.

Definitions: skills, qualities and competence

The OED (2012) defines being skilled as 'trained to do a particular task'. Certainly one of the aspects of counsellor and psychotherapy training is to facilitate the acquisition and development of skill to enable competent practice. The OED defines competence as, 'the ability to do something successfully or efficiently'. We might therefore assume that a 'good' counsellor or psychotherapist is one who has the ability to 'do a particular task successfully and efficiently'. While few would dispute the assertion of this statement, it is rather two-dimensional and does not fully reflect the full essence of being a therapist. We might train a therapist to use questions 'efficiently and effectively', but that would not necessarily enable them to do it compassionately, or empathically, or with care. Similarly, a surgeon might be well-trained to conduct an operation 'successfully and efficiently', but there is more to being a successful surgeon that safely wielding a scalpel: we might also judge 'success' and 'efficiency' by the surgeon's capacity to talk to patients, to reassure them and to explain, clearly and accessibly, the procedure they are about to undertake.

Thus there is something about the qualities of a therapist that acts as an important context for the application of skills. The OED defines quality as, 'a distinctive attribute or characteristic possessed by someone or something'. In defining an effective counsellor or psychotherapist we are assuming they possess:

- the appropriate qualities to undertake their role
- the appropriate level of training to undertake their role
- the ability to deliver their role using key skills.

When these three aspects are taken as a whole, we might assume that a therapist is competent. McLeod (2009, p. 613) states that it is 'essential to view counsellor competence as a *developmental* process'.

He suggests a 'composite model consisting of seven distinct competence areas' (p. 613). These are:

1 Interpersonal skills
2 Personal beliefs and attitudes
3 Conceptual ability
4 Personal 'soundness'

5   Mastery of technique
6   Ability to understand and work within social systems
7   Openness to learning and inquiry.

(McLeod, 2009, p. 613)

In general terms I might also add to this list:

• Capacity to self-reflect
• Willingness to be open to challenge from others
• Ability to identify personal areas of competence
• Capacity to identify limits of competence, or when competence is temporarily impaired.

McLeod's seven areas of competence include the sound acquisition of knowledge and the capacity to understand and apply relevant theory and interventions. Additionally, interpersonal qualities and personal beliefs and attitudes are an important aspect of being a therapist. These might include:

• Honesty
• Being empathic and warm
• Being interested in the wellbeing of others
• Being non-judgemental
• Respecting and accepting of others, and of self
• A commitment to self-awareness and self-development
• Integrity and a willingness to think ethically both personally and professionally
• An ability to communicate interest and attentiveness
• Capacity to hold a sense of hope
• Flexibility.

These are the types of qualities referred to earlier as an important context for an effective counsellor or psychotherapist. A therapist, therefore, might have the ability to learn skills and interventions and deliver them effectively and efficiently, yet without the types of personal qualities outlined above, their work will be experienced as mechanistic rather than fluid and relational.

The final aspects of this discussion related to the definitions offered above are centred on efficiency. The OED defines 'efficient' as, 'achieving maximum productivity with minimum wasted effort or expense'. In counselling and psychotherapy terms, the idea of 'productivity' might be defined in terms of 'successful outcomes'. Yet (as is discussed later in this book) a client's definition of a 'successful outcome' might be very different from that of the therapist which, in turn, might be very different again for the employing agency. Consider the three brief scenarios in Boxes 3.8 to 3.10.

CASE STUDY 3.8
Alan

Alan is a 42-year-old man attending counselling because of bullying at work. After a number of sessions Alan decides that he is financially unable to leave his job and asks for the focus of counselling to be on how he can support himself until the bullying stops. Alan's counsellor, who works for an EAP, hopes that Alan will be able to 'stand up' to the bully and make a complaint at work. However, the counsellor works with Alan on coping strategies in the context of Alan stating he will not make a complaint at work and will 'put up with it'.

CASE STUDY 3.9
Janine

Janine is in a violent relationship. Her partner emotionally, physically and sexually assaults her. She is unwilling to report these incidents to the police because she 'loves' her partner and believes that one day the abuse will stop. Janine wants to use counselling, based within a domestic violence agency, to help find ways of living with this.

CASE STUDY 3.10
Jacob

Jacob is a 20-year-old university student. He does not enjoy his course and, even though only being half-way through his first year, knows he does not wish to pursue his subject after university. He attends the university counselling service and, after some sessions, decides to leave university.

In each of these scenarios the measure of 'successful outcome' will be different. For Alan, success will constitute learning to live with bullying, whereas for his counsellor it might be to make a stand, while the employer will want Alan to be effective in his work. Janine does not wish to leave her partner and so, while understanding the devastating impact of domestic violence, may define successful counselling in terms of learning to cope. 'Success' for the counsellor might be for Janine to make a decision to get out of the relationship. Finally, for Jacob 'success' might consist of having the confidence to leave his course; however, for the university – focused on retaining students – this would not be a 'successful' outcome.

Skills

A therapist may be warm and empathic, but without the right skills might not be able to effectively communicate that to the client. The skills of counselling and psychotherapy therefore, remain integral to the effectiveness of the therapist.

It is important to make a distinction between counselling and the use of counselling skills. Amis (2011, p. 113) defines counselling as 'Agreed, structured and contracted sessions with a trained counsellor. The core objectives are supporting the client and working towards change with the use of counselling skills.' She defines counselling skills as 'a range of communication skills varying in difficulty that are used in general interactions or more skillfully in the caring professions'. Amis's distinction concerning the context in which the skills are used (whether within the context of a general, 'helping' role, or instead within an agreed and structured therapeutic relationship) is helpful. Many helping professionals, such as nurses, social workers or teachers, for example, will undertake counselling skills training. Amis is right in citing counselling skills as 'communication' skills, as counsellors and psychotherapists cannot claim communication as a unique selling point given that as relational beings, humans communicate all the time (with greater or lesser effectiveness). However, counselling skills might consist of communications skills that are enhanced and developed. Nurses, social workers and teachers, for example, can find their work enhanced by developing their core communication skills.

Many of the chapters in this book discuss counsellor and psychotherapist skills, including: contracting, establishing contact, evaluation and reviewing, working with specific presentations and recognising and working with relational dynamics.

Inskipp (2012) distinguishes between 'inner' and 'outer' skills as shown in Figure 3.4.

Inner	Outer
Observing	Attending
Listening	Greeting
Body scanning for:	Active listening:
awareness of body sensations	paraphrasing
emotions	reflecting feelings
thoughts	summarising
images	
Impartial witnessing	Asking questions
Discriminating	Contracting
purpose stating	
preference stating	
Reflecting	Clarifying counselling/psychotherapy and therapeutic role
Technical skills of audio recording and introducing clients to this	

FIGURE 3.4 Inner and Outer Skills

Whether counselling skills should be taught specifically, or be more integrated into learning, is a disputed point. Ivey (1971) argues in support of the specific learning of skills, while Geldard and Geldard (2005) instead propose a more integrated approach to learning. Different courses will approach this question based on the personal preferences of the trainer and the modality being taught. It is, however, helpful to have a clear view as to which skills constitute micro-skills (as opposed to macro-skills that consist of the wider skills of therapeutic practice covered elsewhere in this book). Amis (2011, pp. 111–12) offers the following list of micro-skills:

- Active listening: the capacity to hear the detail of what the client is saying, how they are saying it and what they are not saying
- Attending: noticing the presentation of the client during the session, such as pauses, hesitations, and other communications
- Empathy: to see the world through the client's perspective; taking an 'as if' position
- Unconditional positive regard: accepting of the individual unconditionally, but not necessarily condoning everything they say or do
- Congruence: the capacity and willingness to be open and honest with the client about how they are being experienced in the session (but not about the therapist's own thoughts and opinions)
- Summarising: to encapsulate briefly the main and salient points of the client's narrative
- Paraphrasing: to summarise, often using some of the client's words, particular aspects or sections of their narrative so they are able to check meaning and inaccuracies
- Challenge: the capacity and willingness to challenge a client's position or perspective to help the client move from a position of being stuck with something. This can include empathic challenge
- Advanced empathy: taking empathy to the 'next level' by connecting with the unspoken meaning of the client's narrative
- Encouraging strengths: highlighting areas of particular competence or ability
- Highlighting conscious or unconscious interactions/'edge of awareness': highlighting aspects of the client's behaviour, thinking or feeling that might be beyond the client's immediate knowledge or understanding and bringing it from their edge of awareness into the 'now'
- Reflection: offering back to the client, in their own words, specifics sections of their narrative so they can be encouraged to reflect on meaning and intention
- Exploration: perhaps using questions and other skills, encouraging the client to ask questions from their perspective or narrative

- Non-verbal: eye contact, position, breathing etc. and what they communicate to the client
- Silence: allowing quiet time for reflection, or for the client or therapist to be fully present in the space – can be unsettling for therapists, particularly when new to practice
- Focus: bring particular aspects of the client's narrative or presentation to their attention.

Let us now look at some of these key skills in action, using in each case a short passage of therapy transcript to illustrate them. These are also available in a **PowerPoint presentation** on the companion website.

Client	I think of talking to her about it sometime but ... ehm ... well, I'm not sure what I would ... I guess I'm not sure how I would put it or how she might ... well, react I suppose.
Therapist	You're not sure how she might react if you say something, and I also notice how much you hesitated and paused in saying that; really quite tentative.
Client	Yes, I do feel quite tentative about it. I'm really not sure if it's the right thing to do.

FIGURE 3.5 Attending

Attending

Here the therapist not only reflects back to the client the expression about not knowing how 'she will react', but also highlights the client's pauses and hesitations (which are linked to their concerns).

Client	It just feels so big. I can't even bring myself to think about it. All too much for me to think about.
Therapist	I have a real sense of how overwhelming this feels. Just so frightening and enormous.
Client	Yes, it feels so frightening.

FIGURE 3.6 Empathy

Empathy

The therapist here introduces the word 'overwhelming' to characterise their sense of how this might feel for the client, seeking to understand the situation from the client's perspective. The client hears this as strongly affirming their experience.

Congruence

Client	I know I've talked about this so many times before, you must feel that we go over the same ground. I'm always talking about the same things.
Therapist	I am aware of sometimes feeling a frustration in revisiting things we have talked about, and I wonder if that means anything for your experience too?
Client	Yes! Yes, I feel so frustrated with things – I get stuck with my frustration rather than the things themselves. It's more about what happens with my feelings isn't it!

FIGURE 3.7   Congruence

The therapist here takes a risk in naming the client's experience as 'frustration', which could easily be experienced by the client as critical. However, by linking it to the possibilities of the client's experience too ('I wonder if that means anything for your experience?'), the therapist creates an opportunity for the client to explore and clarify their own process a little more. Congruence always needs to concern a dynamic within the relationship, rather than merely the therapist's own views on life.

Summarising

Client	We've been together for about five years now and, well ... it doesn't seem to be going anywhere. I'm not sure I want to finish it, and I can't imagine another five years like this. It gets so boring at times and un-stimulating – I know I sound horrible saying that about him, but there you go. That's what it feels like [*sighing*] ...
Therapist	So you're struggling with a relationship that you can't imagine will go anywhere but feel quite ambivalent about what to do about it. You seem to make judgements about your feelings about it too, when you say 'I know I sound horrible', and then you sigh?
Client	Yes, I suppose I do make judgements about myself. I think that's probably something I do a lot: I have feelings about things but then give myself a hard time and don't trust them.

FIGURE 3.8   Summarising

The therapist offers a summary of the client's narrative, using in the process non-verbal (paralinguistic) sounds (sighing) and implied meaning ('I know I sound horrible') in what the client is saying. The summary includes more than just the words. This helps the client begin to explore a wider issue of self-judgement.

Paraphrasing

Client	If I got on with my manager more the job wouldn't feel so awful. I mean ... getting up in the morning I just wonder what she's going to be like today. Seems to influence so much what sort of day I'm going to have.
Therapist	Your manager has a lot of influence over how you experience being at work. If your relationship with her was better, work would seem much more manageable.
Client	Yes, she's quite dominant isn't she! Stupid that one person should have such control.

FIGURE 3.9   Paraphrasing

The therapist paraphrases the client's narrative, sometimes using the client's words and phraseology to do so. This provides the client with an opportunity to reflect on the meaning and implications of what they are saying and to move forward with their exploration.

Challenging

Client	I'm just not any good at anything ... I can't organise and manage anything. It's like I am incapable of doing anything well.
Therapist	You say you're incapable of organising and managing, and I think back to when you talked about how you manage your two children on your own – getting them to school so you can go to work – that sounds like a lot of managing and organising!
Client	I suppose, I'd not really thought of that as meaning anything.

FIGURE 3.10   Challenging

The therapist offers a direct challenge to the client's position by referring to things they have said previously. This is different to simply trying to make the client feel better (e.g., 'Oh, I'm sure you can organise things well. I'm sure you can!'), which never has any real benefit.

Advanced empathy

Client	I miss him so much, I can't hardly think of the fact that he has gone. All that time looking after him and now he's not here. But it was so tiring, there's a part of me as well that thinks ... oh, I mean ... I miss him so much all the time.
Therapist	The loss is unbearable at times. And there might also be a part that feels relief from how tiring it was; difficult having those feelings?
Client	Yes, it is a relief as well. I couldn't imagine saying that to anyone, I thought I'd feel so guilty.

FIGURE 3.11   Advanced Empathy

The client tentatively begins to talk about feelings that lead to guilt and shame ('... there's a part of me ...'), but finds them too hard to express. The therapist picks up on this and, from an empathic position, helps the client begin to name the feelings ('... might be a part that feels relief ...') and then acknowledges how 'difficult' it is to have such feelings. The client hears this 'permission' to name the difficult feelings.

Encouraging strengths

Client	I kind of feel stuck. Y'know, I wonder how I'll manage and carry on with all this stuff going on. I feel so depleted in some ways.
Therapist	You feel stuck and depleted, and yet you have coped with so much too. You talked about the things you do to look after yourself, which might be really important here?
Client	Those things do help, yes. I forget them sometimes y'know. I forget I can do those things too.

FIGURE 3.12   Encouraging Strengths

The therapist, using reflective skills, highlights the difficulty of the client's situation but then encourages the client by referring back to a previous session when they had talked about what the client does to take care of herself. This encourages the client to recall these things and begin to draw some strength from them – this immediately begins to help with a sense of depletion, although those feelings are acknowledged too.

Highlighting conscious or unconscious interactions/'edge of awareness'

Client	We ended up having this almighty argument – it was awful. She was going on about what I should do about stuff and ... well ... I just blew – lost it! Another relationship ended ... again!
Therapist	I'm thinking about the other times when you have 'lost it'; I'm thinking about how often it seems to be something to do with being told what to do, about not being in control?
Client	Oh goodness yes! Yes, it is! I hate it, I hate being told what to do. My sister always used to do that to me when I was younger – always pushing me around. I'd really get pissed about it.

FIGURE 3.13   Highlighting conscious or unconscious interactions/'edge of awareness'

The client has not made any links himself concerning the arguments he has in relationships. The therapist tentatively offers a link – not in a way that interprets the client's narrative, but rather as a way of holding similarities together for the client to reflect on them. This has a profound impact on the client, who suddenly begins to make connections.

Reflection

Client	Sometimes I just feel utterly hopeless. Like a big cloud descending on me – just overwhelmed. Utterly, utterly overwhelmed.
Therapist	Like a big could descending – utterly overwhelmed.
Client	Yes, it's so smothering.

FIGURE 3.14 Reflection

The therapist uses the client's narrative without adding anything new: they just reflect the words back for the client to hear. This helps the client to make more sense of their experience and move forward, in this instance to a sense of being 'smothered' by their hopelessness.

Exploration

Client	I look in the mirror and I feel so disgusted. I mean, I feel so fat and ugly and the rest of my body... well ... y'know, it's awful.
Therapist	Can you tell me a little bit more about the rest of your body – what is it about your body that is awful?
Client	I'm too tall and too fat. I think I am completely out of proportion – it's all so ugly.

FIGURE 3.15 Exploration

While the exploration here doesn't lead to any new insight or resolution, it does provide the client with an opportunity to be more specific about how they feel about their body. This extra detail may be important for the client and therapist to use in subsequent sessions.

Focusing

Client	There's the job – that's rubbish and I really hate it. It just gets me down so much. I wondered about moving away and doing something different. I've always fancied living in a big city and ... well, do you think it would be a good idea?
Therapist	The job gets you down so much. I wonder if you could tell me more about what it is about the job that gets you down?
Client	The hours are so long and I just end up feeling exhausted. I never feel that I recover from it and am always tired. I can't enjoy the rest of my life.

FIGURE 3.16 Focusing

The client names an important area of concern and then becomes distracted by the thought of living in the city. It would be easy here for the therapist to follow that line and miss the issue about the job. Here, however, the therapist focuses the client, which helps the client be more specific about what it is they find difficult. The issues of moving may return in subsequent sessions.

Summary

The above passages demonstrate generic micro-skills in action. While some might appear to overlap a little (and they probably do, as in the case of summarising and paraphrasing), there are subtle differences. However, their common intention is to facilitate the client's self-exploration. They require practice and sometimes they won't work. Knowing how best to make use of these skills can also be challenging. Over-using particular skills can be unhelpful as this can undermine the emotional potency. I have given examples elsewhere (Reeves, 2010a) of an overuse of reflective skills with suicidal clients, where there can be a need for explorative skills to help the client consider their experiences in more detail.

These generic skills can be rendered unhelpful and meaningless if used without compassion, integrity and warmth. Imagine any of the therapist statements above if delivered coldly or without feeling: their intention would be lost and the client is likely to feel, at best, untouched and, at worst, misheard and misunderstood. Fundamentally these micro-skills help the therapist communicate their understanding of, and connection with, the client. In these circumstances, with a therapist demonstrating the personal qualities already outlined, the therapeutic relationship can be profoundly powerful in helping the client to move away from a position of despair or hopelessness.

DISCUSSION QUESTIONS

1 By what means do you assess your competence to work as a counsellor or psychotherapist?

2 What personal qualities do you have that contribute to your ability to develop relationships?

3 How might you know if your capacity to work and thus your competence as a therapist was impaired?

4 How do you monitor your use of micro-skills and ensure that you use them in a careful and considered way?

4

Professional Settings and Organisations

4.1 INTRODUCTION

CHAPTER OVERVIEW

The purpose of this chapter is to consider the working contexts of counsellors and psychotherapists. Specifically, it outlines the types of setting in which counselling and psychotherapy are offered and discusses the impact that the setting may have on the therapist's and client's experience and the ways in which organisational policy and procedure shape the type and nature of therapy offered. Additionally, the chapter considers the challenges and benefits of working independently.

The popular assumption about counselling and psychotherapy has perhaps been that they are activities offered by people who work in private practice, accessed only by those who can afford to pay. Stereotypes often perpetrated by the media – films, books and music – have reinforced a view that therapy is something for people who perhaps have too much time and money on their hands. Many people will relate to the idea that a therapist is an important lifestyle accessory, together with a nice car, personal trainer and a fake tan. For a very small minority of people this 'reality' might have some truth. For the overwhelming majority of people who see a counsellor or psychotherapist, however, the truth is very different. For them, therapy provides an opportunity to deal with often profound personal distress or trauma or to access help that is respectful and offers options to accompany or replace medication or hospitalisation.

This is not to say that the option to pay for counselling or psychotherapy is a myth either. Private practice – or independent practice (i.e., independent from an employing organisation) – is an important division of the counselling and psychotherapy profession. Many independent practitioners might also work in organisational settings (e.g. health or social services or voluntary agencies), while others will work exclusively in independent practice while seeing a full range of people and difficulties. The point here, however, is that the stereotype of counselling and psychotherapy often offers the view that therapy is only available if paid for privately, whereas in reality the provision of therapy is now much more diverse, and accessible.

For many decades counselling and psychotherapy were only available from independent practitioners for the majority of people. As was discussed in Chapter 1, the development of counselling and psychotherapy as a professional activity, and the emergence of models of practice beyond traditional psychoanalysis, has provided a greater opportunity for therapy to be provided differently, over shorter periods of time, and in different settings. The traditional model of three or more sessions of psychoanalysis per week over many years proved both financially and practically prohibitive to the wider population. Treatments that were more focused, shorter-term, cheaper and problem-specific enabled their applicability to different settings and client populations.

Slowly, counselling and psychotherapy began to move into focus and was adopted by other professional groups and settings. For example, in the early days of UK social work, hospital almoners adopted what we might now define as counselling skills (Bell, 1961). Such skills became increasingly apparent in other professions, such as nursing, teaching and also psychiatry, which had traditionally adopted a very traditionalist medical model of 'treatment'. As an aside here, some writers argue that as counselling and psychotherapy have emerged into the mainstream, and within contexts that were traditionally medical, the philosophical basis of counselling and psychotherapy has become diluted and medicalised, moving away from the understanding of human experience, certainly within a humanistic paradigm (Olney, 2010).

The purpose of this chapter therefore is to see counselling and psychotherapy in context. Much of the literature in counselling and psychotherapy focuses on what happens between the therapist and the client. In this very intimate dyad, two people meet and share a human encounter, albeit one framed by the assumptions and 'rules' of counselling and psychotherapy. The importance of critical thinking in counselling and psychotherapy here is paramount (Feltham, 2010). Even in independent practice, where there is no employing organisation exerting influence and control over the sessions, there is still a context to the work. The 'context' is multi-faceted and will be intrapersonal, interpersonal and societal in nature. While not an exhaustive list, Box 4.1 provides suggestions as to the contextual factors that might shape and inform the therapeutic process.

BOX 4.1   THE CONTEXT OF COUNSELLING AND PSYCHOTHERAPY

- Age
- Gender
- Culture
- Spirituality
- Sexuality
- Ability and impairment
- How the family was/is constituted
- Family history and current dynamics
- Personal history and upbringing
- Employment or unemployment
- Living situation, e.g. alone, with partner, children
- Friends and availability of support
- Financial situation
- The room in which therapy is offered
- Whether therapy is free or paid for
- The theoretical orientation of the therapist
- The 'organisational' setting, e.g. health, social services, third sector, independent
- Potential dual relationships.

All of the factors highlighted in Box 4.1 will be present in the room, either explicitly or implicitly. All will need to be attended to, again either explicitly or implicitly. Other chapters in this book consider some of these factors in more detail. This chapter looks at the more structural and systemic aspects of counselling and psychotherapy. The first section of the chapter, Working Contexts: Types and Significance, defines more clearly the working contexts of counselling and psycho-therapy organisations: the different types; purpose and function; profile of presenting clients and problems; types of counsellors and psychotherapists working in them, including typical qualification profile; implications.

Next, Procedures, Policies and Guidance examines how organisations of differ-ent types and purposes might develop and create procedural guidance that informs the type and delivery of counselling and psychotherapy, and what the positive and negative implications of such policies might be for therapists and clients alike. It discusses how the theory that underpins counselling and psychotherapy might be usefully applied to organisational thinking and help inform an understanding of organisational dynamics and, finally, how therapy itself is being shaped by the needs of organisations, such as the development of coaching allied to therapy.

The following section, Managing Organisational Expectations, looks at how counsellors and psychotherapists might respond to organisational expectations in a way that is consistent with the ethical expectations of practice. For example, therapists often struggle with contradictions between the expectations of organisations and what they themselves believe to be the core principles of therapy (e.g. confidentiality); they may find it difficult to maintain what they consider to be ethical practice in the face of employer demands.

Finally, in The Independent Practitioner, we go full circle back to the early days of counselling and psychotherapy practice – private or independent practice. In viewing independent practice as an 'organisational setting' within its own right, this section will consider the highlights and challenges of working independently – how that apparent freedom from imposed constraint can liberate practice as well, yet also present extremely difficult dilemmas for practitioners to respond to – and ways in which such practitioners may develop their work to support ethical practice, themselves and their clients.

As will be seen throughout this chapter, the influence of the organisation on counselling and psychotherapy resembles the tide: at times it is very apparent, an inexorable force carrying everything inevitably in its way; at other times it is hidden but still as powerfully present – an undercurrent that, if ignored, would potentially lead in the wrong direction. Counsellors and psychotherapists must pay careful attention to their context to best ensure that the heart and soul of therapy remain intact.

4.2 WORKING CONTEXTS: TYPES AND SIGNIFICANCE

SECTION OUTLINE

The purpose of this section is to give an overview of the different types of organisations counsellors and psychotherapists might work in, how they are structured (at a macro and micro level), their purposes and functions, and how all this may shape the nature of client work. Additionally, the section discusses the qualifications and experience required for working in each setting and the overall implications for practice.

Organisations come in a variety of shapes and sizes. There is no one 'type' of organisation: even those within a common 'frame' (health care, for example) may differ greatly from setting to setting or across geographical locations. A therapist

working in a primary care setting in the south of the UK may have a very different experience from another working in the north – even from someone working
in another team within the same setting. The complexities and layers of differences
across settings appear limitless, yet while the intricacies will often be multi-faceted
there are sufficient commonalities to help us understand organisational dynamics
and culture and, therefore, help us manage practice accordingly.

From the perspective of economics, we can distinguish five 'sectors' of organisation as follows (Fellman et al., 2007):

- Primary: the production and harvesting of food and goods from the earth, e.g.
  grain, coal, etc.
- Secondary: the manufacturing of goods, e.g. textiles, chemicals
- Tertiary: the service industries, e.g. health care, law, etc.
- Quaternary: intellectual industries, e.g. government, research etc.
- Quinary: the highest level of decision making in society, e.g. in government and
  health care.

This way of classifying organisations clearly delineates the various functions organisations serve in society. We can place counselling and psychotherapy within the
tertiary level – delivering services to people – while placing counselling and psychotherapy research in the quaternary level. As a microcosm of the bigger picture,
the counselling and psychotherapy profession also has its own quinary level where
the 'big' decisions are made.

If we focus on the tertiary level, where counselling and psychotherapy are positioned, we can further differentiate contexts. Generally, in economic terms, the
tertiary level includes such activities as health care, law, media, tourism, banking and
insurance. While we might find counselling and psychotherapy provided by
employers in all these settings, it is perhaps helpful to consider these in terms of
categories of settings, rather than simply as an undifferentiated tertiary level activity.
The types of settings in which counselling and psychotherapy may be categorised

are: (1) the statutory sector, including health and social services; (2) education; (3)
the 'third sector'; (4) workplace and employment; and (5) independent practice. These
are also summarised in a **PowerPoint presentation** on the companion website.

The statutory sector

In the UK, the 'statutory sector' is a term used to include centrally funded health and
social services, particularly the National Health Service (NHS) and social services
departments. By centrally funded, I am referring to government-funded organisations, particularly where services may be offered underpinned by a legislative requirement (e.g. mental health and child protection). However, such services are not
exclusively provided by statutory agencies. For example, post-adoption counselling may
be provided by a number of different agencies outside the statutory sector, while

still working within statutory parameters. In health care, counselling and psycho-therapy services may be found across a wide variety of different settings. They include:

- Primary (general) care (in General Practice settings), including specialist services located within primary care, e.g. well-women/men services
- Secondary (specialist) care, including:

  - in- and out-patient mental health services
  - cardiovascular units
  - spinal injury units
  - fertility and maternity units
  - head injury units
  - child and adolescent services
  - pain management units
  - services for older people
  - hospices
  - learning disability units

- Improving Access to Psychological Therapies (IAPT) services – a government-funded initiative for the treatment of depression and anxiety delivering approved psychological therapies at 'low intensity' (guided self-help; bibliotherapy) and 'high intensity' (therapist-delivered interventions) levels

Social services departments are tasked with the assessment of social need and delivery of social care. Here, counselling and psychotherapy services may be found in:

- Adult services, including:

  - mental health
  - learning difficulties
  - physical impairment
  - older people's services
  - generic 'intake' or 'one-stop shop' centres

- Children and family services, including:

  - child protection
  - family support
  - children's centres
  - family therapy services
  - child and adolescent units
  - sexual abuse support units.

The above list is not exhaustive. It does, however, provide an overview of how the delivery of counselling and psychotherapy provision is distributed across a wide range of services and client groups within one 'sector' of employment.

Education

One might think that counselling and psychotherapy in education settings focuses solely on the needs of younger people. In fact, however, education has become a lifelong process: thus therapy services in education settings work across the life span. The following settings may be included in the category of 'education' in the UK:

- Primary education: typically from the ages of 5 years through to 11 years
- Secondary education: typically from the ages of 11 years through to 16 years
- Further education: typically from 16 years. Traditionally young people leave school and progress to further education settings, e.g. 'sixth form' within schools, or further education colleges providing pregraduate training. However, further education colleges also offer adult education opportunities and the profile of students typically falls outside the 'traditional' view. Additionally, many further education colleges now also provide undergraduate-level education.
- Higher education: traditionally undergraduate for 18–21-year-olds and postgraduate study; however, as in further education, the profile of higher education students has changed dramatically, with many returning to education later in life.

Provision of counselling and psychotherapy in education settings is not a new phenomenon. Schools-based counselling can be traced back many years, with a recent resurgence of schools counselling building on a growing evidence base (Cooper, 2009, Cooper et al., 2010, Cooper et al., 2012). Likewise, counselling and psychotherapy in further and higher education settings has been established in many UK institutions for more than 40 years, with many of the leading theorists and writers emerging from that field (Reeves, 2012).

The 'third sector'

The National Audit Office (2012) define the 'third sector' as 'non-governmental organisations that are value-driven and which principally reinvest their surpluses to further social, environmental or cultural objectives. It includes voluntary and community organisations, charities, social enterprises, cooperatives and mutuals'. Previously known as the 'voluntary sector' (and still called that by many), the third sector typically comprises charity-based voluntary organisations, which can also employ paid staff. They can be found in a wide variety of social, health and political contexts, and will often make counselling and psychotherapy available either as a voluntary or paid service. Contexts in which the third sector operates include:

- Adoption services
- Mental health services
- Child and family services
- Services for older people

- Services for people with learning or physical disabilities
- Services meeting specific social or cultural need (e.g. for specific cultural groups or groups defined by sexuality)
- Services for specific demographic groups (e.g. young males, street workers, asylum seekers).

Not all such services will offer counselling and psychotherapy as defined in the context of this book. For example, the Samaritans, a long-established and well-known charity supporting suicidal people, would not define their service as counselling or psychotherapy, though by virtue of providing careful listening they do utilise many counselling and psychotherapy skills.

Workplaces

Counsellors and psychotherapists have been established in workplace settings for many years. There is an increasing evidence base to support their efficacy in such settings (McLeod, 2010a). By 'workplace settings' I am specifically referring to companies or organisations, including many well-known UK major retailers, or public service organisations such as the police or other emergency services, where counselling is provided for employees. Many human resources departments will be aware of the psychological needs of employees, and will have access to counselling and psychotherapy services either in-house (i.e., therapists employed by the company or organisation) or via an Employee Assistance Programme (EAP).

An EAP is a private company that contracts with another organisation to provide counselling and psychotherapy and to case manage referrals. They will receive referrals from the organisation, often through human resource departments or occupational health settings, arrange for an assessment of need and, depending on the outcome of that assessment, will employ a therapist to provide the therapy. Counselling and psychotherapy is typically time-limited and provided with a specific focus of enabling the client – the employee – to address whatever difficulties might prevent them from working effectively (or perhaps facilitate a return to work following a period of sickness). A diagrammatic representation of how an EAP facilitates therapy is provided in Figure 4.1.

Figure 4.1 shows the relationships within the tripartite membership of the therapy. [A] will refer to [B] because of concerns about the employee's psychological wellbeing and their capacity to undertake the work for which they are employed. [B] will identify a suitable therapist, [C], who will meet with the employee (client) to assess them and undertake therapy within given parameters (including the number of sessions, focus of problem, and the limits of confidentiality and liability). At the end of therapy [C] will provide [B] with details of the outcome (the level of disclosure of the details of therapy will typically have been agreed at the outset), who will, in turn, communicate with [A]. The therapist's

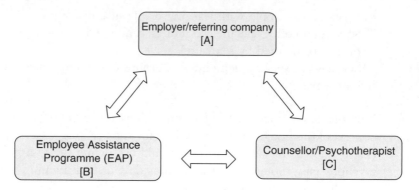

FIGURE 4.1   EAP Referral Routes

contact with the original referring agency – or employer [A] – will usually be very limited, if indeed there is any at all. As can be seen, the EAP [B] is the over-all case manager.

A benefit to the employer of such an arrangement is that they do not need to employ (on their own payroll) a counsellor or psychotherapist with the on-costs (e.g. pension, national insurance, and liability insurance) that would entail. Nor does the employer need themselves to possess the relevant expertise to assess and deliver a therapy service. Instead, they delegate those responsibilities to a special-ist EAP who, with the therapist, manages the therapeutic aspects of the work. A positive outcome is that the client/employee is able to address their difficulties sufficiently to enable them to return to work – or an alternative outcome, which may include termination of employment, may be reached.

Some major companies have led the way in developing ethical, respectful and responsive therapeutic provision for their employees, creating a benchmark for excellence in workplace counselling and psychotherapy. Others, it has been claimed, have only made such provision available following high profile legal cases where employers have been subject to successful civil litigation by employees who have sought redress for psychological injury caused through stress as a conse-quence of alleged poor support systems. Indeed, in the UK the Health and Safety Executive (HSE), which is the statutory body that oversees health and safety issues at work, states the following about stress on their website (HSE, 2012):

Employers should be concerned about stress because:

- They have a legal and moral duty to ensure that their workers and others that visit their premises are not injured or made ill because of the work they do.
- Staff absence and loss of productivity has a financial impact on their business.
- Certain elements of poor work design (for example where an employee has little or no control over the work they do or where there is little support

from managers or colleagues) have been shown to have a real impact on staff performance and reliability, even before an individual takes time off.

- It has an adverse impact on staff retention and recruitment, again causing additional costs to the business.
- Indemnity Insurance premiums may increase, and there may, in severe cases, be issues about litigation by those experiencing the stress.

Independent practice

It may seem surprising to include independent practice in a chapter on counselling and psychotherapy in organisations. Doing so helps to remind us that working independently does not mean that the therapist is not liable for providing a safe, accessible and appropriate service to potential and actual clients. I include independent practitioners here because my proposition is that working independently demands the same level of care and attention to working practices as does working for an employing organisation – even though the therapist is self-employed and is therefore responsible for their own working practices and procedures.

The benefits of working independently include:

- Working from a preferred location, including home (if suitable)
- Preferred hours of working
- Total autonomy over client load and other commitments
- Ability to work entirely consistently with a preferred theoretical model
- Ability to decide on and then implement the parameters of counselling and psychotherapy (other than when otherwise subscribed by legislation)
- Ability to develop own working practices, including preferred ways of working.

However, there are also a number of challenges. They include:

- The cost of suitable room hire, or of ensuring one's home is suitable for counselling and psychotherapy
- If working from home, the careful management of potential intrusions and unplanned self-disclosure
- Dependence on client referrals for income
- Lack of administrative structure and support
- Lack of organisational support, both pragmatically (e.g. provision of room, reception, administration), and procedurally (in organisations, well-written guidelines for working with challenging clients, e.g. those at risk of suicide, can often be experienced as supportive)
- Responsibility for health and safety of client when on own premises
- Advertising responsibilities and costs
- Lack of co-workers leading to a potentially isolated working experience
- Additional health and safety concerns, e.g. greater potential for lone working.

Many independent practitioners also work in organisational settings, thereby gaining benefits from different settings. In independent practice it can often take some considerable time to build a client base, either through careful advertising or 'word of mouth' referrals (i.e., clients enquiring on recommendation of others). There are organisations for independent practitioners that aim to provide support and information for members. For example, BACP Private Practice (formerly the Association for Independent Practitioners), a division of BACP, was established in 1977. At the time of writing the division's mission statement clearly outlined its priorities and commitment to independent practice (AIP, 2012):

> AIP is the division of the British Association for Counselling and Psychotherapy (BACP) that supports members who are primarily in, or about to embark upon, counselling or psychotherapy independently, including those who work in voluntary agencies. The division has the following goals:
>
> • To provide a supportive, encouraging and integrative network with opportunities to exchange ideas, work ethics, methods, and styles
> • To alleviate the loneliness of the independent practitioner by disseminating relevant information, providing tips and techniques and revitalisation
> • To engage in and encourage constructive dialogue about the profession of counselling and psychotherapy, including explanation and discussion of BACP developments
> • To offer therapists an opportunity to interact with the wider world of counselling and psychotherapy
> • To protect clients by promoting BACP standards and ethics.
>
> The division provides a supportive network as well as training with an emphasis on maintaining clear boundaries and having sufficient support and supervision.
>
> AIP provides an interactive sense of professional belonging for all members of our multi-cultural therapeutic community. Equal opportunities are an integral part of this division's philosophy.

While the independent practitioner might become isolated, there are systems available to offset that danger and provide an important network and professional community through which support can be accessed.

Qualifications and experience

In the UK, all working contexts require that counsellors and psychotherapists are trained and qualified to at least a Diploma level. Many organisations now require in addition a certain amount of working experience, which may or may not include a number of training hours (i.e., hours accrued while on a training placement). It is not uncommon for employing agencies to ask for BACP, COSCA or equivalent individual accreditation (or at least eligibility for the same). This in effect means that applicants must possess at least 450 hours of supervised practice. For psychotherapists, the minimum requirement is registration on the UKCP register of psychotherapists, which entails completion of a full psychotherapy training programme.

While for many organisations these qualifications are sufficient, increasingly some require that applicants have specific working experience in the particular field or possess specialist qualifications. For example, many employers working with children and young people will require a specific diploma or additional training in working with such a client group and will not accept a generic diploma that, for the most part, qualifies the graduate to work with an adult population. Other examples might include post-adoption counselling, where specific training is required, or in IAPT services where all employees at both low and high intensity levels of intervention will be required to complete the respective training.

It is therefore important to consider preferences concerning working environments prior to training. Many people entering counselling and psychotherapy training do not have an interest in a particular client group or setting, in which case the generic diploma in counselling or psychotherapy is sufficient for their needs. However, where there is a preference or interest, it is essential that trainees research the requirements for their specialism to ensure the training they are due to embark on is appropriate for their needs. Too many graduates of counselling and psychotherapy programmes complete their extensive and expensive training only to discover their qualifications do not equip them, as they stand, for their chosen working context. Consider the scenarios outlined in Box 4.2.

CASE STUDY 4.2
Ashrim and Stephanie

Ashrim decided to undertake a counselling training following her own experience of counselling for fertility problems. She found her own counselling to be immensely helpful, providing her with the space and opportunity to explore her difficulties in conceiving. She began a diploma in counselling at a local further education college because the times of the course suited her working patterns and travelling was kept to a minimum. She completed her placement at a local higher education institution and enjoyed the work. Her long-standing desire was to specialise in working with children. When looking at job opportunities she quickly discovered that her qualification was insufficient for her to apply for the available jobs as employers were asking for practitioners with specific qualifications and experience in working with children.

Stephanie worked as a support worker with adults with mental health problems during her training to be a counsellor. Her course was a person-centred training diploma at a well-regarded local education provider. She was motivated to undertake training because she was aware how

(Continued)

(Continued)

little opportunity there was for her clients to talk about their problems; they were mostly 'maintained' through the use of medication. On qualifying, she found that there were no job opportunities for her in mental health. She did, however, notice a number of counsellor positions advertised in health care settings, including IAPT services. She was dismayed to find that most required her to have undertaken some training in CBT. She had insufficient experience to compete for those remaining jobs where CBT was not a prerequisite given the number of applicants for each position.

PAUSE FOR REFLECTION

1   What are your thoughts about Ashrim's and Stephanie's situations?
2   What steps might they have taken, prior to undertaking training, that would have been helpful?
3   In reflecting on your own current situation, what do you know already about the working contexts in which you might like to find employment?
4   What steps might you be able to take now to enhance your employability (for example, finding a training placement that provides the specific experience you require)?

Implications of working contexts

There are a number of implications for the therapeutic process – some positive, some negative – for counsellors and psychotherapists who work in organisational settings. They include:

- Role conflict
- Organisational dynamics
- Parallel process between organisation and therapy process
- Different values between organisation and those of therapy
- Competing expectations
- Stress and burnout
- Terms and conditions of employment.

Let us explore these in more detail.

Role conflict

In organisational settings, role conflicts can arise. BACP's Ethical Framework (BACP, 2010) makes clear the need to avoid role conflicts or dual roles wherever possible.

When working as a workplace counsellor or psychotherapist it is very difficult not to find yourself in a situation or role that might conflict with your work as a therapist, unless the role of therapist is clearly defined and that is all you are there to do. In my own working setting as a counsellor in a university my colleagues and I are able to offer a wider contribution to the institution through consultation, membership of professional committees and working groups, or presenting training sessions. It is not uncommon to find oneself in a setting with a former or current client.

It is important to manage potential role conflicts at the commencement of therapy, and discuss with all potential clients fully and honestly the likelihood of these arising, and how they can best be managed if they do. A sensible, pragmatic approach that respects the autonomy and confidentiality of the client is paramount. Where role conflicts can be avoided, they should be, otherwise planning for the eventuality can minimise harm to all parties.

Organisational dynamics

Groups bring their particular dynamics, re-enacting histories and scenarios with individuals taking particular positions within them. This is also true in organisations, which are likely to have their own identity, way of being, ways of 'doing things' and thus written and unwritten 'rules' for employees. Those transgressing can often be scapegoated, suffering enormous stress and psychological harm as a result. Organisational dynamics are not necessarily negative, however, and many function to serve the organisation and employee well. It could be argued that the 'healthier' the dynamic, the more likelihood the organisation has of succeeding (Levi, 2010; Ringer, 2002).

When it does go wrong, however, the consequences can be significant. Walton (2008) refers to the 'toxic workplace', where the toxicity includes 'workplace bullying and harassment in its various forms, deception and fraudulent dealings, the forced imposition of unrealistic workloads and the fostering of disruptive internal competition resulting in bitter and destructive "turf" battles' (2008, p. 9). Walton (p. 15) states that a toxic working environment is identified:

(i)   through the behaviour of an organisation's key personnel,

(ii) by the rules and regulations formally established governing people's behaviour and ways of working, and

(iii) how these rules are implemented in practice.

Counsellors and psychotherapists in organisational settings need to be aware of the dynamics in their particular organisations, as these are likely to be present in their clients' narratives. Supporting staff caught in this form of dynamic can be extremely challenging and can push both the boundaries of the therapist and also therapy itself.

Finally, where a counselling or psychotherapy service is embedded within an organisation (i.e., where it is paid for by the organisation and thus part of the organisational system), the service can inadvertently become the 'trashcan' (as it were) of the organisation, containing all that the organisation struggles with and wishes to dispose of. Employees struggling with organisational difficulties or personal problems can be 'sent for therapy' to 'sort themselves out'. The organisation can project its own difficulties onto the employee or therapy service, thus not attending to issues that need addressing.

Parallel process between organisation and therapy process

The term 'parallel process' is discussed in detail in Chapter 11 of this book. Here we may summarise by saying that it describes the process whereby a dynamic or process within therapy is unconsciously acted out in supervision (for example, a client who is angry in therapy might be presented angrily in supervision by their therapist). The dynamic of parallel process can also be present in workplace counselling, where the influence of the organisation is unconsciously acted out either by the client or therapist. Good management and supervision of counsellors and psychotherapists in the workplace facilitate the recognition of parallel process and bring it into the awareness of the therapists.

Differences between the values of the organisation and of therapy

Most obviously, such differences can occur where the priority of the company or organisation is to make a profit (as opposed to non-profit voluntary or 'third sector' settings, where the priority might be financial survival). Counselling and psychotherapy services may be seen as not contributing to this wider ethos, instead supporting 'malingerers' and 'deadwood' that get in the way of success. This dynamic might also be present in statutory settings or 'third sector' organisations. For example, counselling services within university settings often have to justify their existence by demonstrating their contribution to student retention, where the institution does not readily recognise the contribution counselling may have made to the student's decision to remain on their course or in achieving academic success. In social services or health care settings, where the purpose of the organisation is about the care and treatment of vulnerable people, the needs of the 'helpers' can easily be overlooked or not recognised. Counselling and psychotherapy provision, either in-house or via an EAP, might be provided only to safeguard against litigation (Jenkins, 2008).

It is important that counsellors and psychotherapists find a way of communicating with the organisation how their input can contribute to the success of the organisation, in whichever way that may be judged, without losing what is integral to the role of counselling and psychotherapy. Higher education counselling is a case in point, where successful services learn to use the language of the organisation, demonstrating their unique contribution to its function, while continuing to work in a way that is consistent with the ethics and values of counselling and psychotherapy.

Competing expectations

The management of organisational expectations is discussed more fully later in this chapter. Here the challenges may be summarised as outlined by McLeod (2008, p. 419):

- Being pressured to produce results desired by the agency rather than the client
- Maintaining confidentiality boundaries
- Justifying the cost of the service
- Dealing with isolation
- Educating colleagues about the purpose and value of counselling
- Justifying the cost of supervision
- Avoiding being overwhelmed by numbers of clients, or becoming the 'conscience' of the organisation
- Avoiding the threat to reputation caused by 'failure' cases
- Coping with the envy of colleagues who are not able to take an hour for each client interview
- Creating an appropriate office space and reception system.

Stress and burnout

Stress in organisational settings is well documented (Mellor et al., 2011; Weinberg et al., 2010). Counsellors and psychotherapists will often find themselves responding to staff who are working under a great deal of stress – whether or not the organisation could be defined as being a 'toxic workplace' – or are perhaps off sick through stress-related problems. It is particularly difficult for counsellors and psychotherapists when working with such clients to know how best to support their client, particularly when there are clearly defined in-house causes for the stress (e.g. bullying and harassment or excessive workloads) – much as it is when supporting any client whose social situation is a major contributor to their levels of distress.

Counsellors and psychotherapists too need to pay attention to their own levels of stress. Being the 'container' for others' distress can have profound effects, including burnout and other mental and physical health consequences. While self-care is a requirement of BACP's Ethical Framework (BACP, 2010) that does not necessarily mean that all counsellors and psychotherapists are good at taking care of themselves or have self-care strategies in place that work effectively. There are also particular challenges when we experience stress in the workplace (who do we go to?). In some organisations, employees are able to refer themselves for therapy without the permission of their line manager, while in other settings a line manager referral is required. Unless we are able to pay for our own therapy, or have access to free or reduced-fee therapy locally (without lengthy waiting lists), we must ask our employers to make the necessary arrangements for the provision of their own therapy. This can cause difficulties around confidentiality (finding a counsellor in the locality who is not known) and can also raise concerns in the employer as to our suitability to be delivering therapy to others. It is not uncommon for others to expect their therapists to be invincible! The issues of self-care and stress are discussed in more detail in Chapter 10.

Terms and conditions of employment

At the time of writing there are no national terms and conditions of employment for counsellors and psychotherapists in the UK. The consequence of a lack of a national pay structure and terms of employment for therapists is that there is huge variation between posts. There are many situations where therapists employed to do the same work in comparable organisations are given very different terms and conditions of employment.

While you may be keen to take employment following qualification (often having spent a long time searching for it), it is important to carefully consider the terms of the employment and whether they are acceptable. As newly qualified therapists, if we do not have previous experience in an allied profession (e.g. social work or nursing), we may find we have to work in a voluntary capacity for a while to build suitable and sufficient experience for employment. This is discussed further in Chapter 13.

As can be seen, the organisations in which counsellors and psychotherapists are based profoundly influence and shape the work of therapy. While there are many challenges to negotiate, there are also many benefits to working in a setting with colleagues, structures, clearly defined (and appropriate) procedures, as well as an interesting mix of potential clients.

DISCUSSION QUESTIONS

1   What experience do you have of working in organisations? What do you consider to be the positives and what have been the challenges?
2   How has your work in organisational settings influenced your decision to become a counsellor or psychotherapist?
3   Which types of settings most interest you? Why?
4   How might you manage the challenges of your preferred setting? In particular, how would you ensure you took appropriate steps for self-care?

4.3 PROCEDURES, POLICIES AND GUIDANCE

SECTION OUTLINE

Many types of organisations develop procedures, policies or guidance documents to help streamline activity and ensure a consistency of approach. Many therapy agencies do the same to support therapists in their work with clients. This section considers (a) the differences between procedures, policies and guidance, (b) the ways in which they can be developed successfully, and (c) how to manage conflicts (when they arise) between such documents and the work of therapy.

While for some the existence of policy and procedural documents can feel overly restrictive and prescriptive, limiting the free flow and autonomy of counselling and psychotherapy, for others they provide an invaluable structure in which clients can be responded to consistently and fairly. There are few policy or procedural guidelines that determine the detail of what happens in the therapy session (although they do exist): rather, they mostly attend to the macro issues that therapists can struggle with. There are of course 'manualised treatments', often in therapies such as CBT but also latterly in person-centred therapy/experiential therapy, such as in the Counselling for Depression research (Hill, 2011), used in health care settings such as IAPT services. These aim to standardise the type of interventions used by therapists within the context of a specific modality and philosophical approach: they are discussed further in Chapter 12 and are distinct from the organisational policy or procedural documents discussed here.

WEBSITES

Counselling for Depression Online Learning:
www.bacp.co.uk/learning/Counselling%20for%20Depression/
Curriculum for Counselling for Depression:
www.iapt.nhs.uk/silo/files/curriculum-for-counselling-for-depression.pdf

Counsellors and psychotherapists report that policies and procedures can be experienced as supportive when responding to particular clients – for example, those at risk of suicide (Reeves, 2010a). In such an event they can guide both therapist and client through an assessment or explorative process and offer ways forward to help support the client through their personal crisis. For the therapist, they can provide 'checkpoints', ensuring all salient and important areas are considered and all options explored. Generally, however, it is probably fair to say that policies and procedures tend not to enjoy a good reputation, often associated with overly-bureaucratic systems that have no place in a free-flowing human exchange.

A move away from a more procedural and directive approach can be seen in how counsellors and psychotherapists are informed in their work. For example, BACP used to produce guidance in the form of a Code of Ethics and Practice for its members, providing concrete guidance and advice as to how to incorporate ethical thinking into practice and defining in concrete terms what was and was not deemed permissible in therapeutic work. This has been replaced by a new *Ethical Framework for Good Practice in Counselling and Psychotherapy* (first published in 2002, with the latest revision in 2010), which deliberately took a different position: it provided a looser, less prescriptive framework by which therapists could consider their work. Likewise, COSCA (2011b) offers its members a *Statement of Ethics and Code of Practice*, and UKCP publishes an *Ethical Principles and Code of Professional Conduct* document (UKCP, 2009).

What is certain is that written procedures and policies are here to stay – and over the last couple of decades have enjoyed a new lease of life in the context of targets, 'deliverables' and benchmarks that have peppered government policy and, in turn, the work of the organisations in which counselling and psychotherapy find themselves embedded. It is worth therefore considering a definition of each kind of document.

Policy

One definition of policy is 'a definite course of action adopted for the sake of expediency, facility' (Dictionary.com, 2012), while another dictionary defines policy as 'a course or principle of action adopted or proposed by an organisation or individual' (OED, 2012). Applied to counselling and psychotherapy services therefore, a policy document would be one that outlines a 'course or principle of action' developed by the therapy service or funding organisation. In practice this would mean that the therapist would work within the context of a particular policy that defined aspects of their work or service. Therapy policies might specify:

- Who is eligible to receive a service
- How counsellors or psychotherapists are recruited or employed
- How anti-discriminatory working practices might be employed
- The limit to the number of therapy sessions offered to a client
- How the therapy service liaises or communicates with outside agencies
- How 'at risk' situations are viewed.

It is important that these documents are known to the counsellor or psychotherapist from the commencement of their employment to ensure the best opportunity of adherence to the policy.

Procedure

One definition of procedure is 'an act or a manner of proceeding in any action or process; conduct' (Dictionary.com, 2012), while another defines procedure as 'an established or official way of doing something' and 'a series of actions conducted in a certain order or manner' (OED, 2012). Applied to counselling and psychotherapy services this would determine how certain therapy tasks are to be undertaken or how particular clients are to be responded to in defined situations. Examples of therapy procedures might cover:

- How clients are received and registered by the service
- How clients are allocated to therapists
- Whether clients are assessed at the commencement of counselling or psychotherapy, and if so how this is to be undertaken
- How situations are managed when boundaries of confidentiality are reached, e.g. responding to suicide risk, or child protection
- Responses to third party enquiries and the release of information.

Some of the above procedures are probably less contentious (e.g. the registration of clients) while others more so (e.g. the procedure for assessment of clients). Again, it is important that counsellors and psychotherapists are fully aware of any procedural documents that exist at the commencement of their employment to ensure they don't transgress accepted ways of working.

Guidance

One definition of guidance is 'the act or function of guiding; leadership; direction' (Dictionary.com, 2012), while another defines guidance as 'advice or information aimed at resolving a problem or difficulty, especially as given by someone in authority' (OED, 2012). Applied to counselling or psychotherapy, a guidance document might be said to provide a looser form of procedure, where the therapist employs greater discretion in determining a particular course of action or intervention. Guidance might be offered in the following situations, for example:

- How clients at risk of suicide are responded to
- How or whether to implement outcome measures in sessions
- Giving evaluation forms at end of sessions to clients
- How to get the most out of supervision
- How to negotiate and consider particular ethical dilemmas as they arise in practice.

Readers of this book are likely already to have a good idea of what the terms policy, procedure and guidance mean, but these definitions are offered so as to be entirely clear how they are used in the context of this present discussion. This is important because I have become aware in talking to many counsellors and psychotherapists that these terms are often used interchangeably (indeed, I have done so myself) and as a result the implication or consequence of each in practice is potentially diluted. For example, many therapists will talk freely about 'the policy and procedure to do with suicide risk', while the difference between policy (i.e., what is to be done) and procedure (i.e., how it is to be done) is crucial (Reeves, 2010a). For example, many therapists may consider the *policy* on working with suicide risk while overlooking the *procedure*, failing to conceptualise them as different documents. Likewise, in my own writing on working with suicide risk I have argued for the development of *guidance* documents, rather than policy or procedural ones, as I believe they allow therapists much more flexibility in their thinking and interventions and are less likely to leave organisations hoist by their own petard (Reeves, 2010a). So, the use of language and its application here is crucial in thinking about what best works for whom.

Supporting practice

In light of my previous points, the first step in developing a sound policy, procedure or guidance document is to decide exactly which one is best for the task in hand. My assertion would be that counsellors and psychotherapists are likely to be less inclined towards policies and procedures because they limit freedom of thought and action, and are more likely to be drawn toward guidance as it allows for autonomy of thinking and action within wider parameters. The analogy here as proposed by others is that counsellors and psychotherapists are more like cats than dogs: if you have ever tried herding cats, the analogy will make sense! They quite simply do not like being told what to do, even if there might be sense in the telling.

The lesson here therefore is for counsellors and psychotherapists to take an active role in the development of such documents – thus gaining a sense of ownership from the beginning – to achieve the greatest chance of their success. The resistance felt by therapists is perhaps born out of frustration at systems being imposed on them by people who don't fully understand the nature of being a counsellor or psychotherapist, nor the complexity of the therapeutic process. Organisations dedicated to the delivery of counselling or psychotherapy services are, perhaps, best placed to ensure which approach best suits the target situation. They are also best placed to ensure that policies, procedures or guidance reflect the intricacies of counselling and psychotherapy.

Box 4.3 provides a checklist of questions for determining a best course of action.

> ## BOX 4.3   QUESTIONS TO REFLECT ON WHEN DEVELOPING A POLICY, PROCEDURE OR GUIDANCE DOCUMENT
>
> - What is the hoped outcome, i.e., an overarching statement of intent and action (policy); a means by which a task is achieved (procedure); parameters within which decisions can be made in an informed way (guidance)?
> - Who might usefully contribute to the discussions, and are all parties potentially affected by the outcome able to participate and contribute?
> - Are there implications for existing policies, procedures or guidance documents, i.e., do they need to be incorporated into the planning, reviewed or rescinded?
> - Does the planned document appropriately reflect the parameters and culture of the service offered, i.e., taking into account the experience of the counsellors, supervision contracts, capacity of the service to respond to clients, etc?
> - What steps will be taken to ensure any document is clear, accessible and easy to communicate to all involved?
> - Is the proposed document realistic? Does it provide counsellors and psycho-therapists with realistic options, rather than set up unrealistic and often unachievable expectations?
> - How will the proposed document take into account difference, the varying needs of clients and anti-discriminatory and anti-oppressive practice?
> - What review process will be built in, by whom, and how will the outcomes of reviews be implemented in change?
> - Does the proposed document have a 'shelf life', i.e., is it intended for the longer term, or rather a time-limited approach?

Reviewing policies, procedures or guidance

Policies, procedures and guidance documents have a tendency to defy the normal laws of physics, slipping through a space–time continuum to a place where they live a happy and enduring life in the hereafter. Douglas Adams, in his book *The Hitchhiker's Guide to the Galaxy,* talked of 'a planet entirely given over to Biro life forms. And it was to this planet that unattended Biros made their way, slipping quietly through wormholes in Space to a world where they knew they could enjoy a uniquely Biroid lifestyle, responding to highly Biro-oriented stimuli, and generally leading the Biro equivalent of the good life' (Adams, 1979, p. 160). I suspect the same is true for policies, procedures and guidance documents: once written, they never die.

The truth is that such documents are only worthwhile if they still serve a useful purpose, and the usefulness of their purpose can only really be judged if they are reviewed. The review process achieves a number of useful things, in that it helps to ensure such documents are relevant to practice, reflect the current work of the service and therapists, provide an opportunity to consider practice in the light of the latest evidence, and provide a means by which counsellors and psychotherapist can re-engage with them, helping to create a sense of ownership and integration into day-to-day work.

Clearly not all policies, procedures or guidance documents will originate from therapy services. Many therapists find themselves working with documents that have been developed elsewhere: these may be more generic in nature and not necessarily reflective of the realities of the work. It is sometimes possible to re-shape these with counselling and psychotherapy services in mind. If this is possible, it is important to do this in collaboration with the funding organisation. The funders ultimately have the right to decide the nature of the service, assuming it is ethically and legally sound.

Where it is not possible to develop existing documents, it is important that there is dialogue between workplace therapists or services with funders in an attempt to highlight concerns or deficiencies in the implementation of such documents. Counsellors and psychotherapists have reported disregarding policies and procedures when working with suicidal clients, for instance, when they disagreed with the documents (Reeves and Mintz, 2001). Simply disregarding a policy or procedural document is to be avoided: it has the potential to leave the therapist or service in a vulnerable position, potentially putting funding or employment at risk; additionally it might contribute to a case of negligence. Ultimately if a policy or procedural document is so abhorrent to an individual therapist, cannot be influenced or changed, and compromises fundamentally the therapist's beliefs about their work, the therapist must carefully consider their position and whether they are still able to continue with the employment. In this instance the workplace counsellors and psychotherapists are in the same position as anyone else employed to do a job.

DISCUSSION QUESTIONS

1 If you are working as a counsellor or psychotherapist, what policies, procedures or guidance documents exist that inform your work?
2 Of those documents, which ones are consistent with your practice, and which ones are not? What are the major differences?
3 Given the nature of your organisation, how might you be able to influence or participate in the development of such documents?
4 What systems exist to review such documents? If none, how might you offer feedback to your manager or organisation to implement a review process?

4.4 MANAGING ORGANISATIONAL EXPECTATIONS

SECTION OUTLINE

The purpose of this section is to consider in more detail the expectations that organisations might have of counsellors and psychotherapists and how these can be managed effectively to shape positively, rather than damage or undermine, the essential principles of counselling and psychotherapy.

Clarifying and managing expectations of what can be achieved is an important aspect of the work of counsellors and psychotherapists, regardless of setting. From the outset, the role and scope of therapy need to be clearly communicated to a prospective client – in the way the service is advertised and in what information is provided pre-therapy, during the first contact, at the first session and in contracting. Failure to complete this essential task runs the risk of undermining the potential efficacy of therapy, setting possibly unachievable and unrealistic targets, as well as misleading the client about what they might expect. At worst, it means the client is unable to make an informed decision about whether to begin therapy or whether the therapist they meet is the best person to address their concerns.

Very few counsellors or psychotherapists would dispute the assertions above, yet many will begin employment for an organisation without clarifying these points. Often, many issues will already be clear and, where there is already an established therapist or therapy service, such issues will already have been addressed and be in place. However, it is still important to fully appraise yourself of all the factors that inform and shape your work as a therapist in that particular workplace. In the same way as working with an uninformed client, working for an employer without being clear as to their expectations of the employee and what the employee might be able to expect in return, is potentially setting both parties up to fail.

In my work as a trainer around the UK, on many occasions I have heard therapists, when asked about the existence of a policy on a particular subject, respond, 'Oh, I don't know. I'm not sure if we have one.' Likewise, when arranging training sessions I will ask the organiser – often a representative of the agency – how their therapists work in a particular situation, only to be told 'To be honest I've never asked. I'm sure they manage it fine.' This confidence might be well placed, and the level of trust between both parties admirable, but the danger is that at point of difficulty or challenge either party can feel let down by the other. My belief is that both parties – organisation and therapist – are best supported if the following points are clearly and adequately addressed:

- The nature of counselling and psychotherapy and how that reflects the aims of the organisation
- The development of procedures, policies and guidance that impact on counselling and psychotherapy provision
- Clarifying different or competing benchmarks of 'success'
- Whether therapy services offer a planned response versus crisis intervention
- How the principles of counselling and psychotherapy can be/are safeguarded
- How colleagues view the role of counselling and psychotherapy services
- How the counselling and psychotherapy provision is 'positioned', i.e., advertised and established, within the organisation
- How various systems, space and services are constituted
- Expectations of what can realistically be achieved in the time available
- What happens when things go wrong.

Organisational aims

If the organisation is one dedicated to the provision of counselling and psychotherapy, there is unlikely to be a mismatch between organisational aims and the provision of the therapy service. That said, it is not unheard of for there to be a lack of alignment between the employing agency's view as to how counselling and psychotherapy might be provided and those of the therapists providing it. This might include: how clients are prioritised for therapy if there is a waiting list; the charges made and how this system is managed; the type or form of therapy offered; the ways in which vulnerable clients are responded to (e.g. around self-harm and suicide potential); and the number of sessions offered. This last point is one of the most common areas of dispute, with therapists feeling unduly confined to a very brief model or that the number of sessions they are allowed to offer is insufficient to the needs of the client.

Where counselling or psychotherapy are not the primary 'business' of the organisation, as might be the case with health care providers or social services as well as corporations, there are additional expectations to attend to – for example, clarifying the purpose of a therapy service where it does not directly contribute to the acquisition of wealth or financial success. That contribution will be present in all sorts of ways: in education settings, counselling or psychotherapy might help students work more effectively on their studies, or help them remain at university or college when they might otherwise have left; in the NHS, therapy might support a member of staff to meet the needs of patients' more effectively, or perhaps enable them to manage working with distressing or traumatic events; in business, counselling or psychotherapy might provide an opportunity for an employee to deal with stresses that would otherwise impair their ability to work, or might help facilitate an early return to work from sick leave, saving money in sick pay and contributing to an improved self-esteem for the individual.

What is clear in these examples is a two-layered level of need: those of the organisation, and those of the individual. Consider the three scenarios outlined on Box 4.4.

CASE STUDY 4.4
Two layers of need

- **Gerald** works as a sales manager for a multi-national company that makes engine parts. He has experienced a major bereavement and additionally has problems in his relationship. His manager has been concerned about Gerald's performance at work, and in particular falling sales figures and some complaints received from customers about mistakes he has made. Gerald attends counselling on the recommendation of his manager.
- **Annette** is a nurse-practitioner who works with war veterans in a specialist unit. The majority of her patients have returned from war zones with diagnosed post-traumatic stress disorder (PTSD). She has been feeling increasingly depressed and angry and, with the agreement of her manager, has decided to attend for therapy.
- **Jason** is a counsellor in a college of further education. He works full-time in a busy service and regularly sees five or six clients per day, five days per week. His clients generally come from difficult home circumstances and he has to balance a number of competing demands, including confidentiality, safeguarding concerns and risk. He has been referred to a counsellor via an EAP because he feels highly stressed and unable to effectively work with his clients.

PAUSE FOR REFLECTION

1 What commonalities can you find between Gerald, Annette and Jason? And what differences?
2 How do you think counselling or psychotherapy might enable them to work more effectively?
3 What would be the priority for you as a workplace counsellor: their personal difficulties or their struggles at work?
4 What ethical issues do you find in the three scenarios? How might you manage them?

Whether or not the difference between the aims of the organisation and of counselling and psychotherapy could be described as 'competing' will depend largely on each party's willingness to discuss them transparently and honestly. Where issues are not discussed, there is a greater danger of expectation conflict and difficulty.

Development of policies, procedures and guidance

The development of these documents has been discussed more fully earlier. Suffice it to say here that the policies and procedures that exist within organisations, how they have been developed, whether they are reviewed, and whether individual workers, including counsellors and psychotherapists feel that have any degree of ownership of them will be significant in their effectiveness (or indeed whether they are followed at all).

Benchmarks of 'success'

How counsellors and psychotherapists judge 'success' is a moot point. For example, is success when a client reports feeling happier and their problems solved, or perhaps when problems are not solved but the client feels more equipped to deal with them? I remember working with a woman who was in a violent relation-ship. Having left her partner on a number of occasions only to return to him, she announced in counselling that she had made a decision to remain with him, knowing the risks. She felt that counselling had provided her with an invaluable space to explore her own motivations, feelings and thoughts, and after much con-sideration she felt equipped to make an informed decision about her future, rather than one that was 'knee-jerk'. Was this a successful outcome? I thought not at the time, but are not counselling and psychotherapy about empowering clients to make free and informed choices, in awareness, even if we don't like the choices they make?

In the workplace, it is often even harder to determine 'success'. In my work in education as a counsellor, if a client decides to leave university because they have chosen the wrong course, and they have reached that decision through exploration in counselling, I might view that as a 'success'. I might also be pretty confident in assuming that my employer, the university, would have a different view. It is not always easy to define success when viewed at an individual level, but perhaps bet-ter achieved when the bigger picture is brought into view. For example, if all the students I see in counselling decide to leave university, my employers might have good reason to be concerned about my suitability for the post of university coun-sellor. However, if the majority of students I see manage their difficulties effec-tively, perhaps feel better and successfully complete their degree, I might be viewed as a 'good' counsellor.

Measuring success is of course difficult. Evaluation forms, where clients can provide honest feedback about the service they receive, can be an important step in measuring success. If clients report the service as helpful, responsive, supportive of their needs and effective in helping them to manage their personal life and work more successfully, then the therapy service is well placed to demonstrate to the organisation its efficacy. Outcome measures, such as the Clinical Outcome in Routine Measures Outcome Measure (CORE-OM) (a questionnaire consisting of 34 statements completed by clients before, during and after therapy to help benchmark therapeutic change at an individual client and service level) (Evans et al., 2002), can also provide supportive information. For example, if at point of referral 85% of clients are deemed to fall into a clinical population, and at the end of therapy 12% are in a clinical population, the service might be able to argue for its clinical effectiveness.

Research is another important tool for arguing the case for workplace counselling and psychotherapy. There is a great deal of evidence suggesting that therapy can have a positive effect on sickness levels (Gersons et al., 2000; Rost et al., 2005), overall staff absence (Saroja et al., 1999), and the general wellbeing of staff (Iwi et al., 1998). McLeod's (2010a) systematic review of the available evidence is an excellent resource for making use of the available research.

Planned response versus crisis intervention

How clients will be responded to, in what circumstances and how quickly, are important parameters to define. Too often counselling and psychotherapy services try to be too many things, inevitably failing to do any of them successfully. If, for example, organisations are led to believe that all referrals will be responded to in two working days, then failure to achieve that will be viewed as a wider failure. Likewise, if services indicate that they will respond to all situations at all times, then that will be the expectation.

While some counsellors and psychotherapists have experience in working in crisis services, many do not. It is quite wrong to assume that counselling skills are sufficient in themselves to respond to a mental health crisis. While such skills might be integral to a response, I would argue they are insufficient on their own. There is a great deal of literature about crisis response (Johnson et al., 2008; Kingdon and Finn, 2006), and the particular knowledge and skills required to implement such a response successfully and safely.

Where workplace counselling and psychotherapy services advertise their capacity and willingness to respond in crisis situations (e.g. severe mental health deterioration, immediate suicide risk, or threats to others), it is essential that the service has the wherewithal and therapists with the skills to deliver that. Failure to do so can be both dangerous and unethical. It is arguably more realistic, and more consistent with the principles of counselling and psychotherapy, to offer a planned therapeutic intervention, carefully and appropriately contracted, consistent with the service agreements made with the employing organisation. Services need to be clear as to the speed of their response, to whom, and have readily available information to hand as to what services can be accessed at times of crisis (e.g. emergency services in general, organisation-specific emergency services, and mental health crisis teams).

Safeguarding the principles of counselling and psychotherapy

Related to the points above, the importance of retaining the basic principles of counselling and psychotherapy are essential to ethical practice. There are certainly occasions when these principles are clearly challenged or threatened, and in those instances services or therapists must carefully consider their response, drawing on available resources, research and support. Such instances might be when the autonomy, confidentiality, wellbeing or safety of the client or therapist is compromised. However, when the threat is apparent it is more possible to formulate a response. The bigger threat I would suggest is the subtle one, or the one that builds over time, slowly and inexorably eroding the basic tenets of counselling and psychotherapy in a way so insidious as it is hard to notice. These may cause threats to the autonomy, confidentiality, wellbeing or safety of the client or therapist.

The suggestion here is not that such threats are necessarily deliberate. In many instances the intention may be good: trying to ensure more clients are seen, or seen more quickly, or that information is passed around the organisation to help the client more effectively, and so on. What is essential is that through a careful process of review and re-visiting the basics, workplace counsellors and psychotherapists ensure the basic principles are upheld. Those cited in BACP's Ethical Framework provide a good benchmark:

- Being trustworthy: honouring the trust placed in the practitioner (also referred to as fidelity)
- Autonomy: respect for the client's right to be self-governing
- Beneficence: a commitment to promoting the client's wellbeing
- Non-maleficence: a commitment to avoiding harm to the client
- Justice: the fair and impartial treatment of all clients and the provision of adequate services.

(BACP, 2010, p. 3)

Colleagues' perceptions of the role of counselling and psychotherapy

The way in which workplace services educate and inform others about their work is important. They need to take care to:

- Ensure the service is accountable to the ethical principles of counselling and psychotherapy
- Ensure the service is accountable to the employing or funding organisation
- Provide clear and accessible information as to what type of counselling or psychotherapy is provided
- Advertise if other services are available, e.g. consultation; group work; training
- Provide clear and accessible information about the limits of confidentiality and other boundaries of therapy, e.g. when the service is available; if there is a cost; problems addressed etc.
- Provide sufficient information so as potential clients can make an informed choice about accessing the service
- Clarify how the service can be accessed, e.g. self-referral; referral via manager or occupational health service
- Ensure the organisation can meet its obligations under the responsibilities for duty of care in outlining the service that is being provided for the benefit of employees.

Such information additionally helps inform and educate colleagues in the organisation as to the function of the service. It is also important to help colleagues understand why counselling and psychotherapy are structured as they are, why therapists need individual rooms (rather than shared offices) and why adequate time is needed for ethical therapy.

Positioning counselling and psychotherapy provision

The 'positioning' of the counselling and psychotherapy service (i.e., how the service is located in the hierarchy and structure of the organisation) has an important bearing on its future prospects. Workplace counsellors and psychotherapists may not have much control over this, finding that the managers of the organisation have already made these decisions. In large organisations the positioning can be particularly important. In a university setting, for example, whether a counselling service is seen as a wellbeing service, a professional service, or an academic-support service, can be key to its financial future and stability.

In small or non-hierarchical organisations these concerns are less evident. EAPs are clearly positioned outside the organisational structure. While this allows for the EAP to be responsible for internal procedures and systems pertinent to the provision of counselling and psychotherapy, and less liable to be influenced by internal organisational dynamics and issues, some argue that it is easier for the organisation to amputate the unwanted appendage at difficult times.

Systems, space and services

The structure of the counselling or psychotherapy service is integral to its success. Structural issues include:

- How clients access the service
- Whether or how they register for services
- What information is gathered and how it is stored
- Who greets the client on arrival, and whether there is a safe and confidential waiting area
- Access issues for clients with physical impairments
- Communication systems between therapists and administrative staff
- How therapy rooms are accessed
- How therapy rooms are furnished
- The location of therapy rooms and how confidentiality is protected, e.g. not being seen or overheard during sessions
- How therapy notes are maintained and stored
- The use of audio or video recording for training purposes
- How consent is obtained for third party contact, when appropriate or necessary
- How policies, procedures or guidance documents are developed, communicated, stored and reviewed
- The number of sessions offered and how these are reviewed
- How urgent clients are responded to
- Referral systems to other services or agencies
- Evaluation of counselling or benchmarking of services
- How long notes are stored post-therapy, and where
- How old notes are confidentially stored
- Health and safety concerns, e.g. lone working, working with clients at risk.

Some of the points above may be covered by wider organisational policy (e.g. securing confidential data, referral systems, or access to the service). However, counsellors and psychotherapists have a duty to ensure that all aspects of their work as therapists are ethically attended to and that organisational policy is reconsidered if it potentially undermines the ability to work ethically and appropriately.

Realistic time expectations

This issue here relates to the one above: planned response versus crisis intervention. However, it builds on that in that it also addresses the needs of the organisation to have some facility to deal with difficulty and distress quickly and effectively. Counsellors and psychotherapists, and therapy services, must be clear as to what they are able to offer, the timescales of the service, the limits of the service, and then resist and challenge any attempts for these parameters to be re-drawn, where possible. This is obviously not always easy or possible, but the message from therapy services must always be consistent, honest and realistic, in the same way as we would support a client with unrealistic expectations of their therapist or therapy.

When things go wrong

Hard-built reputations for excellence can be quickly lost in the event of a difficulty. Such problems might include:

- The failure to meet the needs of a client
- Having to break confidentiality in the event of concern
- Self-harm, or the suicide of a client
- A client making a complaint
- Administrative errors or oversights
- Failure to properly follow agreed procedures or policies
- Working beyond the agreed limits of the service, e.g. offering crisis response when ill-equipped to do so; accepting referrals that go beyond the competence of the therapists or service
- Failure to work to agreed national ethical principles.

It is important that problems are attended to quickly, transparently and effectively. Where a problem is identified, the tendency can be to cover it up or hope it will just 'go away'. They invariably don't do so and, if left, tend to grow and cause more damage to people and reputations. The service needs to ensure it communicates effectively within the organisational line management structure, informing relevant people of problems in ways that respect confidentiality. My own experience is that when tackled head-on and in an open way, most problems can be quickly responded to and managed satisfactorily, minimising the potential for scapegoating; although sadly this latter phenomena cannot always be avoided.

Counselling and psychotherapy services have the potential to be an enormous asset to any organisation, if constituted thoughtfully and appropriately. Organisations inevitably and rightly will have expectations of therapy services, particularly if they are funding them. While many of these expectations will be consistent with and complementary to the ethos of therapy, some may not. It is important that managers of therapy services, or counsellors and therapists themselves, engage in direct discussions with funders when these issues arise, to ensure expectations are contextually appropriate and based on understanding rather than presumption.

DISCUSSION QUESTIONS

1   In your experience of working in organisational settings, how consistent were the agency's expectations of the therapy service with the ethos of counselling and psychotherapy?
2   How were any discrepancies managed? Which strategies were successful and which ones didn't work? Why?
3   What do you consider to be the three most important considerations regarding working (as a counsellor or psychotherapist) in an organisational setting?
4   What factors might lead you to question whether you could continue to work for an organisation?

4.5 THE INDEPENDENT PRACTITIONER

SECTION OUTLINE

The independent counsellor or psychotherapist is one who is independent of an employing or funding organisation, relying instead on clients paying privately for the service they receive. This section considers factors that contribute to the working of independent practice (as in other forms of organisation), and the strategies that might be implemented to support the independent therapist. Finally, this section provides suggestions for good practice.

Many counsellors and psychotherapists enjoy the freedom of independent practice: being able to create and develop a service entirely consistent with their preferred way of working; setting working hours that match other personal and professional demands; working in a preferred location; and specialising in particular problem areas for client demographics. On the other side of the coin, however, there are some challenges that are inherent in independent practice: the higher potential for professional isolation; dependency on the availability of client work to pay the bills; health and safety concerns (e.g. lone working); and, if working from home, managing potential intrusions into the therapeutic space (e.g. the telephone ringing, doorbell going, other family members intruding in some way).

I have deliberately included independent practice in a chapter on organisations, contradictory though it might seem, to consider independent practice from an organisational perspective. It is my belief that independent practice is a form of organisation, albeit an 'independent' one, and that independent practitioners can borrow ideas and principles from working in organisational settings to help inform and develop their work. It is probably true to say that the majority of independent practitioners also work in an organisational setting and can thus maintain a successful balance of organisation and independence in their work and thinking. There is an increasing tendency for newly qualified counsellors and psychotherapists to establish themselves independently, particularly in the climate of poor job opportunities. I would offer much caution, as independent practice, in my view, demands a level of experience in responding to potential dilemmas and ethical challenges that goes beyond initial training. Newly qualified therapists setting up independent practices should do so carefully and slowly and in regular consultation with an experienced supervisor.

BACP Private Practice (formerly The Association for Independent Practitioners), a division of BACP, provides some useful guidance and support to independent practitioners via pages on the BACP's website and has a regular journal. On the website Jeffers (2012) offers some useful questions to consider when thinking about working in independent practice. With permission, I have reproduced them here, and will focus on a selection of those most pertinent in the context of this chapter (highlighted in bold).

- Do I want to work by myself? If not, who with?
- **What kind of practice do I want to develop? Do I have the confidence to do it?**
- **Premises, where? Is it suitable? Do I need them? Or do I contract myself out? What is the expense here and what are my obligations? What are the health and safety issues?**
- Costs, especially the start-up costs
- Advertising
- Contact details
- What happens in the event of my illness or death?
- Furniture and fittings and decoration
- **Confidentiality**
- Insurance
- Personal and professional development
- **Where to get help and how can I help myself?**
- The clients – what do I do and who do I want and not want to see?
- What happens if a client doesn't show up?
- How can I make assessments – does my training equip me to do this?
- How much do I charge? How do I want payment and when by? What happens if client cannot/does not pay? Where do I keep the monies before banking it?
- Arranging appointments
- Safety – how do I protect myself and ensure safety of clients? What if a client is abusive? What if a client dies whilst being counselled?

- **Record keeping and administration**
- **Supervision**
- BACP – can it help or hinder?
- Being self-employed, what does this mean regarding earnings, tax, insurance etc.?
- Competition – is my practice viable? Does it matter that there are similar practices in the area?
- Time – how much time do I spend on it?
- **Monitoring the service**
- Professionalism – what does it mean for my practice? Can I be business-minded?
- Am I prepared? Or dazed and confused?
- Does my training/approach help or/and hinder my efforts? Do I need more training?
- Where's the excitement – what happens when it's not working – where are the clients? Where's the back-up?
- IT security
- What do I do with my doubts and disorganisation?
- Where does the family come into this?
- How do I look after myself and the other parts of my life?
- How long to keep client records after contact has ceased?
- What to do if clients bring presents?
- How do I handle seeing clients in the street, shop, doctor etc.?
- Legal aspects: do I need to register the business somewhere; confidentiality in case of a court; statutory obligations, e.g. disabled access to premises?
- Contracting with clients
- Contracting service with others, e.g. EAPs – how does this work?
- Winding up the practice
- Complaints from clients and others. What if I want to make a complaint?

What kind of practice do I want to develop?
Do I have the confidence to do it?

This is perhaps the first and most fundamental question to reflect on. Independent practice might include a number of different activities, of which individual face-to-face work is just one aspect. For example, independent practice might include working with couples, groups, online therapy, and consultation and training. Therapy, whether face-to-face or online, might be directed at a particular client group, such as women, or men, or young people, or be offered as a specific therapy around sexuality, culture, disability etc.

The decisions made at this point will be dependent on personal preference, motivations and training. While in the UK it is possible for anyone, trained or otherwise, to set themselves up as an independent counsellor or psychotherapist, in writing this book I am making an assumption that anyone reading it would subscribe to some form of ethical framework that would prohibit working beyond competence and expertise. With that in mind, it is important that, regardless of interest or motivation, the decision to set up an independent practice at all, and then to target it at a specific group or need, would be informed by training, qualifications and experience.

Premises

Care and attention need to be given to where therapy is going to be delivered, and how clients can safely access the premises. By 'safely', I am not only referring to a physical safety whereby premises are maintained in good order with potential hazards attended to, but also to emotional and psychological safety where dignity, confidentiality and autonomy are respected. For example, can the client attend therapy without being overlooked by others in a way that could impair their right to confidentiality; can they access the premises with minimal assistance, or is assistance available should they experience some physical impairment; and once there do they have access to toilet facilities?

If you are hiring premises, are they appropriate for offering therapy; are there reception facilities available, and if not is it possible for you as their therapist to be present to let them in and is there an appropriate waiting area? If you are working at home, is the room sufficiently private where sessions cannot be overheard or inadvertently interrupted by a family member; have you removed all personal material (e.g. family photographs) that would represent an inappropriate self-disclosure; and what steps can you take to minimise or eliminate other potential intrusions into the therapeutic frame (e.g. the telephone ringing or people coming to the door?).

Confidentiality

It is important to be clear how one structures the limits of confidentiality, and how these will be clearly communicated to the client. While there are some limits to confidentiality determined by law (e.g. anti-terrorism legislation or when subpoenaed to court), other areas are more discretionary (e.g. suicide risk, child protection). Here you would need to ask yourself, 'What is your philosophical position and how will this be implemented?' For example, if you are concerned about a client who you believe to be suicidal, and you have contracted to break confidentiality if the client is unwilling to seek specialist support of their own volition (or temporarily does not have the capacity to do so), whom would you contact, and how? How would you ensure that information about a preferred person to contact (e.g. a GP or relative) is recorded?

Clients can sometimes ask their therapists to write letters of support (for example, to housing companies, financial institutions, an insurance company where a claim is being made, or to employers). It is important to consider one's position on this: would you be willing to write such letters and, if so, how would you obtain written consent from your client for you to do so?

Where to get help and how can I help myself?

Working independently can be an isolating experience, particularly if you are not involved in any other work elsewhere. In using the word 'isolating' in the context of work that involves regularly meeting with people, it is important to note clear differences between the type and nature of contact with people who attend for therapy, and other therapists on a collegial basis. It is important that opportunities to meet with others are taken: to discuss professional issues; receive informal support; contribute to an ongoing professional development; share ideas; and explore new initiatives. Associations of independent practitioners are an excellent way of achieving this. Also, independent practitioners have, over recent years, created networks to facilitate such contact. Such networks include practice-based networks, but also practice-research networks, where groups of counsellors and psychotherapists can collaborate in undertaking research initiatives.

Record keeping and administration

While there is no statutory duty to maintain records of counselling or psychotherapy sessions, many therapists now do so as a matter of good practice (Bond and Mitchels, 2008). If you do decide to maintain records, it is important to consider: the level of detail; how you will inform clients that such records will be maintained: how they will be stored securely to meet any obligations under data protection legislation; how long they will be stored post-therapy; and how they will be destroyed.

Similarly, good administrative procedures can be invaluable in managing an independent practice. Compliance with data protection legislation is essential when handling client's identifying information, and securing data against the event of a break-in. Some therapists prefer to manage paper systems, while others work on a computer. Either way, the same considerations regarding confidentiality and security apply.

It is important to hold pertinent information about clients – for example, their name, age, contact address, telephone number, email address, mobile number, General Practitioner (with contact information), and contact details of a relative. It is important when collecting this information to ask clients their preferred means of contact – for instance, in the event of having to cancel a session – and agree how contact will be managed. For example, if you are working at home there is potential for a breach of confidentiality and inappropriate self-disclosure if a client's phone calls are answered by anyone other than the therapist, unless this has been clearly agreed beforehand. Some independent therapists will have a 'pay as you go' mobile dedicated solely to their practice, so that a phone number given out or advertised is not a family or house telephone number where anyone else can answer. In giving out a telephone number it is important that parameters are clearly agreed at the outset of therapy: for example, can the therapist be contacted to talk outside of agreed therapy sessions; when can/should a client contact the therapist; can they ring if they feel suicidal?

Supervision

In the UK supervision is a requirement (albeit not a statutory but ethical one) of counselling and psychotherapy practice. It is therefore important for an independent practitioner to identify and establish a suitable supervisory contact with an experienced supervisor who is able to provide support. Preferably the supervisor should contribute to the decision to establish a private practice and is able to provide valuable support and guidance through the early stages, as well as supervising direct client work.

Monitoring the service

Carefully monitoring independent practice can be extremely helpful in developing it further and ensuring it best meets clients' needs. For all the care and attention given to setting up a practice, often it is the person using it who can best provide feedback about what works well and what might require further attention. Giving thought to designing a simple, self-completed evaluation form at the end of therapy can be very useful. Additionally, using benchmarking tools, such as CORE (discussed earlier), can help monitor client outcomes and be used to inform continuing professional development strategies.

DISCUSSION QUESTIONS

1 How might working independently suit your personal circumstances and how might it complicate them?
2 What factors would you need to consider before setting up your own independent practice?
3 What personal and professional circumstances would have to be managed before you could work successfully in an independent practice?
4 How might you balance working independently with working in an organisational setting? How might the two complement or work against each other?

4.6 CONCLUSIONS

This chapter has carefully considered the context of counselling and psychotherapy. While many other factors will influence and inform the type of therapist you are, your working context – the organisational setting and how counselling and psychotherapy is constructed within it – will profoundly shape, perhaps more than any other, the way you are able to work. There are several aspects touched on in this chapter that are discussed in more detail elsewhere in the book, and it is important to hold all these aspects together when considering the 'bigger picture' of counselling and psychotherapy.

5

Law, Policy, Values and Ethics

5.1 INTRODUCTION

CHAPTER OVERVIEW

The practice of counselling and psychotherapy is positioned within a context of law, policy, values and ethics. Arguably all practice, whichever setting it is located in, is defined both by any specific legislation or policy pertinent to that setting, and by wider ethical principles. The purpose of this chapter is to outline the importance of an awareness of such aspects of practice for all practitioners.

As the client takes their seat in the therapy room and the therapist closes the door to begin the session, it is possible to believe that the outside world is left behind and the only thing that truly exists is the therapeutic process that is about to unfold. Of course, there is an acknowledgement that in virtue of two people meeting (or perhaps more in couple or group therapy) something of the outside world is brought into the space: that which causes difficulty, distress or incongruence, to be explored and reflected on in the intimate encounter.

The more obvious intrusions into the therapeutic space are often discussed and considered by counsellors and psychotherapists – intrusions such as outside noise, interruptions, the state of the chairs, lighting, and so on. We may also be aware of how the expectations of others impinge on our work: employers perhaps requiring brief therapy when we prefer to work longer-term; or the use of outcome measures or evaluation forms that do not sit comfortably with our own preferred way of working. However, there is another level of 'intrusion' that we must attend to, that is not 'left at the door' when the client enters to begin: it comprises statutory control, policy and ethics.

Of course, many would not see such dimensions as 'intrusions'. Most counsellors and psychotherapists embrace the importance of working ethically with clients, even if they don't read documents on ethics too closely. Many are aware of policy or procedural requirements that shape their work and some others are aware that laws also shape how counselling and psychotherapy are practised. Some counsellors and psychotherapists see a profound value in the way that policy, law and ethics both contextualise and contain therapy. For others, though, they are an unwelcome, invisible visitor – one not considered to any great degree during the therapeutic encounter.

There are some overarching ethical principles that inform all work, all of the time. There are also legal imperatives that shape the very nature of counselling and psychotherapy and its delivery. However, there are also specific aspects that might inform work with particular groups or in specific settings. For example, work with young children might differ significantly in policy and practice when compared against work with older people, or people with learning difficulties, or perhaps those experiencing mental health problems. There are commonalities across all such groups, but there are also specific aspects, perhaps defined by law or policy, which are only relevant in particular settings or situations. To illustrate this point, consider confidentiality, widely recognised as an important cornerstone of trust that under-pins all work. Thinking of the importance of confidentiality, reflect on how it might change in its nature and application in the different scenarios in Box 5.1.

BOX 5.1   THE DIFFERENT SHADES OF CONFIDENTIALITY

- **Joanne** is a six-year-old girl seeing a play therapist in a family centre. She talks to her therapist about the 'nasty man next door' who does things to her she doesn't like.
- **Derek** is a 72-year-old man with a terminal illness. He is cared for at home by his partner and social services. During his counselling session he talks of wanting to be dead.
- **Darren** is a 17-year-old man diagnosed with early onset psychosis. He tells his psychotherapists of the voices he hears and how they are telling him to kill himself.
- **Justine** is a 32-year-old accountant. She talks to her counsellor of her guilt at having stolen significant sums of money from a rich client.
- **Taryn** is a 40-year-old counsellor trainee. In her counselling she discloses racist views and talks of never wanting to work with 'black people'.

These simple scenarios each bring a different take on the concept of confidentiality. A widely acknowledged ethical and legal principle is shaped differently by the context in which it is being applied. Here the therapist's understanding of confidentiality needs to be considered in the context of other expectations, which might include legal and policy requirements. For example, child protection, free will, self-determinism and human rights, mental health legislation, criminal law and anti-discrimination: all aspects may have legal parameters, in all likelihood policy or procedural parameters – depending on the context in which therapy is being delivered – and certainly all have ethical implications for the counsellor or psychotherapist to manage. As we can see, the application of such defining factors can be profoundly complex in the context of human experience and the therapeutic process.

This chapter is divided into three main sections. First, Law for Counsellors and Psychotherapists considers how law in general terms shapes the nature of counselling and psychotherapy, from advertising services, through to contracting, health and safety, and the management of specific therapeutic practices. This section provides an overview of key pieces of UK legislation and an account of how legislation is developed and finalised in the UK.

The following section, Social Policy for Counselling and Psychotherapy, considers what is meant by 'social policy' and outlines its relevance for practice. Some examples of social policy developments in the UK are outlined in order to illustrate how policy can, in many instances, have as much influence on what we do as counsellors and psychotherapists as does legislation. Finally, the section Values and Ethical Practice – and When Things Go Wrong takes a closer look at how counselling and psychotherapy organisations develop ethical guidelines, what they mean for practitioners, and what happens when things go wrong. More specifically, using BACP's Ethical Framework as an example, this section discusses how counsellors and psychotherapists incorporate 'ethical thinking' into their day to day work, and how therapy organisations manage complaints when they are received from clients or other therapists.

As can be seen, even from a mere outline of the issues, counselling and psychotherapy practice draws on a complex interplay of philosophy, theory, skills, ethics, policy, procedure and legislation. This, in turn, is shaped and informed by a number of other external factors, including such matters as where therapy is delivered, how it is delivered, and the particular demographic of the clients accessing the service. So, as the client takes their seat in the therapy room and the therapist closes the door on the outside world, ready to focus on the therapeutic process about to unfold, the outside world doesn't stay outside: instead it is present in every interaction and process that takes place between the therapist and their client.

5.2 LAW FOR COUNSELLORS AND PSYCHOTHERAPISTS

SECTION OUTLINE

Counsellors and psychotherapists, like other helping professionals, work in the context of legal imperatives. This section outlines how practice is influenced and informed by law, offers an insight as to how law is developed and finalised, provides an overview of the principal laws influencing therapy, and provides the reader with helpful pointers as to how they can ensure they remain informed and up-to-date.

It is probably better to begin with what this section is not: the purpose here is not to offer a definitive guide to the law that affects the work of counsellors and psychotherapists. I am not legally qualified, my only legal training being in mental health legislation for the purposes of my previous role as a psychiatric social worker. There are better resources available that provide helpful and accessible guides to law; a couple are detailed in the reading listed below. Rather, the purpose is to provide an overview of how the legal process impacts on the work of therapists and to summarise key information counsellors and psychotherapists need to be aware of in their day-to-day work.

It can be easy to forget the legal context of our work, given that essentially our focus is human relationships. While sitting with a client it is easy to temporarily disregard statute, our energies and attention focused instead on what they are saying and on the process of therapy. However, at all times our work is defined by law, and at every moment some aspect of law is present. It is not something we can disregard: rather it is something that requires commensurate attention.

In my own counsellor training, the legal dimensions of therapy were not particularly discussed or explored. The situation has changed over time, with more focus in counselling and psychotherapy training on the legal aspects of work with clients. However, in my contact with trainees (and indeed qualified practitioners), I am not always convinced that we, as a professional group, pay as much attention to law as we might. For example, we may recognise confidentiality as an ethical requirement and be familiar with it in what we agree with clients at the beginning of therapy, but we tend not to think of it as a legal requirement. Likewise, we may understand that clients, on occasions, do not necessarily make informed decisions about their life or wellbeing due to high levels of mental health distress, but we do not necessarily conceptualise that within a legal frame (i.e., in terms of their 'capacity'). Certainly I find when training counsellors and psychotherapists on working with suicidal clients, those who don't know about the Mental Capacity Act 2005 and its implications for decisions regarding the management of confidentiality with a client at risk tend to significantly outnumber those who do. Of course, my comments are generalisations, and there are many therapists who are very familiar with legislative requirements. The point is that we need to acquire at least a basic familiarity with legal concepts and key legislation from day one.

Later in this chapter we will discuss ethics, but it is worth noting at this point the differences between ethics and law. Mitchels and Bond (2010, p. 5) state that, 'Ethical frameworks are not law, and nor are they, in themselves, legally binding. However, as an expression of the shared values of the profession, they will carry weight within the profession to which they apply'. The distinction is clearly made: statements of ethics do not constitute law. However, when judging a counsellor or psychotherapist's behaviour or actions, statements of ethics provide an important means of benchmarking how the profession views appropriate behaviour or action and may, in that sense, even feature in a court hearing: thus the relationship between the two can therefore be very close.

How laws are made

We all know that laws exist, but tend not to think about the process of how law comes into being in the first place. Of course, in the UK much legislation is developed by central government in Westminster, London. However, it is also important to note that many other powers are devolved to the Northern Ireland and Welsh Assemblies, and Scotland has its own distinct legal system and the Scottish Parliament. Specific information about the UK Parliament and the three regional assemblies is available at the following websites.

WEBSITES

UK Parliament: www.parliament.uk/about
Welsh Assembly Government: http://wales.gov.uk/about/organisationexplained/responsiblefor/?lang=en
Scottish Parliament: www.scottish.parliament.uk/visitandlearn/9981.aspx
Northern Ireland Assembly: www.niassembly.gov.uk/Assembly-Business/

It is useful to know the general outlines of this process, as there are opportunities at various stages to make our views known, either as individuals or through a consultation process via our professional organisations. The following provides a general overview of how a law is passed within the UK, drawing on information from the UK Parliament website, and is represented in diagrammatic form in Figure 5.1.

Consultation: Green and White Papers

While the process of consultation is not a requirement of any new law, in general terms this is the first step of the legislative process. A Green Paper is a document issued by government that outlines in general terms ideas and proposals for government policy and legislation. Interested parties, such as charities or voluntary organisations, may be specifically contacted for their thoughts and views. As a counsellor or psychotherapist there are therefore two primary ways in which to voice opinion – either as an individual or via a professional organisation, such as BACP, COSCA or UKCP. A White Paper is published with the same invitation for consultation, but unlike Green Papers, these are more likely to state an intention and are often more specific in their focus.

Draft Bills

A Draft Bill is again typically issued to interested parties in much the same way as Green and White Papers, but as opposed to consultation documents, they are usually a first attempt at a document to be presented to Parliament. A Draft Bill is an opportunity for the government, which is almost always the issuing body for them, to receive feedback and take an opportunity to refine and develop the document prior to parliamentary scrutiny and debate.

Bills

A Bill is a proposal for a new law or a proposal to change or amend an existing law, introduced to Parliament for debate and scrutiny. When both the House of Commons and the House of Lords have passed a Bill, it is passed to the reigning monarch for their approval – it then receives Royal Assent. It is only at this stage that the Bill becomes an Act of Parliament (i.e., becomes law).

There are three types of Bills that can be introduced into Parliament: a Public Bill (including a Private Member's Bill); a Private Bill; and a Hybrid Bill. A Public Bill applies to the general population and is generally introduced by government ministers as part of their parliamentary programme. However, other MPs or Lords can also introduce Public Bills, and these are known as Private Members' Bills (which sit outside the government's policy programme). There are four ways in which a member of the public can express their views on Public Bills, as follows:

- Writing to their MP or a Lord
- Writing to the government department responsible for the Bill
- Lobbying Parliament
- Submitting evidence to the relevant Public Bill Committee.

A Private Bill focuses on changing law as it applies to specific individuals or organisations, rather than the wider scope of a Public Bill. Such bills are usually prompted

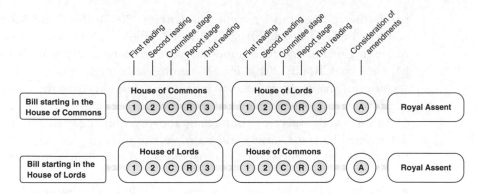

FIGURE 5.1   Passage of a Bill (UK Parliament website, 2012 – contains
Parliamentary information licensed under the Open Parliament
Licence v1.0)

by organisations, such as local authorities, and have to be publicised through local publications.

A Hybrid Bill is a mixture of Public and Private Bills. Changes in law proposed by Hybrid Bills would affect the general population, but also specific individuals or organisations.

Acts of Parliament

An Act of Parliament creates a new law or changes an existing one. It may come into effect immediately following Royal Assent, or may come into effect on a specific date, named in the Act. The full text of Acts of Parliament for all Acts since 1988 can be accessed from the Office of Public Sector Information. Acts that have been amended by other Acts, or are delegated legislation (where changes are made to existing Acts without the government having to push through a new Act of Parliament) are available in the Statute Law Database for all Acts still in force from 1267.

WEBSITES

Office of Public Sector Information: www.legislation.gov.uk/ukpga
Statute Law Database: www.legislation.gov.uk/

The impact of laws on practice

It is not within the scope of this section to provide a comprehensive overview of all the legislation that might be applicable to the practice of counselling and psychotherapy. For this I recommend Jenkins (2007), Bond and Mitchels (2008) and Mitchels and Bond (2010), all of which offer excellent and accessible accounts of key legislation and its relationship to counselling and psychotherapy practice. Mitchels and Bond (2010) list 69 statutes relevant to practice. This does not account for many other statutory instruments that also have the effect of law and need to be considered with equal importance.

Almost every aspect of counselling and psychotherapy will be influenced or determined by law. Consider, for example, the following aspects of the structure, organisation and delivery of a counselling and psychotherapy practice:

- Choosing rooms or a venue for practice, including access, health and safety
- Advertising
- The management of client information and records
- Agreeing a working contract with clients
- Ensuring a client is aware of the service they are receiving, and are able to agree to it
- Record keeping
- Managing the therapeutic process
- Writing information, including 'factsheets', e.g. managing sleep problems, coping with anxiety
- Ensuring confidentiality
- Being clear as to the limits of confidentiality, including statutory expectations of disclosure – prevention of terrorism (Terrorism Act 2000), drug trafficking and drug money laundering (Drug Trafficking Act 1994)
- Monitoring progress and the use of outcome measures
- Contacting third party contact and responding to requests for information
- Evaluating clients and retaining client information post-counselling.

All of the above are subject to some statutory control. If working for an organisation much of the liability will lie with the employing organisation, however, there will still be instances where the individual counsellor or psychotherapist will retain an individual liability (e.g. in the case of terrorism and drug trafficking). If working independently, the individual practitioner will be liable for all aspects of his/her practice and for ensuring that statutory requirements are adhered to. The decision to open an independent practice, sometimes taken by therapists because they cannot easily find paid employment and who see independent practice as a 'short-term solution', is a major step and should be taken with full care and attention to every aspect of work.

The actual legislation that deals with specific aspects of practice will vary, but may focus on client-specific areas or wider practice concerns. For example, legislation pertaining to working with children and young people, or the care of people with mental health problems, or adoption, may make specific demands on practitioners to act in particular ways. Wider scope legislation, not necessarily specifically written with counselling or psychotherapy in mind, is also relevant, though the links between the Act and practice will not necessarily be so apparent. Areas covered by such legislation include negligence, employment, duty of care and contractual law.

Due to the potential pitfalls of failing to meet statutory, policy or ethical requirements of practice, many therapy organisations now require their members to take out personal indemnity insurance, and accreditation by many therapy professional organisations includes a requirement to hold professional indemnity insurance; it is also recommended for those involved in private training. Several insurance companies offer specialist insurance policies for counsellors and psychotherapists, some linked with therapy organisations. While I have worked for a variety of organisations throughout my career, I have always maintained my own indemnity insurance. This hasn't been strictly necessary as, in the capacity of undertaking therapy work for an employer, I have been included on their insurance. However, in this increasingly litigious era it has been a decision I have taken to further protect my work. Certainly it is worth asking for several quotes and ascertaining the level of cover offered before taking out a policy, as policies vary in cover and cost.

In many ways it might appear that working within legislative requirements is less demanding, assuming we are aware of what they are, and legislation deals with certainties and 'givens'. However, the application of law can be profoundly complex and counsellors and psychotherapists should take advice, when in doubt, to ensure they practise in a legally sound manner. The professional requirements of practice – law, policy, values and ethics (discussed later in this chapter) – together provide a complex arena in which counsellors and psychotherapists work. The acquisition and development of competency around theory, knowledge and skills clearly contribute to practice that is appropriate, but of themselves are insufficient for the actual work with clients.

FURTHER READING

Bond, T. and Mitchels, B. (2008) *Confidentiality and Record Keeping in Counselling and Psychotherapy.* London: Sage.

Bond, T. and Sandhu, A. (2005) *Therapists in Court: Providing Evidence and Supporting Witnesses.* London: Sage.

Jenkins, P. (2007) *Counselling, Psychotherapy and the Law.* London: Sage.

Mitchels, B. and Bond, T. (2010) *Essential Law for Counsellors and Psychotherapists.* London: Sage.

5.3 SOCIAL POLICY FOR COUNSELLING AND PSYCHOTHERAPY

SECTION OUTLINE

Like law, social policy is an essential aspect of work for any counsellor or psychotherapist. This section looks at how counsellors and psychotherapists can engage with and influence the development of social policy. In addition, it provides an overview of key aspects of social policy relevant for practice in the UK.

During my own research in developing a training workshop for counsellors and psychotherapists in working with suicidal clients, I piloted a training day that incorporated a number of key aspects required for such work, including personal reflection, research outcomes, good practice indicators and relevant social policy. In evaluating the workshop several months later with participants they remembered most of the session (and thankfully talked highly of it). Consistently across all 250 counsellors involved in this project, however, virtually all of them had forgotten the sections on relevant social policy. Of those that had remembered it, a small handful thought it useful, while the rest talked of 'glazing over' in the session and finding the content thoroughly boring. While I accept the negative impact of social policy might have as much to do with my teaching approach as anything, I suspect it was because of the perception that, as one participant put it, 'It really has nothing to do with what I do with my client'.

While we might focus on the individual experience of distress and difficulty, it is important that we always see the client in the context of their 'system' (i.e., family, friends, housing, employment, health, financial stability etc.). For example, if working with a young person in a school setting, is it really possible not to pay attention to their experience of school, how teaching staff respond to them, what happens at home, their friendships and relationships, and so on? Likewise, if working with an older person who lives alone with little income, is it possible to disregard their relational and financial poverty? If a client lives in poor housing, cannot eat well and has poor health as a consequence, where does therapy fit into that system? The assertion here certainly isn't that counselling and psychotherapy have no place, but rather that they find their place in the bigger picture. Social policy affects us all, and so ultimately it has everything to do with what we do with our clients.

Social policy might be defined as, 'the study of the social relations necessary for human wellbeing and the systems by which wellbeing may be promoted. It's about the many and various things that affect the kinds of life that you and I and everyone can live' (Dean, 2005, p. 1). Social policy, inevitably linked with (but also distinct from) politics, is to do with a wide range of issues, including social care, wellbeing, criminal justice, health care, education and the provision of counselling and psychotherapy. While a policy document does not have the weight of law, and thus can more easily be overlooked, it does often provide the philosophy, structure and rationale for what later becomes law. According to the website of the University of Bristol School of Policy Studies (2011), social policy:

- Is unique in addressing as its core concern people's well being, both as individuals and members of society
- Is an interdisciplinary subject drawing on aspects of sociology, economics, geography, political science, history, law and philosophy
- Considers basic human needs and how society organises itself and responds to these
- Is sometimes referred to as public policy or public administration
- Looks behind the headlines at pressing topical issues such as NHS and welfare reform, poverty and social exclusion, crime and punishment, housing and urban change, health and ageing
- Assesses the way society tackles these concerns through the welfare state, the market, voluntary bodies, and the activities of individuals and their families
- Analyses and challenges policy practices in contemporary society, informs dissent, and encourages you to think critically and progressively about the society and world you live in
- Examines the policy process – how policy is shaped, made, and implemented – within both historical and current contexts
- Debates the future of welfare and the theories and ideologies that drive its provision such as social justice, need, risk, inequality and citizenship.

The influence of social policy on practice

Social policy, then, concerns the relationships that people have with each other, the relationship society has with people, and the way society organises itself to deliver what is needed. It concerns social processes and helps to determine future priorities. All of these points connect with counselling and psychotherapy on a number of levels: philosophical, organisational, interpersonal and intrapersonal. Therapy is fundamentally about how people can live successfully within their worlds and, if we are honest, sometimes how people can live within their limitations. Such limitations may derive from a personal attribute, but more often come from how the individual is placed within society. It is perhaps no coincidence that many of the clients who attend for therapy are 'disadvantaged' in society through one form or another: young people; people with long-term mental health problems; those with alcohol or drug problems; people facing extreme poverty or ill-health.

Whether therapists are agents of social change, or rather agents of social conformity and control, is much debated (Joseph, 2007). The line that exists between these two dimensions is often very fine. For example, I remember first training in social work because I was motivated to be an agent of social change: to support and empower people in making a difference, perhaps moving people out of poverty, or into employment, or advocating for them to receive better health care. Several years into my work as a social worker my role was split between two primary responsibilities: child protection and statutory mental health. On one hand I was 'policing' the care of children and young people, while on the other making decisions to compulsorily detain people under mental health legislation. While I understood that in both of these roles I brought an important social perspective, in my view I had become an agent of the state. This may sound politically extreme (and naïve), and perhaps many would argue factually inaccurate, but my early sense of what I could achieve in my chosen profession did not seem entirely compatible with what I was actually doing. So I decided to leave.

From a sociopolitical perspective it is worth reflecting on our roles as counsellors and psychotherapists to really think about our function and purpose. Consider the scenarios in Box 5.2.

BOX 5.2   THE POSITIONING OF COUNSELLING AND PSYCHOTHERAPY IN A SOCIETAL CONTEXT

- **Julianne** is a counsellor working in a statutory mental health setting. Working as a member of a multi-disciplinary team, her role is to provide individual therapy for people with long-term mental health problems and to alert other team members when a client experiences mental health deterioration.

- **Dennis** is a counsellor working within an Improving Access to Psychological Therapies (IAPT) service. He is able to deliver up to a maximum of 12 sessions of individual counselling to clients diagnosed with depression, but must then refer on to secondary care services if outcome measures indicate little improvement.
- **Sharon** works in a child and family centre. She is required to report any concerns over child protection, whether or not she has permission from the client to do so.
- **Germaine** works with an EAP, offering time-limited counselling to employees. She is required to provide reports and an assessment of an individual's fitness for work at the end of her counselling.
- **Sandra** works in independent practice. She offers a contract of confidentiality that would not require her to disclose suicide potential or child protection concerns.

We can see a number of important themes in the above scenarios. It seems that counsellors and psychotherapists are positioned differently in their role depending on where they are based. For example, working in a statutory service against working independently often brings about important differences in therapist responsibilities. A philosophical underpinning of our work as therapists might mitigate the expectations of our role. That is to say, while at a micro level our work might be about the development of the individual and free choice, at a macro level we might be required to work within certain parameters that would go against a client's preferred outcome. Chapter 4 provides a fuller discussion of these challenges.

Implementation of social policy

While social policy has a profound effect on how we are positioned in relation to our task, it also greatly shapes the ways in which counselling and psychotherapy are structured and delivered and the detail of what we do in our work. IAPT in the UK is a very good example of how counselling and psychotherapy services have undergone major structural change (Clark, 2011). There is much debate as to the efficacy of IAPT services (Rizq, 2011; Rogers, 2009), but what is certainly true is that they have profoundly shaped the form and nature of counselling and psychotherapy provision in the UK for people with depression and anxiety.

This implementation of social policy also has the potential to create far-reaching changes to counselling and psychotherapy at a much wider level. For example, a further instance of social policy implementation concerns the NICE guidelines for the psychological therapies. The National Institute for Health and Clinical Excellence (NICE) has produced a number of guidelines, drawing on evidence-based practice, for the provision of psychological treatments for a range of client presentations. At the time of writing there were 27 guidelines available, ranging from anxiety and alcohol dependence through to schizophrenia and self-harm, with a further nine in preparation. Taking one specific example, the place of counselling within the treatment guidelines for depression has meant that health care providers view counselling as much more of a peripheral option than was perhaps the case prior to the publication of the guidelines.

WEBSITE

NICE: www.nice.org.uk

The development and implementation of social policy, whether specifically related to counselling and psychotherapy, or with a wider scope, is of great importance to practitioners. For example, for counsellors and psychotherapists working in higher education settings in the UK, current government policy on university tuition fees and the funding of education will profoundly shape the nature of services, as well as the issues explored in sessions. At the worst-case level, it has already seen the closure of some counselling services in these settings. For therapists working with people who are unemployed, or unable to work due to physical or mental health difficulties, alterations made in the benefit system, including benefits for people with disabilities, again will see significant changes in the funding of therapy provision as well as in the concerns and anxieties clients present with.

Engaging in the development of social policy

While counsellors and psychotherapists might not be in a position to individually change the shape of policy, counselling and psychotherapy organisations are better placed to ensure that the voice of the profession is heard. For example, organisations with a large membership – such as BACP, with a membership base of around 40,000 counsellors and psychotherapists – are well-placed to participate in consultation initiatives and represent the views of the membership. It is important therefore that practitioners, while making their own contribution to debates, also lobby their member organisations and ensure that as a member they take the time to express opinions and thoughts and to feed back on the effect of change.

Policy development is not confined, however, to central government initiatives. Many employers, such as health and social care settings, voluntary organisations and education settings, for example, will develop local policy that will shape the nature of service delivery. Where possible, counsellors and psychotherapists can look to gain membership of policy development groups and committees. In this way the unique perspective that can be brought by counsellors and psycho-therapists can be offered, and experience gained through the narratives of clients shared.

The purpose here has been to demonstrate how important social policy is to the work of counsellors and psychotherapists, to provide evidence of how policy can profoundly change the nature of therapy services and what is offered to clients, and to help you think about how to inform yourself of policy that has impact on your work and also play a part in the development of policy in the early stages.

DISCUSSION QUESTIONS

1   How relevant do you think social policy is to your work? Why?
2   Which policies influence your work (a) indirectly and (b) directly?
3   How much of your work involves acting as an agent of (a) social change or (b) social control or conformity? Why?
4   What steps could you take to (a) reflect critically on existing social policy and (b) participate in shaping future policy?

5.4 VALUES AND ETHICAL PRACTICE – AND WHEN THINGS GO WRONG

SECTION OUTLINE

All counselling and psychotherapy is based on important principles and values. In addition, the ethical frameworks and expectations of regulatory and professional bodies are essential to all aspects of therapeutic work with clients. This section presents an overview of ethical documents. It encourages consideration of how ethical practice might be incorporated into day-to-day work and prompts the reader into personal and professional reflection into personally held views, values and beliefs. Finally, this section discusses what happens when things go wrong and outlines ways of working with situations to minimise harm.

As counsellors and psychotherapists we are taught early on in our training of the importance of the values and ethics of our work. Arguably those early intro-ductions to ethical thinking do not speak of the complexity of their application to practice, particularly when such teaching takes place prior to the practice placement beginning. It is hard to think about how ethics will present in our work when we have little client experience to draw on. We can certainly appreciate the 'big deals' of ethics, such as not causing harm to a client, not exploiting clients financially or sexually, and so on. However, the real application of ethical practice often takes place in the nuances of our work, in the fine detail where, as practitioners, we are required to think through difficult dilemmas and situations.

With respect to working with suicide risk, I once wrote of BACP's *Ethical Framework for Good Practice in Counselling and Psychotherapy* (BACP, 2010) as a 'hall of mirrors, reflecting back any chosen reality' (Reeves, 2004, p. 28), tending not to trade in certainties, but rather in the nuances about which I talked before. As we have already outlined, there are a number of documents issued by therapy's professional bodies to counsellors and psychotherapists to provide ethical guidance. For the sake of simplicity I will take BACP's Ethical Framework, which I will use as an exemplar ethical guidance document throughout this section. The Ethical Framework replaced the previous Code of Ethics and Practice, moving away from a prescriptive approach to the application of ethical thinking, rather instead providing a structure in which counsellors and psychotherapists could reflect on problems and situations as they arose.

This is not to say that the Ethical Framework contains no certainties, for it certainly does. But in the re-writing of BACP's ethical expectations of its members Tim Bond and his collaborators took into account the sheer scope of difference in working contexts and thus the form and nature of the ethical dilemmas that might arise. It was no longer possible to construct a 'rights and wrongs' document that would suffice for all practitioners most of the time. Instead, the Ethical Framework had to reflect that counsellors and psychotherapists were working in a range of settings, with a range of clients, and were working in many different ways.

But back to the nuances of ethical thinking: let's consider six dilemmas, all taken from the Ethical Dilemmas column in BACP's *Therapy Today* magazine and also available on the companion website. They are outlined in Boxes 5.3 to 5.8 (reproduced with permission).

BOX 5.3   DILEMMA ONE

Matthew works as a counsellor in a large organisation. He has been seeing a member of staff due to work-related stress for some time. He receives an anonymous letter about his client, which states that it is important he knows the client has 'mental health problems'. It then goes on to detail things the client has allegedly said or done in the workplace. The client does not know this letter has been sent and Matthew does not wish to cause the client further distress by declaring it, given that it is anonymous.

BOX 5.4   DILEMMA TWO

Khalil is a counsellor who works for a specialist agency supporting adult survivors of sexual abuse. His client, Angie, discloses abuse perpetrated by a family friend when she was eight years old. She has recently discovered that the alleged abuser has moved in with her aunt, who has a child – a boy aged 11. Angie has never disclosed her abuse to her family and does not wish to do so now. The agency policy is to provide total confidentiality to clients, apart from when legally obliged not to do so. Angie minimises any current risk and states that she only told Khalil because of the agency policy to protect her confidentiality.

BOX 5.5   DILEMMA THREE

Suzanne has worked in a primary care counselling agency for four years and has become good friends with a colleague there, Michelle. Michelle is a highly respected and liked member of the team. Suzanne discovered recently that Michelle has been drinking heavily, and for some time. While she appears to be sober at work, Suzanne is fearful for Michelle's clients and her capacity to work professionally. Michelle became distressed when asked about this, and begged Suzanne not to say anything to her manager – she would 'lose [her] job and become unemployable'. Suzanne feels torn between trying to support her friend to turn things around personally, and the wellbeing of her clients, which increasingly seems to be compromised.

BOX 5.6   DILEMMA FOUR

During supervision your new supervisee informs you that he is unable to attend the next session as he is a member of the British National Party (BNP) and is attending their next conference. You have not had any concerns previously regarding his suitability as a trainee counsellor. However, on researching BNP's policies and constitution you find that the BNP are implacably opposed to multiculturalism, Islam and anti-discrimination laws. Could this be in direct conflict with BACP's own Ethical Framework and the policies of the trainee's education provider? If so, what actions need to be considered, if any?

BOX 5.7   DILEMMA FIVE

You work as an independent practitioner in your own home seeing clients for counselling. You have been seeing Joy for three months. She initially made contact

(Continued)

(Continued)

with you on the recommendation of an infertility support group she was attending. She and her partner had been trying for children but have been told that in all likelihood this is not going to be successful. The counselling appeared to be progressing well and Joy was beginning the difficult process of talking about her grief. The last time you met with Joy she was angry and distressed. She had noticed a photograph of you and your children on the wall. She felt that this was an inappropriate self-disclosure and did not feel able to talk to you anymore. She walked out of the session half-way through.

BOX 5.8   DILEMMA SIX

Emma is a qualified counsellor. Recently she received messages from a client via her Facebook account. Emma assumed her account was private and wasn't aware that clients would be able to contact her via this forum. Her client, Sam, sent messages to her privately and made comments about her profile picture. Although Emma and Sam contracted clear boundaries at the start of the working relationship this is an area that wasn't discussed. Emma is unsure how to deal with this issue as she is still working with Sam and is due to see him this week.

These dilemmas cover a range of ethical difficulties, including the management of confidentiality, third-party information, child protection, competency, self-disclosure, the management of therapy when offered at home, and the setting of boundaries. When we think of these issues in isolation we can, perhaps, be afforded some degree of certainty and confidence in our position. For example, it might be right to break confidentiality when we are concerned about the safety of a child, or that we would stop or suspend our practice if we felt unable to work safely because of our own distress, or that we would manage boundaries clearly and unambiguously and never transgress them. Yet the dilemmas above speak of the profound difficulties we can face when thinking of our responsibilities and potential actions in real-life situations, especially difficult situations we might inadvertently find ourselves in.

PAUSE FOR REFLECTION

1 Should Matthew tell his client about the letter he has received?
2 Should Khalil pass on her concerns about child protection?
3 Should Michelle talk to her manager about Suzanne's problems?

> 4 As the supervisor, how would you respond to your supervisee's statements?
> 5 How would you respond following Joy's leaving the counselling distressed?
> 6 What should Emma say to Sam, if anything, about her Facebook page?
> 7 Overall, which aspects of the Ethical Framework might inform your responses to the questions above?

In this context one can see the difficult task that the Ethical Framework and other such documents have to achieve – the balance between accessibility and simplicity, and complexity and applicability. At times of difficulty or uncertainty, counsellors and psychotherapists often look to such documents for concrete answers, whereas in fact the answers lie in the shades of grey. However, such documents can provide an invaluable tool when used, say, in supervision or in discussion with colleagues and peers, to explore the generalities of practice so that the principles of ethical thinking can be incorporated into day-to-day practice. BACP's Ethical Framework begins by discussing the values of counselling and psychotherapy, followed by the ethical principles and then personal moral qualities.

The values of counselling and psychotherapy

According to the BACP's Ethical Framework (2010, p. 2), the values of counselling and psychotherapy include:

- Respecting human rights and dignity
- Protecting the safety of clients
- Ensuring the integrity of practitioner–client relationships
- Enhancing the quality of professional knowledge and its application
- Alleviating personal distress and suffering
- Fostering a sense of self that is meaningful to the person(s) concerned
- Increasing personal effectiveness
- Enhancing the quality of relationships between people
- Appreciating the variety of human experience and culture
- Striving for the fair and adequate provision of counselling and psychotherapy services.

The Oxford English Dictionary defines values as 'principles or standards of behaviour; one's judgement of what is important in life' (OED, 2012). As can be seen from the Ethical Framework therefore, values are more generic principles that underpin all counselling and psychotherapy, regardless of modality, client group or working context. They are not intended to provide specific answers to specific questions, but rather set a philosophical context for all therapeutic work. Here we see that the values of counselling and psychotherapy are based on: rights, dignity and safety; the quality and effectiveness of human (and therefore therapeutic) relationships; acknowledgment of and respect for difference; alleviation of suffering; and fairness.

Counselling and psychotherapy services can therefore be judged against these values in determining whether they meet the minimum expectations and standards of the Ethical Framework. Of course, the enforcement of compliance with the Ethical Framework is applicable only to agencies or practitioners who are members of BACP. Likewise, compliance with ethical principles and benchmarks would be the same for members of other therapy organisations, such as UKCP, COSCA, BABCP, BPS and so on. Members of UKCP, for example, work to the *Ethical Principles and Code of Professional Conduct* (UKCP, 2009); each member organisation (e.g. Association for Cognitive Analytic Therapy) has its own code of ethics. The UKCP's document covers the following areas:

- Best interests of clients
- Diversity and equality
- Confidentiality
- Conduct
- Professional knowledge, skills and experience
- Communication
- Obtaining consent
- Records
- Physical or mental health
- Professional integrity
- Advertising
- Indemnity insurance
- Complaints.

The Ethical Framework states that, 'values inform principles' (BACP, 2010, p. 2). It identifies the following principles (2010, p. 3):

- Being trustworthy: honouring the trust placed in the practitioner (also referred to as fidelity)
- Autonomy: respect for the client's right to be self-governing
- Beneficence: a commitment to promoting the client's wellbeing
- Non-maleficence: a commitment to avoiding harm to the client
- Justice: the fair and impartial treatment of all clients and the provision of adequate services
- Self-respect: fostering the practitioner's self-knowledge and care for self.

Finally, in outlining the fundamental premise in which any guidance for counselling and psychotherapy needs to be based, the Ethical Framework outlines personal qualities essential for ethical practice (2010, p. 4). These are:

- Empathy: The ability to communicate understanding of another person's experience from that person's perspective
- Sincerity: A personal commitment to consistency between what is professed and what is done
- Integrity: Commitment to being moral in dealings with others, personal straightforwardness, honesty and coherence
- Resilience: The capacity to work with the client's concerns without being personally diminished
- Respect: Showing appropriate esteem to others and their understanding of themselves
- Humility: The ability to assess accurately and acknowledge one's own strengths and weaknesses
- Competence: The effective deployment of the skills and knowledge needed to do what is required
- Fairness: The consistent application of appropriate criteria to inform decisions and actions
- Wisdom: Possession of sound judgement that informs practice
- Courage: The capacity to act in spite of known fears, risks and uncertainty.

The context for ethical thinking is therefore determined at a philosophical, institutional, individual and personal level. If all these aspects are in place, counselling and psychotherapy, in its organisation and delivery, is likely to be ethical and provide the client with the best opportunity to address their difficulties safely and respectfully. Any transgression from these principles potentially positions either the agency or individual practitioner in an unethical situation, where harm or unfairness is likely to result.

How such values, principles and qualities are to be acquired is another question, however. For example, if we consider the list of personal qualities above, it might be fair to argue that competence can be acquired through the provision of high-quality training, where trainees can integrate new knowledge and practise skills. Resilience may be encouraged through the supported exposure to daily professional challenges while on a practice placement where effective supervision is in place. It is less certain whether humility or respect can be taught: are these qualities something that may be acquired through a training curriculum? There seems to be a difference between what we do, and how we are. Whether good counsellors and psychotherapists are born or trained is a much-visited debate (Wheeler, 2002). Certainly, given the right conditions – which might include supervision, challenge, high-quality teaching, and time for reflection – the individual trainee can acquire and develop a range of personal qualities that would contribute to their capacity to work effectively and ethically. Agencies and individual practitioners can also ensure that services are provided fairly and equally, that clients are not discriminated against, and that the delivery of counselling and psychotherapy is respectful, focusing on the development of the client's capacity for self-determination and autonomy. However, there is an interesting philosophical debate over how much also relies on an individual's personality traits and their capacity to change, which perhaps also lies at the very heart of the ethos of counselling and psychotherapy itself.

When things go wrong

Things sometimes go wrong. That is to say, clients may feel that they have received a poor service, or in some way feel damaged by their experience of counselling or psychotherapy. This is sometimes intentional, but often unintentional. **Key aspects** are also available on the companion website. Likewise, therapists may feel let down by their supervisors, or one therapist might identify something in another they believe to be unethical. Often areas for complaint arise from unintended harm (i.e., an action or actions not intended to cause damage or harm to another, but experienced as such nevertheless). Examples where this might be the case are outlined in Box 5.9.

CASE STUDY 5.9
Unintended harm

- **Saya** is a counselling trainer. Due to procedural and assessment changes within her college she is forced to make changes to the training curriculum. This means that a previous piece of work already submitted is now discounted. The trainees on the course feel angry that this change has been made without any prior consultation or warning.
- **Jenny** is a psychotherapist working in independent practice. Her fees for therapy have been set for some time, and when considering this she realises that she must increase her fees to remain financially viable. She increases her fees with little notice to her clients, causing anger and distress.
- **Alan** is a counsellor in a further education college. As part of his role he is asked to join a Welfare Committee. At his first meeting he bumps into a client of his who is also on the Committee. Alan's client feels embarrassed and uncomfortable. Alan had not discussed with his client at the beginning of counselling how he and his client might manage 'boundary issues' (e.g. meeting outside on campus).

The examples in the boxes above highlight situations where the recipient of a service (trainee or client) felt disregarded and subsequently angry because of a process they believed to be mismanaged. In ethics terms, such situations might represent some of the values of counselling not being met: ensuring the integrity of the practitioner–client relationship; enhancing the quality of relationships between people; and striving for the fair and adequate provision of counselling and psychotherapy services for the client, for example. In terms of principles, the situations might represent a failing in being trustworthy; beneficence; and non-maleficence, for example. At a personal quality level, the situations might represent a lack of empathy, sincerity, integrity and respect, for example. The harm caused in these situations, however, arises more out of oversight than from deliberate intent. That is not to lessen the seriousness of the scenarios, for any situation in which a person feels upset or that harm has been done needs commensurate attention. They illustrate, however, that working or acting unethically can happen as a consequence of lack of thought, as much as from intent.

Situations can arise where, through the deliberate intention of the counsellor or psychotherapist, harm is caused. The scenarios of Susie, John and Suky in Box 5.10 illustrate such situations:

CASE STUDY 5.10
Intentional harm

- **Susie** is a counsellor who works in independent practice. She insists that clients pay in advance for their sessions (up to 12 sessions), but will often cancel sessions with no notice and refuses a refund.
- **John** has worked as a psychotherapist for several years. He often finds himself sexually attracted to clients and believes that, if managed carefully, sexual relationships with ongoing clients can be helpful so that they can 'experience a positive sexual experience'.
- **Suky** works as a counsellor in a health care setting, working with people with long-term mental health problems. She offers individual 'psychodynamic counselling' and a variety of therapy groups. Her employer believes she is qualified in both individual and group therapies, whereas in fact Suky has never had any training.

In these scenarios serious harm is caused to clients through an intentional act, such as financial or sexual exploitation, or misrepresenting services or qualifications. The values of counselling and psychotherapy undermined here include: respecting human rights and dignity, protecting the safety of clients and alleviating personal distress and suffering. Some of the principles of counselling and psychotherapy that have been disregarded include: being trustworthy, beneficence, non-maleficence and self-respect, for example. Finally, it could be argued that the therapists in the scenarios above did not demonstrate any of the personal qualities required for ethical practice. Sadly, while the scenarios outlined here appear extreme and unlikely, they do occur.

Complaints procedures

Where harm was unintentionally caused, or perhaps a complaint arises out of a misunderstanding, therapy organisations will in the first instance often look towards
mediation as a means of finding a successful way forward. This is often the first step
in problem-resolution as there is recognition that a full complaints hearing can be
a painful and distressing experience for all concerned, and that it often isn't the
most efficient way of reaching resolution. However, mediation is only a realistic
option if all parties are willing to participate and are positive about its likely chance

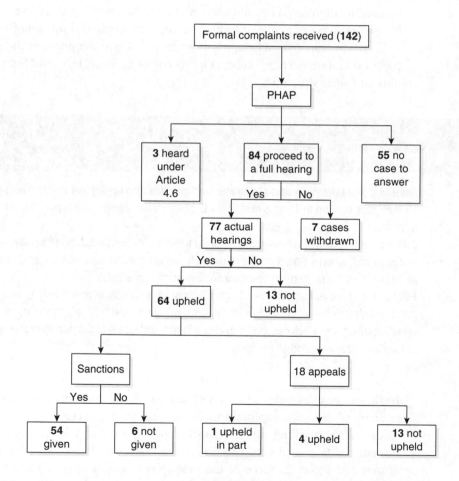

FIGURE 5.2   BACP complaints received – the complaints process. PHAP = Pre-
Hearing Assessment Panel; Article 4.6 = serious allegations, e.g.
exploitation or sexual abuse of clients (Kehle et al., 2008, p. 13)

Note: Khele, S., Symons, C. and Wheeler, S. (2008) 'An analysis of complaints to the British Association for
Counselling and Psychotherapy, 1996–2006', *Counselling and Psychotherapy Research*, 8 (2): 124–32.
Reproduced with permission from Taylor & Francis Ltd (www.tandfonline.com).

of success. If this isn't the case, or if intentional harm is suspected or the complaint raises particularly serious concerns, a complaints process is often the way forward.

All of the major UK and international therapy organisations have formal complaints procedures. Khele et al. (2008) conducted an audit of complaints received by BACP between 1996 and 2006. The research group found that there were 84 complaints that had been taken to a full formal hearing and that, after further analysis, concluded that male members of the Association were disproportionately complained about, and most complaints received were from people already involved in counselling. The numbers of complaints received was 'tracked' through the complaints process – the details of this can be seen in Figure 5.2.

Symons et al. (2011) explored in more detail Article 4.6 complaints, and Figure 5.3 provides an overview of such complaints between 1998 and 2007.

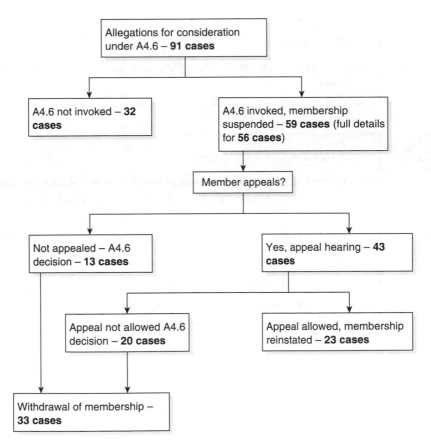

FIGURE 5.3   Article 4.6 complaints between 1998 and 2007 (Symons et al., 2011, p. 253)

Note: Symons, C., Khele, S., Rogers, J., Turner, J. and Wheeler, S. (2011) 'Allegations of serious professional misconduct: an analysis of the British Association for Counselling and Psychotherapy's Article 4.6 cases, 1998–2007', *Counselling and Psychotherapy Research*, 11 (4): 257–65. Reproduced with permission from Taylor & Francis Ltd (www.tandfonline.com).

Working ethically provides clients with the best opportunities for them to safely address difficulties, for counsellors and psychotherapists to maintain a sound and self-respectful practice, for agencies to provide non-discriminatory services, and for the profession of counselling and psychotherapy to retain credibility and authority. This, in turn, ensures that people seeking help can do so in the knowledge that there are systems in place to ensure standards and respond when things go wrong.

As has been demonstrated, ethical thinking – based on sound values and principles – is rarely a clear cut process where there are definite answers or clear ways forward. An ethically reflective approach is essential for the sound practice of counselling and psychotherapy, and this demands that practitioners take opportunities to consider their work and the decisions/interventions they make.

Further reading

Bond, T. (2010) *Standards and Ethics for Counselling in Action*, 3rd edn. London: Sage.

DISCUSSION QUESTIONS

1　To what extent do you think human qualities (such as integrity or respect) can be taught and to what extent are they fundamentally rooted in a person's personality? Why?
2　Which serves a counsellor or psychotherapist better: (a) a framework or guidance document based on ethics or (b) a code of practice outlining how practitioners should and shouldn't act? Why?
3　What, in your view, are the most important aspects of ethical practice?
4　How do you incorporate ethical thinking into your daily work?

PART TWO

THE THERAPEUTIC RELATIONSHIP

6

Clients and Presenting Issues

6.1 INTRODUCTION

CHAPTER OVERVIEW

While each client will present with a different story and experience, there are commonalities between the ways in which clients present that are helpful to understand in practice. The purpose of this chapter is to (a) outline many of the problems that clients may present with, (b) discuss theoretical ways of understanding distress and (c) identify pertinent knowledge and skills for practitioners.

There is certainly something unique in how we each tell our life stories. For example, I am a football fan and regularly go to watch my beloved team, Aston Villa FC. It never surprises me that, on reading the various accounts of the match afterwards, I am left wondering whether I attended the same game. Somehow, a player I believed to have performed terribly turns out to have been a sensation! While that might say something about my understanding of football, I suspect it speaks more about the ways in which our individual perspectives shape our view of the world. We can witness or be a part of the same event, yet the experience of it will vary greatly from person to person. We filter perception through our own perspectives, minimising some parts and privileging others.

One of the tasks of counselling or psychotherapy is to hear the stories of our clients, paying attention to what is, and what is not, said, and also to how the process of telling the story sheds light on other aspects of the client's experience. I have worked as a therapist for more than 20 years and heard many accounts of the same type of human experience, whether that be bereavement or loss, relationship difficulties, or isolation, for example. However, while the underlying 'events' that the clients have experienced may be comparable, the experience of it may be profoundly different.

Herein lies the problem of writing a chapter on presenting issues. An entire book would still be insufficient to truly capture the complexity and richness of the stories we tell. However, there are elements of the underlying problems that can be synthesised into discrete forms of knowledge that can help us hear stories in particular ways. Here, however, we immediately step onto dangerous philosophical ground, where there is much debate over the dangers of reductionist approaches to human experience. That is, the moment we begin to distil commonalities between people's accounts and experiences, we reduce their potency and uniqueness; thus we gain a diagnosis but 'lose' the person.

The first section of this chapter, Psychopathology and Diagnostic Structures, discusses what is meant by the term psychopathology, as well as considering the philosophical implications of that term for how we understand and work with human experience. In counselling and psychotherapy the term is consistent with (and informs) work in some orientations, while for others it will be an anathema that runs profoundly against their conceptions of counselling and psychotherapy. The difficulty here is that the moment we separate out particular aspects of living and label them 'presenting issues', we risk dislocating them from the narrative of people's lives. While there may be similarities between how people structure and conceptualise their experience of, say, depression, there are dangers in assuming that depression will impact on all people in the same way. As counsellors and psychotherapists we must, I suggest, privilege the uniqueness of clients' experiences and not become symptom-driven.

Why, then, a chapter on presenting issues? In short, the answer is: because I believe that we can be better placed to privilege the narrative of the client if we can draw also on general knowledge and insight of the commonalities of our experience. Let me illustrate this point further. Consider the way we experience repeating situations. I do not encounter each repeating situation in my life as if it were for the first time. For example, when I go to the football match I know there will be important aspects of previous such experiences that I will draw on to help me negotiate the current one efficiently – for example, the nature of the journey to the ground, the best place to park my car, when to take my seat, when to avoid queues, and how to leave the ground safely. If I didn't retain this information I would, no doubt, spend my time looking at maps, trying to find somewhere to park and generally standing in queues. However, there will be unique aspects in each occurrence – such as the people I might encounter, the weather, the match itself and, of course, the result. I can still allow myself to experience the uniqueness of the experience within the parameters of familiarity and transferability of experience and knowledge.

The same applies to working with clients. It is helpful for me as their therapist to understand that when people are depressed they may experience similar things, such as a sense of hopelessness, fatigue, loss of appetite, loss of sex drive and disruption to their sleeping patterns, and so on. However, I can still allow myself to hear their individual sense of their experience and what that means for them. I can draw on strategies that may help them, while also encouraging them to find their own particular ways of living with and changing their personal distress. By knowing the generalities, I am better placed to hear each narrative distinctively. I can have a better sense of their context and how that might shape the nature of their living.

It is, without doubt, a fine balance to walk. The hope here is that you, the reader, will be able to assimilate information from a general position that will, in turn, help you and your client to make sense of the specific. The chapter begins by considering the principles that underpin psychopathology and diagnosis, before considering the following client presentations:

- Anxiety and panic attacks
- Depression
- Post-traumatic stress disorder
- Eating disorders
- Loss and bereavement
- Suicide and self-harm
- Sexual problems
- Psychosis
- Personality disorders.

Each section provides, where appropriate and available, the diagnostic criteria for the presentation in question, as well as a discussion of how such issues might present in day-to-day work. Of course, the list could be much longer, but here I have drawn together a discussion of some of the most common presentations in counselling and psychotherapy.

6.2 PSYCHOPATHOLOGY AND DIAGNOSTIC STRUCTURES

SECTION OUTLINE

This section defines the term 'psychopathology' and discusses its relevance to the practice of counselling and psychotherapy. The concept is placed in the theoretical and philosophical context of the anti-psychiatry movement, as well as current mental health practice. Additionally, accepted protocols of diagnostic structures are described, together with a discussion of their relevance (or otherwise) for counselling and psychotherapy.

The Oxford English Dictionary defines 'psychopathology' as both 'the scientific study of mental disorders', and 'features of people's mental health considered collectively: mental or behavioural disorder' (OECD, 2012). Lemma (1996) begins her discussion of psychopathology by stating that 'Any attempt to define what psychopathology is presupposes that we really know what normality is' (1996, p. 1). This is an interesting and important point, given that in the daily work of counselling and psychotherapy an understanding of 'normal' (in the sense of what the individual's experience of themselves and their life was like before the issues arose that brought them to therapy) is essential to helping the client. It is dangerous, and potentially unethical, to assume that simply because a client's views, thoughts or behaviour differ from one's own, they are therefore 'not normal' and are thus potentially psychopathological.

In daily application the term 'psychopathology' generally describes thoughts, feelings or behaviour that: (a) fall outside the person's usual range; (b) fall outside a socially acceptable range of behaviour; and (c) have the potential to be explained from within an illness model, using a diagnostic frame. Here (a) is probably least contentious, while (b) and (c) can be highly contentious. They fall into the areas that those taking an anti-psychiatry position have identified as most troublesome. If an individual's thoughts, feelings or behaviours do not fit within what society deems an acceptable range that does not mean that they are 'mentally ill'. Here it is helpful to consider this in the case scenario outlined in Box 6.1.

CASE STUDY 6.1
Julian

Julian was a 58-year-old male living alone. His relationship had ended many years before and he was not interested in finding another. He had little contact with friends and family, generally preferring his own company. He had a long 'mental health history': he had been admitted to hospital previously, with his agreement, for periods of depression, self-harm and suicide risk. Neighbours, who generally were cautious of contact with Julian because they believed him to be a 'psycho', contacted his GP because they were concerned over his behaviour. Julian lived in a group of flats and, over recent weeks, had become increasingly agitated by the behaviour of his neighbours, who he claimed were transmitting voices into his house. His GP undertook a home visit and, following this, recommended admission to hospital. Julian refused and so a statutory mental health assessment was undertaken. The mental health worker undertook an assessment of Julian's mental health state and made a decision to admit him to hospital because of concerns over Julian's increasing irrational thoughts and his levels of agitation towards his neighbours. The fear was of potential physical violence. Julian was compulsorily admitted to a mental health unit for further assessment.

The primary reasons for Julian's compulsory admission to a mental health unit can be summarised as follows:

- His previous mental health history
- Concerns expressed by his neighbours
- His behaviour therefore being viewed as out of the 'normal' social range
- His belief that neighbours were transmitting voices into his flat (potentially evidencing delusional beliefs and possibly schizophrenia)
- An increased threat of violence towards his neighbours.

On the basis of this account, it would appear that an admission, although distressing for Julian, would afford the best opportunity for a fuller assessment of his apparently deteriorating mental health and might, on balance, reduce the risk of a significant and harmful deterioration of the situation. I was the statutory mental health worker on this occasion and, to this day, I still recall my horror when it was later discovered that a neighbour was operating illegal and non-licensed transmitting equipment in her flat. I had made assumptions about Julian's mental health state based on an insufficiently thought out view of what mental health meant. While this was my personal error, it also provides a shocking depiction of how the idea of psychopathology can be ill-defined and poorly applied.

The assumptions that were made in this scenario included the following:

- The concerns expressed by the neighbours were genuine, as opposed to motivated by a wish to have Julian removed from his flat
- The assessment undertaken by the GP was based on a previous knowledge of Julian and his mental health
- Julian's frustration with the neighbours was unreasonable and without justification
- Julian's claims that the 'voices' in his flat were due to auditory hallucinations (as opposed to actual voices)
- The propensity to violence was higher due to Julian's previous mental health problems (whereas in fact Julian had never been violent – the stereotype of 'madness = violence' was clearly prevalent)
- The situation therefore was out of the ordinary, beyond 'normal', and thus psychopathological.

What Julian's scenario illustrates is that making sense of another's experience is fraught with dangers – and the range of 'normality' always has the potential to challenge previously held assumptions. The debates that rage around the understanding of mental health and mental distress tell us something of the situation that Julian found himself in.

What is a diagnosis?

The OED defines diagnosis as 'The identification of the nature of an illness or other problem by examination of the symptoms', and 'the distinctive characterization in precise terms of a genus, species or phenomenon'. In counselling and psycho-therapy terms, a diagnosis would both 'identify the nature of an illness' by its 'symptoms', such as particular ways in which a client presents, and would addition-ally 'characterise a phenomenon'. This is less contentious when applied to physical ill-health. In the dominant Western culture the diagnosis of cancer, coronary heart disease or diabetes, for example, would be seen as an accepted form of medical practice; a necessary step prior to the application of appropriate treatment. (Other cultures, however, would not so readily subscribe to this view of human health, using instead a conception of a holistic continuum of wellbeing.)

There is greater debate around the application of the principles of diagnosis to mental health (Ellerby, 2007; Newnes et al., 1999). Many commentators vehe-mently reject the 'illness model' and diagnosis, viewing all forms of emotional distress as aspects of human experience rather than pathological processes. Proctor (2007) challenges the assumption that the same diagnostic process that applies in physical health can be applied to mental health. He writes: 'there is no physical test which can establish the presence of mental illness or disorder. Therefore diag-nosis in mental health relies on the professional making observations and judge-ments about how a patient behaves, and about the thoughts and opinions she/he expresses' (2007, p. 105).

These views are consistent with the anti-psychiatry movement that gained momentum in the 1960s through the work of people such as Foucault, Szasz and Laing. The anti-psychiatry movement developed a strong critique of psychiatry, summarised in Box 6.2.

BOX 6.2   CRITICISMS OF ESTABLISHED PSYCHIATRY ACCORDING TO THE ANTI-PSYCHIATRY MOVEMENT

1 Medicalisation through the application of psychiatric diagnosis to understandable human reactions to particular situations
2 Through the misuse of 'science' and positivist enquiry, exclusion of other approaches to responding to mental health distress
3 Imbalance of power between practitioner and patient, with the patient's voice often dismissed as another aspect of their pathology
4 Use of psychiatric diagnosis to control and manage particular social groups (e.g. gays and lesbians)
5 Diagnosis based on ill-informed 'science' where the subjectivity of the diagnosti-cian is masked by the apparent objectivity of the diagnostic principle
6 Profound stigmatising of psychiatric diagnosis
7 Underlying control of psychiatry by pharmaceutical companies with a vested interest in the perpetuation of the illness model of human experience.

I worked in a mental health setting for many years and was very aware of how different perspectives on mental health divided those who were otherwise tasked with working together. It was certainly true that those models adopting a medicalised approach to mental 'illness', such as psychiatry and clinical psychology at the time, were the dominant force. My work as a mental health social worker, drawing rather on developmental and social models of mental health, was seen as more ancillary to the 'proper' scientific approaches. While professionally I never believed in such demarcated positions, I was often left aghast at treatment plans that focused only on the use of psychotropic medication, apparently disregarding factors such as a person's socioeconomic status.

Counselling, psychotherapy and psychiatric diagnosis

In general terms, whether or how counsellors and psychotherapists adopt the principles of psychiatric diagnosis into their thinking is likely to be dependent on their core model of training. Their perspectives on psychiatric diagnosis will, however, also be informed by such factors as:

- The working context of the therapist
- Other core training the therapist may have received, such as social work or nursing
- Other professional experiences of working in settings where diagnostic structures were adopted
- Continuing professional development
- Personally held views about mental health.

However, it is helpful to consider here a modality-specific perspective of diagnosis, based on core philosophical underpinnings of the particular therapy model and how that model is delivered in a training setting. For example, the general division between modalities with respect to psychiatric diagnosis is likely to fall between, on the one hand, the cognitive-behavioural and psychodynamic models, generally more aligned with diagnostic structures of mental illness, and, on the other, the humanistic models (e.g. person-centred or existential approaches), which are generally more aligned to a human experience approach of mental health. Merry (2002, p. 75) wrote that 'issues concerning psychological assessment and "diagnosis" are complex, but the person centred approach tends to view these activities as unnecessary and even harmful to the development of a counselling relationship'.

There are, however, many person-centred therapists who work very effectively in mental health settings, both in terms of accommodating the principles of diagnostic thinking into their work (without necessarily working proactively with diagnosis), and being a full member of the mental health team. While Sommerbeck (2003, p. 33) writes that 'psychiatric diagnosis is of no issue in client-centred theory and therapy', she does offer extremely useful points about how an awareness of diagnostic structures can be helpful to the person-centred therapist. The following list draws on her suggestions:

1   Counsellors will often receive questions from clients about diagnoses they have been given. 'It is important that the therapist is able to accommodate such a request for information in a qualified way when he deems it appropriate' (p. 33).
2   In psychiatric and medical settings, diagnosis is the dominant language, 'and the client centred therapist must be able to communicate in the language with other staff and professionals when working in this culture' (p. 33).
3   Counsellors need to be aware of the range of treatments that might be offered to clients. 'The client centred therapist will quickly experience the necessity of psychiatric diagnostics for many treatment modalities, especially for the psychopharmacological treatments that help many clients, in combination with psychotherapy, or without psychotherapy' (p. 34).
4   Diagnosis is often central when considering the liberty of a client under mental health legislation. A counsellor needs sufficient awareness of this to contribute usefully to that discussion, particularly in relation to client suicide potential.

The positioning of psychiatric diagnosis in counselling and psychotherapy set out above provides a context for the rest of this chapter. Each subsequent section focuses on a primary presenting issue. Where available, the diagnostic criteria for the presenting issue in question will be outlined, drawing on the *Diagnostic and Statistical Manual of Mental Disorders*, 4th edition (text revision) (DSM-IV-TR, herein after referred to simply as DSM) (American Psychiatric Association, 2000). The other main diagnostic manual, the International Classification of Diseases: Volume 10 (WHO, 1992), is less widely used in mental health services in the UK.

Whatever their modality, counsellors and psychotherapists are not diagnosticians and even if sympathetic with diagnostic structures would not be expected to confer a diagnosis on a client (in the UK, GPs, psychiatrists and occasionally clinical psychologists formulate client diagnoses.) The focus here is rather on how diagnostic structures can inform our thinking as therapists, without adopting reductionist positions or becoming diagnosis-driven. The intention is that, regardless of modality, we remain 'person-centred' in the widest possible sense of the phrase.

The DSM defines 'mental disorder' as:

> a clinically significant behavioural or psychological syndrome or pattern that occurs in an individual and that is associated with present distress (e.g. a painful symptom) or disability (i.e., impairment in one or more important areas of functioning) or with a significantly increased risk of suffering death, pain, disability, or an important loss of freedom. (p. xxxi)

It goes on to say, 'this syndrome or pattern must not be merely an expectable and culturally sanctioned response to a particular event, for example, the death of a loved one. Whatever its original cause, it must currently be considered a manifestation of a behavioural, psychological, or biological dysfunction in the individual. Neither deviant behaviour (e.g. political, religious, or sexual) nor conflicts that are primarily between the individual and society are mental disorders unless the deviance or conflict is a symptom of a dysfunction in the individual' (p. xxxi).

Interestingly, DSM is very clear about making a separation between disorder and political beliefs – and yet it is the use of mental health diagnoses against those who challenge some of the accepted positions of society that is one of the biggest criticisms of the diagnostic model of mental illness; that people whose behaviour challenges or is different from the majority can too easily be pathologised.

The DSM definition also very clearly does not make a separation between 'mind' and 'body'. Again, one of the criticisms of a medical model of psychiatry has been its tendency to view 'mind' and 'body' separately, as opposed to seeing individuals more holistically. The DSM states, 'there is much "physical" in "mental" disorders and much "mental" in "physical" disorders' (p. xxxi). This criticism of a diagnostic approach therefore is perhaps more about the application of the system rather than the system itself. If this is the case this may speak a little of one of the other major criticisms of psychiatry, which is power imbalance; leading to situations in which one does *to* another as opposed to doing *with*. Each counsellor and psychotherapist must consider in what ways, if at all, this information is of relevance to them in their work with clients.

DISCUSSION QUESTIONS

1 What is the relationship between your model of training and psychopathology and diagnosis? To what extent are they compatible? Why?
2 What do you know of your local mental health support? How would you or your clients access it?
3 How relevant is a medicalised perspective of mental health to your work? If it isn't relevant, how would you work with a client who views that differently?
4 To what extent do diagnostic categories, used in general terms, inform your work as a counsellor? How does this influence your work positively or negatively?

6.3 ANXIETY AND PANIC ATTACKS

SECTION OUTLINE

Anxiety and panic attacks frequently present as problems in counselling and psychotherapy. Often clients will seek quick solutions, particularly when they are experiencing panic attacks that can be very frightening and come as a surprise. This section defines what is meant by anxiety and panic, outlines the typical 'symptoms' of a panic attack, and considers how clients might be supported to better understand their anxiety and manage panic more effectively.

Definitions

Anxiety is perhaps one of the most overused and misunderstood terms. An attempt at defining it highlights one of the most common difficulties facing a therapist when presented with a client who says they are 'anxious': the phrase can mean so many different things to different people. My experience of anxiety may be very different to yours in how it is experienced emotionally, psychologically and physically. Hallam (1992, p. 2) offers several characterisations of anxiety, as follows:

- An unpleasant quality of subjective experience, varying from 'tension' to 'terror'
- An awareness of imminent danger or harm whether or not its sources can be specified
- An experience of bodily sensations associated particularly with activation of the autonomic nervous system
- A strong urge to flee to a place of safety
- A lack of control over fine motor movements
- Thoughts of a worrying or unpleasant nature over which there is little control
- An inability to think clearly or act in a coordinated manner, especially in novel, conflictual or threatening situations.

In DSM a number of discrete conditions fall under the banner of 'anxiety disorders', namely:

- Panic attack (discussed in more detail below)
- Agoraphobia: 'an anxiety about, or avoidance of, places or situations from which escape might be difficult (or embarrassing) or in which help may not

be available in the event of having a Panic Attack or panic-like symptoms' (p. 429)

- Panic disorder without agoraphobia: 'characterized by recurrent unexpected Panic Attacks about which there is persistent concern' (p. 429)
- Specific phobia: 'characterized by clinically significant anxiety provoked by exposure to a specific feared object or situation, often leading to avoidance behavior' (p. 429)
- Obsessive-compulsive disorder: 'characterized by obsessions (which cause marked anxiety or distress) and/or by compulsions (which serve to neutralize anxiety)' (p. 429)
- Post-traumatic stress disorder: 'characterized by the re-experiencing of an extremely traumatic event accompanied by symptoms of increased arousal and by avoidance of stimuli associated with the trauma' (p. 429)
- Acute stress disorder:'characterized by symptoms similar to those of Posttraumatic stress disorder that occur immediately in the aftermath of an extremely traumatic event' (p. 429)
- Generalized anxiety disorder: 'characterized by at least 6 months of persistent and excessive anxiety and worry' (p. 429)
- Anxiety disorder due to a general medical condition: 'characterized by prominent symptoms of anxiety that are judged to be a direct physiological consequence of a general medical condition' (p. 430)
- Substance-induced anxiety disorder: 'characterized by prominent symptoms of anxiety that are judged to be a direct physiological consequence of a drug of abuse, a medication, or toxin exposure' (p. 430)
- Other kinds of anxiety disorders 'that do not meet criteria for any of the specific anxiety disorders defined ...' (p. 430)

In diagnostic terms it is not accurate to describe anxiety *per se*, but rather to think more specifically in terms of which anxiety is being presented and its context. As will be reiterated throughout this chapter, counsellors and psychotherapists are not expected to be diagnosticians, but rather can use the above information to help them think about a client's experience of anxiety and in turn help the client to understand their own experience more specifically. It is not possible to explore each form of anxiety here, so I will focus on generalised anxiety disorder, as this presents so regularly in counselling and psychotherapy services.

Generalised anxiety disorder

The diagnostic criteria for generalised anxiety disorder are detailed in Box 6.3.

BOX 6.3 DIAGNOSTIC CRITERIA FOR GENERALISED ANXIETY DISORDER

A Excessive anxiety and worry (apprehensive expectation), occurring more days than not for at least 6 months, about a number of events or activities (such as work or school performance).

B The person finds it difficult to control the worry.

C The anxiety and worry are associated with three (or more) of the following six symptoms (with at least some symptoms present for more days than not for the past 6 months; NOTE: only one item is required in children):

   i restlessness or feeling keyed up or on edge
   ii being easily fatigued
   iii difficulty concentrating or mind going blank
   iv irritability
   v muscle tension
   vi sleep disturbance (difficulty falling or staying asleep, or restless unsatisfying sleep)

D The focus of the anxiety and worry is not confined to features of an Axis I disorder, e.g. the anxiety or worry is not about having a panic attack (as in Panic Disorder), being embarrassed in public (as in Social Phobia), being contaminated (as in Obsessive-Compulsive Disorder), being away from home or close relatives (as in Separation Anxiety Disorder), gaining weight (Anorexia Disorder), having multiple physical complaints (as in Somatization Disorder), or having a serious illness (as in Hyphochondriasis), and the anxiety and worry do not occur exclusively during Posttraumatic Stress Disorder.

E The anxiety, worry, or physical symptoms cause clinically significant distress or impairment in social, occupational, or other important areas of functioning.

F The disturbance is not due to the direct physiological effects of a substance or general medical condition ... and does not occur exclusively during a Mood Disorder, a Psychotic Disorder, or a Pervasive Developmental Disorder.

(American Psychiatric Association, 2000, p. 476. Reprinted with permission from the *Diagnostic and Statistical Manual of Mental Disorders*, Fourth Edition, Text Revision (© American Psychiatric Association 2000).

As outlined in the diagnostic criteria, anxiety can also present as part of another type of presentation, such as in obsessive–compulsive disorder (OCD) (discussed in more detail in another section) or panic disorder. However, for many people their experience of anxiety will be quite general. The one misleading aspect of drawing on the diagnostic category perhaps is (A) where it states '... about a number of events or activities ...' (p. 476). My own experience is that many people who attend counselling or psychotherapy with anxiety cannot necessarily link their experience with a particular event or situation, and it is this nondescript nature of anxiety that causes most concern. People will often say something like, 'I have no idea where this comes from'. Often a little more exploration may uncover a situation or event that might explain the symptoms, such as levels of stress at work, or relationship difficulties. At other times the cause(s) can be harder to find. An experience of anxiety is detailed in Box 6.4.

CASE STUDY 6.4
Jenny

Jenny attends for counselling. She states that she feels 'wound up' all the time, and notes physical symptoms including: upset stomach, feeling 'jumpy', racing thoughts, struggling to sleep. She says she feels very stressed but cannot understand why. She feels it is causing her difficulties in life as she cannot concentrate or focus on her work. In therapy Jenny talked of pressures at work and having recently been working under the threat of redundancy. She made connections between her stress at work and other areas of her life. With this insight in addition to working on relaxation techniques, Jenny began to feel stronger and calmer.

Panic attacks and panic disorder

If you have ever experienced a panic attack you will already have some sense of how frightening an experience it is. Like anxiety, the term is overused, often describing a situation that the individual is particularly unhappy about (e.g. 'I felt in a panic when we started to argue'). However, an actual panic attack describes a set of physiological symptoms that can, at the time, feel life-threatening (even though they are not). DSM (p. 432) list a number of symptoms of a panic attack, including:

- palpitations, pounding heart, or accelerated heart rate
- sweating, trembling or shaking
- breathing problems
- chest pain or discomfort

- nausea
- feeling dizzy, unsteady, lightheaded, or faint
- derealization (feelings of unreality) or depersonalization (being detached from oneself)
- fear of dying.

Any one of the above symptoms may be associated with serious physiological conditions and, if in doubt, the client should be referred to their medical practitioner to examine whether there is an underlying disease. The DSM talks of three 'types' of panic attacks: unexpected panic attack (not associated with a situational trigger); situationally bound panic attack (in response to a situational trigger); and situationally predisposed panic attack (when the attack is linked to a trigger, but the panic is not invariably linked to the trigger). Panic disorder is a distinct condition under which panic attacks will occur. In diagnostic terms, panic disorder can either be associated with agoraphobia, or not. Box 6.5 outlines the diagnostic criteria for panic disorder without agoraphobia.

BOX 6.5   PANIC DISORDER WITHOUT AGORAPHOBIA

A   Both (1) and (2):

1   recurrent unexpected panic attacks
2   at least one of the attacks has been followed by 1 month (or more) of one (or more) of the following:

   a   persistent concern about having additional attacks
   b   worry about the implications of the attack or its consequences (e.g. losing control, having a heart attack, 'going crazy')
   c   a significant change in behavior related to the attacks

B   Absence of agoraphobia
C   The panic attacks are not due to the direct physiological effects of a substance, (e.g., a drug of abuse; a medication) or a general medical condition, (e.g., hyperthyroidism)
D   The panic attacks are not better accounted for by another mental disorder, such as social phobia (e.g., occurring on exposure to feared social situations), specific phobia (e.g., on exposure to a specific phobic situation), obsessive-compulsive disorder (e.g. on exposure to dirt in someone with an obsession about contamination), post-traumatic stress disorder (e.g., in response to stimuli associated with a severe stressor), or separation anxiety (e.g., in response to being away from home or close relatives)

(American Psychiatric Association, 2000, p. 441. Reprinted with permission from the *Diagnostic and Statistical Manual of Mental Disorders*, Fourth Edition, Text Revision (© American Psychiatric Association 2000).

An example of a client reporting panic attacks is detailed in Box 6.6.

CASE STUDY 6.6
Simon

Simon had what he describes as his first panic attack four months ago. Since then, he has had a number of others, describing situations in which he feels out of control, with: awareness of beating heart; nausea; sweating; dizziness; fearing collapse or death; and a strong urge to run or escape. He is now avoiding situations in which he fears a further panic attack might occur. In discussing this in therapy Simon talked of having been unwell with a virus for some weeks. He recalled a situation when, in a meeting, he feared vomiting but did not feel able to leave the room – he felt trapped. This discussion was helpful to Simon, who also worked on developing breathing techniques and worked at not avoiding anxiety-provoking situations.

Working therapeutically with anxiety and panic

There are a number of strategies that clients can learn to help them initially cope with anxiety and panic and then to reduce symptoms. Much depends on the motivation of the client and how they wish to solve the problem. I will often talk of a 'broken leg' metaphor with clients: the pain of the broken leg corresponds with the symptoms of anxiety and panic, while the broken bone is the cause of the problem. Painkillers can be given to dull the pain of the broken leg (they correspond to strategies for coping), while the actual broken bone needs attending to, to facilitate healing (this corresponds to providing an opportunity to explore the cause of the anxiety and panic). Some clients opt for strategies only, while others want to take an opportunity to talk about their problems also.

There are a number of useful strategies for clients to try, including:

- Relaxation techniques, perhaps using a relaxation CD or other music
- Guided imagery (i.e., talking the client through an imagined place they associate with calmness)
- Use of self-help books and online resources
- Breathing exercises, such as the 'rescue breath' (one deep breath taken in, then blown out hard), followed by steady breathing, (e.g. breathing in on a count of 3, and out on a count of 3)

- Exercise (to help regulate breathing and manage excessive adrenaline)
- Avoiding stimulants (e.g. caffeine-based drinks and alcohol)
- Ensuring good sleep routines
- Positive self-talk (e.g. I am going to be alright; nothing bad is going to happen to me; I can cope with this situation)
- Meditation techniques, such as mindfulness
- Medication: as a short-term strategy to cope with very high levels of anxiety, a GP may prescribe beta blockers to help reduce the immediacy of symptoms.

It is important not to encourage clients to take lots of deep breaths as a means of coping with high anxiety, as this can cause dizziness and replicate the feelings of a panic attack. It is helpful to work through these strategies with clients, informing them that some are very 'hit and miss' affairs (finding the specific relaxation technique that works can involve trial and error). Also, providing the client with information about anxiety and panic to help them understand the physiological process can be immensely supportive. For example, understanding the physiological 'chain response' of a panic attack, such as it beginning with rapid, short breathing, which is likely then to lead on to physiological symptoms such as those detailed above, can help the client understand their process while it is happening. I will often ask clients to imagine a situation in which they might have experienced a 'fight or flight' response, such as crossing a road and not seeing a car coming. Having safely got to the other side of the road I then ask clients to imagine what they would be experiencing. They will typically describe many of the 'symptoms' of a panic attack. This helps to position a panic attack as a normal response, albeit to an abnormal event or situation.

We might all understand anxiety in different ways when working with it thera-peutically. My own view is to see anxiety as a 'blockage' to feeling, as opposed to a feeling of itself. We often mistakenly call anxiety a feeling, when it is instead a set of physiological responses associated with particular psychological states. I have found that by thinking of anxiety in terms of 'blockages', or absence of feelings, clients can be supported to think beyond their anxiety to help them consider their actual feelings. I will often ask clients, 'If you weren't feeling anxious, what might you feel instead?' – and then encourage them to speculate about alternative feel-ings. This can often provides clients with an opportunity to reflect on anger, hurt, isolation, fear, rejection or loneliness, for example. This discourse provides an open door to often profound in-depth therapeutic work and can, if successful, help reduce anxiety and panic significantly.

Finally, clients often wish to get to an anxiety-free state and will be fearful of anxiety returning. It is important to help clients think about anxiety positively, so that it is not always associated with negative states. It helps here to talk about anxiety as an important human state that can bring benefits too. For example, if preparing for an interview or when presenting to a large group of people, a certain level of anxiety can help motivate and concentrate to achieve a good outcome. It is when anxiety becomes excessive, disproportionate or not explained by a situation that it can become problematic. It is therefore helpful for clients to think about their 'tolerance level' – what level of anxiety might they tell themselves is 'normal' for them (and thus something they can work proactively with), and how would they therefore know when their anxiety is getting too high?

Counselling and psychotherapy can act as an important resource for supporting clients with anxiety and panic, and it is therefore not surprising that they are included as a treatment of choice within UK primary care therapeutic services.

WEBSITES

NHS Direct (Anxiety): www.nhs.uk/conditions/Anxiety/Pages/Introduction.aspx
Mind (Anxiety): www.mind.org.uk/help/diagnoses_and_conditions/anxiety
Royal College of Psychiatry (Anxiety and Phobias): www.rcpsych.ac.uk/mentalhealthinfo/problems/anxietyphobias/anxiety,panic,phobias.aspx

DISCUSSION QUESTIONS

1 Think of a time when you have been anxious or have felt panic. What did you experience: (a) emotionally; (b) behaviourally; and (c) physiologically?
2 What strategies help you to deal with high anxiety or panic?
3 What is the priority for you when working with high anxiety or panic: symptom reduction or psychological exploration? Why?
4 How might the diagnostic criteria for general anxiety disorder and panic disorder support your thinking and interventions? If not at all, why?

6.4 DEPRESSION

SECTION OUTLINE

Depression is one of the most common diagnosed mental health problems in the UK and internationally. Almost all counsellors and psychotherapists will work with clients who experience depression. This section defines what is meant by depression, provides an overview of the research evidence for the treatment of depression, and considers how counsellors and psychotherapists can support depressed clients.

Definitions

According to the National Health Service, depression is internationally the fourth biggest cause of disability and disease (NHS, 2012). According to the Mental Health Foundation (2012), mixed depression and anxiety are the most common mental health conditions. However, 'depression' is a term so widely used (and misused) that its real meaning has been diluted. Many people talk of feeling depressed, yet feeling down or unhappy is a very different experience to depression. It is worth exploring with clients who describe themselves as depressed whether or not they have been diagnosed with depression, or whether they are using the term in a more loosely descriptive way. That is not to say that without a diagnosis an individual's experience of depression is not valid. It is, however, worth discussing in more depth what they mean by depression (e.g. nature, frequency, severity and time since onset).

As with anxiety (discussed earlier in this chapter), depression deserves careful definition. Gilbert (2007, p. 5) defines depression across four different aspects of functioning:

Motivation: Apathy, loss of energy and interest: things seem pointless, hopeless

Emotional: Depressed mood, plus emptiness, anger or resentment, anxiety, shame, guilt

Cognitive: Poor concentration, negative ideas about the self, the world and the future

Biological: Sleep disturbance, loss of appetite, changes in hormones and brain chemicals.

This is a helpful outline as it clearly delineates depression across different aspects of functioning. It is too easy to assume that depression is a psychological process only, whereas depression will cause disturbance across the whole of a person's experience. The experience of depression can often be described as mild, moderate or severe.

DSM classifies depression as a mood disorder alongside bipolar disorders (the combination of 'high' states – mania, and 'low' periods – major depression) and substance-induced mood disorders. It outlines criteria for major depressive disorder, dysthymic disorder and depressive disorder (not otherwise specified). However, it is worth beginning with an examination of the criteria for major depressive episode, which then informs diagnostic criteria for major depressive disorder and dysthymic disorder. The criteria for major depressive episode are detailed in Box 6.7.

BOX 6.7   CRITERIA FOR MAJOR DEPRESSIVE EPISODE

A Five (or more) of the following symptoms have been present during the same 2-week period and represent a change from previous functioning: at least one of the symptoms is (1) depressed mood or (2) loss of interest or pleasure.

   1 depressed mood most of the day, nearly every day, as indicated by either subjective report (e.g. feels sad or empty) or observation made by others (e.g. appears tearful) (NOTE: in children and adolescents, can be irritable mood)

   2 markedly diminished interest or pleasure in all, or almost all, activities most of the day, nearly every day (as indicated by either subjective account or observation made by others)

   3 significant weight loss when not dieting or weight gain (e.g. a change of more than 5% of body weight in a month), or decrease or increase in appetite nearly every day (NOTE: in children, consider failure to make expected weight gains)

   4 insomnia or hypersomnia nearly every day

   5 psychomotor agitation or retardation nearly every day (observable by others, not merely subjective feelings of restlessness or being slowed down)

   6 fatigue or loss of energy nearly every day

   7 feelings of worthlessness or excessive or inappropriate guilt (which may be delusional) nearly every day (not merely self-reproach or guilt about being sick)

   8 diminished ability to think or concentrate, or indecisiveness, nearly every day (either by subjective account or as observed by others)

   9 recurrent thoughts of death (not just a fear of dying), recurrent suicidal ideation without a specific plan, or a suicide attempt or a specific plan for committing suicide

B The symptoms do not meet criteria for a Mixed Episode

C The symptoms cause clinically significant distress or impairment in social, occupational, or other important areas of functioning

D The symptoms are not due to the direct physiological effects of a substance (e.g. a drug of abuse, a medication) or a general medical condition (e.g., hypothyroidism)

E The symptoms are not better accounted for by bereavement, i.e., after the loss of a loved one, the symptoms persist for longer than 2 months or are characterized by marked functional impairment, morbid preoccupation with worthlessness, suicidal ideation, psychotic symptoms, or psychomotor retardation.

(American Psychiatric Association, 2000, p. 356. Reprinted with permission from the *Diagnostic and Statistical Manual of Mental Disorders*, Fourth Edition, Text Revision (© American Psychiatric Association 2000).

Though these broad descriptors offer a good starting point for understanding major depression, they do not necessarily provide the detail of the individual's experience. It is important to explore with the client what their own particular experience might be. For example, the application of the above criteria to an individual's experience may include loss of interest in sex (libido) or relationship difficulties, periodic or longer episodes of crying, loss of interest in family, loss of interest in hobbies or work, inability to concentrate or motivate to undertake work, gastric disturbance, and so on. The NICE guidelines for depression (NICE, 2009) acknowledge that many people will fall below the criteria for major depressive episode by virtue of the fact that not all of the diagnostic criteria will be met. Even where a DSM diagnosis for major depressive episode cannot be made, the experience of depression can be disabling for the individual. NICE calls this 'subthreshold depressive symptoms' (p. 17).

A major depressive disorder describes a major depressive episode that is differentiated from other major disorders, such as schizophrenia or delusional disorder. A major depressive disorder can be a single episode, or recurrent. A major depressive disorder would not be considered recurrent if 'there is an interval of at least 2 consecutive months in which criteria are not met for a Major Depressive Episode' (DSM, p. 375).

Dysthymic disorder, or dysthymia, describes 'a chronically depressed mood that occurs for most of the day more days than not for at least 2 years' (p. 376). Additionally, for such a diagnosis in the previous 2 years the person must not have been symptom-free for any longer than 2 months at a time. Further, when depressed, the person must have experienced two or more of the following:

- poor appetite or overeating
- insomnia or hypersomnia
- low energy or fatigue
- low self-esteem
- poor concentration or difficulty making decisions
- feelings of hopelessness.

Dysthymic disorder is therefore a long-standing depression characterised by low mood. It can be described as having an early onset if it began before the age of 21 years, or late onset if it began at 21 years or older.

Causes of depression

There is much debate over the causes of depression, which speaks of the philosophical divides inherent in the field of mental health, discussed earlier. For example, a purist medical model of psychiatry might consider depression to have biochemical cause, such as deficiencies in serotonin levels (a neurotransmitter that is said to be pivotal in brain function and mood). In contrast, a purist social model might explain depression as a reaction against social conditions – poverty, poor health and depriving living conditions, for example. A purist psychological perspective might instead argue that depression is a consequence of inter- or intra-personal struggle, perhaps resulting from early childhood experiences, upbringing or a state of inner incongruence. I have worked in services where practitioners have taken a single, purist position on depression and have seen any other explanation as an anathema to their own understanding. I have known counsellors and psychotherapists to take a strong position against a medical explanation of human distress, preferring instead to privilege their own perspective. Indeed, it is not uncommon to hear counsellors and psychotherapists denounce anti-depressants and actively discourage clients from considering them as a treatment option.

There now seems to be a general shift in how depression is understood (and therefore treated), with greater acceptance that all perspectives have something useful to offer. When working with clients therefore it is helpful to pay attention to all factors of their narrative, including physical and social factors, in helping to build as informed a perspective with your client as possible.

Treatment for depression

There is a considerable evidence base for the psychological treatment of depression (Cuijpers, et al., 2011; Nieuwsma et al., 2011), and in the UK there has been the development of a 'stepped care' approach. That is, different severity levels of depression are responded to with different levels of treatment; the individual having their level of care 'stepped' up according to the severity of their depression and how they have responded to treatment. The NICE Depression guidelines (NICE, 2009) outlines this stepped care approach, as shown in Figure 6.1.

Each level will have available certain types of treatments deemed appropriate for the severity of depression. In summary, the treatments for each level are as follows:

Step 1: Recognition, assessment and initial management, including the provision of psycho-education

Step 2: Recognised depression – persistent subthreshold depressive symptoms or mild to moderate depression, including the provision of: individual guided self-help (based on principles of CBT); computerised CBT; group physical activity programmes; and CBT. Medication (anti-depressants) is generally not advised at this level

Step 3: Persistent subthreshold depressive symptoms or mild to moderate depression with inadequate response to initial interventions, and moderate and severe depression,

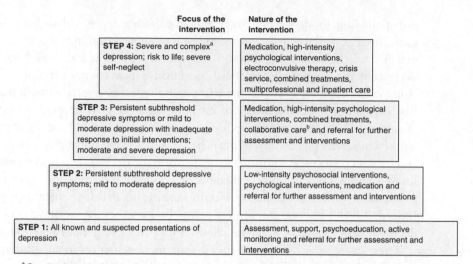

	Focus of the intervention	Nature of the intervention

STEP 4: Severe and complex[a] depression; risk to life; severe self-neglect

Medication, high-intensity psychological interventions, electroconvulsive therapy, crisis service, combined treatments, multiprofessional and inpatient care

STEP 3: Persistent subthreshold depressive symptoms or mild to moderate depression with inadequate response to initial interventions; moderate and severe depression

Medication, high-intensity psychological interventions, combined treatments, collaborative care[b] and referral for further assessment and interventions

STEP 2: Persistent subthreshold depressive symptoms; mild to moderate depression

Low-intensity psychosocial interventions, psychological interventions, medication and referral for further assessment and interventions

STEP 1: All known and suspected presentations of depression

Assessment, support, psychoeducation, active monitoring and referral for further assessment and interventions

[a] Complex depression includes depression that shows an inadequate response to multiple treatments, is complicated by psychotic symptoms, and/or is associated with significant psychiatric comorbidity or psychosocial factors.
[b] Only for depression where the person also has a chronic physical health problem and associated functional impairment (see NICE Clinical Guideline 91: Depression in Adults with a Chronic Physical Health Problem: Treatment and Management (2009)).

FIGURE 6.1   The stepped care model for treating depression (NICE, 2009, p. 33)

including the provision of: anti-depressants; CBT; interpersonal therapy (IPT); behavioural couples therapy; and counselling or short-term psychodynamic therapy (for patients who decline all the previous options)

Step 4: Complex and severe depression, including the provision of: referral to mental health services, including in-patient care, crisis resolution, and home treatment services.

The guidelines contain much more detail about the specific delivery of such and should be referred to (space does not allow for a fuller discussion here). However, this overview sheds light on some of the main criticisms of the guidelines in what some claim is an over-reliance on CBT, with 'counselling' (typically referring to person-centred counselling) and short-term psychodynamic approaches recommended only for those with mild to moderate depression who have already declined other options. This certainly seems to position counselling as a 'last gasp' option, disregarding what many claim is an extensive evidence base for these interventions (Elliott and Freire, 2008; Gibbard and Hanley, 2008). My own experience of working in mental health services is that many clients talked of great benefits from having received counselling: this does seem to be supported by research, albeit research that does not meet the accepted level for NICE.

There are initiatives to build an evidence base for counselling with IAPT services, with BACP developing manualised guidelines for the delivery of person-centred therapy for depression (Hill, 2011), and arguments for the development of RCTs to investigate the efficacy of counselling for depression (Cooper, 2011).

Counselling and psychotherapy for depression

It might be asserted that a range of counselling and psychotherapy models can potentially offer clients both relief from their symptoms, and as importantly, choice. At a time when life can feel out of control and there is a diminished sense of person efficacy, the capacity to make choices about treatment options seems too great an imperative to limit. I would suggest however, regardless of orientation, that there are key features to consider when beginning work with a depressed client, or in ongoing work. They include:

- Ensuring that the client understands the nature of therapy being offered and the nature of its intention to help
- Undertaking a careful assessment (in whatever way consistent with your model of practice), paying attention to those factors that might indicate depression
- Where depression is suspected but not yet diagnosed, carefully considering suggesting to the client that they additionally consult with their GP (remembering that no one single approach to supporting depression is necessarily the 'right' one). If the client does not wish to speak to their GP, that should be respected, unless high risk is suspected – see later in the chapter for details
- Taking a holistic approach to working with depression, remembering that social and physical factors are as relevant and important to the client as psychological ones
- Ensuring that sessions are scheduled for when the client is best able to make use of them (for example, early morning sessions might be difficult for a client with disrupted sleep patterns)
- Ensuring that you ask the client about any prescribed medication. While you do not need to be an 'expert' in medication, it is helpful to ask questions such as, 'How does your medication affect you?' Again, this can help inform the nature and timing of counselling to best help the client
- Ensuring regular reviews so the client can monitor their own progress
- As with anxiety, helping the client to understand the nature of their fluctuating mood so that they can determine their own 'tolerance level'. That is, monitor and understand their mood and the normal fluctuations day by day
- Paying careful attention to the risk of suicide or self-harm, both strongly associated with depression.

Following these general pointers, clients can be greatly helped by the provision of counselling and psychotherapy, both to understand the nature of their experience and also to help reduce the disabling effects of it. Counselling for depression is also discussed in Chapter 12, with the development of the Counselling for Depression resources by BACP (see Websites below for more information).

W E B S I T E S

Depression Alliance: www.depressionalliance.org/
Mind (Depression): www.mind.org.uk/help/diagnoses_and_conditions/depression
Royal College of Psychiatrists (Depression): www.rcpsych.ac.uk/mentalhealthinfoforall/problems/depression/depression.aspx
BACP Counselling for Depression: www.bacp.co.uk/learning/Counselling%20for%20Depression/index.php

DISCUSSION QUESTIONS

1 What physical, social and psychological factors might trigger a period of depression?
2 What do you think are the benefits and difficulties of a stepped care approach to working with depression?
3 How helpful do you consider the diagnostic criteria for the different types of depression to be for work with clients?
4 How might you and your client assess collaboratively their experience of depression?

6.5 POST-TRAUMATIC STRESS DISORDER

SECTION OUTLINE

Both post-traumatic stress disorder and acute stress disorder are responses to highly stressful or traumatic events. Our understanding of traumatic responses and the associated treatments have (relatively recently) developed considerably. This section defines post-traumatic stress disorder and acute stress disorder and considers some of the counselling and psychotherapy approaches that can benefit clients.

Definition

I write in the section overview that post-traumatic stress disorder (PTSD) and acute stress disorder (ASD) are relatively new diagnoses. In terms of their psychiatric classification they are, emerging only in the 1950s and 1960s. However, the phenomenon of a major psychological response to traumatic events has been known of for many decades, and experienced for centuries, even though conceptually understood differently prior to knowledge of how the 'mind' developed. Over the course of the 20th century PTSD was called different things at different times. For example, soldiers returning from battle in World War One were described as having combat fatigue or shell shock, whereas in the American civil war the term 'soldier's heart' was coined. For all of these different terms, the same psychological processes were being described, including:

- Re-experiencing: flashbacks, nightmares, or repetitive distressing images or symptoms
- Avoidance: a strong desire to avoid situations where the original experience occurred
- Hypervigilance: difficulty in relaxing and being very aware of potential stressors; easily startled
- Emotional numbing: cutting off from feelings, sometimes feeling guilty and appearing introspective
- Other symptoms: which can include depression, anxiety and panic, and phobias. (NHS, 2011)

From other sections in this chapter, such as those on depression, and anxiety and panic it will be quickly apparent that there are important overlaps between a diagnosis of PTSD and generalised anxiety disorder. Differentiating between these diagnoses is an important aspect of assessment. The clear existence of a recent trauma is obviously indicative that the person may be experiencing PTSD, however matters are not necessarily that straightforward. For example, PTSD has been associated with childhood sexual abuse (Jonas et al., 2011). An adult client presenting in counselling and psychotherapy might not disclose their previous experiences of abuse, and yet may be experiencing psychological distress in the present. The link between their early traumatic experience and their current presentation might not be apparent and so an important process may be overlooked.

The DSM defines PTSD as:

the development of characteristic symptoms following exposure to an extreme traumatic stressor involving direct personal experience of an event that involves actual or threatened death or serious injury, or other threat to one's physical integrity; or witnessing an event that involves death, injury, or a threat to the physical integrity of another person; or learning about unexpected or violent death, serious harm, or threat of death or injury experienced by a family member or other close associate. (p. 463)

It is important to note that, for a diagnosis of PTSD, there needs to be 'recurrent and intrusive' (p. 468) memories of the traumatic event for more than one month following the event, which leads to a number of psychological consequences, including: sleep disturbance, irritability, difficulty in concentrating, and an exaggerated startle response. Acute stress disorder is defined as, 'the development or characteristic anxiety, dissociative, and other symptoms that occurs within 1 month after exposure to an extreme traumatic stressor' (p. 469).

As can be seen, the primary difference between a diagnosis of PTSD and ASD is timescale: a PTSD diagnosis can only be made after a minimum of one month duration, whereas a diagnosis of ASD can only be made up to a maximum of one month.

PAUSE FOR REFLECTION

Consider your responses to the diagnosis of PTSD and another psychiatric diagnosis (depression or psychosis, for example). PTSD is more widely 'accepted' in counselling and psychotherapy approaches, whereas, for example, a diagnosis of psychosis is more likely to be philosophically rejected as medicalising human experience. Why do you imagine some diagnoses are more acceptable than others? What is your view?

The emerging influence of neuropsychology and trauma

While trauma has, for many years, been seen as a psychological process, a great deal of research over the years has identified an important physiological dimension too, with an understanding of brain function central to our understanding of how traumatic memories are processed. While it is not possible to present the findings in detail here (I recommend some further reading at the end of this section), it is possible to present a summary. To do this, knowledge of a little basic brain physiology is required. The relevant information is outlined in Figure 6.2.

The development of neuropsychology has provided further insight into how and why traumatic memory differs from non-traumatic memory and thus how counselling and psychotherapy can, in turn, be developed. The following section discusses counselling and psychotherapy for PTSD in a little more detail.

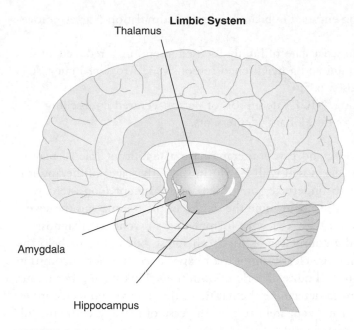

The **thalamus** receives sensory information of an event and turns that information into brain 'language'. It is then processed by the **amygdala** which processes the emotional significance of the event, while the **hippocampus** provides mediating information – declarative memory (e.g. seeing a lion in real life will invoke a 'fight or flight' response (amygdale-driven), whereas seeing it on television will not (amygdala response is mediated by information from the hippocampus). In trauma, this system is interrupted and thus the person experiences an amygdala-driven response not mediated by the hippocampus (e.g. this is not happening now; I am not in the same situation). Traumatic memories are stored in two separate but interacting systems: verbally accessible memory (VAM: conscious representation of event) and situationally accessible memory (SAM: unconscious representation of event)

FIGURE 6.2   How the brain processes memory

FURTHER READING

Vasterling, J.J. and Brewin, C.R. (2005) *Neuropsychology of PTSD: Biological, Cognitive, and Clinical Perspectives.* London: Guilford Press.

Counselling and psychotherapy for PTSD

The UK NICE guidelines (NICE, 2005) for PTSD identify the following treatments:

- Cognitive-behavioural therapy
- Exposure therapy: a means of confronting trauma memories
- Cognitive therapy: to become aware of and modify negative cognitions
- Stress management: such as relaxation, breathing, positive thinking etc.
- Eye movement desensitisation and reprocessing (EMDR): developed by Shapiro (1989), the aim of EMDR is to help the client reprocess their memory while

at the same time being engaged in bilateral physical stimulation (e.g. eye movements, taps, tones etc.).

- Hypnotherapy: to 'induce a state of highly focused attention, a reduced awareness of peripheral stimuli and a heightened responsiveness to social cues (suggestability)' (NICE, 2005 p. 56)
- 'Supportive' counselling: NICE's definition of person-centred counselling
- Medication: typically the use of anti-depressants.

As can be seen, counselling and psychotherapy have a significant role to play in the support for someone diagnosed with PTSD. In the early stages of therapy, it is helpful for the therapist to undertake some form of assessment (consistent with the therapeutic model used) to determine the nature of the trauma and the severity of symptoms. This is not with a view to formulating a psychiatric diagnosis, as that is not the role of the counsellor or psychotherapist, but rather to help the therapist and client think more clearly about their experience. It is not uncommon for a traumatised client to feel quite chaotic in both their thinking and behaviour. An early assessment helps to determine the nature of the trauma and to identify a trauma if it is not immediately apparent (e.g. in the case of therapy with an adult survivor of childhood sexual abuse).

Providing a safe and predictable space for the individual to consider their thoughts and feelings is very important. In my own experience, clients have not always wanted to re-visit their traumatic experience. Unless you have the necessary experience and skills it is important not to pursue this line of exploration as the danger of re-traumatisation (experiencing the same level of distress as during the original trauma), is high. I have known many clients who have chosen not to talk about the specific details of their experience and yet, by their own account, have felt significantly stronger and better able to cope because of therapy. Again, it is important (consistent with your therapeutic model and way of working) to provide space and time to consider specific coping strategies – not dissimilar to when supporting a client experiencing high anxiety or panic – as a means of addressing some of the worst feelings. If a client can feel that they are better able to cope with and survive their feelings, the world becomes a less frightening place and the symptoms of trauma can reduce.

Therapist self-care and vicarious trauma

All counselling and psychotherapy involves hearing a client's story and paying attention to their detail. Inevitably, working with a client who has experienced a major trauma can involve listening to highly distressing or shocking accounts. For example, hearing details of abuse, assault, of clients having been involved in a major disaster, can be profoundly distressing both for the client and therapist alike. I recall my own distress while working in a mental health crisis team of visiting a woman who had witnessed a road traffic accident involving her five-year-old child. As she talked in detail, recounting her worst memories, I can still recall the impact her story had on me, and the nightmares that followed for a while.

Vicarious trauma (McCann and Pearlman, 1990), describes the impact on the 'helper' (e.g. therapist, support worker, GP) because of an empathic supportive relationship with a trauma survivor. It may be defined as:

> transformation in the helper's inner sense of identity and existence that results from utilising controlled empathy when listening to clients' trauma-content narratives. In other words, Vicarious Trauma is what happens to your neurological (or cognitive), physical, psychological, emotional and spiritual health when you listen to traumatic stories day after day or respond to traumatic situations while having to control your reaction. (Vicarious Trauma Institute, 2012)

This can, over a sustained period, lead to 'burn-out', where the 'helper' is no longer able to create or sustain an empathic helping relationship and instead experiences anger, resentment and distress when exposed to someone else's psychological needs. The need for therapist self-care is important (and indeed an ethical requirement) in all therapeutic relationships. This is particularly the case when working with trauma. Self-care is discussed in more detail in Chapter 10. In summary, it involves:

- Ensuring good quality supervision is in place with an experienced supervisor
- Seeking personal therapy, if required
- Managing client caseloads to ensure there isn't an over-representation of trauma work
- Taking breaks from practice, as and when required
- Having access to peer support (mindful of confidentiality), to discuss and share the impact of work on 'self'
- Creating a clear distinction between 'work' and 'home', ensuring one doesn't intrude on the other
- Putting in place clear self-care strategies, such as time for hobbies like walking and music, ensuring there is time for physical exercise
- A space for debriefing work soon after sessions have finished.

Trauma is very likely to present to most counsellors and psychotherapists in their work. An understanding of what is meant by PTSD and ASD can support you in your work with such clients. As with all work, it is important to refer on to another therapist or specialist agency if the needs of the client outweigh your competence and ability to meet them.

WEBSITES

NICE (PTSD): http://guidance.nice.org.uk/CG26/Guidance/pdf
Mind (PTSD): www.mind.org.uk/help/diagnoses_and_conditions/post-traumatic_stress_disorder
Royal College of Psychiatrists (PTSD): www.rcpsych.ac.uk/mentalhealthinfo/problems/ptsd/posttraumaticstressdisorder.aspx

DISCUSSION QUESTIONS

1 What types of situations might constitute a 'trauma'?
2 From the list you have developed for the previous question, what are the main similarities and differences between situations?
3 How might you assess for trauma when beginning to work with a client?
4 How does your preferred model of working help you to understand trauma and how to work with clients who present with PTSD or ASD?

6.6 EATING DISORDERS

SECTION OUTLINE

The number of clients presenting in mental health settings with eating disorders has increased significantly over the last ten years or so. Counsellors and psychotherapists are very likely to meet clients who present with disordered eating. This section: (a) identifies the primary eating disorders; (b) explores how they might present in counselling and psychotherapy; (c) discusses appropriate assessment; and (d) outlines some models for treating eating disorders.

Definition

Many therapists will talk about eating disorders, using the two primary diagnostic categories, anorexia nervosa and bulimia nervosa, without ever having really considered what those diagnostic categories mean. Likewise, it is not uncommon for clients to present in counselling and psychotherapy, telling their therapists that they have an 'eating disorder' that might, on further exploration, mean that they have lost their appetite. Like 'depression', the term 'eating disorders' has moved from the specialist language of mental health into the mainstream and, in the process of doing so, has lost some of its meaning and potency.

As with depression it is, however, important not to become diagnosis-centred. When a client talks of their 'eating disorder', whether or not their presentation meets the diagnostic criteria for the label, they are telling something of their experience of themselves and their lives, and must always be listened to. Nevertheless, it is useful to begin our discussion of eating disorders here by clearly outlining diagnostic definitions.

Anorexia nervosa is defined by DSM as applying to 'an individual [who] refuses to maintain a minimally normal body weight, is intensely afraid of gaining weight, and exhibits a significant disturbance in the perception of the shape or size of his or her body. The individual maintains a body weight that is below a minimally normal level for age and height' (p. 583). Bulimia nervosa, as defined by DSM, refers to 'binge eating and inappropriate compensatory methods to prevent weight gain. In addition, the self-evaluation of individuals with bulimia nervosa is excessively influenced by body shape and weight' (p. 589).

The two diagnostic categories are similar when outlined in DSM, but are essentially differentiated by the fact that anorexia bulimia is focused on weight reduction through fasting, whereas bulimia nervosa is characterised by binge-eating and the management of weight and body size through purging or non-purging type behaviours. This point is important because it has been my experience that many assume an individual has bulimia nervosa only if they are also self-inducing vomiting. In my own experience of working with young people with bulimia, many will present with a non-purging type and may instead be involved in excessive exercise. We also need to differentiate eating disorders from body dysmorphia, which involves poor body image and a set of beliefs about parts of the body being particularly ugly. While this can include being overweight, it does not involve behaviours that would be defined as anorexic or bulimic.

Causes of anorexia nervosa and bulimia nervosa

The causes of both anorexia nervosa and bulimia nervosa are many and will vary greatly from individual to individual. There has been extensive research into both the causes and treatment of anorexia and bulimia (Morris, 2008; Thompson-Brenner et al., 2009). The relationship between a media representation of how women should look and the 'size 0' 'ideal' for models is worthy of mention. Feminists have argued that the male-dominated 'ownership' of the female body has contributed to high numbers of women with poor body image, low self-esteem and thus motivations to manage their body size and weight through controlling their food intake (Fallon et al., 1996). Women particularly are introduced to the socially accepted concept of diets and dieting (and the multi-million pound industry that supports it) in early adolescence. Recent research has also pointed to the potentially damaging effect on the development of self-esteem in the early sexualisation of young girls, through the selling of particular types of clothing, make-up and diets (Papadopoulos, 2010).

A similar trend can be observed for males. Whereas the 'body-image industry' was typically a female-centred one, advertisers and publishers have recently realised the potential money available in targeting male body image. Perhaps there is no coincidence in the increasing numbers of young men presenting with anorexia, bulimia and poor body image since the plethora of men's health magazines hit the stands. Whereas for females the 'perfect' tends to centre on body size, for men 'perfect' tends to focus on body shape, with the 'ideal male' possessing the six-pack, broad shoulders and well-muscled body. For women and men alike, the pressure to conform to society's image of what female and male should be is enormous and can lead them into self-destructive and potentially life-threatening behaviours (Papadopoulos, 2010). In my own work I have seen many women with disordered eating and have noticed over the last ten years an increasing number of young males presenting for therapy too.

Counselling and psychotherapy for eating disorders

Throughout the UK, and internationally, there are specialised eating disorder services. These services combine a range of therapeutic approaches to the treatment of eating disorders, thus providing the client with a holistic approach, utilising a variety of treatment options, rather than relying on one single way. Holistic approaches will take into account the physical as well as emotional wellbeing of the client and will provide for careful monitoring of the person's physical health.

Severe eating disorders can be life-threatening. If someone's weight drops below a certain threshold specific for that individual's gender, age and other physical factors, the danger of death is very high. While it is avoided if at all possible, the option remains for an individual to be admitted compulsorily to a mental health unit under mental health legislation for assessment and treatment, which can include feeding. While these are exceptional circumstances, they show the need for careful medical monitoring of the physical wellbeing of someone with an eating disorder.

Eating disorder services provide monitoring in situ and, if at all possible, it is advisable to suggest to a client they speak with their GP about arranging a referral (usually eating disorder services require a GP referral as opposed to one from a therapist). However, while eating disorder services exist and generally are the preferred course of treatment for someone with eating-related problems, they are generally under-funded and therefore have long waiting lists. The two options that remain therefore are to begin counselling and psychotherapy while a client is waiting for their refer-ral to an eating disorder service to be accepted, or to contract for therapy as an alternative to a referral.

If working with someone who has an eating disorder, a careful assessment should be undertaken (or an informed exploration of the nature of the prob-lems consistent with orientation is made). The NICE guidelines for the treatment of eating disorders (NICE, 2004a) identify the following broad areas for assessment:

- Current and past physical health and treatment
- Cognitive abilities
- Any present physical disabilities
- A historical and current assessment of family and interpersonal relationships
- Mental state and personality factors
- Social circumstances and supports
- Occupational and social functioning
- Educational and vocational needs.
  (NICE, 2004a, p. 36)

From the point of view of counselling or psychotherapy, the following additional factors should be considered:

- Understanding of the therapeutic process and willingness to engage
- Willingness for the appropriate and informed liaison between therapist and others involved in providing care (e.g. GP)
- Preferably a recent health check by a GP and plans for ongoing monitoring of physical health needs
- Clearly defined and agreed boundaries of confidentiality should physical or mental health seriously deteriorate
- An agreement between therapist and client about the focus of the therapy (which might or might not be eating or food).

The final point in the above list is interesting to note. While many of the psycho-logical therapies recommended for people with eating disorders focus on the behaviour of the eating (or not eating) and the client's attitude to food, some argue that instead it is better to focus on the cause of the problem (e.g. low self-esteem; family history; traumatic event; socioeconomic factors), rather than the symptoms related to the cause (e.g. the eating disorder itself). The approach will in part depend on your orientation and how you prefer to work. Many of the psychological treatments recommended in the NICE guidelines make use of CBT or cognitive or behavioural approaches. If this is consistent with your preferred model of working then it would be entirely appropriate to focus on the nature of the behaviour and facilitate change at that level. If, however, your orientation would not normally include such approaches, an exploration of the underlying issues might be more appropriate.

In my own practice I tend not to focus on the eating disorder *per se*, nor on the use and misuse of food. I actively and openly move away from discussion of 'good' or 'bad' food (as clients often term it), and instead focus on their wider sense of self, seeing the eating disorder as a means of coping with underlying distress (not dissimilar to that of self-harm or self-injury). I am not suggesting this is the 'right' approach, and certainly the use of CBT approaches is well evidenced (Fairburn, 2008), however it is an approach that has worked with many clients. Where a client specifically wishes to focus on their disordered eating, however, it is always advisable to suggest they speak with their GP for a referral to a specialist service for eating disorders if you do not have the necessary knowledge and skills to undertake such specific work.

As with many serious mental health problems, counsellors or psychotherapists should begin therapy with clients who experience such problems only if they are competent to do so and have the support of a suitably experienced therapy supervisor. A range of interventions have the potential to be of help to clients with eating disorders, but the likelihood of improvement is enhanced if a holistic approach is adopted, such as psychological treatments, physical health care monitoring, family therapy, sound dietary advice and social support. This integrated approach is probably best achieved through a specific eating disorder service. However, a range of counselling and psychotherapy approaches can provide such clients with the necessary space and time to explore not only their behaviour, but also the origins of their behaviour and the nature of their distress.

WEBSITES

Mind (Eating Problems): www.mind.org.uk/help/diagnoses_and_conditions/eating_distress
Beat: www.b-eat.co.uk/
Royal College of Psychiatrists (Eating Problems): www.rcpsych.ac.uk/mental healthinfoforall/problems/eatingdisorders.aspx

DISCUSSION QUESTIONS

1   What do you consider to be the main causes of eating disorders, and why?
2   How would you work with a client with an eating-related problem? For example, to what extent would you prefer to focus on the eating problem itself or on the underlying causes? Why?
3   Are there any specialised eating disorder services in your locality? If so, what do you know about the services they offer and how they accept referrals?
4   How would you monitor therapeutic progress when working with a client who presents with an eating disorder? How would you use supervision accordingly?

6.7 LOSS AND BEREAVEMENT

SECTION OUTLINE

Loss and bereavement are arguably an unavoidable aspect of living. We will all experience loss (in whatever form) and bereavement at some stage in our lives. For many this is a difficult process that they will work through in their own time and way. For others, however, bereavement can present particular difficulties and they might turn to counselling or psychotherapy to help them through. This section defines loss and bereavement and then considers (a) when the process might become difficult for clients and (b) how counselling and psychotherapy can help.

Definitions

Cruse Bereavement Care, a UK counselling and support charity, states:

> bereavement will be the most psychologically distressing experience we will ever face. Grief is what we feel when somebody we love dies. The death of a significant person is a devastating loss. Everyone experiences grief differently and there is no 'normal' or 'right' way to grieve. How we react will be influenced by many different things, including our age and personality, or cultural background and religious beliefs, our previous experiences of bereavement, our circumstances and how we cope with loss. (Cruse, 2012)

Bereavement can be the death of someone close to us, but also the loss of something else in our life that had a significant place in it, such as a job, family pet, house etc. Grieving is the process we go through after a bereavement; the process of adjustment and mourning that will ultimately enable us to make a psychological accommodation for the loss we have experienced.

With these definitions in mind, it is clearly apparent that each one of us will, at some stage in our lives, experience bereavement and be thrown into the profound process that is grieving. Certainly when my own father died of cancer I found myself in emotional turmoil, awash with anger, rage, but also a sense of hopelessness and apathy in the face of something I couldn't easily reconcile or explain. I held on to the notion that this was a 'normal' process, albeit an extremely distressing and unwelcome one, and trusted that I would navigate my own way through it, even though every moment of grief was new and unknown. And so it happened: the sharp pain of loss gave way to a dull ache which, in turn, gave way to an eventual acceptance of the reality of his death. I had worked through my grieving. That said, there are times now when the sharpness can return, unexpectedly, but that is the nature of grief. We understand the process of grief not as an ordered and sequential one, passing each 'stage' neatly and in order, but instead one in which we move between stages and over time.

The grieving process

Much has been written of the grieving process and our understanding of this has changed over time (Kubler-Ross, 1973; Worden, 2009). Even in my own working lifetime the perspective we have on grieving has shifted dramatically. I recall being taught that the stages of grieving begin at point A, and move slowly and carefully, point by point, until the final stage is reached. We now understand that the process of grieving is much more chaotic – and less ordered – than that. We can move backwards and forwards between different stages, but the direction of travel may still be a healing one. While there are commonalities behind the shared human experience of grief, there is now a much greater acknowledgement of the individual and unique journey we each travel. As the Cruse quotation has it, our journeys are 'influenced by many different things'.

There are several different 'takes' on the stages of grief. Box 6.8 outlines a six-stage model.

BOX 6.8   SIX STAGES OF GRIEF

Shock and denial: In the immediacy of loss we can deny the reality of it, a psychological anaesthetic against the awfulness of what we are experiencing.

Pain and guilt: As the 'anaesthetic' wears off we are left with unbearable pain, sometimes associated with a sense of guilt about what we might or might not have said or done. In traumatic circumstances there can be 'survivor guilt', where we feel we should have died instead.

Anger and bargaining: The pain can turn into rage, and a sense of fury at the injustice of what we have experienced. As a means of ameliorating that we turn to bargaining: 'I would do anything to turn back time.'

Reflection and loneliness: We become more self-reflective, sometimes turning away from the 'external' world and moving into a lonelier 'internal' one.

Reconstruction: We begin a process of putting the pieces back together, and for the first time having a sense of future and hope.

Acceptance: We begin to accept the reality of our loss and accommodate it into our life (but not 'getting over it').

These stages are probably recognised by everyone reading this who has experienced loss. Some of the stages might not be experienced at all, while others might be experienced more acutely or severely. Some people never reach full acceptance, never quite reconciling themselves to their experience, but still managing to get on with their lives successfully and relatively happily.

When grieving gets 'stuck'

The premise of the subtitle above is that grief is a dynamic and moving process, shifting between different stages. Knowing when the 'normal' process of grief is becoming problematic, perhaps when someone finds it difficult to move on, is extremely difficult. It is not uncommon for people to present in counselling and psychotherapy having felt the same thing (such as anger or denial) for many years. These feelings can be very confusing and distressing; the person intellectually knows their feelings or responses are unhelpful and are getting in the way of them living their life, yet feels unable to shift anything. This is sometimes known as 'complicated grief'; the person needs help to function more effectively.

The DSM notes that sometimes grief may present as a major depressive episode, as the symptoms (such as feelings of sadness, poor appetite or weight loss) are very similar. Defining a 'normal' grief reaction is difficult because of differences of age, gender and culture, for example. There will be different rituals and accepted behaviours according not only to macro cultural differences, but also micro differences (such as region or geographical area). A socially acceptable response for a young male may be very different to the acceptable response for an older female. Much is dependent on the contextual defining factors of the individual concerned. Therefore, any attempt to judge 'abnormal' must be seen within the context of what is 'normal' for that individual. Careful assessment here is important. DSM states that a diagnosis of major depressive disorder is not given unless the symptoms are present at least two months after the loss. Additionally, the DSM (pp. 740–1) identifies the following six indicators for differentiating between a 'normal' grief response and a major depressive episode:

1   Guilt about things other than actions taken or not taken by the survivor at the time of death
2   Thoughts of death other than the survivor feeling that he or she would be better off dead or should have died with the deceased person
3   Morbid preoccupation with worthlessness
4   Marked psychomotor retardation
5   Prolonged and marked functional impairment
6   Hallucinatory experiences other than thinking that he or she hears the voice of, or transiently sees the image of, the deceased person.

Counselling and psychotherapy for loss and bereavement

Few would doubt the benefits of counselling and psychotherapy for bereavement and loss and much of the work of the counsellor and psychotherapist in practice will be to do with these areas of human experience. Western culture does not allow death and dying to sit comfortably within it: there is much focus on the avoidance of ageing and of death itself. Even in language it is difficult to talk of death or dying: one relies instead on euphemisms such as 'going to sleep' or 'passing on' to communicate an otherwise stark reality. Beyond bereavement through death, other losses often prove too difficult for us to talk about – physical illness and unemployment, for example. Many people will be aware of how difficult it is to talk to family or friends about their feelings, finding that counselling and psychotherapy provides a rare and invaluable space to explore their deepest distress.

We should not underestimate the importance of simply listening attentively and providing an uninterrupted space for the client to talk about their loss and subsequent feelings. Many clients will reflect on the restorative factor of being heard and of freeing themselves of the perceived shame of grief. It can be helpful too for counsellors and psychotherapists to 'normalise' the grief process, perhaps by providing information about the stages of grief, and by giving 'permission' for the person to grieve without the imperative of time constraints. One of the most common phrases I have heard in therapy over the years has been 'I should be over it by now'; simply affirming the right of the individual to take their own time in processing their experience can be therapy enough.

The psycho-educational aspect should not be underestimated. Many bereaved clients will come to counselling and psychotherapy in a state of chaos and confusion, perhaps never having experienced such profound feelings before. The sense of relief I have seen on faces as I have outlined the process of grieving and the feelings it might stir can be palpable. Timing is important too, however. My own work in a university setting often sees young people attending for 'bereavement counselling' immediately following the death or loss. While clearly a careful assessment needs to be made about their individual support needs, generally our advice is to take some time and to allow the grieving process to happen. It is my own view that counselling or psychotherapy for grief very early on in the process is generally not helpful. The danger is of pathologising what is essentially a normal human experience, and of trying to facilitate a person's exploration of their feelings when perhaps they are still emotionally 'anaesthetised'. Affirming the availability of later support when they are ready for it (and not at the behest of another) is often all that is needed in those early stages.

Finally it is important to keep an open mind about the potential for other mental health distress. Given that loss and bereavement has an enormous psychological impact, it is entirely possible that the process of grieving will trigger other mental health needs, such as depression (as outlined previously), trauma or occasionally psychosis. The counsellor or psychotherapist needs to keep such possibilities in mind and, if in doubt, to suggest to the client that they consult with the GP if any presentation seems to fall outside a 'normal' range (for the individual).

Continuing bonds

Continuing bonds challenges the primary assumptions of existing theories of bereavement and grieving (Klass et al., 1984). It has been argued that previous theories about loss and adjustment have focused on the task of the individual to break the attachment with the deceased person as a means of accommodating and ultimately accepting the loss. The theory of continuing bonds, however, asserts that the task of grieving is to find a new attachment to the deceased individual, and that the attachment – or bond – is continuing. According to this view, we essentially redefine our relationship with the deceased person, as opposed to viewing it as at an end. If the continuing bonds theory is viewed within the context of theories of attachment, it makes a great deal of sense. The attachment to the individual is formed and remains, even if that individual is no longer physically present. The nature and form of the attachment can change to accommodate the new circumstances (Field et al., 2005).

How we understand bereavement and loss for clients can be importantly shaped by our own reflections of loss and the processes we subsequently worked through. Certainly, my own experience of my father's death has been extremely important in helping me to empathise (but not identify) with clients I have seen. Empathy, congruence and acceptance remain important principles in providing a stable base from which clients can step out of the chaos.

WEBSITES

CRUSE Bereavement Care: www.crusebereavementcare.org.uk/
Mind (Bereavement): www.mind.org.uk/help/diagnoses_and_conditions/bereavement
Royal College of Psychiatrists (Bereavement): www.rcpsych.ac.uk/mental healthinfoforall/problems/bereavement.aspx

DISCUSSION QUESTIONS

1 Think of an important loss in your life. How did it make you feel and how did you cope?
2 What might be the signs of a grief that is 'stuck', and how would you respond?
3 Consider your own counselling or psychotherapy context: how do macro and micro cultural differences inform (a) your understanding of grieving and (b) your client's understanding of grieving?
4 How might you incorporate the continuing bonds theory into your work with bereaved clients?

6.8 SUICIDE AND SELF-HARM

SECTION OUTLINE

Working with clients who present at risk of suicide or who self-harm can be personally and professionally challenging for counsellors and psychotherapists. This section considers what is meant by suicide and self-harm and how these might present in therapy. It then outlines strategies that practitioners can employ when working with these issues.

We can explore the topics of suicide and self-harm through the cases of Adrian and Evene in Boxes 6.9 and 6.10.

CASE STUDY 6.9
Adrian

Adrian is a 23-year-old man who has recently experienced a relationship breakdown. In counselling he talks of relationships never working for him and how people will always let him down. He has been feeling depressed for some time and feels increasingly hopeless. He says that it would be much better if he were 'out of people's way'.

CASE STUDY 6.10
Evene

Evene is 31 years old. She attends counselling because of what she describes as low self-esteem. She doesn't get on with her family, feeling that her mother has never really been interested in her. Her father left the family home when she was nine. She has been self-injuring for several years (cutting her arms and legs), and wants to try to stop.

In these two scenarios we can see how suicide and self-harm present quite differently: one an expression of hopelessness and of not wanting to live, while the other is about a means of survival and coping, albeit a strategy that has run its course. Adrian cannot see a way forward and appears to have lost any sense of his value in other people's lives, while Evene wants to put self-harming behind her and possibly find a new way of being. However, both scenarios in their different ways present challenges for the practitioner, including:

1   How to find a way of talking about suicide
2   How to find a way of talking about self-harm
3   How to make use of 'risk factors' to help inform support options
4   How to manage issues of confidentiality when risk is presented
5   How the therapist copes with their own responses to suicide
6   How the therapist copes with their own responses to self-harm
7   How the therapist makes use of consultation and supervision to inform practice.

Suicide

The World Health Organisation (WHO) defines suicide simply as 'the act of deliberately killing oneself' (WHO, 2012b). The definition of suicide is probably less helpful to counsellors and psychotherapists than a definition of suicidal, which is much more complex. Suicide is a completed act, whereas 'suicidal' refers more to a state of being. It is determining this state of being that is perhaps most difficult and challenging for therapist and client alike. Constraints of space do not permit a fuller exploration here of what suicidal means; that can be found in Reeves (2010a) and Leenaars (1994). However, suicide risk can present in several ways:

- Suicidal thoughts can be in response to an immediate or ongoing crisis, e.g. illness, trauma. A decision can be made to end one's life, with the person working to that event in a planned and thoughtful way, such as in the managing of personal affairs and writing suicide notes.
- Suicidal thoughts can be ongoing and persistent. Keeping in mind the possibility of ending life can, for many, be sufficient in helping them stay alive.
- Suicidal thoughts can emerge from profound mental health distress, such as depression and psychosis, for example.
- Suicidal thoughts can be fleeting and transient – more general in nature and never developing with any degree of intent.
- Suicidal thoughts can be impulsive – in immediate response to a short-term crisis, and can diminish and go as quickly as they were triggered – this is particularly the case for young people who, in general terms, are less likely to have the emotional resilience to cope with crisis.

While the above points run the danger of reducing a very complex human process, they do provide a general overview of how suicidal potential might present.

Self-harm

Babiker and Arnold (1997, p. 2) define self-harm as 'an act which involves deliberately inflicting pain and/or injury to one's body, but without suicidal intent', while the National Institute for Health and Clinical Excellence state that self-harm is 'self-poisoning or injury, irrespective of the apparent purpose of the act' and that 'self-harm is an expression of personal distress, not an illness, and there are many varied reasons for a person to harm him or herself' (NICE, 2004b, p. 7).

Babiker and Arnold's definition draws out a distinction between self-harm and suicidal ideation when they state '... but without suicidal intent'. A generally held view is that self-harm is usually used as a coping strategy against profound or overwhelming feelings of distress (anger, hurt, rage, low self-esteem) and is a means of living, rather than dying. A report by the Royal College of Psychiatrists in the

UK stated 'an act of self-harm is not necessarily an attempt or even indicator of suicide, indeed it can sometimes be a bizarre form of self-preservation' (Royal College of Psychiatrists, 2010, p. 6). However, it is important to keep in mind that on occasions self-harm can be sufficiently severe or chaotic that the behaviour becomes a risk to life, with or without that intention. Certainly self-harm is correlated with a higher risk of suicide.

Terms such as self-harm and self-injury are, inaccurately, used interchangeably to describe the same behaviour. Specifically, self-injury is a term used to describe specific injury caused to the person through a self-directed act (such as cutting, burning, breaking etc.), whereas self-harm can describe a wider range of behaviours that cause harm indirectly (such as over-exercise, binge drinking or sexual risk taking). The difference here is whether harm is caused directly and immediately, or whether harm is indirectly caused. Harm can, of course, also occur as an act of omission, such as starving or lack of self-care.

The relationship between self-harm and suicide

In accepting the broad definitions given above, it is worth keeping in mind that they are not mutually exclusive. It is an easy mistake for counsellors and psychotherapists to believe that self-harm/self-injury generally concerns coping and living, whereas suicide generally concerns wanting to die. Consider the case example in Box 6.11.

CASE STUDY 6.11
Suzanne

Suzanne is a 29-year-old woman who has experienced severe mental health distress for many years. She is known to mental health services and contacts a 24-hour crisis line regularly. She has, for some time, taken small overdoses that usually result in her attending a hospital Accident and Emergency department for treatment. On exploration she is clear that this behaviour is not with an intent to die, but rather is a form of self-harm. As time progresses her actions become more severe in an attempt to achieve the same emotional response. That is, Suzanne begins to take bigger overdoses to elicit the same personal response. This continues until it becomes clear that the overdoses Suzanne is taking have high potential to kill. Suzanne's self-harming has become life-threatening; her actions are no longer simply about living.

This is an interesting situation, taken from my own working experience as a counsellor. When I explored it with Suzanne, she had not consciously made the link that her behaviour had become life-threatening. She was genuinely shocked when she realised this was the case. It was important for me as her therapist to keep open this possibility and not assume that self-harm is always about self-preservation. It is important for us to carefully explore with clients their thoughts, motives and feelings. Of course, this situation might have spoken of Suzanne's unconscious or passive wish to be dead, which was important to pick up in our work together.

Risk factors

Known risk factors are important knowledge for counsellors and psychotherapists to possess, though they should not become risk factor-driven. It is very easy to tick a few boxes of a risk assessment form and consider that an exploration of risk has been conducted. I have argued elsewhere for the importance of a full and open dialogue with clients about suicide and self-harm (Reeves, 2010a). Table 6.1 presents a summary of risk factors.

TABLE 6.1   Suicide risk factors

Gender: e.g. males generally present with greater risk across age groups
Age: e.g. males aged 14–25 and people over 75 years
Relationships: single, widowed, divorced, separated
Social isolation
Psychopathology (including):
   Schizophrenia
   Mood disorders, including depression
   Psychosis
   Post-traumatic stress disorder
   Affective disorders, including bipolar affective disorder
   Organic disorders
   Personality disorders, e.g. sociopathy, aggression
   Alcohol and drug use
   Hopelessness
Occupational factors, e.g. unemployment, retirement
History of childhood sexual or physical abuse
Adult sexual assault
Specific suicide plan formulated
Prior suicide attempt and/or family history of suicide or suicide attempts
Physical illness, e.g. terminal illness, biochemical, hormonal
Bereavement or recent trauma
Significant and unexplained mood change
Self-harm

Source: Reeves, 2010a, p. 33

It is not possible to accurately gauge the risk of suicide of a client simply through the consideration of these factors, although many risk assessment questionnaires attempt to achieve just that. Rather, it is important for the counsellor or psychotherapist to be willing to ask their client about suicide or self-harm in a way that opens dialogic doors. Asking someone whether things ever get so bad they have considered hurting themselves as a means of coping, or of ending their life, will not put the thought into their mind if it wasn't there before. Instead, it will quickly and effectively communicate to the client that talking about suicidal feelings or self-harm is okay. It will help tackle the silencing stigma or shame that often permeates all talk about such topics. Of course, it is not possible to give here any blueprint of how that dialogue should take place: the phraseology offered is my own and is consistent with how I work. It is important, in supervision and discussion with colleagues, to reflect on how you can ask those questions in a way consistent with how you work.

Key points for practice

Counsellors and psychotherapists should keep the following guidelines in mind when working with clients who are suicidal or who self-harm:

1 Be aware of personally held views about suicide and self-harm, as these will be present in work with clients.
2 In the case of self-harm, challenge the 'them and us' thinking. That is, there aren't, on the one hand, people who self-harm and then, on the other, 'us': we all self-harm to a greater or lesser extent. Reflecting on what we do to cope with feelings that might be harmful can help us achieve a greater connection with our clients.
3 Understand that working with risk can provoke anxiety in the practitioners. Anxiety is not necessarily a 'bad' thing because it can help focus our thinking. Overwhelming anxiety and terror, however, will prevent effective working relationships.
4 Consider whether and how working context and the agency in which you work require any particular form of response to clients at risk (e.g. referral for a specialist assessment).
5 Be aware of the implications of the contract of confidentiality agreed with clients and how the boundaries of those would be managed at times of risk.
6 Be aware of local agencies and mental health services that might be recommended to clients at risk and know how to access such services at times of crisis.
7 Understand relevant policy and research with respect to suicide and self-harm (e.g. suicide prevention strategies).

8   Ensure you are aware of legal and ethical parameters to working with risk.

9   Consider how you will record risk when it presents in therapy sessions, and keep a detailed record of how and why you responded as you did.

10 Always be prepared to ask the 'suicide question' or be willing to talk about self-harm in sessions.

Counsellors and psychotherapists should keep in mind that having the confidence to talk to clients about their most difficult thoughts can be profoundly facilitative and, of itself, reduce levels of risk considerably. For a client to know they can talk freely to their therapist about thoughts or feelings that might otherwise remain unnamed can be very freeing.

DISCUSSION QUESTIONS

1   What are your own views about suicide? (For example, do you believe people have the 'right' to kill themselves if they decide to? Would there ever be exceptions to this?)

2   When stressed, angry or upset, what might you do to cope that would indirectly be harmful? How might this insight inform your work with clients around self-harm?

3   What is your organisation's policy concerning risk? If you are working independently, what are your strategies for working with risk?

4   How might you ask a client about their suicidal thoughts or about self-harm? What factors might prevent you from doing so?

FURTHER READING

Reeves, A. (2010) *Counselling Suicidal Clients*. London: Sage.

WEBSITES

Mind (Suicide): www.mind.org.uk/help/diagnoses_and_conditions/suicidal_feelings
The Samaritans (Mental Health and Suicide): www.samaritans.org/your_emotional_health/publications/mental_health_suicide.aspx

6.9 SEXUAL PROBLEMS

SECTION OUTLINE

Clients with sexual problems often attend counselling and psychotherapy, but feel confused, embarrassed or ashamed about naming their problems. It is important for counsellors and psychotherapists to be both comfortable and confident in talking to their clients about sex and to have some knowledge of sexual difficulties that might present. This section outlines the main sexual problems and provides suggestions for ways of supporting clients with them.

Definitions

Like every other aspect of human experience, sex and sexual problems can present in counselling and psychotherapy sessions. Sometimes clients will be very clear about the nature of their difficulties, while at other times they will present with a number of issues but sexual difficulties will emerge as the therapy progresses and clients feel more comfortable in naming them. Certainly talking about sex and sexual difficulties can present clients with high levels of discomfort and a sense of shame. For all the sexual promiscuity and precociousness of today's society, talking intimately about actual sexual experience and difficulties seems to remain as taboo.

For the purposes of this section I refer to sex as something that either happens for the individual in isolation, or between people. I specifically include here all relationships and sexual experiences, regardless of sexual orientation. Sexual intimacy and subsequent difficulties are as relevant in same-sex relationships as they are in straight relationships. Much of the older literature on sexual difficulties (which still is used to an extent in informing today's therapeutic practice) assumes a heterosexuality that excludes many peoples' experience of their relationships. I specifically include an individual's relationship with themselves sexually, with respect to intimate touch and masturbation, as often this is where difficulties can emanate from and, in turn, start to be addressed.

The human sexual response cycle

Before considering sexual problems, it is worth thinking about sexual experience. The DSM outlines four primary stages of the human sexual response cycle:

desire – excitement – orgasm – resolution (p. 536). This is outlined in Figure 6.4, with an explanation of each stage given. The cycle is similar for both males and females at various stages, but differs importantly too.

Desire: Both males and females will fantasise about sexual activity and will move into a desire to have sexual activity.

Excitement: As the level of sexual excitement increases, there will be accompanying physiological changes. In males this will include tumescence of the penis (swelling) and subsequent erection. In females this will include vasocongestion of the pelvis, vaginal lubrication and expansion, and swelling of the external genitalia.

Orgasm: A peak of sexual pleasure psychologically and physiologically. In males there will be a sense of ejaculatory inevitability (a sense of 'no going back'), followed by ejaculation of semen. In females there are contractions of the wall of the vagina (outer third).

Resolution: Muscular relaxation and sense of physical and emotional ease. Males move into a 'refractory' period where further erection and orgasm are impaired (the time of refraction varies). Females may be able to respond to further sexual stimulation almost immediately.

It is helpful for counsellors and psychotherapists to understand the normal sexual response cycle so that sexual problems can be located within it – and, additionally, so that problems can be differentiated between males and females, where appropriate. This is particularly helpful for a therapist working with a different gender client where identification with sexual experience might not be as easy.

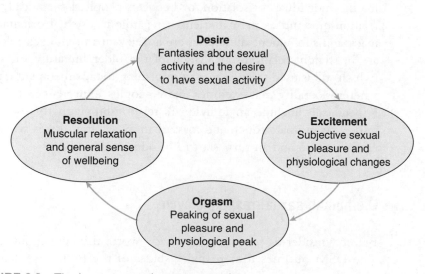

FIGURE 6.3 The human sexual response cycle

Overview of sexual problems

Here I outline a number of primary sexual problems, informed by diagnostic criteria (based on DSM) given where appropriate. It is not my intention to discuss sexual orientation here, as to do so would locate it as a problem, which it isn't. Chapter 9, Working with Diversity and Difference, explores issues for counsellors and psychotherapists in working with gay, lesbian, bisexual and transgendered clients, but in the context of acceptance rather than pathology.

DSM (pp. 536–7) outlines four types of sexual problem that may be distinguished, as follows:

- Lifelong type: where the sexual problem is present since the onset of sexual functioning
- Acquired type: where the sexual problem develops after a period of normal functioning
- Generalised type: where the sexual problem is not limited to certain types of stimulation, situations, or partners
- Situational type: where the sexual problem is limited to certain types of stimulation, situations or partners (but can also include during masturbation).

Hypoactive sexual desire disorder can occur with both males and females and describes deficient or absent sexual fantasies and desire for sexual activity. A judgement of 'deficiency' is made by a clinician taking into account factors such as age and the context of a person's life. We should note that the problem 'causes marked distress or interpersonal difficulty' (p. 498). Sexual aversion disorder relates to persistent or recurrent extreme aversion to, and avoidance of, all or almost all sexual contact with a sexual partner. Again this is applicable to both males and females.

Arousal disorders are differentiated between males and females. For males, there is male erectile disorder, which describes a 'persistent or recurrent in ability to attain, or to maintain until completion of the sexual activity, an adequate erection' (p. 545). For females there is female sexual arousal disorder, which describes a 'persistent or recurrent inability to attain, or to maintain to completion of the sexual activity, an adequate lubrication-swelling response of sexual excitement' (p. 543). We can see here that the differentiation is based purely on physiology.

Orgasmic disorders are again differentiated between males and females. For males, the male orgasmic disorder describes 'persistent or recurrent delay in, or absence of, orgasm following a normal sexual excitement phase' (p. 550). The same set of criteria applies for females also, but goes on to state that, 'Women exhibit wide variability in the type or intensity of stimulation that triggers orgasm' (p. 547). Again, the clinician's judgement here is crucial in deciding whether female orgasm would be 'reasonable for her age, sexual experience, and the adequacy of sexual stimulation she receives' (p. 547). The danger of subjectivity is clearly high.

For males specifically, an issue sometimes discussed in counselling and psychotherapy sessions is premature ejaculation. This phrase refers to the 'persistent or recurrent ejaculation with minimal sexual stimulation before, on, or shortly after penetration and before the person wishes it' (p. 552). I would broaden this definition to include any stimulation, without it necessarily being linked to penetration. This would then include: (a) instances where couples do not wish penetration and (b) masturbation. I have certainly seen many males for whom premature ejaculation during masturbation is problematic and causes 'marked distress or interpersonal difficulty' (p. 552).

Both males and females may experience dyspareunia, which describes genital pain associated with sexual intercourse. Vaginismus is an involuntary contraction of the muscles surrounding the outer third of the vagina when any form of penetration is attempted (not necessarily by a penis). Substance-induced sexual dysfunction describes distress or interpersonal difficulty in males or females when sexual problems are experienced related directly to the use of drugs or medication. Four specific aspects may apply in this instance: impaired desire; impaired arousal; impaired orgasm; and sexual pain. Finally gender identity disorder, again pertinent for both males and females, is a 'strong and persistent cross-gender identification (not merely a desire for any perceived cultural advantages of being the other sex)' (p. 576).

Paraphilias

We will not go into detail on the paraphilias; any therapeutic work with such presentations is quite specialised. However, it is worth noting them here. DSM defines paraphilia as 'recurrent, intense sexually arousing fantasies, sexual urges, or behaviors generally involving 1) nonhuman objects, 2) the suffering or humiliation of oneself or one's partner, or 3) children or other nonconsenting persons, that occur over a period of at least 6 months' (p. 566). The main paraphilias are:

- Exhibitionism: the exposure of one's genitals to a stranger
- Fetishism: the use of non-living objects (the 'fetish') for sexual excitement or gratification
- Frotteurism: touching and rubbing against non-consenting persons
- Paedophilia: sexual activity or arousal with a child. In diagnostic terms the individual with paedophilia must be aged 16 years or older and at least 5 years older than the child
- Sexual masochism: the act of being humiliated, beaten, bound, or otherwise made to suffer during sexual desire or activity

- Sexual sadism: the act of inflicting psychological or physical suffering on another during sexual desire or activity
- Transvestic fetishism: cross-dressing, usually with masturbation
- Voyeurism: observing unsuspecting individuals, usually strangers, who are naked, in the process of undressing, or engaging in sexual activity.

Counselling and psychotherapy for sexual problems

Sexual and relationship therapy is widely acknowledged to be a specialist field with discrete knowledge and theory. In the UK, one of the leading organisations for sexual and relationship therapy is the College of Sexual and Relationship Therapists. There are other leading therapy providers, including Relate. For a counsellor or therapist without specific training, experience, or supervision in working with sexual problems, it is generally advisable to refer clients on to specific services. These are often available either through the voluntary sector or the NHS in the UK, although waiting lists can be high and clients may not wish to use such services, fearing the identification of their problem or experiencing a perceived stigma. Clients may wish to explore their sexual problems in the context of therapy they know or with a therapist they trust. For this reason it is important that therapists have sufficient knowledge to support any work.

It is important in the first instance to keep in mind that there may always be a physiological cause for any sexual problem, rather than assuming it is necessarily psychological. Any of the problems outlined above may be symptomatic of serious underlying health problems. For this reason it is always important to suggest to clients they speak with their medical practitioner to ascertain whether there is any disease or other physiological problem. Only with that clarification should a therapist proceed with working with sexual problems.

Sexual problems can often be identified early on in counselling and psychotherapy, during the assessment. Some modalities might work against a therapist asking their client about sex. In my own practice I ask all clients during the assessment about libido (sex drive) and sex. It never fails to surprise me how often sexual problems are acknowledged at this stage, whether or not they then become the focus of the therapeutic work. Simply asking the question early on, confidently and without embarrassment, can communicate to the client that it is okay to talk about sexual problems. The client is then able to decide whether they wish this to be the focus of their work and it is important the therapist follows the client's lead on this, whether to discuss or not.

Talking through issues can provide the client with an important space to name and explore their sexual anxieties. It may be possible to identify early causes for sexual anxiety, such as abuse, sexual assault, or early humiliating sexual experiences. Likewise, talking also provides an opportunity to provide important information to clients about sex, and to debunk myths and other misleading information. It is certainly the case in my working environment, particularly with younger people with limited sexual experience, that anxieties about sexual performance and the 'shoulds' and 'oughts' can serve as preventative factors on the development of sexual confidence and esteem. For example, I see many young, male clients experiencing erectile problems rooted in anxieties about sexual performance.

There are a number of helpful strategies that clients can use to help develop sexual confidence. These can be used either with a partner or alone during their own sexual exploration and during masturbation. If the client feels comfortable to, they can be discussed in therapy. Strategies might include:

- Increasing sensation or focus during touch or masturbation
- Providing clear and accessible information about sex, physiology and the realities of 'performance'
- With a partner, experiencing non-sexual touch and intimacy to help build confidence in self, body-image and being with another
- For males, masturbation techniques that can help slow down sexual excitement and thus address premature ejaculation
- Couple therapy where both people can discuss sexual anxieties, expectations and fears.

It is not possible here to provide detail of all strategies that can be successfully used to support sexual problems, and I would recommend following these up via the websites listed at the end of this section. The main point here is that counselling and psychotherapy can provide an excellent forum for clients to be supported with sexual problems. Such work demands sensitivity, empathy and confidence from the therapist to help provide a space in which clients will feel comfortable enough to share their fears and thoughts.

WEBSITES

CORST (College of Relationship and Sexual Therapists): www.cosrt.org.uk/
Relate: www.relate.org.uk/home/index.html
NHS (Male sexual problems): www.nhs.uk/Livewell/Goodsex/Pages/Male sexual dysfunction.aspx
NHS (Female sexual problems): www.nhs.uk/Livewell/Goodsex/Pages/Female sexualdysfunction.aspx

DISCUSSION QUESTIONS

1 What specialist sex therapies are available in your community and how are they accessed?
2 What factors might make talking about sex (a) difficult or (b) comfortable for you?
3 What resources could you access to help improve your knowledge and confidence concerning working with sexual problems?
4 What steps might you take to support yourself in helping clients explore sexual difficulties?

6.10 PSYCHOSIS

SECTION OUTLINE

Psychosis can be a frightening thing for individuals to experience and can present with particular challenges in counselling and psychotherapy. This section outlines what is meant by psychosis, how it might present and what options counsellors and psychotherapists have for working with clients with psychosis.

Definitions

I will outline some important information about psychosis here. I will clearly state that, in the majority of instances, it will be necessary to seek the help of specialist intervention if psychosis is suspected as the majority of counsellors and psychotherapists are not based in settings where they could work effectively with psychosis. However, it is included here as it is important for you to be able to understand how psychosis might present so that you can make informed referrals to specialist services, and also have an overview of some of the treatments. Clients will sometimes be fearful as to what might happen next following referral, and it is important you are able to engage in an informed discussion with them.

The Royal College of Psychiatrists outlines a number of possible symptoms of psychosis. Not all will necessarily be present and there is no one single test for psychosis. They note that a person with developing psychosis may:

• Hear, smell, feel or see things that other people do not (hallucinations)
• Have strange thoughts or beliefs which may make the person feel they are being controlled, persecuted or harassed (delusions)

- Have muddled or blocked thinking (thought disorder)
- At times seem unusually excited or withdrawn and avoid contact with people
- Not realise that there is anything wrong with themselves (lack of insight).

Additionally, they note that others might observe that the person concerned:

- Has problems understanding reality and thinking clearly
- Talks to themself and/or appears to be listening to something else
- Has problems communicating effectively
- Loses interest in their personal appearance and life in general
- Is restless, irritable or tense and anxious
- Avoids other people
- Is aggressive or violent (in a minority of cases)
- [Can] Be very high 'manic' or very low 'depressed', or
- [Can] Swing from one state to the other (manic depression).
  (Launer and Foster, 2005, p. 2)

Psychosis develops over three main stages: prodrome; acute; and recovery. In the prodrome stage the signs and symptoms might be very difficult to detect and often this stage is missed by friends and family who note changes, but not of any real significance. In the acute phase symptoms are much more apparent, and may include hallucinations or delusions. In the recovery phase individuals respond to treatment, which is likely to consist of medication or some form of therapy, or typically a combination of both.

The charity Rethink – a mental health charity – provides some important facts about psychosis on its website (Rethink, 2012). For example:

- Psychosis often strikes young people
- Psychosis distorts the senses, making it very difficult for the person to tell what is real from what is not
- The risk period of first-episode psychosis is age 14–35 but it is most common in the late 'teens and early 20s
- Men and women are affected with equal frequency, but for men the age of onset for psychosis is often earlier than for women, in the 'teens and early 20s
- For women the age of onset can be later; half of the women who develop psychosis start their difficulties in their early 20s
- Early assessment, education and treatment greatly improve outcomes for the individual and their family

- The word 'psychosis' is used to describe a mental health problem that can affect the brain, so that there is a loss of contact with reality. When someone develops a mental health problem in this way it is called a 'psychotic episode'
- About 3 out of every 100 people will experience a psychotic episode, making psychosis more common than diabetes. Most people make a full recovery from the experience.

Assessment for psychosis

Many counsellors and psychotherapists have not received the specialist training that would equip them to appropriately and adequately assess for psychosis. Such an assessment is complex and detailed and often takes place over a period of time. It is rare for psychosis to be assessed and diagnosed quickly, unless a person is in an acute phase where their presenting symptoms are likely to be more evident. Early Intervention Services, particularly designed for speedy referral and assessment of people with early symptoms of psychosis – particularly young people – are specifically skilled and equipped to undertake a full assessment of the individual's needs. Such services have proved themselves to be effective both in diagnostic terms but also in formulating treatment plans to quickly manage early symptoms, helping to lead to a quicker recovery and reduce the chances of future relapse.

In almost every instance it is inadvisable for a counsellor or psychotherapist to try to assess and treat for psychosis in isolation, unless they are based within a specialist team and are tasked with that particular expectation. It is possible for early symptoms of psychosis to be detected in a therapy assessment, where an individual's day-to-day functioning can be discussed in some depth as well as their understanding of themselves and their world explored. A counsellor or psychotherapist might detect inconsistencies in presentation, or perhaps be concerned about how the person constructs their world: there might be indicators here of the onset of a psychotic process. It is important not to assume this is the case: if in doubt the best course of action is to discuss concerns with the client (without necessarily naming psychosis as a possibility), and to discuss a referral on for more specialist assessment. I caution here against actually naming psychosis as a possibility with clients, as counsellors and psychotherapists are not diagnosticians and should always be very wary about using diagnostic terminology in a way that might imply an actual diagnosis. Rather, it would be better to explain to the client that it would help, in establishing the best form of treatment, for a further assessment to be undertaken.

Consider the case of Angelina, outlined in Box 6.12.

CASE STUDY 6.12
Angelina

Angelina is a 20-year-old student. She recently began counselling and has been working well. As her counsellor you have noticed that over recent weeks she has appeared more agitated, a little restless in sessions, and is more unkempt than when she first presented. You have mentioned your observations to her and while she was attentive, did not believe them to be of any significance. She presents at one session in a very agitated way: she is unsettled, makes little eye contact and is apparently distracted. She has brought a diary in which she has made 'notes'. She asks if she can read some, and does so quickly and with little breath. She describes being concerned about her reflection in the mirror; that it seems distorted and sometimes to be laughing at her. She fears that people might be watching her and is very unsettled by this. She is able to have a clear and rational conversation about this and says that she knows some of this 'sounds a little mad'.

This case, drawn from my own working experience, is an excellent example of the possibility of early-onset psychosis. The following points are noteworthy in her presentation:

- Angelina's age – she is young (the first episode of psychosis often happens to younger people)
- Gradual deterioration in her physical presentation
- Gradual deterioration in her emotional wellbeing, with some increasing agitation
- Possible lack of insight into the changes in her presentation
- Little eye contact, and increased agitation, in the latter stages
- Possible distortions in her self-perception and view of the world
- Possible evidence of some paranoia
- However, some insight into her thought disturbance.

None of these, in themselves, is sufficient evidence of psychosis. To mention to Angelina the possibility of psychosis without being in the position to do so authoritatively has the potential to cause more harm and unnecessary distress. However, it would also be wrong to disregard Angelina's presentation and to continue counselling without any further assessment. At this stage there is no justification for breaking confidentiality, as there is no evidence to suggest that Angelina is of any danger to herself or others. Therefore the best course of action would be for the therapist to identify their concerns with Angelina and to request permission to arrange a more specialised assessment, either via her

GP or in discussion with an Early Intervention for Psychosis team. If Angelina refuses permission to consult her GP or mental health service then, at this stage, that must be respected. However, the counsellor or psychotherapist would continue to monitor her mental and physical wellbeing carefully and discuss their concerns with a supervisor.

Should Angelina appear to be developing psychosis and move out of the current prodromal stage into an acute stage, it would be essential for her therapist to alert mental health services as quickly as possible, as it is unlikely she would retain capacity to do that for herself. However, it would be important for the therapist to obtain Angelina's consent for this referral, wherever possible. She is unlikely to have real insight into her own predicament and early intervention offers the best likelihood of Angelina responding to treatment and moving into recovery, as well as decreasing the chance of relapse.

Treatments for psychosis

A number of psychosocial interventions have been developed for the treatment of psychosis. While psychopharmachological treatments used to be the front line option, they are now used in conjunction with a range of other treatments very successfully. The prognosis for people with psychosis is significantly better than a couple of decades ago. Rethink (2007) outlines the following ways of treating psychosis:

- Medication
- Education
- Family support
- Hospitalisation
- Rehabilitation programmes
- Self-help groups
- Nutrition, rest and exercise
- Talking therapies.

Let us examine these each in turn.

Medication

The medication offered to people with psychosis, as with many mental health conditions, is used less to treat the underlying condition, but rather to alleviate the symptoms. The symptoms of psychosis can be profoundly distressing and the chances of improvement and recovery during the acute phase of psychosis are significantly lessened if people remain frightened or distressed by their symptoms. Reducing symptoms is therefore an important part of a person's recovery.

Education

Like many situations, the more we understand the problems we face the better equipped we are in tackling them. Many counsellors and psychotherapists, depending on their way of working, are likely to include in their sessions psycho-education, where clients are provided with information that informs them about the situation in which they find themselves. For example, understanding the processes of bereavement can be very reassuring for someone grieving for the first time. The same is true of psychosis, where understanding that their experience is explicable can be very reassuring.

Family support

A criticism of counselling and psychotherapy is that it can, on occasions, be very individualistic. That is, it may focus solely on the distress and development of the individual without always taking into account their living situation or other significant relationships. Yet an individual can only truly develop and make changes if they can also understand themselves in context; seeing themselves in their 'system' of relationships and living. For people with psychosis this also applies and the need to include significant others (e.g. parents, siblings, other family members and friends), where appropriate, in the care of the individual is important. This is a particular challenge for counsellors and psychotherapists, who may find it very difficult, in virtue of their specific role, to communicate with family and friends freely. A mental health team is better equipped to do this, with therapy embedded as part of the wider support picture.

Hospitalisation

There are occasions, particularly for people in an acute phase of psychosis, where hospitalisation is required to ensure their safety. This is obviously the last alternative but, on occasions, an individual's level of distress and lack of insight is such that safe containment in a therapeutic environment is the best and only possible alternative. This would be with the individual's consent wherever possible. However, mental health legislation does provide the circumstances for an individual to be compulsorily admitted to hospital if there is no alternative and it is in their best interests. The law requires that mental health teams always aim for the least restrictive alternative.

Of course, a hospital admission is not always because of a mental health crisis. There are times when individuals will request an admission to hospital, or where such an admission is desirable to monitor and amend medication. It can also provide the person with opportunities to participate in group or individual therapy.

Rehabilitation programmes

When an individual has been in hospital or in receipt of residential support, a period of rehabilitation where there is the option to participate in a range of psychosocial and therapeutic activities can help provide the right environment for the person to rebuild confidence and self-esteem, and can provide a bridge between high levels of care and independent living.

Self-help groups

The importance of self-help groups can be seen right across the spectrum of presenting issues, including psychosis. Having the chance to meet with others who have gone through, or are currently going through, similar experiences can be extremely affirming and supportive. It provides an opportunity to share experiences and support each other, as well as discussing practical strategies for coping and suggestions for future support. Inevitably there can be an element of exposure in talking about personal problems with others in such an open way, but many self-help groups are very aware of this and take active steps to encourage the individual's involvement and participation.

Nutrition, rest and exercise

A combination of factors – good eating patterns with nutritionally high-value food, plenty of rest and also some exercise – can contribute to the individual's sense of well-being. As is the case for many people experiencing mental health distress, basic patterns and structures of living, such as eating and sleeping patterns, can be seriously disrupted. This can quickly leave the person feeling both physically and emotionally depleted. Offering an individual support to begin to re-establish these patterns is very important.

Talking therapies

Of course, the value of talking therapies cannot be overstated. Ranging from effective listening through to more structured counselling and psychotherapy, the value of talking about experiences is well established. As current UK health care policy reflects, cognitive-behavioural treatments (CBT) and psychodynamic therapy are highly valued as a means of supporting a person with psychosis. However, many other valuable approaches, and particularly some of the humanistic approaches such as person-centred and gestalt for example, have been marginalised, with their efficacy and appropriateness questioned.

It is an irony that certainly before the current emergence of CBT and the preferred treatment choice across many client presentations, person-centred therapy was ground-breaking in its application for people with a diagnosis of schizophrenia. Rogers's extensive writing about his work with such people was both innovate and paradigm-shifting at the time and the 'outcomes' – as we would seem to term it now – were excellent (Rogers, 1962). It is my personal hope that such humanistic approaches begin to create the evidence base that will bring them back into the mainstream and thus give people with psychosis a wider range of options for support.

The emergence of psychosis can be immensely distressing for anyone. Typically, its onset affects people in their late adolescence and early 20s and can have a devastating effect on their lives, self-confidence and self-esteem. While counselling and psychotherapy have much to offer people living with this experience, it is best delivered within the context of a well-planned, collaborative package of care that is multi-disciplinary. Counselling or psychotherapy alone is unlikely to provide all that is needed for someone with psychosis, but within such a package it can make a major difference both to their current sense of self and their future hopes.

WEBSITES

Mind (Understanding psychotic experiences): www.mind.org.uk/help/diagnoses_and_conditions/psychotic_experience
NHS (Psychosis help): www.nhs.uk/Conditions/Psychosis/Pages/Introduction.aspx
Royal College of Psychiatrists (Psychosis in young people): www.rcpsych.ac.uk/mentalhealthinfo/youngpeople/psychosis.aspx

DISCUSSION QUESTIONS

1 Reflect on times in your life when you have felt out of control or when your worldview was different to how it usually is. How did that feel and what did you need?
2 What are your thoughts when working with a client who has a diagnosis of 'psychosis'?
3 When you begin counselling or psychotherapy with a potential client, how much attention do you give to the possibility of psychosis and, if you suspected it, what would you do?
4 What are the mental health services specifically for psychosis in your area, e.g. Early Intervention Teams, and how would you access them for your client, if needed?

6.11 PERSONALITY DISORDERS

SECTION OUTLINE

A diagnosis of personality disorder is as much a political as psychiatric one, it has been claimed. This section outlines the diagnostic structure of personality disorder, provides a brief overview of the main aspects of each of the personality disorders and considers treatment options. It also considers criticisms of 'personality disorder' as a diagnostic category.

Definitions

There are 10 specific personality disorders outlined in the DSM. In general terms, a personality disorder is defined as 'an enduring pattern of inner experience and behavior that deviates markedly from the expectations of the individual's culture, is pervasive and inflexible, has an onset in adolescence or early childhood, is stable over time, and leads to distress or impairment' (p. 685). We can see from aspects of this clinical definition where controversy around the diagnosis might begin. Consider, particularly, the following part: '[a] pattern of inner experience and behavior that deviates markedly from the expectations of the individual's culture'. Even in the rare event of an exclusively single-culture society, this would still be potentially problematic because no clarity is provided concerning individual difference. In a multicultural society, attempting to define the 'expectations' of the individual's culture is even more difficult and dangerous. While the definition does locate the behaviour of the individual within their own cultural context, it is still difficult to define, given the shifting nature of culture and expectation. The term has the potential to be mis-used to undermine those that take a different position from the 'norm'. It has the potential therefore to silence and stifle individual difference. Other aspects of the definition do not necessarily help: 'has an onset in adolescence or early childhood' possibly describes the formation of everyone's personality; 'is stable over time' probably describes most people's experience of themselves; and 'leads to distress or impairment' is a state perhaps not unfamiliar to many who feel frustrated at repeated ways of being they would prefer to be different. I certainly tick the boxes of the major part of this definition! In short, the clinical definition is vague, non-specific and open to abuse.

More clarity emerges, however, when we consider the ten specific forms of personality disorder. The DSM (p. 685) identifies them as follows (together with an eleventh, catch–all, category, i.e., 'personality disorders not otherwise specified'):

1 Paranoid personality disorder: is a pattern of distrust and suspiciousness such that others' motives are interpreted as malevolent.
2 Schizoid personality disorder: is a pattern of detachment from social relationships and a restricted range of emotional expression.
3 Schizotypal personality disorder: is a pattern of acute discomfort in close relationships, cognitive or perceptual distortions, and eccentricities of behaviour.
4 Antisocial personality disorder: is a pattern of disregard for, and violation of, the rights of others.
5 Borderline personality disorder: is a pattern of instability in interpersonal relationships, self-image, and affects, and marked impulsivity.
6 Histrionic personality disorder: is a pattern of excessive emotionality and attention seeking.
7 Narcissistic personality disorder: is a pattern of grandiosity, need for admiration, and lack of empathy.
8 Avoidant personality disorder: is a pattern of social inhibition, feelings of inadequacy, and hypersensitivity to negative evaluation.
9 Dependent personality disorder: is a pattern of submissive and clinging behaviour related to an excessive need to be taken care of.
10 Obsessive-compulsive personality disorder: is a pattern of preoccupation with orderliness, perfectionism, and control.
11 Personality disorder not otherwise specified: is a category provided for two situations: 1) the individual's personality pattern meets the general criteria for a personality disorder and traits of several different personality disorders are present, but the criteria for any specific personality disorder are not met; and 2) the individual's personality pattern meets the general criteria for a personality disorder that is not included in the classification (e.g. passive–aggressive personality disorder).

The DSM offers specific diagnostic criteria for each personality disorder, and it is worth visiting the manual for that detail. The above overview of each personality disorder raises some important questions, some of which are addressed in the detail of the specific criteria. For example, at what level would an individual's presentation warrant a 'personality disorder' diagnosis? I find that several of the criteria would apply to me at various times and in various contexts: that would not necessarily mean, however, that I have a personality disorder. Rather, it demonstrates how encompassing these terms can be. Note too the rather broad-brush phraseology of the category 'personality disorder not otherwise specified'.

The case of borderline personality disorder

To illustrate how the DSM provides specific criteria for each diagnostic category, I will focus on borderline personality disorder (BPD). This is probably one of the most contentious of the personality disorder categories because of its widespread application. The DSM diagnostic criteria for BPD are detailed in Box 6.13.

BOX 6.13   DIAGNOSTIC CRITERIA FOR BORDERLINE PERSONALITY DISORDER

A pervasive pattern of instability of interpersonal relationships, self-image and affects, and marked impulsivity beginning by early adulthood and present in a variety of contexts, as indicated by five (or more) of the following:

1 frantic efforts to avoid real or imagined abandonment. Note: do not include suicidal or self-mutilating behavior covered in Criterion 5
2 a pattern of unstable and intense interpersonal relationships characterised by alternating between extremes of idealisation and devaluation
3 identity disturbance: markedly and persistently unstable self-image or sense of self
4 impulsivity in at least two areas that are potentially self-damaging (e.g. spending, sex, substance abuse, reckless driving, binge eating). Note: Do not include suicidal or self-mutilating behavior covered in Criterion 5
5 recurrent suicidal behavior, gestures, or threats, or self-mutilating behavior
6 affective instability due to a marked reactivity of mood (e.g. intense episodic dysphoria, irritability, or anxiety usually lasting a few hours and only rarely more than a few days)
7 chronic feelings of emptiness
8 inappropriate, intense anger or difficulty controlling anger (e.g. frequent displays of temper, constant anger, recurrent physical fights)
9 transient, stress-related paranoid ideation or severe dissociative symptoms.

(American Psychiatric Association, 2000, p. 710. Reprinted with permission from the *Diagnostic and Statistical Manual of Mental Disorders*, Fourth Edition, Text Revision (© American Psychiatric Association 2000).

A critique of BPD diagnosis

Many have criticised both the validity and application of BPD as a diagnostic category. Proctor (2007, 2010) has been one of the most vocal critics, writing that,

> Many girls who self-injure are likely to end up being diagnosed with BPD, as self-injury is a highly stigmatised form of behaviour, which challenges many of society's norms and expectations. Women's and girls' distress can be understood as a response to our experiences in a society where power is shared unequally between men and women. Referring to a large body of feminist

work, BPD is situated in a long history of responses to women's distress, denying the impact and extent of childhood sexual abuse. The diagnosis of BPD is criticised for focusing attention on the individual woman, rather than on the context of her life. (Proctor, 2007, p. 117)

Thus one of the main criticisms of BPD is that it has been primarily applied to women rather than men (Proctor, 2010). Proctor additionally argues that many of the women who have been diagnosed with BPD are rather survivors of childhood sexual abuse, with 'symptoms' such as self-injury and suicidal ideation typical of those experiencing such early trauma.

Added to this are my own experiences of mental health settings, where I would certainly concur with Pilgrim's (2001, p. 255) assertion that 'in British mental health services it is very common for PD [personality disorder] to be anything that cannot be accounted for in a patient by mental illness. PD is a dustbin category of problematic "behaviour" as judged by significant others or staff'. I have known of situations where individuals have been diagnosed with BPD because, according to the psychiatrists, 'nothing else seems to fit'. I was also aware of a situation once, following the appointment of a new psychiatrist tasked with reducing patient numbers, for a large number of patients (mostly women) to be re-diagnosed with BPD and discharged from the mental health service because the accepted view at that time was that BPD was not treatable. These are obviously extreme examples taken from my own practice experience, but they do, to an extent, support some of the criticisms made of the diagnostic category, but particularly the application of it.

Counselling and psychotherapy for people with BPD

Treatments for people with personality disorders have progressed significantly over the last couple of decades. Twenty years ago, it was not uncommon to hear that people with such diagnoses could not be treated, but this has changed and a number of options are now available. Medication is often offered as a means of symptom management, rather than treating the cause of the problem. The presumption with a personality disorder is that the problem lies within the structure of an individual's personality, rather than as a consequence of biochemical change or dysfunction. Some people are offered therapeutic community support, where they live for several months within a strict therapeutic regime of individual and group work, along with collaborative living and conformity to group rules and expectations. The availability of such services appears under threat, perhaps because they are expensive and demand a high time commitment from staff and funders.

Individual counselling or psychotherapy are typically offered in the form of CBT or, increasingly, a psychosocial intervention called dialectical behaviour therapy

(DBT). DBT combines traditional CBT techniques with additional approaches (e.g. the development of distress resilience techniques). It is not uncommon for clients to attend mainstream counselling or psychotherapy services with a diagnosis of personality disorder (or, if without a formal diagnosis, their own suspicion they have one). Reflecting the information age, people will often fear a diagnosis because of information they have read on the Internet and come to see a therapist with a wish for that fear to be confirmed or rejected. As stated earlier in this chapter, it is not the role of a counsellor or psychotherapist to offer this to a client: if this is what the client is wanting, they would be better referred to their GP for further discussion.

That is not to say that counselling or psychotherapy has no place for people with such a diagnosis, for that is far from the case. The same principles of therapy would be applied as to any client encounter, that of respect, empathy, professionalism, ethical practice and clearly negotiated boundaries. How or whether counsellors and psychotherapists view personality disorder diagnoses as relevant to their practice is likely to be strongly informed by how they view psychiatric diagnosis more generally. Certainly, it is hard to disregard the criticisms of some aspects of the personality disorder group, more particularly BPD. However, there may be aspects of personality styles that can helpfully inform thinking, if not drive it.

WEBSITES

Mind: Understanding Personality Disorders: www.mind.org.uk/help/diagnoses_and_conditions/personality_disorders

Royal College of Psychiatrists – Personality Disorders: www.rcpsych.ac.uk/mentalhealthinfoforall/problems/personalitydisorders.aspx

DISCUSSION QUESTIONS

1 What are your views about the definition of personality disorder? How might it be made more specific?
2 How might you understand your own personality style with reference to the 10 types of personality disorders outlined here?
3 Reflecting on your own client work, what trends of personality styles (if any) have you noticed?
4 Consider borderline personality disorder: to what extent do you see it as a valid diagnosis or as a political and social means of discrimination and oppression?

7

Managing Aspects of the Therapeutic Relationship

7.1 INTRODUCTION

CHAPTER OVERVIEW

To help establish a safe, appropriate and ethical therapeutic relationship, counsellors and psychotherapists need to consider how to manage each part of the process – from before the first session, through using questions and making an assessment, contracting, the early stages of the relationship, goal-setting and reviewing, to post-therapy. This chapter discusses each of these parts in turn, identifying aspects that can serve as the foundation and structure for therapy, regardless of theoretical orientation.

This chapter discusses a number of key factors that all counsellors and psychotherapists, regardless of their theoretical orientation, must consider to help establish appropriate, safe and ethical therapeutic relationships with their clients. If we use the metaphor of house building, then if the bricks represent the details of therapy and the particular therapeutic skills that facilitate the process, the elements considered here represent the mortar between the bricks. Without the mortar for stability and security, the bricks will always run the risk of falling down.

It may sometimes feel cumbersome to attend to this level of detail: there can be a temptation instead to get straight into the immediate pull of the client's narrative. This is often very compelling and the desire to support someone experiencing high levels of distress is very instinctive. Clients too will often not wish to dwell too long on contracting, but rather move into telling their story in the hope of some relief or answers. However, as I hope will become clear throughout this chapter, the greater level of attention paid to these particular aspects, the greater level of security in the relationship, the greater level of containment and support for the client, and ultimately both you and client can be 'held' more effectively in your mutual endeavour.

We begin at the very beginning. The first section, Before the First Session, outlines what you need to consider before the client ever walks through the door. This includes early contacts with clients and pre-therapy publicity. The section also considers how we create a space in preparation for face-to-face and online meetings. The next section, Using Questions and Making an Assessment, discusses an area often contentious in counselling and psychotherapy: whether it is helpful or not to use questions as a form of intervention, and how (or whether) you might undertake an assessment early on. Theoretical orientation and modality will profoundly shape whether the use of questions or assessment have any place in the therapeutic process. My aim here is to provide some thoughts in a modality-neutral way in the hope that, regardless of your orientation, you might be able to integrate certain aspects into your therapeutic work for the benefit of your clients.

The next section, Contracts and Fees, discusses the thorny issues of money – how fees may be set and collected, and how the whole issue of fees can be negotiated and contained in an appropriate contracting process. The argument here is that good contracting provides the client with sufficient information to make an informed decision whether to enter into therapy at all and, if they do, both you and your client are entirely clear as to the parameters within which the therapeutic relationship is contained. This, I argue, affords both parties with the greatest degree of security in the event of confusion or disagreement later on. Finally, I suggest that contracting should not be an isolated event at the beginning of therapy, but rather a process that is alive throughout, available as a therapeutic tool, when appropriate.

Early Stages of the Relationship outlines the factors that help to establish the relationship with clients in the early stages of therapy. Goal-setting and Reviewing examines how, once the therapeutic relationship is established, you can ensure work is conducted at the client's pace. The section focuses on the particular needs of therapy and the aspects of their problems they hope will change, and how progress and pacing can be collaboratively monitored through the use of reviews.

Currently there is a great deal of pressure in the UK, in the face of increasing waiting lists and reducing financial support, for therapy providers to consider different ways of providing help. The section Working Long Term or Briefly looks at the relative merits and difficulties of open-ended counselling or psychotherapy against briefer ways of work. More specifically, the factors that you might need to address to work briefly successfully are identified. In Managing Endings the importance of paying careful attention to how endings in therapy are addressed is discussed. A distinction is made between planned endings, set in place typically from the outset of therapy, and unplanned endings, which may occur at any point. The impact on us of unplanned endings is considered.

Finally, After the Client Has Left considers how we can maintain professional practice, meeting caseload management obligations and maintaining a high level of professional accountability, while also ensuring we continue to take full opportunity to reflect on the work to contribute to our growing body of knowledge and experience.

7.2 BEFORE THE FIRST SESSION

SECTION OUTLINE

Client work begins even before the client has entered therapy. From referral onwards, a counsellor or psychotherapist will be communicating with a potential client. This section considers at what point a person becomes a 'client' and what steps need to be taken to ensure appropriate contact.

As we have mentioned elsewhere in the book, the therapeutic process extends well beyond the beginning and end of the therapeutic hour and also beyond the first time a client arrives for counselling or psychotherapy or the time they leave after the final session. These points in time represent false parameters: our professional and ethical obligations to our clients are much wider. Whether we work in an organisation or independently, how our service is communicated to clients affects their perception of what therapy might be like and how we might be experienced as therapists. The way information is written, how it is presented, the type of font used in publicity material, all say something about our approach and who we are. Whether our style is 'chatty' or friendly, or instead to-the-point and business-like will influence clients' perceptions. These perceptions will then be brought into the therapy space.

Pre-therapy information

Pre-therapy information can take various forms – for example, an advertising flyer or a website. Typical contents include:

- Information about what counselling or psychotherapy is and who it is for
- Information about charges and fees
- Details about what happens in the first session
- Self-help information
- Information about confidentiality
- Details on counsellors' or psychotherapists' training, qualifications and membership of professional bodies
- Contact details.

The information needs to be tailored for the intended audience. As an example of tailoring, consider the writing of this book. I have in mind people who may be considering a training in counselling or psychotherapy, people already in training, or those newly qualified who are developing their practice. I have tried to imagine the sorts of information that would be most helpful to such groups and to write it as if we might be having a conversation. Here the writer's (my) 'position' is that of a practitioner drawing on working knowledge, rather than taking an overly academic perspective – I have tried to bring myself into my writing rather than only writing in the third-person. Of course, whether I have succeeded with any of my intentions is ultimately your decision – and that is the point: you will interpret my intentions and what you imagine I am like based on how I have presented myself in my writing. This is just as true for information intended for prospective clients of our service. We need to consider, therefore, how much we wish to be present in our pre-therapy information, for that is likely to signal something about how much we wish to be present in our therapeutic relationships.

Creating a space: face-to-face therapy

In any setting the importance of a safe, respectful space cannot be overstated. The place that the client will come to will communicate something about how you intend to care for them. In saying this, however, I am very aware that space is not something we always have control over. In some organisational settings where space is at a premium, or where counselling and psychotherapy are not perhaps understood as well as we might like, space can easily be compromised. It is not unheard of for therapists to find themselves allocated rooms with glass walls, where confidentiality would be compromised, or rooms with no natural light and more than a passing resemblance to a broom cupboard! We can argue our case, but sometimes have to make the best of what we have, unless ethical working is not possible.

Where we do have some control over our working space, we need to attend to the 'big' things, especially:

- How the client will access the room and, if they have a disability, what adjustments can be made to facilitate safe access
- How the client's confidentiality can be respected when they come to see you
- Whether suitable toilet facilities are available and accessible to the client
- Whether the room is sufficiently heated or ventilated
- Whether there is a confidential space where therapy cannot be overheard
- Whether clients are likely to be inhibited because of thin walls or people walking past the door
- Whether the chairs are comfortable (you will be spending a great deal of time sitting in one of them) and of sufficient quality to cope with regular use
- How you will manage your own safety. How would you summon help in an emergency? Who knows your working timetable (without names of clients) so that your safety can be monitored?
- Whether there are waiting and reception facilities. (If not, have you informed clients that, because there are no waiting facilities, they will be allowed in only at their designated time?)

Other details matter too. Ask yourself these questions:

- Are you qualified to do what you say you will do? You have a duty of care to your clients that demands you are able to deliver what you say you will deliver.
- Is there adequate and appropriate insurance in place to cover the activities you offer (for example, individual therapy, group therapy, training, workshops, hypnotherapy)?
- Have you put in place appropriate and sufficient supervision with a supervisor who is sufficiently qualified and experienced?
- Have you ensured that all information about your service is accessible to clients in a form they can later refer to (i.e., not verbal information only)?
- If you are a member of a professional body, is your practice and work consistent with any ethical requirements made of you?
- Have you considered all important aspects so that you can contract fully and openly with your clients?
- Have you ensured that, if necessary, you have a means of referring on to other services? (Do you know what services exist in your area and how to access them, including in crisis situations?)

Creating a space online

Not all therapeutic encounters happen face to face. There are an increasing number of online therapists – counsellors or psychotherapists who offer therapy to individuals via online mechanisms such as email and synchronous chat ('real time' discussion, either in chat room type environments or using dedicated software). The same professional standards apply, including care of the client. Every aspect discussed in this book will apply to those working online.

This applies to the matter of creating the therapeutic 'space'. While clients do not go to a particular venue for therapy as they would with face-to-face sessions, they do connect with their therapists in very similar ways. There is a growing body of research on online counselling and psychotherapy that asserts the value of the online therapeutic relationship and how, with a skilled therapist, the same degree of intimacy, relational depth and thus therapeutic change can occur (Baker and Ray, 2011; Hanley, 2012; King et al., 2003).

None of this happens by accident, however, and intrusions into the therapeutic space must be managed carefully. Indeed, it could be argued that the danger for intrusion when working online is greater. In face-to-face work the therapy room becomes a metaphor for care and attention. We would not imagine wandering in and out of the room, allowing other people to be around, or responding to a text message while the client is present. We would immediately acknowledge that as unprofessional, unethical and profoundly disrespectful of the client. The same degree of attention is required when working online. If based at home that means ensuring the computer is in a separate room, where you will not be disturbed. It also means ensuring you prepare for the online session in exactly the same way you would as if the client was due to arrive at your door. You need to ensure that the space and time is free from interruption and that your focus and attention is entirely on what is happening for the client, and between you and the client. For a full discussion of the issues related to working online, including guidelines for working professionally and ethically, see Anthony and Goss (2009).

DISCUSSION QUESTIONS

1   What publicity do you or your service make available to clients? How would you respond to it if you were yourself a prospective client of your service?
2   Consider how the information provided is written: what does it communicate about you or your service?
3   Consider the therapeutic environment: how much control do you have over it and how fit for purpose is it?
4   Which other aspects would you need to consider with your client group for creating a suitable space?

7.3 USING QUESTIONS AND MAKING AN ASSESSMENT

SECTION OUTLINE

Not all counsellors and psychotherapists are comfortable with asking their clients questions. However, all will make some form of assessment, either explicitly or implicitly. This section outlines important aspects of assessment and considers how assessment approaches might be integrated into various modalities.

Throughout the time that I have been involved in counselling and psychotherapy debate has raged as to the appropriateness of asking questions and the place of assessment – especially in person-centred therapy. I am very well aware that simply including a section with the words 'questions' and 'assessment' runs the risk of alienating a significant group of readers. I hope therefore that those of you who question the place of this section in a book on counselling and psychotherapy will stick with me and find something of value.

For some, the use of questioning in therapy, particularly person-centred therapy, is a contentious issue. However, I might suggest that a well-placed question, for the purposes of clarification or exploration, can be of great value. I would also suggest that assessment has a very important role in therapy, but that it needs to be collaborative so that the client benefits as much from the learning as the therapist. I acknowledge that all will not agree with this position, but let me outline my views in a little more detail.

Using questions

The use of questions can go hand-in-hand with the role of assessment, particularly in the early stages of therapy. Questions should never be posed for the sake of asking them and should not be used for the purpose simply of satisfying the curiosity of the therapist. While curiosity is not necessarily a bad thing, we need to be clear about why we are curious and what it is we really want to know (and for whose benefit). We can try to understand our curiosity a little more in supervision before exposing the client to an interrogation to make ourselves feel better.

When therapy is time-limited or brief, careful and judicious questions can provide much-needed focus and direction, enabling sessions to be used wisely and to their full potential. If working to a five-session model for example, there may be insufficient time to allow all necessary information to emerge – important facts might become apparent only right at the end, when there is little time for client or therapist to respond appropriately. In this instance questions can help structure thinking and facilitate a collaborative and transparent approach to the focus of the work. See the section on goal-setting for a more detailed view of this.

Questions may have a direct, factual focus (such as who, when, how) to help the therapist quickly build an understanding of the client and their difficulties, and to establish the social context (family, support network, work circumstances, and so on). Alternatively, questions may have more of an indirect, facilitative focus (such as I wonder if; could you tell me a little more about; what is your sense/understanding of?). Alongside skills such as paraphrasing and reflection, questions can be an important aspect of a counsellor or psychotherapist's intervention choices.

Making an assessment

In some therapeutic approaches the therapist's role clearly involves assessment of the client, identification of the problem and formulation of a solution. The therapist here might assume an 'expert' position, using their skills and knowledge for the benefit of the client. This approach does not easily transfer to the more humanistic or pluralistic models where the client's understanding of their own distress is privileged above that of the therapist. This does not necessarily mean, however, that assessment has little or no place in the work of a humanistic therapist.

As I have argued elsewhere (Reeves, 2008), we all assess, all of the time. We make judgements about our life, about situations, and about others to enable us to navigate through our world as efficiently and expediently as possible. We do not approach each situation as if it were never encountered before. Instead we use transferable knowledge to assess the new situation and act accordingly. I believe the same is true of therapists, although we might act on our assessments differently, or attempt to bracket them so that they play less of a direct role on our future actions. While I might like to think of myself as entirely non-judgemental, I know that isn't the case: I am a product of my own upbringing located within a culture laden with stereotypes and particular ways of seeing the world. It is extremely important that I am aware of how I might 'short cut' a new assessment of things and impose inappropriate or inaccurate information into a new situation. I explore these concepts further in Chapter 9, Working with Diversity and Difference.

As a therapist, I privilege my client's understanding of themselves and use that as a starting position for our work together. However, there may be information that is relevant to how I understand my client's distress that my client might need me to know but not be aware of its importance. For example, if my client is taking medication that means it is difficult for them to 'get going' in the morning, it might be helpful for me to suggest afternoon appointments. I do not need to be an expert in medication (nor indeed sanction its use); simply asking a client, 'Are you taking any medication at the moment and, if so, how do you find it affects you?' could be invaluable in establishing therapy in a way that better meets their needs. Finding out how well (or not) a client is eating, sleeping, whether they are in a relationship, whether they can talk to anyone about their problems, how they are coping at work (or why they are off sick from work), or how they feel about themselves, and so on, can all be invaluable in helping me enter into a client's world sooner rather than later. Of course, all of this assumes that I am willing and able to ask my client appropriate questions, at an appropriate time, and in an appropriate way.

It should be stressed that this does not bring an inquisitorial style to my therapy. I do not shine lights into my client's eyes as I strut around the room barking my questions! For me, true assessment is a collaborative process, where I can find out more about the client and their difficulties, they can find out more about themselves and their difficulties, and they can find out more about me and the therapy on offer. We ask each other questions, and ask questions of ourselves. It is a shared venture rather than one 'done' to another. My experience has been that clients often come back from early sessions saying how helpful they had found the process of assessment; that they had begun to understand themselves quite differently and that no one had taken the trouble to find out as much before. Figure 7.1 outlines the areas that might inform an assessment process. **Figure 7.1** is also available on the companion website.

Presenting problems	What is the client's problem/difficulty – how do they define it? How long has the client experienced problems for?
	How severely do they experience their problems (a 0–10 scale is often helpful) and does this change? If so, what factors make things get better or worse?
	Are the problems specific or do they cause difficulties in other areas of the client's life?
	Have they tried any strategies to improve things? If so, have these been successful?
Functioning and social support	Is the client experiencing any problems with sleeping, appetite, sex, concentration, motivation, energy levels? If so, are these problems new or long-standing?
	What support does the client have (e.g., family, friends, colleagues)?
	Does the client feel able to access support at particular times of difficulty? If not, what inhibits them from talking to someone about things?
	How does the client feel they are coping with daily demands (e.g., job, studies, other responsibilities)?

Family and relationships	Who is in the client's family? (Sometimes it is helpful to draw a genogram – i.e., a pictorial representation of the client's family – to quickly highlight important relationships and dynamics)
	How much contact does the client have with family, friends and colleagues? Is the client socially isolated?
	How would the client describe the quality of their personal relationships?
	Is there a history of previous significant relationships?
Medical/ psychiatric history	Has the client ever experienced emotional/psychological difficulties previously? If so, when and what was the nature of them?
	Does the client use alcohol or drugs to cope with their problems? If so, how does this affect the client's mood/perception of themselves?
	Is the client taking any prescribed medication for their problems? If so, how does this medication affect the client's mood/perception of their problems?
	Has the client experienced, or does the client experience currently, any medical conditions that they attribute meaning to in relation to their psychological distress?
	Has the client ever been given a diagnosis in relation to their psychological distress?
Sense of self	How would the client describe their degree of self-confidence?
	How would the client describe their sense of self-esteem – do they like who they are?
	Does the client feel valued by others?
	How does the client feel/think about their physical self (their body image)?
Risk	Does the client have any thoughts of suicide? Are these thoughts long-standing, impulsive or persistent?
	How does the client manage their thoughts of suicide? How do they not act on them?
	Does the client hurt themselves in any way as a means of coping with their problems?
	Has the client ever hurt anybody else or feel as if they might want to hurt someone else?
	Does the client appear to be looking after themselves or are they self-neglectful?
Psychological mindedness	What has brought the client to therapy now?
	What does the client understand about therapy?
	What does the client hope for from therapy – what do they want to change?
	How does the client relate to you in the session (e.g. eye contact, understanding your questions)?
	Does the client have an 'emotional language' to draw on?
	Might the client benefit from short-term, long-term or group therapy?
	Do you have the capacity and experience to work with this client and their presenting problems (e.g. do you need to refer to other specialist services or for another form of therapy)?
	Does the client appear willing and able to engage in the therapeutic process?

FIGURE 7.1   Outline structure for assessment at the beginning of counselling (Reeves, 2008, pp. 67–8)

The questions listed in Figure 7.1 are not intended to be worked through sequentially with clients. Rather, the hope is they provide an overview of the types of areas that might helpfully be explored in a collaborative assessment process. Neither is an assertion being made that by not asking questions around such areas the therapist is being neglectful of the client's needs. The suggestion is that, rightly or wrongly, assessment is a process conducted collaboratively and transparently and can be of enormous help to the client in helping them to think about their own distress and difficulties in a systematic way.

> **DISCUSSION QUESTIONS**
>
> 1 What in your view are the arguments for and against using questions in counselling and psychotherapy?
> 2 What factors might make a question facilitative, and what might make it unhelpful?
> 3 If you conduct assessments with your clients, consider what works well and what doesn't.
> 4 How might you make an assessment a collaborative venture?

7.4 CONTRACTS AND FEES

> **SECTION OUTLINE**
>
> Careful contracting is essential to ensure the wellbeing of both client and therapist. It underpins all aspects of therapy. The process of discussing the contract will help ensure that the client can make an informed choice as to whether to enter into therapy at all. The therapeutic contract is best seen as something alive within the therapeutic process, as opposed to a static entity that, once agreed, is never referred to again. This section considers how counsellors and psychotherapists can use the contracting process therapeutically, the types of issues that might be covered by the contract, and how to keep the contract 'alive' during therapy.

Most trainees I have worked with during their placement have arrived with an understanding of what a client contract is and when it should be agreed: it is an agreement between counsellor and client regarding the parameters of therapy, discussed and agreed usually in the first session. They have had opportunity to practise the sorts of things they might say during the contracting process during their classroom-based sessions, and are keen to ensure the process is completed satisfactorily by the first session. Like all experiences of transferring theory to practice, there are factors to consider beyond the basic principles they have learnt.

Why contract at all?

As Sills (1997, p. 5) states, 'the therapeutic relationship, with its inevitable power imbalance and its capacity to arouse very deep and disturbing issues, is in particular need of structure and order to contain it. The contract helps to provide this structure'. Many professional organisations view contracting as an ethical imperative: the BACP's Ethical Framework (2010, p. 5) states that 'Good practice involves clarifying and agreeing the rights and responsibilities of both practitioner and client at appropriate points in the working relationship'. It adds that '[p]ractitioners who respect their client's autonomy ... engage in explicit contracting in advance of any commitment by the client ...' (p. 3). From these points we can summarise a number of important reasons for contracting. We may say that it:

- helps clarify both practitioner and client's rights and responsibilities
- helps clarify the responsibilities (and rights) of the organisation (where therapy is provided by an organisation rather than an independent practitioner)
- respects the client's autonomy
- helps ensure that clients make an informed choice about entering into therapy
- clarifies practical considerations (e.g. fees, timing of sessions, venue, length of each session, number of sessions offered, implications of cancelled sessions or missed sessions etc.)
- helps set boundaries, such as confidentiality
- helps contain the process of therapy, which might be difficult or distressing for the client.

Several years ago I attended a workshop that examined complaints against therapists. I learnt that the type of therapist most complained about was the independent practitioner who relied on verbal rather than written contracts. Counsellors or psychotherapists working in organisations might often be frustrated by the procedures and protocols they find themselves having to work within, but they do offer both the practitioner and client a degree of protection in the event of dispute or disagreement (assuming they have been followed). Independent practitioners must therefore take clear steps in ensuring aspects that inform their practice are clearly communicated to the client.

The second aspect of this complaint 'profile' was the use of verbal rather than written contracts. Many clients, when they first arrive for therapy, may be anxious, distressed or confused and, no matter how clearly or articulately the therapist outlines the contract, it is unreasonable to assume clients will be able to remember this detail. It is therefore essential that you make available to the clients in written form (or in a form accessible to the client to take away, e.g. audio version or braille) all aspects of the contract agreed so that the client can consider the implications of the contract for them with space and without pressure. This helps protect the client and ensures they are able to make an informed choice about therapy, and helps protect the practitioner in the event of a dispute over what was agreed.

Likewise, it may become necessary during the course of therapy to vary the terms of the contract (e.g. an increase in fees or a change of venue or time); this requires negotiation. It is important to ensure this information too is available to the client in a written or accessible form and that sufficient notice is given for the client to adjust their expectations or make alternative arrangements, if necessary.

How and when to contract

In many ways the process of contracting begins before the client even enters the therapy room. Pre-therapy information, such as leaflets or web-based information, will constitute a contract. For example, if a service states on the web that it offers free, unlimited counselling, it would not be possible then to charge the client for sessions or tell them they can only receive six sessions free before a charge is made. It is important to do what we say we will do and not to promise anything we are unable or unwilling to do. Whether the client seeks counselling within an organisation or with an independent practitioner, it is very likely they will arrive with expectations, partly based on information they have already read.

For clients to make an informed choice about whether to begin therapy they need as much information as possible early on in the process. For that reason, contracting needs to begin with the client directly during the first session. Some therapists like to begin with this discussion before inviting the client to talk about their difficulties, while others prefer to do it later on in the session, allowing the client to begin. Whatever is planned may need to change quickly in response to the situation as it develops. For example, I have experienced many occasions when clients arrive in a very distressed state and there is barely sufficient time to say 'hello' before they begin to talk about their difficulties. My own view is that it is not appropriate to interrupt a client in such a situation, given there is a diminished likelihood of them being able to take in much information. Rather, allow for an appropriate time during the session to gently take the client's attention to the contract. It is very important that clients are given space and time to consider how their therapy will be shaped and that contracting is as collaborative as the fixed parameters allow.

Of course, clients are likely to arrive with expectations based on fears, anxieties and hopes. The purpose of contracting, therefore, is to ensure the client's expectations are both realistic and deliverable by the therapist. By 'realistic' I am referring to the goals and hopes they might have about how their problems will be addressed with counselling (I will discuss this further later on in the chapter). By 'deliverable', I am referring to the therapist's willingness and ability to deliver what is promised. For example, a therapist might say their therapy is time-limited and that six sessions will be available at a certain cost per session. This is deliverable, in that the therapist is able to meet these parameters. However, if the therapist says that they can guarantee the client will feel better after six sessions, this would be both unreasonable and, in all likelihood, misleading.

However, it is important to challenge the idea that contracting is something that takes place only at the beginning of therapy. The client's situation may have changed over time where a re-negotiated contract is desirable. For example, a client may wish to reduce the frequency of sessions if they feel improvements are being made, or perhaps the time or day of sessions. All these need to be incorporated into a new contract. Likewise, the practitioner's circumstances may demand changes that need to be negotiated with the client.

My own experience of working with clients at risk of suicide or self-harm suggests that a detailed exploration of the boundaries of confidentiality can also provide a structure within which to explore risk. In this sense the contract can also be used as a therapeutic tool as well as an administrative or procedural one. For example, in the dialogue presented in Figure 7.2 the contract is referred to in helping the client, Alex, to consider the nature of suicidal thoughts. Here the counsellor is able to use the initial discussion about the contract and the meaning of suicide risk to help Alex think more about his own thoughts and his level of distress. The contract is brought into therapy in an active and applied way, rather than an isolated dialogue that only informs the process of therapy from a distance.

What the contract might include

The exact contents of a contract will depend on the context in which counselling or psychotherapy is being offered. For example, in the university setting in which

Alex	Sometimes I feel just ... rubbish. I just wish I could go to bed and not wake up – just disappear ... if you know what I mean?
Therapist	I think I know what you mean. Sometimes we just don't want to be around any more, but aren't sure whether it is something we want to actively do to ourselves, or just to happen.
Alex	In what way? How d'you mean?
Therapist	Well, remember when we first started counselling and I explained about confidentiality? [Yes] I made a distinction between having thoughts about wanting to be dead, and having plans or an intention to kill ourselves. The first one can illustrate how bad we are feeling, while the second talks more about our intention to kill ourselves.
Alex	Yes, I remember that.
Therapist	I wonder what your thoughts are, and what they mean to you?
Alex	Ehmm. That's interesting. I don't want to do anything to kill myself ... I mean ... I don't intend to kill myself or actually want to die, now I think about it. I just want the pain to stop; to go away. It's like I want to sleep it away.
Therapist	You don't want to kill yourself – to do something specific to end your life, but you are tired of how you feel and just wish it could go away?
Alex	Yes. That's right.

FIGURE 7.2 Using the Contract as a Therapeutic Tool

I work counselling is offered free at the point of delivery. Thus, while our contract will outline confidentiality, number of sessions, frequency and means of contact, for example, it does not need to make any reference to fees. An independent practitioner will need to address issues of fees and payment clearly to avoid any future confusion. The following list represents the types of things that might be included in a contract, depending on the setting:

- Who the therapist will be
- How to make contact with the therapist, and in what situations (email, phone etc.)
- How to contact the client (email, phone), and whether messages can be left
- The name and contact details of a GP, or a friend/relative who the client would be happy for the therapist to contact in the event of an emergency
- Any specific needs (e.g. access) and how these will be accommodated, if possible
- How many sessions will be offered, if there is a limit
- How long each session will last, and the frequency of sessions

- The fee for each session (if applicable), including cancellation fees and fees for missed sessions
- Whether cancelled or missed sessions are included in the total number offered (regardless of fees)
- How holiday periods will be managed
- The nature of therapy being offered (e.g. modality, scope)
- Where therapy will take place, and how the client should arrive
- The limitations of confidentiality and the circumstances in which confidentiality may be broken
- Whether the therapist works to any ethical guidelines
- What to do in the event of a complaint
- Whether review sessions are to be held, and their frequency
- How therapy can be cancelled, including the length of notice required (if any).

Fees

In an organisational setting, it is likely that the organisation will decide the fee structures and how monies will be collected. If working independently, these decisions clearly fall to the therapist to resolve. The amount charged for a session is obviously an important business decision, and one most likely informed by the prevailing fee structure locally. For example, if the majority of independent practitioners charge in the range of £40–£50, it would not make business sense to charge in the range of £90–£100, unless specific reasons warrant such a fee. It is important too to consider carefully whether: (a) sessions are charged for on a session-by-session basis, retrospectively or in advance; (b) fees will be charged for cancelled sessions, missed sessions and for holiday periods; and (c) whether initial or assessment sessions are charged for or are free of charge. All of these decisions need to be clearly communicated to the client before they arrive for a first session.

DISCUSSION QUESTIONS

1   In your setting, what are the main considerations that would need to be covered in a contract?
2   How do you communicate the details of the contract to the client? How could the contract be made more accessible?
3   How do you undertake a discussion about the contract and when do you do so?
4   How does your theoretical orientation inform your approach to contracting?

7.5 EARLY STAGES OF THE RELATIONSHIP

SECTION OUTLINE

This section explores the challenges of the early stages of counselling and psychotherapy, including the development of a therapeutic alliance and ways of facilitating the client. Ways of working to help the client engage with counselling or psychotherapy are considered, as well as challenges that therapists might need to overcome so that the early relationship is not undermined.

Much will have already happened by the time you sit with your client to begin the process of exploring with them the issues that have brought them into counselling and psychotherapy. It is likely they will have a number of expectations, hopes and anxieties about the process of therapy, some of which may have been attended to by reading thorough and appropriate pre-therapy literature, and perhaps by talking to you on the telephone or by email when arranging the appointment. Certainly all of the important questions about the nature of counselling and psychotherapy with you will have been addressed during the contracting process, which may also form an important aspect of initiating an early therapeutic relationship. If you put time aside to assess with the client their needs and expectations, the therapeutic discourse will already have started and the relationship begun to develop.

We need to keep in mind what research tells us about what clients know and expect of counselling, for we can often assume they know much more than they actually do. Pipes et al. (1995), LeSurf and Lynch (1999) and Lambert (2008) all note in their studies the level of apprehension about counselling and psychotherapy clients will experience as they attend for their first few sessions. This certainly affirms my own experience of beginning therapy with people, many of whom know very little about what happens. As I have outlined previously, they may assume I will be an Austrian man with a beard asking them to lie on a couch, telling me the first thing that comes into their head, or what they see in ink blots. While there are, of course, many excellent Austrian therapists, and some will use a couch and free association, and others may indeed use ink blot tests, the stereotype probably says very little about the realities of most of the counselling and psychotherapy clients will access.

The most common problems concerning preconceptions about counselling or psychotherapy, as outlined by Lambert (2008, p 50) are:

- An ambivalence and uncertainty about seeking counselling or psychotherapy,
- Having doubts about the therapist's motives and awareness of the power differences,

- Social and cultural perspectives, which may be different from those of the therapist,
- Stigma and negative influence of peers and family on exploring emotions, and fear of delving deeper.

Often with a huge sense of relief clients will say towards the end of the first session, or after a couple of sessions, they feel less anxious about coming and that it 'really wasn't as bad as they feared'. It is very easy for us to forget from time to time that although we may be very familiar with the language, culture, nature and form of counselling and psychotherapy, most people will not be: they may instead make assumptions based on stereotypes, media representations, or what they have read on the Internet. The first task then, is to ensure our language is accessible, and that we avoid unnecessary jargon and assume nothing.

Lambert (2008, p. 51) has identified a number of key skills required in early sessions to help initiate and develop an early therapeutic relationship. These are:

- Listening carefully to the client without making assumptions
- Exploring with the client what he or she hopes to gain from counselling or psychotherapy
- Describing your own approach to counselling or psychotherapy and being clear, in the light of the aims you are exploring with the client, as to the possible benefits and limitations
- Being clear about the practicalities of counselling and psychotherapy within your organisation or practice (for example, the client's idea of how long therapy will last, the number of sessions available, fee arrangements, tape-recording of sessions, and note-taking)
- Discussing issues that may arise in connection with confidentiality and supervision.

I would supplement Lambert's list with the following thoughts:

- If asked about your approach, give sufficient information to provide a full answer without slipping into a lengthy lecture about the relative pros and cons of your model, the underlying philosophy and key theorists.
- Be willing and able to talk about how you like to work without becoming overly theoretical about it. (For example, 'I like to offer feedback to people during sessions', or 'I particularly focus on what you are saying to help you think about your situation more', or 'I may sometimes offer my own interpretations of what you are saying, which we can discuss'.)
- Ensure you allow plenty of time for clients to ask questions, and perhaps prompt questions if they are unsure or reluctant to ask. (For example, 'Sometimes people

like to know a bit more about what I mean by confidentiality' or 'Is there any-thing you would like to know about what happens in sessions?')

- Ensure you provide choices and that clients have permission to make choices. (For example, clients may prefer to work with a female or male counsellor, or might prefer to see someone else.)
- It is very difficult to back out of counselling or psychotherapy, so give your clients breathing space to think about what they would like to do. (For example, 'I think it is important to take time to think about whether you are happy to continue – don't feel as if you have to make a decision now if you are not sure.')

Pace

It is important to work at the client's pace and not to 'rush ahead'. This is often a particular challenge for trainees new on a placement who are keen to practise their skills and what they have been learning in a 'real-world' environment. It is important to develop a rapport, which hopefully will have started during a con-tracting or assessment process, so that the client can tell their story and carefully, and sometimes slowly, outline their particular difficulties. Often a great deal of shame will be associated with emotional difficulties or a distressing set of experi-ences, so time and care is needed. While exploration and challenge are important, these need to be carefully pitched so as not to rush a client or leave them feeling overwhelmed.

Particular challenges arise when working within a brief model where there is less time to allow this process to occur naturally. It is helpful in this instance for therapists to be more directive and outline to their clients from the very beginning the time scale and the implications that might have. However, even in brief therapy it is perfectly possible to allow space for clients to tell their story without rushing them. In working at the client's pace it is important to check the client's expectations and understanding of the process and, in doing so, negotiate with the client how best to proceed and what aspects of their story they would like to focus on.

Challenges in the early stages

Perhaps the greatest threat to an early therapeutic relationship derives from unex-plored assumptions about counselling or psychotherapy, or about the therapist themselves. As Lambert (2008) notes, clients may assume the therapist has particu-lar techniques they might employ, or a hidden agenda, or the therapist has made assumptions about the client's difficulties they are not talking about. The therapist needs to demonstrate from the very beginning that they will be transparent in their thinking and approach and collaborative in their interventions. However, there may be some therapeutic approaches where this would be contraindicated, such as in psychoanalysis where the therapist abstains from disclosure or a personal presence. Clients attending for such therapy will have been provided with that information from the beginning (and preferably before they attend their first session) so they can make a choice about whether that particular approach is best for their needs.

The therapist might bring assumptions or stereotypes about clients or presenting problems that do not reflect the reality of the actual client or their experience. The importance of supervision here cannot be overstated as a place for such assumptions and stereotypes to be named and explored. This may be particularly challenging to the therapist who may feel their own sense of shame in naming them, fearing judgement from their supervisor. However, if they are not named and fully explored there is a high chance they will be acted out in sessions with clients. This situation will quickly inhibit the development of a safe and trusting therapeutic space.

DISCUSSION QUESTIONS

1 What steps do you take to ensure clients have the necessary space and time to identify and express their expectations, hopes and anxieties about counselling?
2 What steps do you take to ensure that you explore your own expectations, hopes and anxieties about counselling with a particular client?
3 How do you begin to establish a therapeutic relationship with a client? What are the key skills required?
4 How do you ensure that you are working at the client's pace (especially if you are offering time-limited therapy)?

7.6 GOAL-SETTING AND REVIEWING

SECTION OUTLINE

The identification of particular goals or hopes for therapy is an important part of the therapeutic process, as is knowing when and how to review therapy. This section explores the issues pertinent to goal-setting and reviewing so that counselling or psychotherapy can remain a collaborative, beneficial process.

While the setting of goals might be assumed to be associated specifically with cognitive-behavioural approaches, it is arguably embedded within all therapeutic modalities. The terminology might be different in that the term 'goals' might not be used, but arguably most therapists, most of the time, are concerned with the client's expectations and hopes from therapy. We might think of goals as desired outcomes, or targets, or simply what the client wants for themselves. Humanistic approaches that are client-centred are focused on the client's direction for therapy. The suggestion here is that some time be taken in the early stages of any therapeutic relationship to explore with our clients what their hopes might be, and incorporate them into the therapeutic process. Of course, clients might not be able to clearly articulate their goals, or differentiate particular goals from a more generalised wish to feel better. The skill of the therapist can be used to help encourage clients to think differently about their problems so they have a better idea of where they want to head.

Bordin (1979) has suggested that failure to help clients explore their 'wants' from therapy can lead to clients feeling disappointment and frustration. As a result, early attempts at developing a therapeutic alliance might flounder. According to O'Carroll (2008, p. 105), this early process might prove difficult because:

- Clients find it difficult to see future goals through the fog and confusion of their current world problems and their personal problem experiences.
- They may see their goals as in conflict between goals about changes to their world problems and goals about changes in their problem experiences.
- If many goals are identified, clients and therapists may be unclear which are and which are not relevant to the process of counselling and psychotherapy.
- Clients may often look to the past to define their goals, before their world problems or their problem experiences began.

Bordin (1979) identified a number of key aspects for the therapeutic alliance (later discussed by Dryden, 2008):

Bonds: the nature and form of the bond between therapist and client, which will include attitudes of the therapist and how they are experienced by the client; the attitudes of the client and how they are experienced by the therapist; the interpersonal styles of both therapist and client; the concepts of transference and countertransference (discussed further in Chapter 8)

Views: these include the views held by therapist and client on issues such as:

The nature of clients' psychological problems

How can clients' problems best be addressed

The practical aspects of counselling

Therapists' views are influenced by their therapy approach

Clients' views about therapy

Effective therapy occurs when the client's views are similar to the therapists'

Goals: the objectives of both the client and therapist that go beyond wanting to feel better, and wanting to help

Tasks: activities carried out by the client and therapist with a view to achieving the agreed goals

Helping to define goals

Moving on from the starting point of the client generally wanting to feel better, the task of the therapist is to help the client differentiate a little more about what would help them feel better, and how that might be achieved. This is particularly true for time-limited or brief therapy, where there is less chance all problems will be addressed: there is a need instead to focus on primary difficulties that might lead to the greatest possible change. A number of important considerations need to be borne in mind when helping clients to think about their goals. They include the following:

- Goals need to be as specific as possible, so that, for example, 'I don't want to feel anxious anymore' is worked through until 'I don't want to feel anxious when meeting my friends' is reached. In this example the client has been supported to move away from a generalised hope (of not wanting to feel anxious anymore), to a more specific goal (where the specific situation(s) in which anxiety is particularly experienced is named).
- Goals need to reflect aspects of the client's life over which they have the power to change. So, a goal of 'I want my father to listen to me more' falls outside the client's capacity to achieve, in that this would demand changes in the father's behaviour, which the client is unable to fulfil. Instead the client may have a goal of 'I want to be able to notice more effectively when my father has time so I can be more selective of when I tell him things'. In this example the client is defining aspects of their own behaviour they have the capacity to change, rather than aspects that fall outside of the client's will.
- Goals need to be realistic and achievable rather than unrealistic and aspirational. It is important to be clear about the goal, and ensure that the goal is achievable, so that the tasks can be set accordingly. If we take the example given previously,

'I don't want to be anxious when meeting with my friends', the goal here is both realistic and achievable. ('I want all my friends to like me' would be unrealistic and aspirational). The client and therapist can then set tasks for them both to work through as 'stepping stones' towards the goal. In this instance, this might include: identifying what aspects of contact with friends trigger anxiety and what the anxiety means for the client; an exploration of the relationship between therapist and client to help explore relational dynamics that might hinder the client (mediating external and internal client goals – see Dryden, 2008 for a fuller discussion of these); and things the client might do outside therapy to facilitate change, such as spending time with one friend and noticing changes while using self-support strategies discussed in therapy.

- Goals need to be regularly reviewed to determine change and whether they remain relevant. As therapy progresses the original goals may change as the client feels they progress or as different priorities emerge. It is important to regularly revisit goals to ensure therapy remains relevant for the client.

Reviewing

I can think of times over the years when, as a client, my own therapy has become aimless and without direction. It is very easy to slip into a routine of counselling or psychotherapy and not question its relevance or purpose. Time passes and it becomes harder to step back and ask questions of the process. Clients can find themselves trapped in open-ended therapy that no longer meets their needs, but it is too difficult to extricate oneself from it: perhaps for fear of disappointing the therapist, or of making them angry. Goals that were once set have long passed their 'sell-by date' and real change and insight is a thing of the past.

A review can:

- help keep the client's needs central to the process
- provide an opportunity for the client and therapist to think about what has changed
- offer a chance for client and therapist to reflect on what is working in the relationship, and what isn't
- communicate to the client their central importance in the process and that their needs remain key
- provide an opportunity for things previously unsaid to be brought into the open
- provide an opportunity for metacommunications (Rennie, 1998), where the process of how client and therapist talk to each other is itself talked about

- generate a time for new goals and tasks to be set
- provide an opportunity for client and therapist to check they are working to the same agenda
- provide a space to ask whether it is time to finish and, if it is, to plan for that.

The concept of reviewing needs to be introduced from the first session and built into the contract. This ensures that reviewing is culturally embedded into the therapeutic relationship. Introducing a review into counselling or psychotherapy without warning runs a high risk of the client feeling judged on their 'performance', thus compounding any sense of shame they may experience. It is also important that the review process considers all aspects of the therapy relationship, including the part the therapist plays in that. You might usefully prepare for reviews by exploring these considerations in your own supervision first.

Which questions are included in a review will depend on modality. They might include the following:

- How are you feeling now by comparison to when we started?
- Thinking about the initial goals we set, what are your thoughts about them currently?
- How relevant are they for you at this stage in your life?
- What things do you think have changed positively for you?
- What things do you think you continue to struggle with?
- Are you able to say all the things you need to say here?
- What about what happens between us during sessions – how we talk to each other, how we cope with disagreements, whether you feel listened to?
- What do you think are the most helpful things about our counselling or psychotherapy?
- What do you think are the least helpful things about our counselling or psychotherapy?
- If we were to arrange more sessions, how would we best use them?
- Has a point come for you where taking a break or ending counselling or psychotherapy would be helpful?

The dialogue informed by such questions needs to be a collaborative one, in which the therapist is able to give permission to the client to be honest about their experience by taking their own risks. The more I have been able to put my 'self' into the review and occasionally offer my own thoughts initially, the more the client has felt able to be honest about their own part of the process. This has typically led to a relational exploration of some considerable depth. As a result, a well-managed review process can facilitate a level of change and take the relationship to a new level, which might otherwise not have happened.

7.7 WORKING LONG TERM OR BRIEFLY

SECTION OUTLINE

Therapy may be open-ended (with no limit to the number of sessions offered), time-limited (with a specific number of sessions offered), or brief (i.e., with only a few sessions offered). This section considers what is required by each approach and what factors therapists need to keep in mind when working in each way.

The idea of brief therapy is essentially a new one, with little consideration given to it in the UK before the early 1990s (Feltham, 2012). In the UK many organisations have adopted brief, or time-limited, models of therapy. Feltham (2012) notes that the terms brief and time-limited are generally used interchangeably and typically refer to therapeutic approaches that are: (a) designed by nature to be delivered briefly; or (b) approaches not specifically designed to be brief therapy, but are delivered as such. In this section I will make three distinctions:

• open-ended therapy: where there is no time limit placed at the commencement of therapy but rather the number of sessions is dictated during a review process or by client direction
• time-limited therapy: where the number of sessions offered is limited by theoretical/modality direction, such as cognitive-behavioural therapy (generally offered over 16 sessions)
• brief therapy: where only very few sessions are offered – this can run from so-called 'single session therapy', through to six or eight sessions maximum, as a rule.

There is a fine line between the definitions of time-limited and brief therapy. Here I simply wish to differentiate between those therapies designed to be delivered briefly, and those not but delivered briefly all the same. This is an important distinction when exploring the application of such approaches in practice because it is not uncommon for therapy, normally not associated within a time-limited frame, to be delivered over a limited number of sessions without any accommodation being made on behalf of the counsellor or psychotherapist for the change in focus. As the old saying goes, it is difficult to put a quart into a pint pot. Thus for time-limited or brief therapy to be most effective, some changes to how the therapy is delivered need to be made, as it is generally not helpful to work in the same way in brief therapy as you would in open-ended therapy.

Failing on the part of the practitioner to adjust is a classic mistake: it can make brief therapy a frustrating endeavour for therapist and client alike. I can certainly recall many instances of practitioners new to brief therapy bemoaning its usefulness during supervision: the client's problems remained unresolved; the work was too superficial; the client didn't have time to talk about their problems in any meaningful way; and working briefly was ultimately incongruent with an underpinning therapeutic philosophy, for example. In such instances, brief therapy can be experienced as the antithesis to 'good' therapy and as something that is generally imposed on the therapist by an organisation too focused on the importance of numbers and not the individual.

Open-ended therapy

Open-ended therapy is perhaps the idea most associated with counselling and psychotherapy – where counsellor or psychotherapist meet with the client and the process of therapy is allowed to take its time in development, sometimes over several years. Indeed, psychoanalysis (as discussed further in Chapter 3) is intended to take time, typically involving two or three sessions per week over many years. This allows for the full development of transferential dynamics and, therefore, as Feltham (2012, p. 560) outlines, time to search for the 'putative origins of symptoms; preoccupation with clients' early histories; perfectionism; dwelling on mainly in-session phenomena; infantilisation and dependency; the apparent aimlessness of free association; transference neurosis; and recognition of the economic convenience of long-term paying clients'. He adds that the principles of brief therapy are the 'reversals' of these factors (p. 560).

Taken literally, many humanistic theories might be expected to require an extraordinary amount of time to successfully complete. If counselling or psychotherapy is truly person-centred, for example, surely it would only end when the client is ready for it to? Likewise, why work, not within the 50 or 60 minute session, but rather (as some therapists have chosen to do) for as long as the client is experiencing benefit?

The research evidence does not necessarily support the premise of the efficacy of open-ended counselling or psychotherapy. Kadera, Lambert and Andrews (1996) noted in their study that 22% of their participants recovered after eight sessions of therapy, while the earliest recovery noted was after two sessions. Hansen, Lambert and Forman (2002) reviewed a variety of evidence and noted that between 57.6% and 67.2% of clients improved within an average of 12.7 sessions. One might argue, on the basis of this evidence, that there is little benefit in working long term with clients and that all counselling or psychotherapy would be better structured around 12 sessions. However, experience would suggest that there are clients for whom longer-term therapy is very effective, particularly when a focus is retained through the use of regular reviews.

The last decade has certainly seen a shift in focus in the UK from many services willing and able to offer long-term or open-ended counselling or psychotherapy to just a few, usually located within the third sector. Many organisations in health, social care, education and the third sector have also been forced to cut the number of sessions offered to clients as a means of managing over-demand for therapy. Outside independent practice it is rare indeed to find many such services now.

Brief therapy

As we have established, much counselling and psychotherapy provision in the UK is, whether through design or necessity, now structured around brief working, ranging anywhere from single-session therapy through to 14–16 sessions maximum. An increase in the popularity of counselling and psychotherapy, a greater acknowledgement of the viability and efficacy of the psychological therapies generally, and reducing budgets are all contributing factors to this trend. Alongside this is a deliberate choice made by some therapy providers for the efficacy of brief therapies, supported by a clear rationale (Dewan et al., 2012).

In an overview of brief therapy, Feltham (2012, pp. 560–2) highlights the following areas for therapists to consider:

- Assessment: brief therapy is generally most successful with people who have mild to moderate problems with clear presenting difficulties, who are motivated, psychologically minded, and who possess a reasonable level of coping and with good support from family and friends.
- Belief in the approach: the counsellor or psychotherapist must be committed to the idea of delivering brief therapy (rather than feeling it having been imposed on them). When fully committed to the benefits of brief therapy, clients are more likely to be helped to engage in a time-limited endeavour.

- Developing the therapeutic alliance: therapists must be willing and able to focus on establishing a sound therapeutic relationship as early as possible. The importance of collaboration between practitioner and client is stressed. This can be achieved through clear contracting, being honest with the client about realistic expectations of what is likely to be achieved, and a shared focus and goal(s).

- Being focused and active: whereas, in open-ended work, non-directiveness and a full exploration of history and problems is possible, brief therapy does not allow for this. Helping the client to focus on key problem areas that can be worked with leads to the best likelihood of a positive outcome. This will often mean 'parking' other concerns (i.e., acknowledging their importance for clients, but agreeing they will not be the focus of therapy and thus need to be temporarily 'parked').

- A skilful use of skills: working as one might in open-ended therapy but instead simply doing it in a fewer number of sessions is unlikely to be a satisfactory experience for either therapist or client. Instead, a greater degree of pragmatism is required, with the counsellor or psychotherapist being more directive or active than they might ordinarily be.

- Parsimony: Feltham describes this as 'the practice of making the least radical intervention necessary and the most obviously indicated' (2012, p. 561). This demands that the therapist looks towards the least intervention necessary. This might include no intervention at all (one should not simply assume the client needs therapy).

- Time as a form of focus: in the same way that clients can feel contained by the 50 or 60 minute therapeutic hour, knowing when it starts and stops, the same can be true for brief therapy. In my own experience, clients have reported liking the focus of brief work and feeling contained knowing the number of sessions they have, even though that isn't many.

- Specific techniques: while many interventions from open-ended therapy can be effective, interventions designed specifically for brief work can be particularly beneficial. For example, the miracle question from solution-focused therapy, helping the client to consider expectations in relation to their current problems, paradoxical interventions, and scaling questions (when clients self-score their problems and consider the factors required to facilitate change) can all be beneficial.

- Preparing for ending: Feltham (2012, p. 562) outlines a number of factors that are key to ethical and effective brief therapy, including:

  - realism about end results and disappointment
  - discouragement of dependency on the therapist and a focus on self-coping
  - preparation for possible relapse by focusing on strategies
  - the possibility of follow-up sessions
  - evaluation of outcomes.

When a counsellor or psychotherapist is able to utilise these aspects and integrate them into their way of working, they are best placed to help facilitate change and growth for their clients. It is, however, unhelpful to view brief therapy as simply the consequence of financial expediency imposed on the unwilling therapist, as it can, when employed skilfully, offer clients viable options for change.

DISCUSSION QUESTIONS

1   What are your thoughts about open-ended and brief therapies? What factors inform these views?
2   How might you adapt your current way of working to brief therapy? Or, if you have already done so, how did you achieve it?
3   What clients might make most effective use of brief therapy? Why?
4   What do you see as the potential difficulties of open-ended therapy?

7.8 MANAGING ENDINGS

SECTION OUTLINE

Endings are an inevitable consequence of beginnings. The question of the ending of the therapeutic relationship requires attention from the moment a counsellor or psychotherapist begins to work with a client. Some endings are planned, others are unplanned and unexpected. This section considers planned and unplanned endings and the considerations therapists need to keep in mind when working with all types of endings.

The moment we begin counselling or psychotherapy with a client, we have an ethical and professional duty to plan for its end. Unless we envisage therapy with a client to be a life-long process, the end of therapy is one inevitability we must address. When we consider the process of counselling and psychotherapy in our training, we often bring to mind a neat and sequential process of beginnings, middles and ends. Certainly for many clients this will be the case, and the end of therapy will be carefully planned and anticipated by both client and therapist in advance of it happening. Together we will be aware that it is approaching and we will collaboratively bring the therapeutic exploration to a close, tying up final loose ends before saying goodbye.

On placement, however, we can quickly realise that endings can often arrive unexpectedly. They may take us by surprise, sometimes leaving us feeling bereft and questioning our interventions and the integrity of the therapeutic relationship. We might not have had the sense of a 'middle', which only becomes apparent in the context of when and how the therapy finished. Sometimes there might not be a middle at all, with clients terminating therapy after one session. In short, we have both planned and unplanned endings to consider, and both need anticipating carefully.

Anticipating endings

I have discussed earlier in the chapter the importance of contracting. The careful management and anticipation of the ending of therapy is an excellent illustration of why contracting is so important. The most effective way of working towards an end ethically and professionally is to name it at the beginning. It is extremely helpful to clients for the end to be discussed as it helps shape realistic expectations and provides containment for the client to either consciously or unconsciously work within. As stated elsewhere in this chapter, we all accept the importance of informing clients of the timing of therapy, so if we begin seeing a client at 2.00 pm, for example, they will be very aware that the session will finish at 2.50 pm or 3.00 pm (or whatever has been agreed). When in counselling myself as a client, this knowledge has provided me with an opportunity to pace my disclosure and subsequent exploration. The same is true for the wider process of counselling and psychotherapy.

Some would argue that, with some presentations, knowledge of when therapy will finish is a therapeutic imperative. For example, many would believe that in bereavement counselling a defined and agreed finish provides the client with an opportunity to work towards another 'end', perhaps giving them an invaluable opportunity to do this 'end' differently from the bereavement. Likewise, others have argued that when working with clients who have experience of sexual abuse, an end-point for therapy is essential. When they were being abused, clients often would not have known when it was going to stop; having an agreed end-point in therapy enables them to have a degree of control that perhaps was not available to them previously. The contracting stage of counselling and psychotherapy is therefore the obvious place for endings to be discussed.

Planned endings

A planned ending is where the end point of therapy is determined from the outset and both therapist and client work towards the ending. Planning for the end of therapy will often be a balance between a number of factors, including: the needs of the client; the hopes and expectations of the client regarding the length of therapy; the assessment of the therapist; the preference of the therapist for how long they typically like to work; and, if therapy is located within an organisational setting, the fixed parameters of how many sessions can be offered. Sometimes this balance works well, where all aspects coincide without problem. Often however, some compromise might need to be made, either by the therapist or the client. For example, the client might arrive to counselling expecting long-term help, only to be disappointed to discover that they will only be able to attend for six sessions. Likewise, the therapist might prefer to work in an open-ended way (i.e., without limiting the number of sessions from the outset), but work in an organisational setting where only a limited number of sessions are allowed – see the previous section on working long term or briefly for a fuller discussion. Other difficulties may arise with planned endings. Box 7.1 outlines work with Anya as an example. A further **two case examples** are available on the companion website to further illustrate planned endings.

CASE STUDY 7.1
Anya

Anya has been seeing her counsellor, Deb, for seven sessions. Anya originally attended therapy for relationship problems and, while these have been mostly addressed, she and Deb have begun to talk about Anya's future and how uncertain and anxious she feels. Counselling is provided in a voluntary agency where the policy is to offer clients eight sessions. Deb explained this to Anya at the beginning, and it is written in the contract. Deb is ambivalent about time-limited therapy and enjoys working with Anya. Deb is also aware that there is only one session left, but is finding Anya's exploration fascinating. Likewise, Anya had not anticipated talking about these issues in counselling, but is finding it very helpful. She is upset and disappointed that counselling is due to finish, and requests further sessions. This request is declined by the agency because Deb acknowledges the original presenting issues have now been addressed.

PAUSE FOR REFLECTION

1 What are your thoughts about how Deb has managed the planned ending? What might she have done differently?
2 Why might Deb have managed this ending in such a way?
3 What are the implications for Anya in finishing counselling at this stage?
4 What issues does this scenario raise concerning the difficulties of planned endings?

While the ending with Anya was carefully planned from the outset, it is possible to see in this scenario how easily such planning can be undermined and the possible implications for both therapist and client. It raises the issue that, for a variety of reasons that might not include mis-management by the therapist, when the planned ending actually comes around it may not be welcomed by either party. It is important for you to keep the planned ending in sight, just as you would the ending of any one session, and plan accordingly. It is not helpful for clients for you to facilitate a deeper exploration of new issues when therapy is coming to an end. Rather, consolidating change, discussing future strategies for coping and reviewing progress might be more helpful. Ultimately, planned endings might bring disappointment and frustration, just as they might bring consolidation and looking forward. The response to these feelings is as much a therapeutic task as anything that took place previously.

Unplanned endings

Unplanned endings can happen for a variety of reasons. An unplanned ending is any ending of therapy that was not foreseen or predicted from the outset. Two case examples of unplanned endings are available on the companion website. Robson (2008) has provided a helpful summary of why therapy might end unexpectedly. This is outlined in Table 7.1. This outline is helpful because, as therapists, we might assume unplanned endings will be the result of client behaviour or withdrawal; whereas, while clients may withdraw from therapy for a variety of reasons, therapists can also cause unplanned endings. It is important for us to consider our own vulnerabilities, such as changes to our employment status, changes in our domestic circumstances, ill-health or death.

TABLE 7.1   Possible reasons for unplanned endings

For the client	For the therapist
May feel they are not ready to continue therapy; may not be convinced therapy will work; may not be convinced that therapy is worth the pain/hard work/financial cost	The therapist leaves the agency that employs them – voluntarily, through redundancy or being sacked
May feel they have finished but are reluctant to discuss this with the therapist; may be uncomfortable with the therapist but unable to say	The therapist moves away from the area
Illness	Illness
Crisis in their life	Crisis in their life
Death (including suicide)	Death (including suicide)
May have been ambivalent about therapy to begin with	
Runs out of money	
Life changes, such as a new job, or moving away	
Another, perhaps free, source of help becomes available (e.g., therapy from a GP practice)	

Source: Robson, 2008, p. 200

Elsewhere I have written extensively about an unplanned ending with a client due to her suicide (Reeves, 2010a). This type of ending is certainly feared by many therapists. Likewise, it is important to pay particular attention to the wellbeing of clients if therapy is ended unexpectedly by the therapist. For therapists working in organisational settings there are likely to be protocols in place to manage ongoing client work. However, for independent practitioners it is essential they have plans in place for the management of their caseload in the event of illness or sudden death, including suicide.

As therapists we are often left with lots of unanswered questions that need to be processed. When clients don't return to counselling or psychotherapy we may experience a number of thoughts and feelings. These are outlined in Table 7.2.

TABLE 7.2   Emotions experienced by therapists following unplanned endings

Endings precipitated by the client	Endings precipitated by the therapist
Self-doubt (guilt, along with feeling inadequate/insufficient/incompetent)	Guilt
Worry about the wellbeing of the client	Worry about the wellbeing of the client
Relief	Relief
Confused as to the best thing to do	Confused as to the best thing to do
Frustrated/irritated/cross	Frustrated/irritated/cross
Hurt and sad	Sad

Source: Robson, 2008, p. 201

As we can see, the feelings therapists may experience can be similar if the client or therapist initiated the unplanned ending. It is important for therapists to fully address these feelings, by talking to colleagues, peers or more specifically in supervision. Counsellors and psychotherapists will often look for answers and certainty following an unplanned ending, and often answers will not be found. We must be able to consider all possibilities and respect the client's right to end in a way and at a time of their choosing.

DISCUSSION QUESTIONS

1   How do you discuss endings with your clients?
2   How do you prepare clients for planned endings? How might you manage situations where either you or the client does not wish to end as planned, yet there is no choice?
3   How do you support yourself following an unplanned ending initiated by a client?
4   What plans do you have in place should you need to end therapy with clients unexpectedly, perhaps in the event of serious illness or death?

7.9 AFTER THE CLIENT HAS LEFT

SECTION OUTLINE

Once counselling or psychotherapy sessions have finished, there may still be unfinished business for the therapist to attend to. Understanding the impact of work, learning from successes or mistakes, and transferring skills and knowledge into new relationships are all important matters. Additionally, the business of keeping records and respecting confidentiality continues to require attention long after therapy has finished. This section explores these issues, identifying ways in which counsellors and psychotherapists can continue to respect the integrity of the therapeutic relationship.

Our commitment to ethical, professional practice and accountability to our clients does not finish when therapy does. While we might no longer be meeting regularly with our clients and the active therapeutic relationship has finished, there remain several aspects we need to pay attention to. These fall into three distinct areas:

1   Case management
2   Professional accountability
3   Therapeutic reflection.

Case management

When counselling or psychotherapy ends, a number of case management considerations require immediate and ongoing attention. Clearly the task of ending will focus on helping the client to safely 'close' personal material so that they can leave therapy with as few 'loose ends' as possible. This might include helping clients to consider strategies they have learnt during therapy and ways in which they might support themselves in the future.

However, it is important not to overlook the practical aspects of ending counselling. Where a charge is made for counselling or psychotherapy, all financial aspects must be completed. This might include ensuring that all sessions have been charged for, refunds (if any) have been made, and receipts have been issued where required. These should be dealt with before the client leaves the final session, so that the ending process is not impinged upon by practical discussion and it is not necessary to contact the client, once finished, to settle any remaining financial issues.

It is important to reassure clients about any records that have been kept. This requires information on how they will be securely retained, for what purpose and for how long. How long written notes need be retained following the end of counselling is difficult to be clear about. The Association for University and College Counselling (AUCC) (Lawton et al., 2010, p. 9) guidelines for university and college counselling services states that the following should be considered:

- The Data Protection Act 1998, which states that sensitive data should not be kept for longer than is necessary.
- The ability of the service to store confidential records safely and securely over time.
- The purpose for which the notes are kept (i.e., their therapeutic purpose).
- The content of the therapy and the possibility that a client's records might be needed in the future (e.g. for a criminal case or civil suit, in a claim for compensation, or in an internal university or college procedure such as an academic appeal or formal complaint). The length of time needed to retain records in such scenarios is extremely difficult to predict. There are different time limitations on cases brought before the courts (see Bond and Mitchels, 2008, pp. 72–8).

There are tensions here, given that the Data Protection Act 1998 states that sensitive data should not be kept for longer than is necessary, while notes might be important for a therapist in providing information to court at a later date or in dealing with a complaint. Some services retain only minimal information while therapy is ongoing, and shred all information at the end of therapy. Others will store therapy notes for three or five years, or sometimes longer. If notes are retained, it is important (and a legal requirement) that they be stored securely to safeguard the client's confidentiality and identity. If counselling is located within an organisational setting, the policy of the organisation (who must comply with data protection requirements) will dictate whether and how notes are retained. Independent practitioners must decide for themselves how long they wish to retain notes, if at all, and ensure clients are fully informed of this policy.

Finally, the therapist should discuss with the client before the end of therapy whether and how the client wishes to be contacted in the future. Some clients may be interested to hear about other therapy services, such as the future provision of workshops or groups. Other clients may not wish to be contacted at all. If clients are to be contacted post-therapy, the counsellor or therapist needs be clear with the client in what circumstances this would take place, and how the client would prefer contact to occur. Obtaining written client consent for such contact would be important.

Professional accountability

The duty of professional accountability to clients does not end when the ongoing direct work does. Indeed, the same level of care is required post-therapy as was demanded during therapy. This includes such matters as how the therapist responds to any subsequent contact from the ex-client, whether future contact has been agreed and the client's confidentiality.

As I have argued at several points in this book, client confidentiality, and the appropriate management of confidential information, is one of the most fundamental aspects for retaining trust. Without trust, therapy is likely to fail. The same level of confidentiality is expected post-therapy as was agreed pre- and during therapy. Without the client's written permission, it is not permissible (either ethically or legally, unless required to do so by a court) to disclose any information about a client. This would include information the client has disclosed during therapy, or even the information that they attended for therapy at all. If a request for information is received from a third party, it is important, wherever possible, to seek written permission from the client to release such information. Additionally, the specific level and extent of that disclosure needs to be agreed with the client (i.e., what is to be said, about what, to whom, and when).

There are times when it is not possible to obtain permission from an ex-client: perhaps the client has moved and you no longer have their up-to-date contact information or perhaps the client has died. In such instances the best course of action is to assume consent would not be given and to politely refuse to provide such information. If a request is made by a court of law (via a subpoena) then the therapist has to comply. However, careful discussion needs to take place in supervision (and with a manager if therapy was located in an organisational setting) about the nature of the disclosure, before the disclosure is made. A full discussion about the management of confidentiality can be found in Bond and Mitchels (2008).

Therapeutic reflections

Over time, counsellors and psychotherapists develop a body of experience and knowledge based on previous work with clients. While each client will bring unique challenges and opportunities, with different stories and experiences, there is an opportunity for a significant amount of learning that can underpin transferable skills. It is therefore important to see the end of therapy as an opportunity to reflect on the process of therapy: what worked well; what was difficult; what facilitated change; what hindered it; and what, if the time could be repeated, would or could be done differently.

Supervision provides an excellent opportunity to step back and reflect on the bigger picture of your practice. An experienced supervisor, who has an opportunity to get to know you and your work, will be invaluable in helping you to make links between different client experiences and to consider how to transfer learning from one situation to another.

However, reflection on your work need not be confined to supervision. Talking in more general terms (again, with respect to the client's confidentiality) with colleagues, peers or professional networks can trigger fascinating learning. Reading around particular issues raised by clients and attendance at conferences or one-day or short workshops can further facilitate learning and help you gain different insights into work completed. Each therapeutic relationship brings something new to the table, and post-therapy can provide a space where you can really begin to see the wood for the trees.

DISCUSSION QUESTIONS

1 How do you currently prepare for therapy to end, bearing in mind your professional expectations post-therapy?

2 What steps do you take with your clients to prepare for the management of your professional accountability post-therapy?

3 What opportunities do you have to help you reflect on finished work? How well do you use them?

4 What has been your biggest insight, to date, when looking back on therapy that you have been involved in?

8

Challenges in the Therapeutic Relationship

8.1 INTRODUCTION

CHAPTER OVERVIEW

This chapter discusses commonly encountered challenges to the therapeutic relationship. It aims to help the therapist both to identify these challenges accurately and to deal with them positively and proactively. The chapter examines a range of challenges in turn, from transference and countertransference, through dependency, missed appointments and client resistance, to the therapist's self-disclosure.

The success of counselling and psychotherapy perhaps depends as much on how challenges to the relationship are negotiated as on the quality of the relationship between client and therapist itself. The therapeutic relationship has been shown through research to be important for positive therapeutic outcome (for example, Horvath and Bedi, 2002; Martin et al., 2000). However, the quality of relationship is inevitably dependent on how the most difficult aspects are managed. Some clients come to counselling and psychotherapy ready for change, committed to the process, fully open to self-exploration, and willing to trust the therapist throughout the process. Perhaps many more, however, will have fears and concerns about how therapy will be, and how they will cope when faced with aspects of their experience that might be traumatising or shameful.

The purpose of this chapter is to identify challenges to the relationship in counselling and psychotherapy and how therapists can meet them effectively. In some ways the term 'challenges' is a misnomer, in that it might imply something out of the ordinary, or unexpected, or mis-managed, whereas the very opposite is true. It is my assertion throughout this chapter that the aspects discussed are in fact importantly embedded within a therapeutic process: they should be welcomed and made explicit where possible to facilitate a collaborative approach with the client.

The first section, Transference and Countertransference, reflects on these important relational dynamics and how they inform the very relationship on which counselling and psychotherapy is based. There is an acknowledgement that the terms 'transference' and 'countertransference' may be alien to practitioners not trained within a psychoanalytic or psychodynamic frame, but that the dynamics the terms describe are pertinent to all practitioners (however the concepts are subsequently termed).

The next section, Dependency, challenges the common misconception that dependency is inevitably a bad thing in a therapeutic relationship and should be avoided at all costs. Rather, it argues that dependency is not only not bad, but is essential, healthy and unavoidable. The dangers of unacknowledged dependency are highlighted and discussed. This is followed by a section on Missed Appointments and Cancellations. These are often dismissed as merely an administrative aspect to manage: here, however, they are presented as an important communication to be engaged with and treated as an integral part of the therapeutic process.

The next section, The Resistant Client, acknowledges that clients do not all come to counselling and psychotherapy willing and able to engage in a therapeutic process – or, once engaged, may be resistant to certain aspects of self-exploration. The concept of resistance is considered as a therapeutic defence. Suggestions are offered as to how this may be successfully worked with.

The final section considers Self-Disclosure. There is much debate between theoretical orientations about the nature and appropriateness of self-disclosure (i.e., the sharing of personal information by the therapist to the client). This section considers what is meant by self-disclosure, how it can occur both intentionally and through accident, and the ways in which it has the potential, if managed carefully, to be therapeutically facilitative.

It is hoped that by framing these aspects as positive and important parts of the therapeutic process therapists can support themselves, and be supported in supervision, to manage and work with such aspects proactively and positively.

8.2 TRANSFERENCE AND COUNTERTRANSFERENCE

SECTION OUTLINE

This section outlines what is meant by 'transference' and 'countertransference' and how these processes will be present in all therapeutic relationships. In addition, it discusses how the counsellor or psychotherapist may work with transference and countertransference in the context of various modalities.

The difficulty in writing about transference and countertransference is that some readers may feel alienated by concepts considered irrelevant according to their practice or understanding of human relationships. Such is the link between transference and countertransference and psychoanalytic or psychodynamic theory that other modalities, and particularly some of the humanistic traditions such as person-centred for example, see little or no relevance to their working ideas. Though there are obvious exceptions to this (Owens, 2007), generally this holds true.

As a counsellor who has received a person-centred training in the past, I think this is a shame. The insights that thinking about transference and countertransference can provide, if we can only get past the semantics of the terms, are significant. It is my assertion in this section therefore that, however we choose to describe the phenomena, the experience of the relationship by the client and therapist and what they bring to it in terms of previous relationships is very important. I shall use the terms transference and countertransference and hope that readers who do not align themselves to such terms will mentally substitute alternative, or better, terms instead.

Transference

Macaskie (2008, p. 148) describes transference as 'a fundamental process in human relationships which makes use of learning from past experiences'. She goes on to say, 'Transference brings the advantage that we do not need to keep learning everything afresh. The problem is that we may over-generalise from previous experiences of significant relationships, particularly with family members, and behave in new relationships as if they inevitably conform to similar patterns' (p. 148). We can see, therefore, that the client may relate to their therapist in ways that are more representative of, or appropriate to, other existing or previous relationships.

The factors that trigger a transferential response can be wide ranging. They may be clearly apparent or, on the other hand, not so obvious. In basic terms, the therapist may consciously or unconsciously remind the client of a significant figure in their lives because of how they look. It may be that such responses are triggered by behaviours, figures of speech, mannerisms or smells, for example. The client may be very aware of their response and bring it to the attention of the therapist. On the other hand, they may be unaware of their reaction. In turn, the therapist may notice clear reactions and responses from the client and make enquiries about them, or struggle over some considerable time and in supervision to try to make sense of why certain things seem to happen during sessions.

There may be positive or negative transference, depending on the experiences being transferred into the therapeutic relationship. While on one hand a positive transference (from a caring or supportive experience) might appear to be a good thing, it can lead to the client idealising their therapist and receiving challenge with difficulty or as a rebuke or criticism. Likewise, a negative transference might prevent the client from fully trusting the therapist, or from discussing aspects of themselves perceived as difficult or shameful. See the example of Daniel in Box 8.1, where we can see an example of a negative transference of a critical father. An additional case example illustrating transference is available on the companion website.

CASE STUDY 8.1
Daniel

Daniel is 27 years old and decided to come for counselling due to anxiety in social situations. He finds it very difficult meeting people but, once over those initial stages, can build friendships. He engages in counselling well and seems relaxed with his male therapist. His upbringing was a very critical one. Daniel speaks positively of his parents and continues to have a close relationship with them, however he feels that he has been a disappointment to his father. During therapy, the therapist gently challenges some of Daniel's thoughts about himself, which Daniel experiences as highly critical, and leaves him feeling 'demolished'.

In certain approaches, as was outlined in Chapter 3, the therapist will make active use of transferential responses and build interpretations around them. The importance of therapist 'abstinence' – the therapist disclosing nothing about themselves and remaining a 'blank slate' onto which the client can project – becomes apparent. The more the client knows of the 'person' of the therapist, the more diluted the transferential responses will be.

Working with transference

Most therapists will work with transference by attending to what is happening in the relationship and may then, depending on their particular style and orientation of working, bring it to the client's attention. A person–centred counsellor, for example, might bring material that sits at the client's edge of awareness, through the process of immediacy and congruence, so that the client can consider themselves in relation to the therapist; a psychoanalytic therapist might form and offer interpretations to help the client reflect on and challenge particular feelings or behaviour; and a cognitive-behavioural therapist, while paying careful attention to establishing a sound therapeutic relationship, will be less likely to work with the dynamics of the relationship as that is not their direct focus.

It is helpful in supervision to consider the relational dynamics, as a supervisor is able to help the therapist to listen 'between the lines' (Macaskie, 2008 p. 153) of what is happening in the counselling or psychotherapy process. Additionally, the parallel processing that can occur within the supervisory relationship can provide helpful insight into dynamics at play within the therapy. For a fuller discussion of parallel process, see Chapter 11 on Supervision and Consultation.

Countertransference

Symons (2008, p. 244) describes countertransference as 'a psychodynamic term that relates to the emotions of the therapist and how they may be used therapeutically'. She suggests that countertransference 'can be described as the internal responses evoked in the counsellor by the client. The usefulness or not of these internal responses depends on their meaning and whether they are rooted in the counsellor's own pathology or whether they contain unconscious communication from the client' (p. 245). Symons (p. 245) outlines four primary forms of countertransference as follows:

1   Subjective countertransference: when a therapist responds to the person as if they are someone from the therapist's own past (similar to transference, but therapist to client rather than client to therapist)
2   Objective countertransference: responses according to the therapist's experiences that sit within the current therapeutic relationship rather than being informed by others
3   Concordant countertransference: therapist feelings that match those of the clients. This is also termed projective identification, where the client projects 'unbearable feelings ... into the therapist, who then feels the projected emotions as if on the client's behalf ...' (p. 245).
4   Complementary countertransference: where the therapist responds in the way that the client expects them to, based on their assumptions from past relationships.

Person-centred therapists will certainly recognise the concept of objective counter-transference as the mechanism through which they are able to be congruent with their clients – reflecting on their own responses to the client's presence and actions in the therapeutic relationship with the aim of facilitating the client's self-awareness and insight. As stated previously, while the labels applied to particular human dynamics can become a barrier between modalities, there are often greater points of similarity than imagined.

Working with countertransference

The challenge is for therapists to recognise their countertransference and deter-mine how much of their response is related to the dynamics of the relationship (which it will then be important to take back into the relationship), and how much is related to their own experiences and feelings (which will then need to be addressed elsewhere). Depending on the orientation of the therapist, it is impor-tant to find a way of bringing objective countertransference back into the relation-ship so that its meaning and relevance can be explored collaboratively between client and therapist. There are obvious potential difficulties here given that this demands a great deal of honesty and trust between the therapist and their client. See the example of Julie in Box 8.2, a psychotherapist who experiences subjective countertransference in her work with a client. An additional **case example** illus-trating countertransference is available on the companion website.

CASE STUDY 8.2
Julie

Julie, an experienced psychotherapist, experienced the death of her mother four years previously. She had a close and affectionate relationship with her mother but does not feel 'at ease' with her grief. She has been working with her client Sasha for four months, focusing on Sasha's relationship difficulties. Julie has discussed in supervision on several occasions how she has noticed herself working beyond her usual boundaries (e.g. occasionally extending sessions, moving times around at the last minute, etc). It becomes apparent in discussion with her supervisor that Sasha, who is unlike Julie's mother in many ways, does use the same figures of speech and talks in a similar way. Julie realises how she has been drawn into a subjective countertransferential process with Sasha.

It is also important to keep in mind how significant previous relationships may be for the client in informing their experience of the current therapeutic relationship. A negative transference might mean the client does not believe the therapist to be sufficiently trustworthy to hear their feedback and might immediately retreat to a defensive position, while a positive transference might mean the client hears such honesty from the therapist, particularly if it additionally involves a challenge, as highly critical and thus devastating. Such feedback requires careful consideration, but when managed well can provide the client with perhaps the most important opportunity for insight and change.

FURTHER READING

Macaskie, J. (2008) 'Working with transference in counselling', in W. Dryden and A. Reeves (eds), *Key Issues for Counselling in Action*, 2nd edn. London: Sage. pp. 147–59.

Symons, C. (2008) 'Countertransference', in W. Dryden and A. Reeves (eds), *Key Issues for Counselling in Action*, 2nd edn. London: Sage. pp. 244–56.

DISCUSSION QUESTIONS

1   What are your responses to the terms 'transference' and 'countertransference'? How do you understand these terms in the light of your own training?
2   How important do you think it is to attend to potential transference in the therapeutic relationship? Why?
3   What steps do you take to recognise your countertransferential responses?
4   How do you use your countertransference to inform your work with clients?

8.3 DEPENDENCY

SECTION OUTLINE

Clients and therapists can become dependent on each other without being aware of it. Some modalities regard some degree of dependency as essential for facilitating therapeutic change, while other approaches caution against it. This chapter considers the benefits and dangers of dependency and how therapists can pay attention to it.

Dependency is an area of anxiety to trainee and qualified therapists alike – and sometimes for clients too. Whether the therapeutic relationship is becoming a 'dependent' one, what that might mean, and whether that constitutes 'bad' therapy, are concerns often explored in supervision. The concept of dependency is, therefore, often viewed negatively, as something always to be avoided. This one-dimensional view does not incorporate ways in which dependency might be helpful in the therapeutic process, if worked with in awareness and in collaboration with clients.

As indicated, it is not an area of concern exclusively for therapists. It is not uncommon for a client to ask the therapist whether they feel they are becoming dependent on therapy. Sometimes clients may prematurely decide to end therapy for fear of dependency, whereas in fact it might instead be an important part of their therapeutic experience.

What is dependency?

Amis (2008, p. 173) notes that, 'For a number of clients, [the] independent interest and focus can be perceived as a personal caring by the counsellor over and beyond professional responsibilities. The resulting compulsion or reliance upon this process and experience is referred to as dependency.'

PAUSE FOR REFLECTION

Re-read Amis's definition of dependency above and note your responses to it (for example, whether you feel dependency is a good or bad thing).

I ask you to pause here to think about Amis's outline of dependency because I suspect, for many readers, the answer will be more negatively framed. That is, terms such as 'compulsion' or 'reliance' might suggest an unhealthy and unhelpful interpersonal process. In my own case I found that, once I considered my own initial responses to this statement and thought about it more, I realised that it is, in fact, a fairly neutral statement onto which I had projected my own fears and thoughts about what dependency might mean.

Resnick (2004, p. 52) states that 'dependency has often been considered a dirty word and therapists have been criticised for fostering dependency. However, dependency is an essential, healthy and unavoidable quality of any meaningful relationship'. Let's analyse the terms of this statement in more detail.

Dependency is 'essential'

It is helpful here to consider 'meaningful relationships' that are not therapeutic ones, such as those with friends or partners. When I think of my own relationships a degree of dependency is a common factor between all of them. It might be that there are things I look for in my relationship with my partner that I do not need from friends, and vice versa, but as a 'giving and taking' process there are certainly aspects on which I am dependent, such as: love, warmth, approval, affirmation, forgiveness, security and support, to name a few. If these aspects were removed from my close and intimate relationships they would, perhaps by definition, cease to be close and intimate. I would perhaps feel less safe, less supported and less able to place my trust in the other person.

In counselling and psychotherapy we work towards the point where the client can place their trust in the 'person' of the therapist and also in the process of the therapeutic relationship. We ask them to take enormous risks by talking about personally held beliefs and feelings, or exploring difficult and sometimes traumatic past experiences. To do this we offer warmth, approval, affirmation, security, and so on. In placing that level of trust, clients must be dependent on the strength and integrity of the therapist and the relationship to contain and safely hold it. In that sense dependency is certainly an essential aspect of counselling or psychotherapy.

Dependency is 'healthy'

Many clients bring to counselling or psychotherapy a history of abusive, traumatising or simply unhelpful or uncaring relationships. As therapists we may do the same. Many clients will talk of their difficulty in trusting others and in taking the risk in relating to another. For some, the therapy relationship will be the first in which they experience a safe intimacy, with an opportunity to explore their thoughts, feelings and behaviours. This can be a profound experience and can become the springboard for them taking greater risks in their own lives away from therapy.

Even for those clients who have a number of healthy and positive relationships, the therapeutic process still needs to be safe and respecting. Being able to trust another sufficiently to talk about personal and sometimes shameful aspects of themselves requires them to take enormous risks. In this sense dependency is a fundamentally healthy aspect of counselling or psychotherapy.

Dependency is 'unavoidable'

Dependency might be unavoidable, yet it might not occur. It is worth picking apart this apparent contradiction a little more. It may be helpful to view dependency as a by-product of a successful relationship, and a successful relationship is one in which both parties can be open, honest, and feel equally respected and present. When this happens it is arguably unavoidable that there will be elements of dependency for the reasons outlined above. However, not all therapeutic relationships will be successful and, in such scenarios, dependency may not feature. In this sense, therefore, dependency can be seen as an unavoidable aspect of all successful therapeutic counselling and psychotherapy relationships.

Working therapeutically with dependency

To view dependency as an unavoidable, yet healthy and essential, by-product of a therapeutic relationship makes the question, 'Do you think my client is dependent on therapy (or me as a therapist)?' somewhat redundant. A better question, and one that might be more therapeutically advantageous to both the client and therapist is, 'How might we understand dependency in this relationship and the particular features of the relationship that contribute to dependency?' This question opens a number of therapeutic doors and is one that can be successfully explored with clients collaboratively, as well as in your personal reflective space or in supervision.

By making the concept of dependency more accessible (and therefore less daunting) to clients, it is possible to use it as a structure within which relational experiences, fears, patterns and dynamics can be explored. By moving away from the idea that dependency is essentially a bad thing best avoided, it can become more of a liberating idea and, for those clients for whom relationships have been damaging or unhelpful, an affirming one. Consider Mattie (in Box 8.3), who has been working with his counsellor, Jake, for several weeks.

CASE STUDY 8.3
Mattie

Mattie, 19 years old, never knew his father when he was growing up and was the only male in the family, with a mum (with whom he had a close relationship), and two older sisters. He decided to attend for counselling because of low self-esteem and a lack of self-confidence. He gets on with Jake very well and feels that he is making progress. He is starting to feel positively about himself and is slowly building confidence. Jake has discussed with Mattie the possibility of ending therapy, which left Mattie feeling panicky. They discussed this in some detail and helpfully explored Mattie's relationship with Jake as an important male figure in his life and how Mattie feels dependent on Jake.

Dangers and difficulties

It is important for you to regularly consider dependency so that it remains a valuable relational dynamic, rather than a potentially harmful one. The therapeutic relationship can be a seductive one for both therapist and client alike. The intimacy, warmth and sharing that occurs within the therapeutic frame is important, but only in so far as it facilitates that possibility outside of therapy for the client. For therapists, the dangers can include:

1 developing friendships with clients
2 exploiting clients for our own unacknowledged needs
3 blurring the boundaries of a professional relationship
4 failing to manage other relational dynamics, such as sexual attraction, intimacy
5 confusing clients' needs with our own
6 having unrealistic or inappropriate expectations of clients and of their 'commitment' to us as their therapist.

For clients, the dangers can include:

1 believing the therapeutic relationship is a friendship rather than a therapeutic one
2 failing to manage or understand other relational dynamics, such as sexual attraction, intimacy
3 having unrealistic or inappropriate expectations of the therapist and of their 'commitment' to us
4 being unable or unwilling to put energy into other relationships, or rejecting other relationships in favour of the one with the therapist.

Fundamentally we need to ask ourselves about the nature and value to the client of the therapeutic relationship. Amis (2008, p. 180) offers some useful questions for self-reflection or for exploration in supervision. They are:

1 Does my client want to increase the regularity of sessions?
2 Is my client overly familiar with me?
3 Is my client unable to take action without bringing it first to sessions?
4 Is my client suggesting meeting in addition to sessions?
5 Is my client contacting me regularly between sessions?
6 Do I feel that the professionalism of this relationship is being compromised by inappropriate behaviour from the client (or from me as their therapist)?
7 Do I feel that we have come as far as we can but the client is still wanting to attend?
8 Do I feel that I can't address ending the therapeutic alliance for fear of upsetting the client?

As has been outlined, dependency can be a hugely important resource for establishing safe and facilitative therapeutic relationships, particularly when brought into the client's awareness and worked with collaboratively. Ensuring that the therapeutic relationship is clearly and carefully contracted and bound by relevant ethical principles helps create the right environment for dependency to be a facilitative, rather than destructive, aspect of the therapeutic process. Careful attention to the management of endings (see Chapter 7 for a fuller discussion of endings) helps you and the client work with dependency and ensure the move towards independency. There are potential dangers, but with careful management, reflection and supervision, this can be managed effectively.

FURTHER READING

Amis, K. (2008) 'Working with client dependency', in W. Dryden and A. Reeves (eds), *Key Issues for Counselling in Action*, 2nd edn. London: Sage. pp. 172–82.

DISCUSSION QUESTIONS

1 How do you respond to the concept of dependency in counselling and psychotherapy? How are these responses informed by your own experience of relationships?
2 How does your theoretical orientation shape your views about dependency?
3 How do you work with dependency in your therapeutic work?
4 How might you use dependency collaboratively in your work with clients as a structure within which their experience of relationships can be explored?

8.4 MISSED APPOINTMENTS AND CANCELLATIONS

SECTION OUTLINE

Clients will sometimes miss or cancel appointments. It is an important skill for counsellors and psychotherapists to reflect on the potential meaning of such events and manage and respond to them appropriately. This section considers how to manage these situations ethically and appropriately so as to respect the therapeutic process while also meeting organisational requirements.

While it may seem to be stating the obvious to say clients will sometimes not attend or cancel therapy appointments, it is an important statement to begin with all the same. While many training courses allow time to consider the reasons for and impact of missed appointments, there are some trainees for whom such a possibility has never been considered. When experienced in practice, it can quickly undermine confidence. Certainly I have heard many trainees say that, naively, they expected when coming to a placement that clients would engage quickly, attend all sessions, work productively throughout, experience many 'ah-ha' moments (of profound insight), and leave following a well-managed ending fully actualised. Any variation of this leaves them questioning their own competence and capacity to work effectively as a therapist.

Of course, the reality of practice is that while many clients will attend sessions regularly and conscientiously, others will cancel arranged sessions or not arrive for sessions at all without any notification. Some will 'disappear' from therapy – not attending planned sessions and never returning – while others will cancel sessions regularly. Some will forget to pay for arranged sessions, while others will arrive for sessions but will consistently be late. All of this represents communication of sorts, and certainly offers an important insight into both their own process and the process of the therapeutic relationships.

Planning for all eventualities

The management of cancelled appointments and 'Did Not Attend' (DNA) sessions begins at the commencement of counselling or psychotherapy, rather than as a reaction to them during the course of therapy. Some organisations will have a specific policy about missed sessions, particularly where therapy is charged for on a session-by-session basis. The same is often true for independent practitioners where the management of missed sessions is responded to both as a therapeutic issue, but also as a financial/business one.

As with all aspects of counselling and psychotherapy, the importance of clear contracting, supported by an accessible written statement, cannot be overstated. This will include carefully outlining what a DNA means, and what would happen in the event of either repeated DNAs or cancellations. Issues regarding persistent lateness for sessions might also be addressed too. Such agreements might include how much notice is required for a cancelled session (e.g. 24 or 48 hours, or longer), the consequences of cancelling, and what might happen should several sessions be cancelled successively. Likewise, they might specify what would happen in the event of a DNA. Once these agreements have been made, the practical response to such eventualities is clear.

Cancellations

On face value, the management of cancellations sounds straightforward. A client contacts you, within the notice period, and informs you that they are not able to attend. This may trigger certain actions by you, given the agreements made at the contracting stage, including contacting the client by phone, email or text to con-firm the next appointment, or to suggest a next appointment time if one is not already made. If the client has given insufficient notice in line with previous agreements, it may also be necessary for you to inform them that they will still be charged for the cancelled session. My own view is that such communications should always be in writing, so I would advise against discussions of this type happening by telephone. It is important for you to have a clear audit trail of agreements and variations to those agreements, so as to avoid future confusion or dispute.

There are times, however, when cancellations become more problematic and require further exploration. Consider, for example, the case of Anthea in Box 8.4.

CASE STUDY 8.4
Anthea

Anthea, aged 21, self-referred for counselling following a period of anxiety and depression. She had a supportive relationship with her mother, but felt let down by her father who was often away and 'disinterested'. Anthea seemed very motivated for counselling and attended the first two sessions. She then began to cancel sessions – giving sufficient notice as per the original contract – because of 'ongoing family demands'. The pattern then became that she would attend one session, but then cancel the next. On reviewing her attendance it became apparent that she had only attended four out of nine sessions.

While one would imagine that Anthea's attendance pattern would become obvious while it was happening, this is often not the case, and the therapist (me, in this instance) can easily fail to notice the pattern until it has fully emerged. While the client maintained there were clear practical reasons why the cancellations had occurred (and which were all very reasonable and believable), the outcome remained the same: it was impossible to gain a momentum to the therapy and each session became disconnected from the previous one. I wondered whether it also spoke of an important therapeutic issue: the relationship between Anthea and her father was perhaps very present between Anthea and me, as a male therapist. However, it is impossible to appropriately explore such dynamics as a therapeutic issue unless the client is physically present in the sessions to do so, and the therapeutic relationship is sufficiently established to support what might be a difficult process. In the event, Anthea decided against continuing with counselling and it was not possible to take this issue further with her.

Non-attended sessions

A DNA might be classed administratively as an appointment where a cancellation contact was received but with insufficient notice, or where the client did not attend a planned session without notification. For both scenarios, and certainly the latter, it is important for you to have clearly agreed with the client at the commencement of therapy how you will act in such circumstances. It is not uncommon for clients to end therapy by not attending sessions, and their right to end therapy in such a way needs to be respected. However, if several sessions remain planned it is also your right to have clarity about whether those sessions will be attended, particularly if working independently when income is dependent on attendance or where there is a waiting list for therapy.

A sensitively worded email or letter, with a time deadline, is often sufficient. It is important that the client does not feel criticised (and there is sometimes a danger for written communications to be inadvertently punitive in the frustration of a DNA session), but that the parameters are clearly outlined or affirmed. Box 8.5 provides an example of such a communication.

BOX 8.5   A DNA EMAIL

Dear NAME

I am sorry that you were not able to attend your planned counselling/psychotherapy session today (DATE and TIME).

Our next planned appointment is scheduled for DATE and TIME, and I hope you will be able to make it. However, it is important that you confirm your attendance by DATE and TIME otherwise I will not be able to guarantee the appointment and will have to allocate it to someone else.
[alternative: I am aware that we do not have any further appointments arranged. Could you contact me by DATE and TIME to agree your next appointment?].

It may be that you have decided to discontinue counselling/psychotherapy. If this is the case I hope it will be possible for us to arrange an 'ending' appointment. However, if I don't hear from you by DATE and TIME I will assume this is the case and won't contact you again.

Looking forward to hearing from you.

The outline in Box 8.5 can, of course, be amended to reflect the nature of the relationship with the client. The key point is to clearly outline expectations, with a deadline. Clearly setting out a realistic deadline is important, as otherwise there is no clear end-point and the process runs the danger of drifting unhelpfully, or of you making further, unnecessary contacts with the client. Additionally, the charging policy can be added to this email if a charge is made for missed sessions.

Therapeutic process vs. self-reflection

It is very easy to jump to one particular end of the 'therapeutic process vs. self-reflection' continuum. The 'therapeutic process' end is characterised by thoughts such as, 'this is the client acting out', or 'this is typical of the client's behaviour', while the other end of the continuum is often characterised by 'I've really done a bad job', or 'I am not a good enough therapist'. The truth is most likely to lie somewhere in the middle, where the importance of self-reflection about our part of the therapeutic relationship is essential, while also keeping in mind important therapeutic possibilities that might be present in the behaviour, such as in the example of Anthea above. It is too easy to blame the client, or ourselves, where instead there might be something valuable to consider that is worth taking back into the therapeutic process, if it is still ongoing.

FURTHER READING

Dale, H. (2010) *Making the Contract for Counselling and Psychotherapy*. BACP Information Sheet P11. Lutterworth: BACP.

McMahon, G. (2005) *The Essential Skills for Setting up a Counselling and Psychotherapy Practice*. London: Routledge.

DISCUSSION QUESTIONS

1   Does your working organisation have a policy on cancellations or DNAs (or, if working independently, do you)? What is the policy and what is it designed to achieve?

2   To what extent do you currently explore the management of cancellations or DNAs at the contracting stage of therapy? Is this sufficient?

3   How do you communicate with your client about cancellations or DNAs? How does it compare to the example given in this section?

4   How do you create space to consider the 'therapeutic process vs. self-reflection' continuum before you make contact with a client about a cancellation or DNA?

8.5 THE RESISTANT CLIENT

> **SECTION OUTLINE**
>
> In some settings clients may be coerced into attending counselling or psychotherapy. In others, clients may choose to attend but be resistant to exploring personal distress. Counsellors and psychotherapists need to attend to the process of resistance to ensure they respond appropriately or sensitively. This section outlines the issues involved.

As we have discussed elsewhere in this chapter, many trainees when they first attend placement hold the belief that clients are generally motivated for counselling or psychotherapy (because they have sought it out), achieve therapeutic contact and work effectively and efficiently throughout the process, until a mutually agreed and well-managed end has been negotiated. As they quickly learn, this does happen but generally not that often. Instead, the process of counselling and psychotherapy can be immensely demanding for both the therapist and client, with both sometimes engaging fully and, at others, both being resistant to certain areas of exploration.

However, neither is the concept of resistance a binary one. By 'binary' I mean either the client is resistant or not. The challenge in therapy is working with the shades of grey of resistance in which most of us live, most of the time. I deliberately use the term 'us' rather than 'them' (the client), as we need to be open to exploring our own resistance as well as identifying and challenging it in the client.

Resistance

We might define resistant as 'unwilling or hesitant'. This may present at different stages of the therapeutic process, as the three scenarios in Boxes 8.6 to 8.8 illustrate:

CASE STUDY 8.6
Daniel

Daniel is a nursing student in his second year. He has experienced a number of family problems, including his parents separating and disagreements with siblings. He feels angry and confused, and struggles to talk about his feelings. He sees himself as a private person and would rather manage his problems on his own. His personal problems have affected his studies – he has been unable to concentrate and has fallen behind with his work. In a meeting with his Head of Department he is told to attend counselling, otherwise he might not be able to continue on his course. He attends counselling, but really does not want to be there.

CASE STUDY 8.7
Noel

Noel has been attending counselling for several weeks and has been finding it helpful. In his initial session he told the counsellor there was a 'big issue' he needed to explore to be able to 'move forward'. His counsellor has noted that, despite several opportunities for Noel to talk about the 'big issue', he has steered the discussion away from it. The counsellor challenges Noel and highlights what might be his pattern of avoidance. Noel says that he is not sure how to talk about it and changes the subject once again.

CASE STUDY 8.8
Doreen

Doreen has been attending counselling following the death of her partner. She has been coming regularly to sessions for several months and says that while she is not finding out anything new anymore and feels generally stronger, she is not ready to finish. Her counsellor feels that it is time for Doreen to move on, but when this is discussed, she is very unwilling to do so.

In these three scenarios we can see resistance at different stages of the relationship. These are very clear examples of resistance (in many circumstances resistance might not be so apparent during therapy). They all represent clients finding themselves in situations in which they are unwilling or hesitant about continuing. Daniel finds himself in a difficult situation where there are clear difficulties, including his undertaking a professional training that requires him to demonstrate to his course that he is fit to practise, but he is frightened about exploring his thoughts and feelings. Noel is very aware that he is avoiding something of great distress or shame, but does not know how best to proceed; and Doreen does not want to end therapy, perhaps for fear of her own isolation and loneliness.

Working with resistance

The challenge for the counsellor or psychotherapist is to work with the resistance so as to help the client to engage. The caveat here is that the philosophical premise of all counselling and psychotherapy modalities is that therapy is an activity undertaken in collaboration with another, rather than something 'done to' the other, with only very few exceptions. Essentially, if the client does not wish to be a client, they do not have to be and any attempt to engage them otherwise is likely to be fruitless. So the premise here is that the client has, to some degree, an intention to engage in therapy, but is resistant to aspects of it.

It might be helpful then to think of resistance as a form of defence – a means by which the client protects themselves from some real or perceived threat to personal or emotional integrity. Clients might defend themselves for two primary reasons: they have experienced harmful events that have caused emotional/physical harm and so avoid situations where that might recur; or they have been witness to (or fear without experience) harmful events that might cause them emotional/physical harm. In either instance the intention is about survival from harm. For many people the process of therapy might be perceived as potentially harmful: it might indeed be so, of course, if not managed carefully, sensitively and empathically by the therapist.

The perceived threat may be very explicit – for example, 'Can you tell me about your experiences of abuse?' (where the client is invited to talk about a particular event that causes great distress) – or more implicit – for example, 'How do you feel about that?' (where the question is more gentle and non-specific, but the invitation is about honesty of feeling). As counsellors and psychotherapists we can become too feeling-fixated, privileging feelings above all other forms of communication. This might sound a strange thing for a therapist to say, and here I certainly don't deny the importance of feelings, but where the prospect of experiencing feelings is potentially terrifying for the client and results in resistance, it is better to identify alternative ways clients might explore their experience. This is applicable to both male and female clients, but males who, in Western culture, are typically socialised out of expressing feeling, might particularly struggle with a 'feeling-dominated' discourse (Blazina and Watkins, 1996; Levant, 1998; Mahalik et al. 2003).

The paradoxical injunction

The paradoxical injunction is a particular therapeutic means of responding to and managing difficult behaviours. The premise is to encourage the troublesome behaviour, thus reducing it. For example, a child having a tantrum is less likely to have one if actively invited to do so. While there are obvious dangers to this approach and it should be used carefully and following supervision, the philosophy behind it is perhaps useful here in working with resistance.

Put simply, the less the client has to defend against – or resist – the more likely they are to engage in the process on their terms. Taking Daniel as an example, he is reluctant to engage in counselling because he is fearful of talking about his feelings. His fear perhaps is that his counsellor will force him to talk about his feelings in the same way he was forced to attend counselling, or perhaps forced to witness the breakdown of his parent's relationship. He might begin to feel differently should his counsellor say, 'I understand that there are things you might not want to talk about, and that is fine – you don't have to. Perhaps we could do some useful work though on the difficulties you are having with your course, and perhaps help in that area?' If he prefers not to, that is his right and it should be accepted. However, the counsellor's intervention here is much more likely to lead to Daniel engaging in therapy, and he might decide in future sessions to begin to talk about his feelings.

To Noel, the counsellor might say, 'I understand, Noel, that this is a difficult area for you to talk about. It is okay for us to not talk about it if you prefer not to.' The real or imagined pressure is immediately lifted from Noel, and he can then decide whether or not it is an area he will explore. For Doreen, there may be value in exaggerating her unwillingness to end by perhaps imagining what it would be like if counselling sessions didn't end, ever. Doreen may be facilitated to explore her resistance to end through the paradoxical idea of them never ending.

The therapist's resistance

Resistance, therefore, can be seen as an important part of the therapeutic process and as a mechanism through which clients may defend themselves against difficulty. It is additionally important for us to be open to the possibility of our own resistance, perhaps projected on to the client. When we identify resistance in our clients, it is also worth exploring for ourselves and in supervision whether some of the resistance is our own. For example, there will be areas for all of us that prove particularly difficult, where the client's difficulties or problems correlate closely with our own previous or current struggles.

There may also be occasions when we experience our own resistance as a sense of being 'stuck' – not knowing what to say, how to help things move on, or that we have reached the end of the process with a particular client. It might, of course, be true that we are reaching the end of a productive process with a client, which can helpfully be explored in supervision. However, we also need to be open to the idea that instead we are resistant to a particular aspect of the work, or a particular client (possibly due to transferential or countertransferential dynamics) (Fernandes, 2008).

It is very easy to assume that all the difficulties in the therapeutic relationship emanate from the client. Supervision is an excellent space in which we can consider our own part in the difficulties and, in recognising where we may be 'backing off' from contact with our clients or their problems, take our own risks in a therapeutic engagement.

FURTHER READING

Careswell, C. (2008) 'Working with reluctant clients', in W. Dryden and A. Reeves (eds), *Key Issues for Counselling in Action*, 2nd edn. London: Sage.

Fernandes, F. (2008) 'Working with the concept of stuckness', in W. Dryden and A. Reeves (eds), *Key Issues for Counselling in Action*, 2nd edn. London: Sage.

Kindred, M. (2010) *A Practical Guide to Working with Reluctant Clients in Health and Social Care*. London: Jessica Kingsley.

DISCUSSION QUESTIONS

1   Consider a time when you were resistant about doing something. What were you protecting yourself from?

2   How have you experienced resistance in your client work? What are the different ways in which it has presented?

3   How does your theoretical orientation prepare you to understand and work with resistance?

4   How might you apply the concept of paradoxical injunction?

8.6 SELF-DISCLOSURE

SECTION OUTLINE

Some modalities might encourage or sanction self-disclosure by a counsellor or psychotherapist, while others view it negatively. Knowing when or how to disclose a little of the 'self' of the therapist to the client is a delicate issue. This section considers the meaning of self-disclosure and provides parameters you might keep in mind when working with clients.

For some therapists, such as those from a humanistic orientation, careful and limited self-disclosure, with a view to facilitating the client's process, can be viewed positively (Farber, 2006; Rowan and Jacobs, 2002). From a psychodynamic or psychoanalytic perspective, the concept of self-disclosure would be an anathema to the core principles and philosophy of training, where therapist abstinence facilitates transferential dynamics and thus informs interpretation. From a cognitive-behavioural position, self-disclosure might be viewed as an irrelevant concept, given that the relationship facilitates the work, but is not the focus of the work. These are, of course, generalisations, and therapists from these orientations might view the idea of self-disclosure differently. A helpful overview of some key literature in self-disclosure is offered by Henretty and Levitt (2009).

What is meant by 'self-disclosure'

Self-disclosure is typically understood to mean the revealing of personal information by the therapist to the client within a therapy session. This may be factual information about themselves or their lives, or it might perhaps be the disclosure of personally held views or beliefs. However, self-disclosure goes beyond what we might say and can include other aspects about ourselves or our lives. The ethical considerations surrounding self-disclosure can be complex. To consider the different ways in which self-disclosure may occur, reflect on the scenarios in Boxes 8.9 to 8.13. Two further **case studies** exploring issues of self-disclosure are available on the companion website.

CASE STUDY 8.9
Jude

Jude has been seeing her client Antony for several weeks. He began attending counselling following the death of his mother, with whom he had a close relationship. He has found her death from cancer hard to reconcile and continues to feel overwhelmed by his feelings. Jude, whose own mother died four years previously, also from cancer, can identify with Antony's feelings, but acknowledges the differences in the two situations. In one session she briefly tells Antony of her own mother's death and how she coped, in the hope that it will help him.

CASE STUDY 8.10
Becci

Becci works as a counsellor for a young persons' agency. She meets with Danielle, who has recently found out she is pregnant. The father of the baby has told Danielle that he is not interested in supporting her, and Danielle's family, who know of the pregnancy, are vehemently against termination. Danielle is not sure of what to do as she does not know how she will cope once the baby is born. Becci says to Danielle that she believes every woman has the right to make a choice about a termination and, in her view, a termination wouldn't necessarily be 'a bad thing'.

CASE STUDY 8.11
David

David is a counsellor in independent practice. He works from home in a room he has converted into a space for counselling and study. Clients arrive at the main door of his house and he takes them through to the counselling room. David has made his counselling space as neutral as possible, decorating it as an office environment. Carol, his client, seems flustered during her second session. She self-referred for counselling following family problems. She says to David that she noticed a photo of him and his (male) partner on the wall on her way through to the counselling room. She says she is not sure how she feels about 'gay couples' and doubts he would understand her heterosexual relationship.

CASE STUDY 8.12
Baz

Baz works in a further education college. She is careful about boundaries and generally chooses not to disclose any personal information about herself. She logs into her Facebook account and sees a friend request from one of her current clients. The client had made a couple of jokey comments about some of her photos of herself out drinking with friends. Baz has not made any changes to her Facebook security settings and realises that anyone can view her profile.

CASE STUDY 8.13
Steve

Steve is a counsellor in a voluntary organisation. He enjoys his work and sees a range of clients between the ages of 18 and 65. He is a member of an extreme right-wing political party and, while out on a demonstration for them, bumps into one of his clients. His client is clearly shocked and does not quite know how to respond.

PAUSE FOR REFLECTION

1   How do you feel about each of these scenarios? What are the key similarities and differences between them?
2   Are some self-disclosures in these scenarios 'worse' than others? Why?
3   Taking each scenario in turn, what would you have done differently, if anything?
4   Referring to BACP's Ethical Framework (or other framework within which you work), what are the key ethical implications in each scenario?

What you may notice in reading through these scenarios is that some examples of self-disclosure are intended, while others not so. Equally, some are explicit, while others are implicit. By 'implicit' I mean that the self-disclosure not only did not happen intentionally, but that the counsellor was not aware it was happening (e.g. disclosure via a social networking site, or a client viewing a family photograph at home). Certainly in the technological age where lots of information is easily available online, the possibility of accidental self-disclosure is high. It is important that therapists consider what information may be available about them online, but also how the wider environment in which they practise will communicate something of their 'selves'.

Advantages and disadvantages of self-disclosure

Inskipp (2012, p. 88) helpfully outlines a number of advantages and disadvantages of self-disclosure, which I will refer to here.

Advantages

Therapist not seen as perfect

Self-disclosure can act as a model for the client to talk more openly about him- or herself: clients sometimes experience great difficulties in finding ways of expressing their thoughts and feelings in a way that really captures their experience. Clients have the opportunity to see how, through the process of self-disclosure, their therapist is able to express an aspect or part of themselves. Self-disclosure can also build the relationship: the prospect of beginning to tell a stranger personal information can form an early barrier to the development of a therapeutic relationship. Limited and well-timed self-disclosure can help break down that barrier and facilitate the building of trust.

Self-disclosure can shorten the psychological distance between the client and counsellor, producing more intimacy and trust. The client having an opportunity to hear a little about the counsellor's experience can help the client see the 'person' of the counsellor more, bring client and therapist closer together. If the therapist discloses difficulties he or she has overcome (e.g. bereavement, without divulging too many unnecessary details), this can encourage and challenge the client; the therapist holding 'hope' in the face of the client's difficulties can be extremely powerful (Farber, 2006). Providing an example that it is possible to overcome adversity can be immensely powerful, as long as it does not undermine the client's efforts.

Disadvantages

Drawing on the work of Inskipp (2012. p. 89), there are a number of disadvantages to consider when working with self-disclosure. While there may be benefits in you not being seen as 'perfect', too much detail about personal struggles you have experienced may leave the client more vulnerable, with a loss of trust in your strength or robustness and capacity to hear and respond to their own particular difficulties. Additionally, self-disclosure can be too challenging, with an increased degree of intimacy threatening the client. It is often important for a client to have a sense of 'distance' from, as well as intimacy with, their therapist. Having too much information about a therapist's life or beliefs can undermine the safety of the relationship.

– to much details

Clients may see themselves or their difficulties as very different from their therapist's and so will not be encouraged to help themselves: clients may feel misunderstood if a therapist's disclosure does not quite resonate with the client's experience; the client may therefore not be able to identify their own 'agency' for change. Intentional self-disclosure is considered by some therapists to be always poor practice. As stated at the beginning of this section, intentional self-disclosure is contextualised by the orientation of the therapist: some orientations do not condone self-disclosure as a therapeutic technique.

Other therapeutic considerations

If, in principle, you accept that self-disclosure can be of benefit to your client, it may be helpful to keep the following questions in mind:

1 How established is the therapeutic relationship (i.e., is there sufficient robustness in the relationship to manage self-disclosure)?
2 How able is the client to find their own words and meaning in articulating their experience?
3 Will the client's narrative be enhanced by self-disclosure, or will it detract from it?
4 Is the self-disclosure for your benefit, or the client's? If in doubt, don't self-disclose.
5 What feelings do you have about telling the client information about you? What might they tell you about how the client is feeling?
6 Is there any other way of facilitating the client?
7 Is what you have to say sufficiently close to the client's experience so that it might be experienced as facilitative?

Managed carefully and thoughtfully, and delivered sensitively, self-disclosure has the potential to create a sense of intimacy and connection with the client in a way that facilitates their process. However, great care needs to be given, including through the use of supervision, in ensuring that any self-disclosure is rooted within the therapeutic relationship and not driven by personal needs.

FURTHER READING

Rowan, J. and Jacobs, M. (2002) *The Therapist's Use of Self*. Buckingham: Open University Press.

DISCUSSION QUESTIONS

1   Consider a time when you have self-disclosed to a client? To what extent did it help or hinder?
2   What is your view of self-disclosure? How is it informed by your therapeutic approach?
3   What are the key differences between a facilitative self-disclosure and an unhelpful one?
4   How might you use supervision to inform your use of self-disclosure?

9

Working with Diversity and Difference

9.1 INTRODUCTION

CHAPTER OVERVIEW

People who attend counselling and psychotherapy sessions do not form one homogenous group. Instead, they represent the full spectrum of people across socioeconomic status, age, gender, culture, sexuality and disability. In turn, they bring experiences of privilege, power, discrimination and powerlessness. Counsellors and psychotherapists, who will themselves reflect a broad spectrum, need to consider ways in which the therapeutic relationship and process are entwined with this reality. The introductory section contextualises this discussion and outlines the overall structure of this chapter.

Many forces have served to stifle an honest and open exploration of difference and disability over the last few decades. If we take Burch's (Burch and Miller, 1977) four stages of learning – (1) unconscious incompetence; (2) conscious incompetence; (3) conscious competence; and (4) unconscious competence – perhaps society would be somewhere between the conscious incompetence and the conscious competence stage. We generally know what we are doing as a society is wrong and unhelpful in terms of stereotyping and discrimination, though in some ways our society is beginning to do better – although it is always dangerous to apply such general statements to society as a whole. Different societies and cultures are at different stages and within each social grouping there will be broad differences between people's understanding of diversity and their willingness to challenge their potentially oppressive thinking. Sadly, for all our understanding of the process of discrimination and its devastating consequences, many still adopt an unquestioning position and perpetuate discriminatory and offensive values at the expense of others.

As a social worker and then as a counsellor I have had several experiences of attending 'working with cultural diversity'-type courses. The titles of such courses have changed over the years, with the terms 'diversity' and 'difference' probably reflecting current wisdom. However, my experience of participating in such courses – however they have been titled – has essentially been unchanged. Course leaders have fought valiantly in trying to facilitate an honest and open engagement with the process of power, difference and, most importantly, our own 'position' in relation to it. I say fought valiantly because so often they have been greeted with the polished and smooth veneer of 'I am not racist/sexist/homophobic/ageist (etc.) ...', and thus the challenge and potential for important self-reflection is lost. It seems that in an attempt to be so unconditionally accepting of all, we can lose a willingness to go to difficult places and explore those more painful parts that might be so incongruent with our role of therapist. This chapter is based on the view that, however we might like to think differently, we are all a product of our upbringings and the cultures and contexts in which we grew. The power to discriminate and the potential to disempower are aspects of those cultures and contexts.

That is not to suggest that we are unable to challenge or shift from our position through awareness, but rather that we all have the potential, when backed into a corner, to revert to early conditioning and learning. However, the more we are open to and engage with those parts that might draw on reductionist and harmful stereotypes, the more we may be able to counteract and ultimately render harmless those views; like pouring an alkaline solution into acid. Conversely, the less willing we are to turn to those parts of us we would rather not be there, the more likely it is that the acid will remain potent and silently corrosive.

Taking the metaphor just one final step further then, this chapter is about some of the ways in which the social acid of discrimination and prejudice is distilled into our lives through our growing up and how, as counsellors and psychotherapists, we can work towards neutralising its harmful action; how we can really be open to diversity and difference, not only in our personal lives but our professional lives too. The challenge for counsellors and psychotherapists is to find ways of developing and sustaining facilitative therapeutic relationships with people from a diverse range of backgrounds, influences, experiences and understandings of the world. Additionally, we need to consider ways of exploring with clients the complications of the 'meeting point' in therapy: the point at which one world meets with another, that demands negotiation and translation to enable therapeutic contact to be established, maintained and developed.

The use of language, which I will explore in the first section, Power, can either facilitate or hinder change. The ways in which people are described and thus constructed socially have significant consequences for how they are then positioned in terms of power and authority. It is worth paying particular attention to the terms used in the title of this chapter, *diversity* and *difference*. The Oxford English Dictionary defines diversity as 'the state of being diverse; a range of different things' (OED, 2012), while difference is defined as, 'a point or way in which people or things are dissimilar'. We need to ask here, 'Dissimilar and diverse from what?'

We might assume that difference and diversity is anything that diverts from the accepted norm. However, this argument is problematic in that it assumes a 'right' way of being: a gay man, for example, is likely to take exception with an assertion that heterosexuality is the 'normal' position and that being gay is a divergence from that 'norm'. This example highlights well the toxicity of oppression in that some will see heterosexuality as 'normal' and being gay as therefore 'abnormal', while many others would argue that sexuality is not a lifestyle choice but rather an integral part of a person's very being – so each person's sexuality is 'normal' for them, regardless of orientation.

It is therefore simplistic to assume the terms difference and diversity will apply simply to someone who is black, gay, lesbian, transgendered, bisexual, disabled, Muslim, Christian and so on. However, being a member of these communities is likely to bring a greater likelihood of having experienced discrimination and oppression. In the counselling and psychotherapy frame, difference is likely to exist between therapist and client. Both will bring into the room their unique experience of being. It would be wrong to assume, however, that working with difference and diversity assumes the therapist to be in the dominant position and the client in a more passive one: though dynamically that might be true (in that one is assumed to be in a relative position of psychological congruence, while the other in a relative position of incongruence), one needs the help of the other. A disabled therapist with an able-bodied client; a black therapist with a white client; or a Christian therapist with an atheist client will all bring their particular challenges. These three scenarios present situations where difference is apparent, yet the challenges might be as great even when the difference is less apparent, such as a gay therapist working with a lesbian client (both fall into minority groups within a dominant heterosexual culture), or a visually impaired client working with a client in a wheelchair (both fall into a minority group in the context of a dominant able-bodied society). The challenges are often in the nuances of difference, whereas the bridges are the subtleties of similarity and contact.

There are many points of difference and diversity within the human frame. I have selected several of the most common areas of difference that counsellors and psychotherapists might face in their work, but accept that many others exist too, and apologise for their omission. In the section entitled Power, I will outline in more detail how the outcome of discrimination is that in counselling and psychotherapy 'one' holds and retains a position of power while, inevitably, the 'other' is disempowered and can become disenfranchised. The exertion of control by one over the other has peppered humankind over the centuries. This can easily be seen at a macro level, but is typically implemented at a micro – person-to-person – level.

Having set a wider context, the chapter will move on to consider specific areas in which people may experience discrimination and oppression and bring these experiences for exploration into sessions. The section on Sexual Orientation will consider the dynamics that might be experienced in therapy between therapist and client in relation to issues of sexual orientation. The Gender section discusses what the research tells us about men and women's experience of therapy and how gender differences can hinder the therapeutic process, if unacknowledged.

The section Faith and Spirituality considers the importance of faith in the lives of many people and reflects on the place of counselling and psychotherapy in relation to faith and how it may be brought usefully into the counselling process. The section on Culture looks at the Western-influenced counselling and psychotherapy approaches and their relevance for a diverse population. It considers how culture difference can be successfully acknowledged and worked with in sessions. Finally, the section on Disability defines what is meant by disability and considers how language has evolved in an attempt to describe differences in physical and cognitive capability. Additionally, the relational and practical implications of working with people with disabilities will be discussed.

Clearly there will be common themes across all sections. That is, regardless of how people are different, therapy has the potential to meet with and play an important part in enabling change and empowerment. The challenge is on the therapist to consider their part in the process and find ways of ensuring honesty, transparency and integrity in the delivery of services.

9.2 POWER

SECTION OUTLINE

Power (and powerlessness) are not always fully discussed in counsellor training. In fact, some modalities work on an 'equality assumption', where therapist and client are assumed to have equal power throughout the therapeutic endeavour. This section considers these ideas alongside the concepts of institutional and personal power and control associated with the role of counsellor or psychotherapist. It then discusses the potential implications for the therapeutic process.

The definition and nature of power is much debated, yet the consequences of power are all too evident in society. Though people can identify those who hold power and the implications of decisions made by the powerful over the powerless, they may be less willing to identify their own personal power and control over others. Moreover, any groups or individuals who deviate from what society has defined as 'normal' are susceptible to the power of the state and society to control and to oppress. Sometimes such power is made very explicit, as in the apartheid laws in 20th-century South Africa, where black people were oppressed and discriminated against in systematic ways through the use of legislation, violence and fear. However, power can be also exercised implicitly. Such power can be as destructive, causing a loss of employment opportunities, unequal pay for the same job, or unequal access to counselling and psychotherapy services. As George Orwell famously wrote in *Animal Farm*, 'all animals are equal, but some animals are more equal than others'.

Definitions

OED (2012) defines power as, 'the ability or capacity to do something or act in a particular way' and 'the capacity or ability to direct or influence the behaviour of others or the course of events'. Control is defined as, 'the restriction (or direction) of an activity, tendency, or phenomenon'. Oppression is defined as, 'prolonged cruel or unjust treatment or exercise of authority'.

Power might, therefore, be seen as the means through which influence or control is exerted over other(s), while oppression is the exertion of power with an intent to undermine or disempower (i.e., to take power away from). Society is constructed through the use of systems of power as a means of organising and managing functions and tasks. Whether it is possible to have a society without using power as a means of organising and facilitating function is uncertain: some would argue it is not. We might assert that power is not necessarily a bad thing: after all, at a macro level power can be used to liberate and prevent oppression, while at a micro level it may be used, for example, to prohibit acts of violence. However, if we return to Orwell's observation, a danger of power is that it can corrupt and is not always transparent or honest: though we can strive for equality, the equality we achieve might not always be what it appears to be.

Overall, we may say that as power helps construct society, power is also socially constructed; it is a self-propelling process. That is to say that power dynamics contribute to the organisation of community and society. However, in turn we may define power from within a system and thus it is partly defined by the system: it is socially constructed. These two dynamics support each other and can be seen as self-propelling. Society is also bound together by culture, shared values, experience, history and a shared goal or goals. Society is structured through the use of functional systems, such as health, justice, law, employment, education and finance. Each of these systems has power devolved to them from a centralised point (which still retains power itself) so that they can execute their functions effectively and efficiently.

Each system typically has its own structure of hierarchy and control. McLeod (2009, p. 463) states that 'research into the social psychology of humans overwhelmingly supports the notion that power differentials are an unavoidable feature of human social life'. Hierarchy is also a feature of almost all functions of employment in society: each profession has its own structure of power and control, while there also exists a hierarchy between professions (Leavitt, 2004). The 'helping professions', however altruistic they claim to be, are not exempt from this dynamic (Newnes et al. 1999). Certainly, in mental health systems in which I have worked over the years I have seen many battling for their own positions of power. For example, psychiatrists often like to sit at the top of the tree, but have been challenged over the years by clinical psychologists and general practitioners who quite fancy a branch up there too! Social workers may look enviously at clinical psychologists, but be caught up in their battle with mental health nurses who may think they have the edge because their training is rooted in science rather than the humanities (and science always trumps the humanities) ... and so on (perhaps I should apologise here for caricaturing various professional groups). The point is that because of what McLeod called this 'unavoidable feature', none of us is immune and we must all examine ourselves and our role, including those who work in counselling and psychotherapy.

Power in counselling and psychotherapy

Humanistic modalities work to what I might call an 'equality assumption': there is a philosophical assumption that therapist and client begin at an equal point and, indeed, that this equality contributes to the conditions for therapeutic change. However, when we pay closer attention to the structure and form of counselling and psychotherapy, we may see that the institutional power inherent in its provision makes equality nigh on impossible, certainly in the early stages of therapy. Whether therapy is offered in an independent setting, or within an agency, the agency or individual therapist retains control over many factors – over the setting, the time, the frequency and duration, the cost, as well as (to an extent) the form and content of sessions, for example. Though clients are encouraged to define their own parameters, essentially this happens within a context of wider parameters the therapist has already set. The apparent control of the client is defined only in the context of the control the therapist has allowed the client to have. It is a little like taking a mountain walk: we have the sense of freedom, but only within the parameters of public access and private property – stray into the wrong territory and the freedom is quickly removed. Most clients who might ask for open-ended counselling will typically experience their liberty to define their own sense of help quickly curtailed.

Like other professions, counselling and psychotherapy also controls and limits through its use of language and discourse. 'Transference', 'countertransference', 'parallel process', 'EMDR', 'external locus of evaluation/control', 'organismic self' and 'schema' – such terminology does little to promote a sense of inclusivity. Rather, language and discourse play an important function is setting parameters to membership and control over understanding. Clients are welcome to join the club – but only if they do so through the process of therapy. Clients who come to therapy already knowing these terms are sometimes greeted with the knowing smiles of a therapist who already senses a 'psychological defence'.

Counselling and psychotherapy organisations, therapy agencies – and, in turn, their counsellors and psychotherapists – inevitably represent institutional power, and individual therapists will often hold personal power (and be perceived as having this power by clients). That is not in essence problematic: it only becomes so when such power remains unacknowledged and thus unaddressed. In this circumstance power can become oppressive. Consider these dynamics in action in Box 9.1.

CASE STUDY 9.1
Ellis

Ellis is a 19-year-old black, male client who is currently unemployed. He has been experiencing depression for two years and, on the advice of his GP, agrees to go for counselling. He is referred to his local psychological therapies service six months post-assessment. His local young persons' service has recently closed due to a lack of funding. He accesses information about independent practitioners and makes contact with several. He finds the typical cost for counselling in his area, per hour, is around £60. One therapist is willing to offer a concessionary rate for people who are unemployed, at £35 per hour. Ellis does not have any money and cannot afford this option.

PAUSE FOR REFLECTION

1   What aspects of this scenario do you feel Ellis has control over?
2   What aspects of this scenario do you feel Ellis has no control over?
3   What factors impinge on his choices and options for seeking personal therapy?

The following sections of this chapter will illustrate in more detail how power can be used to negative effect and how groups and individuals can be oppressed within social structures because of difference and diversity.

9.3 SEXUAL ORIENTATION

SECTION OUTLINE

This section defines what is meant by sexual orientation and considers how an individual might be positioned in society in virtue of their sexuality. In turn, it considers the implications for the process of therapy at a relational level. The therapist's sexuality will be significant in this relational dynamic, as will the issues of whether (and, if so, how) sexuality is disclosed by therapist or client during a session.

Definitions

Sexual orientation is defined by the American Psychological Association (2012) as follows: 'Sexual orientation refers to an enduring pattern of emotional, romantic, and/or sexual attractions to men, women, or both sexes. Sexual orientation also refers to a person's sense of identity based on those attractions, related behaviors, and membership in a community of others who share those attractions'. This definition concurs with an assertion made by the UK-based charity Stonewall (2012), which states that defining lesbian, gay or bi-sexual is, 'better expressed as "sexual orientation towards people", rather than "sexual attraction to". This reflects the fact that people build committed, stable relationships and is not purely a focus on sexual activity'. Orientations include heterosexual (or being 'straight') as well as gay (where a man experiences sexual and/or emotional orientation towards other men, although the term 'gay' is also sometimes used for women), lesbian (where a woman experiences sexual and/or emotional orientation towards other women), and bisexual (where a man or woman experiences sexual and/or emotional orientation towards both men and women).

The first use of the term homosexuality is disputed in the literature: it has been variously attributed to medicine, law and sociology, depending on the source. What is less disputed is that the term is now seen as outdated and as offensive by some. The use of the term 'homosexual' in medical discourse and its historical links with ideas of disorder and illness means that it has become value-laden. In the UK the terms gay, lesbian and bisexual are preferred: in addition, transgendered and increasingly queer, or 'questioning' are often included (hence the acronym 'LGBTQ') in political campaigning for equal rights under law. Of course, how a person decides to define their own sexuality (if indeed they choose to 'define' it at all) should take precedence.

Sexual orientation is generally viewed as being less of a fixed state but rather experienced on a continuum. The complexities of human dynamics and the power of relational experiences can mean that any one of us may experience orientation towards another of the same or other sex. People may predominantly define their experience at a particular point on the continuum (such as exclusively straight or exclusively gay), but the reality for many is that the experience of sexual and emotional selves is much more complex and subtle. In a society that continues to privilege being straight above all else, experience of orientation that opposes either the dominant view, or a personally held sense of identity, can be profoundly challenging. The experience of 'coming out' (i.e., disclosing sexual orientation to others) and the subsequent rejection, hate, discrimination, violence and ongoing oppression that can follow has the potential to be profound, even traumatic.

It is important to make a clear distinction between sexual orientation, sex and gender. According to the American Psychological Association (2012), 'Sexual orientation is distinct from other components of sex and gender, including biological sex (the anatomical, physiological, and genetic characteristics associated with being male or female), gender identity (the psychological sense of being male or female), and social gender role (the cultural norms that define feminine and masculine behavior)'. People experiencing gender dysphoria (where an individual feels they are trapped within the body of the wrong sex, otherwise known as gender identity disorder, gender incongruence or transgenderism) will often present to counsellors and psychotherapists because of the personal distress they can experience, or perhaps during preparation for gender re-assignment treatment and surgery where therapy is required. For the purposes of this chapter, I will use the acronym LGBT (lesbian, gay, bisexual and transgender) when discussing working with sexual orientation in counselling and psychotherapy.

Training implications

Professional organisations are increasingly recognising the need for counsellors and psychotherapists to take particular steps in understanding the particular challenges LGBT clients face in their daily lives (Grove, 2009). However, whether and how this actually transpires in training courses is under-researched. The profile of LGBT issues in counselling training is generally unclear, although a study by Alderson (2004) of Canadian graduate counselling training found that on average LGBT issues accounted for between 0 and 3 hours of specific attention throughout the duration of training. There is sufficient evidence to support the idea that a lack of specific training for counsellors and psychotherapists can have a detrimental effect on therapy because of issues such as internal prejudice, lack of critical analysis of psychological theories, and lack of knowledge of LGBT issues (Davies and Neale, 1996; Liddle, 1996; Phillips and Fischer, 1998).

A study by Matthews et al. (2005) found that LGBT clients felt more positively about their therapist and the process of therapy if there was evidence that the therapist had either received training or had educated themselves about LGBT issues, did not pathologise sexual orientation, and was proactive in their work around sexual orientation. In a study by Israel et al. (2008), therapist competence in working with LGBT issues was seen to positively affect the experiences of clients who access therapy, particularly around the process of 'coming out'.

Grove (2009, p. 84) has outlined a basic framework for a training curriculum based on a study looking at the competence of newly qualified therapists to work with LGBT clients:

Skills

Develop ways of communicating

Self-awareness

Impact on self

Knowledge acquisition

Political and social context

Understanding others

Counselling and psychotherapy with LGBT clients

Gay affirmative therapy is not a specific model of therapy in its own right, but rather a set of values and ideas. As Malyon (1982, p. 69) describes,

Gay affirmative psychotherapy is not an independent system of psychotherapy. Rather it represents a special range of psychological knowledge that challenges the traditional view that homosexual desire and fixed homosexual orientation are pathological. Gay affirmative therapy uses traditional psychotherapeutic methods but proceeds from a non-traditional perspective.

As such it has the potential to be integrated into an existing approach to counselling and psychotherapy. It has been further developed by the work of authors such as Davies and Neal (2000) and Hunter and Hickerson (2003).

Pixton (2003, p. 214) studied clients' experience of gay affirmative therapy. It was noted that LGBT clients valued the following aspects of gay affirmative therapy:

1   the counsellor communicating a non-pathological view of homosexuality
2   the counsellor providing a space that allows for a full exploration of sexuality
3   the specific knowledge and awareness of the issues affecting lesbian, gay and bisexual individuals and the counsellor's level of comfort in exploring sexuality
4   the counsellor not having barriers of prejudice so being able to connect fully with the client
5   the counsellor being a positive role model for their own sexuality group and enabling the client to be themselves fully in the relationship
6   the counsellor having a holistic view of sexuality.

Many counsellors and psychotherapists will not practise gay affirmative therapy, but will offer an approach that is inclusive and respectful. However, many clients may still experience coming out in therapy as highly risky, for fear of rejection or judgement. Consider the scenario in Box 9.2.

CASE STUDY 9.2
William

William has recently come out as gay to his family. They were angry and rejecting and insisted this was a 'phase' he would grow out of. This has made him fearful of talking to other people about his sexuality, and has caused him distress and confusion. He has started individual psychotherapy with George. He does not know George's sexuality and is fearful about talking about his own sexuality in the sessions, not knowing how George will respond.

PAUSE FOR REFLECTION

1 How relevant is William's sexuality to the process of therapy?
2 How relevant is George's sexuality to the process of therapy?
3 What might the risks be for William?
4 If disclosed, how might George respond, and how might George's theoretical orientation influence this?

It is important not to overlook the place of the therapist in this process. In the context of extensive literature about therapist self-disclosure, little attention has been given to a therapist 'coming out' to their client in therapy (Moore and Jenkins, 2012). For the little there is, there is some debate as to whether self-disclosure about a therapist's sexual orientation is helpful or not. Looking at therapists' perceived risks and benefits of 'coming out' to their straight clients, Moore and Jenkins (2012, p.6) found that overall this was perceived to be potentially problematic with the following themes emerging:

1 respondents' fears of client judgement
2 a need for therapist self-protection
3 self-awareness of the potential impact of their own fears and prejudices on the therapeutic relationship
4 the potential relevance of internalised homophobia, as an overall constraining factor.

The research seems to suggest therefore, that while counsellors and psychotherapists need the same relational skills as they would with all clients, further professional development is helpful in ensuring an empathic connection with LGBT clients, particularly through acquiring knowledge and adopting a proactive positive position about sexual orientation. Therapists need to attend to and be aware of their own prejudices and assumptions about sexual orientation, as otherwise these have the potential to be acted out in sessions, despite the therapist's best efforts not to do so.

http:

WEBSITES

Stonewall, UK: www.stonewall.org.uk/
Queer Youth Network, UK: www.queeryouth.org.uk/community/

DISCUSSION QUESTIONS

1 What have been the main influences, personally and professionally, in shaping your current attitudes towards sexual orientation?
2 What steps do you take to help LGBT clients engage and work with issues relating to their sexuality, if that is the focus for their work? What are the implications for your clients if you don't take any additional steps?
3 Have you ever talked about your sexual orientation in a session with a client? Why not, or what prompted this?
4 Do you think that any therapeutic approach should affirm a particular sexual orientation?

9.4 GENDER

SECTION OUTLINE

This section considers how gender is a powerful dynamic in the therapeutic relationship. Therapists need to carefully consider the influence of gender and the similar and different expectations and fears of female and male clients when they attend for therapy. This section explores what is meant by gender and ways in which it is relevant in the counselling and psychotherapy relationship. It also considers the specific issues that women and men might experience at times of difficulty.

Gender is a dynamic present in all therapeutic relationships, although the nature and extent of its influence in the content and process of counselling and psychotherapy is not fully understood. The following dimensions will be considered here:

1 The definition and construction of gender
2 The shared needs of women and men
3 The challenges for women in seeking help
4 The challenges for men in seeking help
5 Gender-awareness in counselling and psychotherapy.

The definition and construction of gender

An understanding of sex, gender and sexual orientation are often mistakenly truncated into one all-encompassing but ultimately misleading category. Sexual orientation has been defined and discussed above. Here it is helpful to differentiate between sex and gender, as both are key terms. The OED (2012) defines sex as, 'either of the two main categories (male and female) into which humans and most other living things are divided on the basis of their reproductive functions'. However, while this definition refers to biological differences, defining sex is not necessarily easy due to points of uncertainty, such as in situations of genetic confusion, or transexuality. Sarah Wilcox defines a transsexual as, 'someone who identifies as male or female but whose gender identity conflicts with their biological sex – that is, they were born male or have XY chromosomes, but experience themselves as female' (Rankin, 2004). The OED defines gender itself as, 'the state of being male or female (typically used with reference to social and cultural differences rather than biological ones)'.

These definitions therefore offer subtle but important distinctions between our understandings of sex and gender. OED defines femininity as 'the quality of being female; womanliness', and masculinity as 'possession of the qualities traditionally associated with men'. Here we have a multi-layered understanding: sex, gender, femininity and masculinity – each offering something different but linked in some way. These terms are a little more fluid: an individual may be biologically male, identify their gender as male, but not see themselves (or be seen) as masculine – similarly being female is not to be equated with being feminine.

PAUSE FOR REFLECTION

1 Consider what characteristics you would apply to the following terms:

   a Female
   b Male
   c Masculine
   d Feminine.

2 How similar or contradictory are these characteristics? How might many overlap?
3 What are the implications here for gender identity?

In discussing the implications for counselling and psychotherapy, I focus here on the term 'gender'. This is on the basis that an individual's biological sex may not be as relevant as an individual's gender identity (unless sex identity is their primary reason for seeking help), and the implications that has for how they experience and articulate their needs, and how or whether they seek help at times of difficulty. The social and cultural construction of gender can present people with very real difficulties and can be the distinctions on which discrimination and oppression may take place. That is to say, women might struggle to experience the same employment opportunities as men not necessarily because of their biological sex, but rather because of the roles and expectations socially ascribed to being female, or a woman (or feminine). Likewise, men may be more reluctant to talk about their personal problems not because of their biological sex, but again because of the roles and expectations of being male, or a man (or masculine).

The shared needs of women and men

This passage works on the assumption that the psychological needs of women and men are essentially the same, but the ways in which they access help, how their psychological needs will be socially constructed and the implications for the nature of help they receive will be differentiated based on their gender. I suggest that we all need a number of factors to be present to achieve psychological health, including intimacy, confidentiality, trust, presence, touch, relational contact and security. The absence of any of these aspects from our lives can leave us in a state of psychological deficit and thus in a greater state of psychological distress. We are relational beings and thrive on secure and trusting relationships, of whatever form, to be in a state of equilibrium.

We might argue, therefore, that the particular difficulties that women or men experience in expressing their psychological needs are more socially constructed, rather than inherent to a particular sex. That is, being male or female isn't of itself the facilitator or barrier to receiving emotional support, but rather how society views the attributes of being male (masculine) or female (feminine) and the relationship of those attributes to seeking help.

PAUSE FOR REFLECTION

Consider again the list of the needs to be met for psychological health, namely: intimacy, confidentiality, trust, presence, touch, relational contact and security.

1   Which factors (if any) are missing for you?
2   Which other needs do you need in your life to achieve psychological health?

The challenges for women in seeking help

Across most settings, ages and cultures, many more women than men access psychological help (WHO, 2012a). The World Health Organisation states, 'Women are more likely to seek help from and disclose mental health problems to their primary health care physician' (WHO, 2012a). Likewise, many more women than men train to be counsellors or psychotherapists. The attributes usually associated with the practice of counselling or psychotherapy – relational, emotional, expressive, vulnerable, talkative, articulate and feelings-based, for example – are perhaps not coincidentally very similar to those associated with femininity. There is a high level of consistency between the activity of counselling and psychotherapy and those associated with being feminine. Because there is a congruence between the help-seeking activity and the way of 'being' that is socially accepted, it is, perhaps, more socially acceptable for women to enter into such professions, and for women to seek help from such professionals.

However, feminist theorists have argued that support for women over many years has focused on facilitating them back into their gender role, rather than truly focusing on their needs as individuals (MacDonald, 1995). Herein lies an important criticism of counselling and psychotherapy: that it is a subtle but powerful agent of social control. Women over the centuries have been labelled as 'hysterical' and 'mad' if they step outside of their gender roles. Proctor (2007) offers a compelling argument against the diagnosis of borderline personality disorder (discussed in more detail in Chapter 6), in claiming that in its disproportional use with women it pathologises women who have been subject to abuse, oppression and discrimination. Women who step beyond what is accepted of them run the risks of a diagnosis of pathology, medication and potential institutionalisation to 'help' them on the road back to conformity (Proctor, 2007). In short, while women may be freer in seeking help, the help they receive has the potential to direct them back into the confines of a gender role that keeps them oppressed and silent.

WEBSITE

Mental Health Foundation (Women): www.mentalhealth.org.uk/help-information/mental-health-a-z/W/women/

The challenges for men in seeking help

Men are generally under-represented in the helping professions, including counselling and psychotherapy, and are under-represented across all age groups and working contexts as clients of counselling and psychotherapy. Men present a higher suicide risk across all age groups internationally and more men die of suicide every day than women across all age groups (WHO, 2012b). Men are more likely to be over-represented in the criminal justice system, and under-represented in mental health systems (other than where mental health systems 'meet' criminal justice systems, such as special hospitals).

The attributes generally associated with counselling and psychotherapy (as out-lined above) are opposed to those generally associated with masculinity (i.e., being strong, silent, capable, in control, stoic, logical, thought-based, and so on). These gen-der-specific attributes arguably make it difficult for men to access help for mental health distress. Men are instead more likely to be found in alcohol or drug-based services, where anaesthetising distress is preferred to actually talking about it (Cour-tenay, 2000). Mahalik et al. (2003) proposed several masculine 'scripts' (predetermined and socially constructed ways of thinking and behaving specifically related to being male). I have represented these 'scripts' in diagrammatic form, as shown in Figure 9.1.

Mahalik et al. additionally outlined the dangers of these masculine scripts on men's mental health (see Figure 9.2).

The problems for men don't lie simply in an unwillingness to seek help for emotional difficulties, however. Many men have been socialised out of emotional awareness from a very early age. Here Levant (1998) developed the term 'normative male alexithymia'. 'Alexithymia' describes an inability to describe emotions in words and is applied to both women and men. 'Male alexithymia' relates this condition

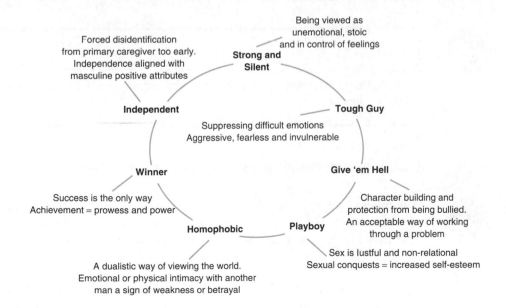

FIGURE 9.1   Masculine scripts

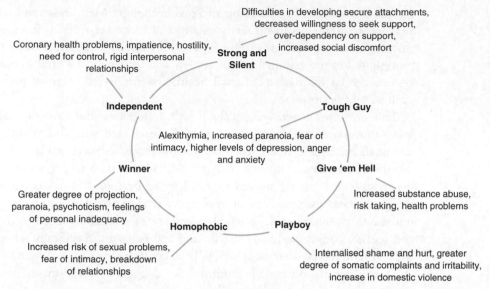

FIGURE 9.2   Problems generated by masculine scripts

specifically to men, and 'normative' generalises that across a wider proportion of men so that, to some degree, the state becomes normalised. This implies that many men experience difficulties in putting emotions into words – though rather than seeing this as a new pathology, it may be more helpful to see this as an aspect of gender role socialisation for men.

WEBSITE

Mind (Men): www.mind.org.uk/campaigns_and_issues/current_campaigns/men_and_mental_health

Gender-awareness in counselling and psychotherapy

A number of steps can be taken to help ensure that counselling and psychotherapy services become gender-aware – that is, engaged with the dynamics of gender and how they might present in sessions, with a commitment to proactively counteract them in service structure and delivery. These include:

1   Wherever possible, ensuring publicity is gender-neutral (i.e., does not promote any particular 'benefit' of therapy that might affiliate more specifically to any one gender role)

2 Wherever possible, ensuring that clients are able to select a female or male therapist

3 Ensuring that access to services is equitable and available to all

4 Encouraging therapists to actively consider gender in their provision of services

5 Encouraging therapists to actively explore the implications of gender in supervision

6 Ensuring that no one 'way of being' is privileged over another (so, for example, the expression of feelings and thoughts are both valued)

7 Encouraging therapists to actively consider clients in the context of gender roles, and how presenting problems might be helpfully understood in that frame

8 Ensuring that the role of pathology, diagnosis and other social functions (such as criminal justice) are critically reflected on as incorporating gender influences

9 Encouraging clients to set their own agenda for counselling and psychotherapy and providing reviews of therapy to allow clients to benchmark progress against their own parameters

10 Ensuring that therapists are open to an exploration of the implications of gender, if client-led.

DISCUSSION QUESTIONS

1 How relevant to you are the terms 'masculine' and 'feminine' in your every day life?

2 To what extent do you actively consider gender in your work with clients?

3 To what extent is your service 'gender-aware'?

4 What additional steps might you or your service take to work with the dynamics and implications of gender?

9.5 FAITH AND SPIRITUALITY

SECTION OUTLINE

This section considers how religion and spirituality can present in the therapeutic relationship. The reader is encouraged to consider, with the help of research and case vignettes, ways of working with different religious and spiritual beliefs and to explore whether, and how, to integrate particular strategies into their work.

Tan (1994, p. 389) states that 'Religion is now recognized as a significant dimension of human diversity that needs to be respected and dealt with appropriately in psychotherapy'. It could be argued that even though faith and spirituality represent core activities or values for many communities, they have been, for many years, under-represented in the counselling and psychotherapy literature. Very few generic counselling and psychotherapy training courses specifically address faith and spirituality in their core training and so therapists are left either to draw on their own beliefs and find ways of integrating them into their practice or, as is more often the case, set aside any consideration of faith, even if it is of importance to the client.

The relationship between faith, spirituality, and counselling and psychotherapy is not always an easy one. For some, faith and spirituality are so much a part of their sense of self that to separate them from personal growth and insight would make no sense. For others, their experience of religious practice has always been associated with an experience of hurt and discrimination and the inclusion of faith and spirituality into therapeutic practice would be an abhorrence. This may be the case, for example, where they have experienced a religious stance on sexuality.

McLeod (2009, p. 487) suggests that 'many of the values and practices of counselling have been derived from the Judaeo-Christian religious tradition'. This further complicates the relationship between faith and therapy. Some have explored the relationship between therapy and the 'new religions', drawing on many of the traditions inherent and integral to religious practice (Kilbourne and Richardson, 1984).

Definitions

The OED (2012) offers two definitions of faith: '(a) complete trust or confidence in someone or something' and '(a) strong belief in the doctrines of a religion, based on spiritual conviction rather than proof'. 'Spiritual' is defined as 'relating to or affecting the human spirit or soul as opposed to material or physical things'; 'having a relationship based on a profound level of mental or emotional communion'; '(of a person) not concerned with material values or pursuits'; and 'relating to religion or religious belief'. Religion is defined as 'a particular system of faith and worship'. Faith and spirituality can therefore be seen as aspects of subscribing to a religious belief, while religion is seen more as the system within which faith and spirituality function. The term spirituality is perhaps more associated with religious conviction, whereas some will talk of having a faith without necessarily subscribing to any religious belief: indeed, they may identify themselves as either agnostic (uncertain as to the existence of God or gods) or atheist (a person who does not believe in the existence of God or gods). For the purposes of this chapter therefore, I use the terms faith and spirituality (rather than religion), so as to include all religions and faiths. The focus of this section is on whether and how faith and spirituality, which might hold particular significance for the therapist or client, is integrated into the therapeutic process. There may be dangers for counsellors and psychotherapists to consider if integrating faith and spirituality into therapy sessions.

The challenges of integrating faith and spirituality into therapy

The integration of faith and spirituality into counselling and psychotherapy practice can be fraught with difficulty and is typically treated with suspicion (Gubi, 2002). Gubi (2009) undertook a study of the use of prayer in counselling and psychotherapy. His participants (counsellors) raised a number of concerns and these generated over-arching themes. Here I draw on and adapt these to outline a number of concerns about the wider integration of faith and spirituality into the therapeutic process. It is important to note that Gubi's study focuses specifically on the use of prayer and, therefore, the following points are my adaptation of his findings. The concerns relate to:

1 Dangers for clients with an underlying psychopathology: for clients with an underlying psychopathology, such as early-onset psychosis for example, concepts around faith and spirituality might be insufficiently 'grounding' and might, inadvertently, exacerbate concerns of anxieties as experienced by the client.

2 Imposing the therapist's faith on the client: whether or not the client holds beliefs consistent with or similar to those of the therapist, the client might not feel able to decline the therapist's reference to faith and spirituality. Even if offered tentatively, it can quickly become an imposition.

3 Accountability of intervention: the integration of faith and spiritual dimensions into the therapeutic frame may be difficult for employing organisations who might feel that following any subsequent complaints the practice was hard to justify, or that it might be inconsistent with ethical frameworks, particularly if the client experienced the integration as an imposition. It may be too easy to mistakenly make assumptions about a client's belief system, or not have the client's consent to explore this area.

4 Faith and spirituality as an avoidance or defence: while it may help the client draw on their own resources, it might also move the focus of work to 'another', or to God or gods. It might inadvertently help the client avoid themselves and thus mitigate against their capacity to engage with coping strategies or change.

5 Difficulties in challenge: linked to the point above, clients may feel unable to challenge the integration of faith or spirituality into sessions because they see it as a strongly held view on behalf of the therapist and do not wish to dismiss or undermine its relevance for them. Ultimately they may 'go along' with it to avoid hurt, but find the intervention unwanted, unhelpful or offensive.

6 Matching faith and spirituality with the client: it may be very problematic to bring together a therapist's faith or spirituality with that of a client, even if the similarities appear apparent. It is not uncommon, even for people subscribing to the same principles of faith, for there to be important divisions and differences.

7 Cultural pressure to accept faith and spirituality: this may be particularly the case if therapy is located in an organisation with a specific faith context, or where therapy is funded by a faith-based organisation even if the therapy offered is non-faith-based. Clients may feel a compulsion to accept faith and spiritual dimensions to the therapy for fear that if they refuse, the therapy will be withdrawn.

8 The routine use of faith and spirituality in sessions: the routine integration of faith and spirituality might override the client's focus for therapy, or change the essence of the relationship from a therapeutic one to a religious one. It is important for counselling and psychotherapy to remain therapy-centred.

9 Using faith and spirituality when it is not part of the client's agenda: this may arise with clients who hold faith-based beliefs, as well as for those who don't.

10 Faith and spirituality as a means of enhancing the therapist's power: as discussed earlier in this chapter, there are inherent power dynamics pertinent to counselling and psychotherapy that are difficult to mitigate, even with awareness. It is likely therefore, the therapist will hold greater power in the relationship, particularly in the earlier stages, and their bringing faith and spirituality into sessions might be a way (consciously or unconsciously) through which their power is enhanced or perpetuated.

As stated earlier, however, there is a growing recognition of the importance and value of acknowledging the dimensions of faith and spirituality in an individual's process of growth and change, particularly when led by the client themselves. The Association for Pastoral and Spiritual Care in Counselling (APSCC), a division of BACP, is active in helping to promote spiritual dimensions in counselling and psychotherapy in a way consistent with ethical principles. There is additionally an increasing body of research that helpfully explores the delicate interface between faith and therapy (Barnett and Johnson, 2011; Nelson and Wilson, 1984; Stein, 2011). Ultimately, ethical practice would require the client's lead on an exploration of faith and spirituality, defined by their parameters and extent. Some pointers for ethical practice in this area, again drawing on Gubi's work, include:

1 Ensuring that a faith-based exploration is client-led and focused

2 Recognising that interventions will not necessarily be driven by faith, but rather informed by faith (if used at all)

3 Ensuring there is sufficient space for the client to move away from a faith-based discussion, when they are ready to

4 Acknowledging cultural pressures the client may experience and ensuring the client does not feel an imperative to follow a particular discourse if they would rather not

5 Ensuring any faith–based exploration is defined by the client's position, rather than the therapist's
6 Helping the client to integrate faith and spirituality with the other, stated focus of their work in therapy
7 Using supervision to explore any motivation to draw on faith and spirituality in sessions.

WEBSITE

Association for Pastoral and Spiritual Care and Counselling (APSCC): www.apscc.org.uk/

DISCUSSION QUESTIONS

1 What is the relationship, for you, between faith and spirituality and your work as a therapist?
2 How might this relationship facilitate or hinder a connection with your client's faith or spirituality?
3 How would you respond to a client who wished to explore their faith in therapy?
4 What steps do you take to reflect on the presence (or not) of faith or spirituality in your work as a therapist?

9.6 CULTURE

SECTION OUTLINE

Culture arguably informs the essence of our being, shaping our up-bringing, experiences, social engagement and our constructs of the world around us. Whether we experience our culture as an explicit part of ourselves, or rather as something more implicit or inherent in our way of being, it will inform much about how we think, feel and process our experiences. Counsellors and psychotherapists work with clients from a wide variety of cultural backgrounds and traditions. Sometimes the struggle to match therapeutic models and theories to an individual's experience and view of the world can be challenging. This section explores what we mean by culture, how it might define the nature and shape of the therapeutic relationship, and how therapists' practice can respect cultural diversity.

Mohamed (2006, p. 50) argues that culture has 'a profound impact ... in defining different aspects of an individual's social and psychological experiences'. Our discussion here is based on recognition of the integral importance of culture in shaping identity, our self-construct (as influenced through our upbringing), our view of the world and how we process experience. For some, culture is an explicit, lived experience that they pay conscious attention to on a moment-by-moment or day-by-day timeline. For others, culture is a way of being that is experienced at a much more integrated and implicit level – one that shapes experience less in awareness and more in process. A client's culture will be powerfully present in all therapeutic relationships and the challenge is for therapists to work with this with awareness and thoughtfulness, regardless of whether the therapist shares the same cultural background.

Definitions

It may be helpful to begin by (perhaps artificially) separating out the terms 'race', 'ethnicity' and 'culture' to enable us to consider the implications of culturally sensitive work. The OED (2012) defines race as, 'a group of people sharing the same culture, history, language' and 'each of the major divisions of humankind, having distinct physical characteristics'. It defines ethnicity as 'the fact or state of belonging to a social group that has a common national or cultural tradition', and culture as 'the ideas, customs, and social behaviour of a particular people or society'. Culture is a social concept, including values, attitudes and behaviours common to a group of people. It seems that ethnicity helps us understand the meaning of race and, in turn, culture helps us to understand the meaning of race and ethnicity. The assertion by Mohamed (2006, p. 51) that culture 'affect[s] the way that we interact with the world, and conduct and define relationships' is particularly relevant when applied to the process of counselling and psychotherapy. For the purposes of this section I have chosen to explore the implications of culture for counselling and psychotherapy practice. However, the discussion will also include the implications of racism and discrimination based on race and culture and how those implications might present in counselling or psychotherapy.

Racism and discrimination

Racism may be defined as 'the belief that all members of each race possess characteristics, abilities, or qualities specific to that race, especially so as to distinguish it as inferior or superior to another race or races' and 'prejudice, discrimination, or antagonism directed against someone of a different race based on the belief that one's own race is superior' (OED, 2012). There are countless examples throughout history where one race or culture has experienced oppression at the hands of another, based on spurious ideological or sociological grounds. An example many people would quickly bring to mind would be the persecution and mass murder of the Jewish, gypsy and lesbian and gay communities and people with disabilities by the Nazis in the 1940s, leading to mass exterminations. As Mohamed (2006, p. 54) states, however, racism 'does not appear to be a stagnant ideology, but adapts to accommodate the socioeconomic needs of the dominant society'. To this I would add political needs and those based on power, with sadly plenty of historical evidence since the 1940s of racism and oppression of one group by another leading to genocide (e.g. during the Balkan wars in the 1980s; Rwanda in the 1990s).

These examples illustrate the devastating effects of racism at a macro level, with systematic and organised policies and actions based on racist beliefs. Equally devastating examples of racism can be seen at the micro level, however: individuals experiencing abuse, attack or insult on a daily basis because of their defined social or cultural groups, or pay or opportunity being denied to people based on their cultural identity.

While counselling and psychotherapy has been used effectively in response to major traumas, such as in Rwanda for example (Cohen et al., 2011; Sakai et al., 2010), most counsellors and psychotherapists will encounter the effects of racism and discrimination in their day-to-day practice in hearing of their clients' experiences of abuse and lack of opportunity. Many people who become counsellors and psychotherapists will also have experienced their own traumas rooted in racism in virtue of their own cultural identity. It is at this point that Western-dominated counselling and psychotherapy models, typically developed by white, heterosexual males in powerful employment, can flounder. By privileging 'self', personal growth and insight as a priority, the system in which the client functions and lives and which, quite often, can include oppressive and discriminatory processes, can be sidelined. It can be too easy to define an individual's experience as stemming from an inner incongruence or pathology without taking into full account the external factors that might be figural in shaping their experience both of themselves and of the world in which they live. It can be very hard, if not impossible, to achieve good mental health in a society that marginalises at best, or represses and abuses at worst, based on cultural identity. The imperative here is for you to take a systemic view of your client's experience and take active steps to understand the context.

Culture, communication and the expression of distress

Research in psychiatry has, for many years, identified important differences between the expression of distress and the definition of mental disorder across cultures

(Lipsedge and Littlewood, 1997). It is widely reported that minority culture groups are over-represented in mental health systems (Thavasothy, 2009); it is essential to contextualise an individual's distress by what is culturally appropriate. Work by Tseng (1999, p. 132) identified three types of therapies internationally: (i) culture-embedded indigenous healing practices, (ii) culture-influenced unique therapies and (iii) culture-related common therapies, more typically the counselling and psychotherapy models primarily utilised in the West (e.g. CBT, psychodynamic).

Even for people sharing a language and culture, the articulation of distress can be profoundly complex and difficult. For therapist and client working across cultures and language, the need for great care in both understanding and relevance is paramount. For understanding, the therapist must carefully check with the client they understand the explicit and implicit meaning of what is being said. For relevance, the therapist must carefully check they do not inadvertently privilege certain expressions and aspects that are consistent with the model of therapy being used, but that might not be consistent with the cultural frame from which the client has experienced, and therefore articulated, them. In short, what might be 'important' for one person might not share the same level of 'importance' for the other.

Developing anti-discriminatory therapeutic practice

Tseng (1999, p. 168-71) and Bhui and Morgan (2007, p. 192) offer helpful guidelines on the development of anti-discriminatory and culturally sensitive practice in counselling and psychotherapy. Therapists should:

1   Consider their preconceptions about the race and ethnicity of the client and of that person's family
2   Recognise that an individual may be quite different from other members of the same racial and ethnic group
3   Consider the sociocultural setting of where therapy is located and delivered and how that might shape the therapeutic process
4   Consider how racial and ethnic differences between themselves and the client might affect psychotherapy; these include:

   i   differences in conceptualisation of mental health and illness
   ii   differences in conceptualisation of the self in relation to family and community
   iii   differences in communication styles
   iv   the client's understanding of therapy and its aims

v   the therapist to reflect on their preferred communications style and how that might facilitate or inhibit the relationship

vi   culturally adjust theories and understanding of psychopathology

vii   be aware of the potential impact on the therapist's and client's value system

viii   be clear as to the goals of therapy

5   Acknowledge that power, privilege and racism might affect interaction with all clients

6   Err on the side of discussion when in doubt about the importance of race and ethnicity and treatment

7   Keep learning about issues of race and ethnicity, and become a 'mini-ethnographer' with clients and the public

8   Notice, apprehend and think through the racial transference so that it is understood, acquires therapeutic value and is not re-enacted in the therapy room.

The first step, however, is for all counsellors and psychotherapists to be aware of the dangers of being 'culturally blind' and adopting a 'one model fits all' approach to delivering therapy. The importance of recognising and working with difference cannot be overstated in ensuring that counselling and therapy is and remains truly anti-discriminatory and respectful of individuals.

WEBSITES

Equality and Human Rights Commission: www.equalityhumanrights.com/
Amnesty International: www.amnesty.org.uk/

DISCUSSION QUESTIONS

1   To what extent do you think discrimination plays a part in developing psychological distress?

2   How culturally diverse is your practice? What steps might be taken to encourage greater cultural diversity amongst your client group?

3   How might you inadvertently adopt a 'one model fits all' approach with your clients? What would be the consequences of this?

4   How do you seek to work in an anti-discriminatory way, and how do you review your progress on this matter?

9.7 DISABILITY

SECTION OUTLINE

Greater awareness of the needs of disabled people has resulted in a higher profile in legislation and policy implementation. In the UK, legislation promotes disabled people's access to services and many sectors of society are taking proactive steps to make their services 'disabled-friendly'. As well as the challenges of physically accessing services for some, the importance of ensuring attitudes that support the delivery of a positive experience are equally important. This is true for counselling and psychotherapy, which disabled people may access to address issues around their disability or to address other, non-related concerns. This section considers the meaning of disability, the attitudinal measures required to ensure that clients receive a respectful service and the practical considerations required to ensure dignity and equality of provision.

According to Reeve (2002, p. 11), 'Counsellors are subject to the same negative images and stereotypes of disabled people as the rest of society. The attitudes and prejudices of counsellors towards disabled people can adversely affect the nature of the client–counsellor relationship when the client is a disabled person – there is sometimes oppression within the counselling room'. This view is supported by Taylor (2010, p. 15), who states that, 'People with learning disabilities have traditionally been denied access to a range of psychological therapies', and by Roosen (2009, p. 1) who noted that, 'Individuals with disabilities have been largely ignored from research and training in the field of psychology'.

The lack of presence of disability in both the research and provision of the psychological therapies perhaps reflects a wider problem, in that people with disabilities have, for many years, been marginalised and overlooked in society. A culture that privileges the able-bodied in music, sport, culture and art, for example, seems to have little space or time for people who do not fulfil the mainstream idea of 'normal'. The reality, of course, is very different: people with disabilities make a significant contribution in all these areas, albeit in a less acknowledged way.

The challenge for counselling and psychotherapy, and for all of us who work in the field, is to embrace ways in which opportunities for people with disabilities to participate in counselling and psychotherapy can be made available, whether that be in training, practice, research or as clients. There is no justification for a continuing invisibility of a significant proportion of society in the ways reported by the writers above.

Definitions

In the UK the Equality Act 2010 aims to protect disabled people and prevent discrimination based on disability. The law defines a person as having a disability if:

1 they have a physical or mental impairment
2 the impairment has a substantial and long-term adverse effect on their ability to perform normal day-to-day activities.

For the purposes of the Act, the key terms are defined as follows:

- 'substantial' means more than minor or trivial
- 'long-term' means that the effect of the impairment has lasted or is likely to last for at least 12 months
- 'normal day-to-day activities' include everyday things like eating, washing, walking and going shopping.

Further guidance is available to help assess disability for the purposes of the Act (see Websites section at the end). The OED (2012) defines disability as 'a physical or mental condition that limits a person's movements, senses, or activities'. Here physical disability might include visual or hearing impairment, illness, mobility impairment or learning impairment, for example. Mental disability might include a long-standing mental health condition, such as schizophrenia, bipolar disorder, or dementia.

The use of language has played an important part in determining and shaping society's view of disabled people. Cavender, Trewin and Hanson (2009), quoting from the American Psychological Association's style guidelines on non-handicapping language, distinguish key terms as follows:

> Impairment is used to characterize a physical, mental or physiological loss, abnormality or injury that causes a limitation in one or more major life functions …

> Disability refers to a functional limitation that affects an individual's ability to perform certain functions …

> Handicap describes a barrier or problem created by society or the environment …

> A disability is a measurable impairment or limitation that 'interferes with a person's ability, for example, to walk, lift, hear, or learn. It may refer to a physical, sensory, or mental condition' (Schiefelbusch Institute, 1996).

It is always problematic when reducing a complex and diverse group of people to a single term, such as 'disabled', when some would see themselves in that way and others not. In my own work over the years people with disabilities have defined themselves in very different ways. The sector I currently work in, higher education, currently offers 'disability support' to people with physical, emotional and learning challenges; some who access such support do so happily, while others resent the term 'disability'. In this section I will use the term 'people with disabilities', given I am referring to specific 'functional limitations' people may experience that have implications for the delivery of counselling and psychotherapy. I make two philosophical assumptions here: that we should always see the person before the disability; and that the notion of disability does not necessarily lie in the individual, but rather in the construction of a society that prohibits free and equal access and opportunity.

Relational challenges for counsellors and psychotherapists

I begin with relational challenges, rather than outlining practical problems initially, as it is too easy to focus exclusively on the practical limitations that might prevent people from working as counsellors or psychotherapists, or of accessing counselling or psychotherapy. We need to critically reflect on the nature of training and service delivery and, in particular, how fears and stereotypes might sometimes be unconsciously used to avoid making services more emotionally accessible. The fears and myths that can haunt people more generally in responding to people with disabilities can be present for counsellors and psychotherapists too. In training, very little time or attention tends to be given to help therapists face such fears. Henry (2007) offers some general guidance in communicating about disability and with people with a disability. Her advice can be summarised as follows:

1   Don't make assumptions about disabilities or people's needs.
2   Ask whether help is needed rather than simply doing something to help.
3   Talk directly to the person, and not a helper, family or friend.
4   Use normal dialogue rather than adapting it, unless asked to do so.
5   Avoid euphemisms for disabilities and take your lead from the person directly about how they talk about themselves.
6   Use 'people-first' language, (i.e., a person with visual impairment, rather than a visually-impaired person).
7   Be sensitive to personal space, particularly when a person requires equipment to aid mobility.

We can too readily assume that the disability itself is the focus of any therapeutic work or the cause of difficulty. According to Oliver (1995, p. 261), 'more often than not it is the client's lack of control over their physical and social environment and not the impairment that causes emotional difficulties'. This statement reminds us that we may play a part, albeit inadvertently, in contributing to a person's sense of lack of control.

CASE STUDY 9.3
Justin

Justin is a 52-year-old man with multiple sclerosis. He attends for counselling following the break-down in the relationship with his partner. They have experienced difficulties in their relationship for some years; their only child moving to university seems to have precipitated the breakdown. Justin has experienced deteriorating physical health and now mostly uses a wheelchair for mobility. His speech is restricted following a stroke two years ago. He now lives alone and is reluctant to have carer support.

Justin has quickly become frustrated with his counselling as the counsellor keeps returning to his physical health while, for Justin, his priority was the ending of a significant relationship and his child moving away. The counsellor is concerned about Justin's unwillingness to accept his physical health needs and that he is placing himself in a vulnerable position. The counsellor challenges Justin about this, suggesting that he is denying the reality of his situation. The counsellor wonders about a possible link between Justin's attitude to himself and the breakdown of the relationship.

PAUSE FOR REFLECTION

1 How would you suggest the counsellor might have balanced more effectively Justin's focus for counselling against the concerns about his physical health?

2 To what extent do you think the counsellor might have allowed his own preconceptions about disability to influence his understanding of Justin's situation?

3 How do you think you might have responded to Justin differently, if at all? Why?

Practical considerations in accessing services

Clients with disabilities may seek counselling or psychotherapy because of their disabilities, perhaps as a process of emotionally adjusting to a newly acquired disability or facing the implications of a long-standing one. Alternatively, they may seek counselling or psychotherapy for a range of other reasons and happen additionally to have a disability. It is important not to become automatically disability-centred, but rather allow the client to frame their own focus, as we would with any other client. The early sessions or assessment will be crucial in determining the nature and focus of the work.

It is important, however, that services and we as counsellors and psychotherapists pay careful attention to how clients can access services, and are aware of aspects of service delivery that might prevent someone from seeking help. Considerations might include:

1 Accessibility of pre-therapy information, such as ensuring written or web-based materials are accessible to people with visual impairment, for example, or are written in a way that is clear and non-jargonistic. This would include ensuring information is presented in an understandable way for people with learning disability so that they are able to make informed choices about whether and how to access therapy.

2 As with pre-therapy information, ensuring that written contracts or agreements for therapy are accessible and understandable, taking additional steps to adapt information so that it becomes so, if required.

3 Ensuring that clients are clear about the parameters of therapy, including what charges are to be made (if any), particularly for clients with learning difficulties or mental health problems where recall or understanding might be impaired.

4 Discussing with the client the timing of sessions and whether certain times are more suitable than others (if, for example, transport is required, or for the availability of carers (if used), or if people are more 'sluggish' earlier or later on etc.).

5 Taking steps to ensure the therapy room is accessible, wherever possible. In the UK there is a statutory responsibility to ensure equality of access to buildings and services, wherever practicable. Consider whether people can access the building and room, whether the chair is suitable, and whether the client is able to access appropriate toilet facilities, if required. If assistance is required for access, it is important to discuss with the client who will be available to provide that assistance and then to ensure that person remains available, if required.

6 Taking steps to ensure appropriate levels of confidentiality, particularly when working with people with learning difficulties, or when using signers or interpreters.

7 Taking steps to ensure clients are clear as to the scope and nature of the counselling and psychotherapy offered, and that, if they so wish, the client can end sessions, or therapy altogether, without difficulty.

Provided one takes these considerations into account and takes a person-first approach, it is entirely possible to ensure that any counselling and psychotherapy provision can fully meet the needs of a person with a disability. It is essential that counsellors and psychotherapists carefully consider their own prejudices and assumptions about disability and use opportunities to discuss these openly and honestly. As stated elsewhere, it is unacknowledged prejudice that has the potential to cause most harm, as it will present in our work in some form.

WEBSITES

Disability Action: www.disabilityaction.org/
The International Disability and Human Rights Network: www.daa.org.uk
The Equality Act 2010 (Guidance): www.equalityhumanrights.com/advice-and-guidance/new-equality-act-guidance/

DISCUSSION QUESTIONS

1   Reflect on the service in which you work. How easy is it for people with disabilities to access your service (from the provision of pre-therapy information onwards)?
2   How many people with disabilities make use of your service? If the numbers are low, why might this be? If higher, what are you doing well and how might you develop this further?
3   Considering the way you publicise your therapy and also your own approach as a therapist. To what extent is your work 'person-first' around disability?
4   What factors in your life have influenced your attitudes to disability?

PART THREE
THE PROFESSIONAL SELF

10

Managing Professional Responsibilities

10.1 INTRODUCTION

CHAPTER OVERVIEW

Beyond direct work with clients, counsellors and psychotherapists have to manage a number of other professional and personal responsibilities while ensuring that their work is ethically appropriate, acknowledges the autonomy of the client and remains personally respectful. This chapter examines a number of challenges to counsellors and psychotherapists' professional practice, whether they are working in larger organisations or in independent practice.

The most obvious frame of counselling and psychotherapy is direct work with clients, whether that be individual face-to-face work, online therapy, or therapy with couples or with groups. The therapeutic 'hour' begins, work commences and then the therapy session finishes. The time is managed carefully and boundaries monitored closely. However, less attention is given to the professional demands of working as a counsellor or psychotherapist and how those too shape both how we are viewed as therapists generally, and the therapeutic work with our clients specifically.

Working in a large organisational setting (for example, the health service or an EAP) might present the most obvious challenges to us in terms of working beyond our specific role with clients. For example, managing confidentiality in a multi-disciplinary team, or writing a report for an employer about counselling under-taken with an employee, presents particular challenges to be carefully negotiated. Likewise, there are challenges within the therapeutic process that can, at times, present practitioners with great difficulty, such as the appropriate use of touch and maintaining appropriate relationships with clients.

The independent practitioner has a number of challenges to manage that might be heightened by their 'independent' status. For example, while an agency setting typically has reception facilities and standardised responses to missed sessions or collect-ing fees, an independent practitioner needs to consider how 'out of therapy' contact (by email or telephone, for example) can be ethically and appropriately managed.

While the process of therapy is complicated enough, counsellors and psycho-therapists, like many other 'helping' professionals, have to carefully consider many issues – for example: what is and is not appropriate for the scope of their work; how to apply the requirements of ethical practice into the real world; how to man-age particular aspects of therapeutic work that might on one hand be helpful, but on the other misconstrued as unwanted or even abusive; and finally, how to pay sufficient attention to their own wellbeing to ensure that they remain emotionally and psychologically available to their clients.

This chapter therefore considers a number of the key responsibilities that we might face in our work. The first section, Communicating with Clients Outside Therapy, considers why we might need to have contact with our clients outside of specific therapy sessions, how we might negotiate and contract for these carefully, and how all that we and our clients do and say has the potential to contribute to the therapeutic process.

The next section, Keeping Relationships Appropriate, discusses how to manage relationships with clients so that they remain safe and respectful. In addition, it considers the management of relationships with others who might make demands or have expectations that challenge the boundaries of therapy. Next, The Profes-sional Self considers our role as a counsellor or psychotherapist in the context of wider systems, as well as our role in promoting the profession and thus enhancing counselling and psychotherapy as a viable choice for people.

The next section addresses one of the areas I am most asked about when work-ing with trainees or newly qualified practitioners. Is it ever appropriate to have physical contact with clients as a means of supporting them without transgressing boundaries? Can one do so while ensuring that one's conduct remains ethically appropriate? The Use of Touch identifies factors to keep in mind and examines how touch can be explored within the therapeutic frame.

Working Within One's Own Competence considers the ethical requirement of working within our professional competence. It considers how to identify where we reach our limits of competence and what actions we can take to support both our clients and ourselves whenever we begin to feel out of our depth.

The final section reflects on what the over-used phrase 'self-care' actually means in practice, what can happen when we fail to take adequate care of our emotional, psychological or physical wellbeing, and how we can integrate good self-care strategies into our daily work. Though these aspects can sometimes be seen as peripheral to the 'proper' client-based work of counsellors and psychotherapists, they are, in fact, essential considerations to help embed ethical integrity into our work. Failing to address these issues comprehensively can lead to burnout, an impaired capacity to meet our clients in their distress, and, consequently, a fundamental failure to offer clients a safe and respectful therapeutic space.

10.2 COMMUNICATING WITH CLIENTS OUTSIDE THERAPY

SECTION OUTLINE

Communication with clients takes many forms. The most apparent, of course, is the actual face-to-face encounter. However, for a variety of reasons we may have to communicate with clients beyond the therapy session, including setting up initial contact, managing cancellations and non-attendance, as well as responding to questions or crises that might emerge during the therapeutic process. This section examines what we need to consider during these times.

When thinking about communicating with clients, we understandably focus on the therapeutic relationship itself and the process of counselling or psychotherapy. The majority of our training will concentrate on the particular skills required to facilitate a therapeutic relationship, including 'micro' skills such as reflection, paraphrasing and summarising. Enormous amounts of time are spent practising these skills and reflecting on the smallest aspects of our interventions and what clients said or did not say. It is right that so much attention is given to this aspect. After all, that is surely what counselling and psychotherapy is about: two people, a couple or a group meeting together to be facilitated through distress or difficulty.

As a supervisor of trainees I am aware, however, that many begin placement with very little thought about the management of communication with clients beyond the therapy hour. Many trainees seem to hold the view that such communication, perhaps by telephone, email, letter or text, for example, is purely an administrative task. My assertion here is that, while such communication is administratively important, it should be viewed as a therapeutic task, equally as important as what happens during the process of therapy itself.

The 'hows' and 'whys' of client contact

Here we need to be clear as to how such communication might take place, and why. There are many reasons why we might need to contact, or be contacted by, clients outside the 'therapy hour'. 'Contact' might come in a variety of forms, including:

- Telephone calls
- Emails
- Letters by post
- Texts
- Contacts via social networking sites (e.g. Facebook)
- Other online contact (e.g. Skype or chat rooms)
- The client unexpectedly calling at your place of work (e.g. office or home)
- Seeing your client unexpectedly (e.g. while shopping, at the gym).

The therapist needs to consider how both parties would prefer to be contacted outside therapy so that difficult situations can be avoided where possible. For example, in my own place of work we routinely ask clients to provide a postal address, telephone number, mobile number and email address, but also ask for them to indicate their preferred means of contact. We have made an organisational decision not to contact clients by mobile phone (either for a voice call or text) other than if notifying them of a last minute change to their therapy appointment (if their counsellor is off sick, for example). This decision was informed by the fact that with the client group using our service (i.e., mostly 17–21-year-olds) the 'turnover' of mobile phones is high, while voicemails are often not customised by the user and therefore it is difficult to ensure confidentiality if leaving messages. In other services or settings it may be appropriate to take a different decision.

Having agreed with the client how they would prefer you to contact them, and the circumstances in which this is likely, it is important to clarify how you would prefer your client to contact you. You may have an email address dedicated to your work as a therapist, in which case this may be the preferred method of contact. Alternatively you might have a 'work' mobile telephone account that you make available. It is important to clearly outline how the client may contact you, in what circumstances, and when. Unplanned contact presents the greatest danger of a breach of confidentiality or an inappropriate self-disclosure (e.g. a family member accessing a home email account and seeing an email from a client, or someone else answering your mobile phone when the client would only be expecting to speak to you). It is essential that any means of communication offered to the client is only available for that purpose. If working within an organisation, reception facilities are often in place to manage such contact. If working independently, further steps will need to be taken. Given the number of secure and free email services available, an account could be set up to which only you have access. Likewise, a pay-as-you-go mobile account could be set up simply for the purposes of client contact. Taking these simple steps can help safeguard the client's confidentiality and provide important parameters for managing such contact.

Additional points to include in a contract for therapy are a specification of the circumstances in which contact will be received and the timing. Some counsellors and psychotherapists offer out of hours contact with clients if crisis situations should arise. This is a decision for each practitioner, following careful discussion with the supervisor that might consider the therapist's capacity and competence to offer such support. My own preference is not to provide such contact, even though I am familiar with supporting people out of hours in crisis as part of my professional background. I find that therapy is best contained within limited parameters, and that in crisis periods clients are better contacting specialist crisis services, or telephone helplines (e.g. The Samaritans). I make information about such services available to clients at the beginning of therapy and additionally make clear that I can only be contacted for the management of sessions using the means outlined in the contract. I am unavailable out of hours: this is personal and professional preference.

Instances in which contact with clients outside planned contact times might occur include:

- Receiving an initial enquiry about counselling or psychotherapy from a prospective client
- Organising a first appointment or assessment appointment
- Sending out pre-therapy information, such as information about ourselves, how we work, or particular aspects that will help define therapy
- Providing websites or other sources of online information about ourselves and our work
- Confirming post-initial session the agreements made (e.g. the contract agreed, confirmation of fees)
- Sending out questionnaires or outcome measures prior to therapy
- Receiving requests from clients to change appointment times or days
- Clients cancelling planned sessions
- Counsellors or psychotherapists having to cancel planned sessions
- Contacting clients following their non-attendance
- Notifying or confirming any changes to the working contract (e.g. increase in fees, change in location)
- Issuing invoices for charges made or receipts for payments received
- Receiving contact from clients when in crisis or when they are highly distressed
- Confirming the end of therapy

- Contacting a client post-therapy – for example, to request access to notes or in response to a request for reports from therapists as part of an insurance claim or court process
- Seeing clients unexpectedly outside therapy sessions.

This list isn't exhaustive: other unexpected reasons might necessitate therapist–client contact. The examples fall into two distinct groups: expected and unexpected contact. By expected contact I am referring to instances where we might know contact will occur or when it is reasonably predicted. Such instances might include contact due to changes in arrangements or when sending out information about therapy. Unexpected contact, when contact might not be reasonably predicted, might include initial enquiries for therapy (we might hope that such contacts will occur, but they will often come at the most unexpected times), or seeing a client outside of therapy, perhaps while shopping, for example. It is probably fair to say that most instances will be expected contacts and therefore can be planned for. The two short vignettes in Box 10.1 illustrate such contacts. There are two additional case examples on the companion website, one each for expected and unexpected contact, to help you reflect on this further.

BOX 10.1   EXPECTED AND UNEXPECTED CONTACT

Expected contact

Mohammed receives an email from a client saying she needs a report for her workplace about the progress of counselling, which is due before the next planned session. She asks if it would be convenient to talk on the telephone for 10 minutes to briefly discuss the content of the report. Mohammed replies saying this would be okay, and a time is arranged for the client to call.

Unexpected contact

Jonah is an independent psychotherapist. He sees clients usually from his local community, accepting referrals from GPs. While out one evening with friends, having had several drinks, he bumps into one of his clients in a club. The client, who is with her partner, is clearly uncomfortable as she has previously told Jonah she does not wish her partner to know she is attending therapy.

It is always important to talk with clients at the contracting stage about unexpected contact outside of therapy and how you would both manage this. Some clients will like a smile and brief acknowledgement, while others would prefer to be ignored. If this is discussed and planned in advance then both client and therapist can be clear as to how each other will behave.

Administration or therapy?

Having considered the 'hows' and 'whys', we need also to reflect on the meaning of contact. I would argue that every form of contact, and in every situation, plays some part of the therapeutic process. From how a client makes contact initially, what they say and the questions they ask, through to how and when they might cancel a session, all situations say something about the client's relational style (i.e., how they interact with their world) that might, at some point, be relevant. Consider the scenario in Box 10.2:

CASE STUDY 10.2
Joyce

Joyce makes contact and requests counselling. She arrives a few minutes late for her first appointment and apologises, saying there was a great deal of traffic and she wasn't sure where she was going. She talks about a number of failed relationships and her frustration at 'never being able to make relationships work'. She had difficult parental relationships and felt hurt by their lack of care and interest. She often felt overlooked and when she did try to engage them in her life this usually resulted in greater hurt and her withdrawal. Out of eight appointments she cancels two with less than 24 hours' notice. She generally arrives a few minutes late on each occasion, citing traffic problems as the reason.

We might speculate over the reasons behind Joyce's cancelled sessions and late arrivals. Perhaps:

- Joyce finds the prospect of all relationships frightening and needs to keep control
- She is frightened of commitment and, while making real efforts to engage, needs to keep 'one foot outside the door'
- Her low self-esteem means that she cannot believe her attendance is important, nor that her absence will be noticed
- She is angry at parental figures, or those who hold power in her life, and unconsciously 'punishes' them through her withdrawal
- Joyce cannot feel valued in relationships and experiences the relational dynamic as challenging and hurtful
- Joyce's life is currently chaotic, representing her inner turmoil
- There is a great deal of traffic.

As therapists we are bound to reflect on and speculate about our client's actions and behaviours – within the counselling frame and beyond it. We work on an assumption that what our client says (and does not say), and how they act (and do not act) will communicate something about how they are in their world and the relationship they might have with their distress or difficulty. What we do with our speculations will depend on our way of working and theoretical orientation. As psychodynamic therapists, we might offer an interpretation to help the client reflect on their actions. As cognitive-behavioural therapists, we might identify behavioural and cognitive problems and focus on the process of change. As person-centred therapists, we might 'hold' our speculations and wait for the client's lead, or instead explore through our congruence the impact of their actions on us, or perhaps instead bring patterns and aspects of what they do from their edge of awareness. Fundamentally we have made the link between what happens outside therapy and what happens inside it.

The link between 'inside' and 'outside' action is apparent with Joyce; though it might be less apparent with other clients, the link is still there. It is imperative therefore that while communicating with clients outside therapy might involve an administrative process, it is recognised as fundamentally and inextricably a therapeutic one and so requires the same commensurate skill and care we would afford contact within a therapy session.

Considerations for communicating with clients

The 'rule of thumb' here is that all communications, however brief or apparently functional, need to be undertaken as if they were being spoken directly to the client. Initial information about you as a therapist or the service you offer, whether that be online or hard copy, needs to communicate your 'self' as practitioner as much as what you charge or where you will meet. The tone (inclusive and warm or rigid and detached) of the contract you write will be important, as will the tone of emails sent. In essence you are indicating how your contract will be implemented in practice across all aspects of your work. Consider the three emails in Boxes 10.3 to 10.5 in response to a client's non-attendance, without notice.

BOX 10.3   EMAIL CONTACT: VERSION 1

Dear Alan

I am sorry that you were not able to attend our scheduled appointment today (DATE/TIME). We have another appointment booked for the same time next week and I will look forward to you attending.

Please do contact me if you anticipate any problems.

Yours
Andrew

Andrew Reeves
Counsellor

BOX 10.4   EMAIL CONTACT: VERSION 2

Hi Alan

Sorry you weren't able to come to our appointment today (DATE/TIME). Hope things are okay with you? We've another booked next week at the same time – hope you can make it. Let me know if there's a problem.

Cheers
Andrew

Andrew Reeves
Counsellor

BOX 10.5   EMAIL CONTACT: VERSION 3

Alan

Well, where did you get to? We were meant to meet and you didn't show up! I'll be here same time next week so hopefully you'll make it too. Give us a ring if you're not able to come.

Thanks mate
Andrew

Andrew Reeves
Counsellor

PAUSE FOR REFLECTION

1   What was your response to each email?
2   Which aspects of each email were positive for you, and which were negative?
3   Imagine conveying each message by speaking directly to the client, rather than using email. How does that change your preference for a particular approach?
4   How is your preference between emails informed by your theoretical model?

As can be seen from the emails in Boxes 10.3 to 10.5, a different tone produces a different type of communication. The relationship you have with your client will be important in deciding how to pitch any particular form of communication, but still grounded in a wider therapeutic process. For those counsellors and psychotherapists who are members of a professional organisation with a defined code of ethics or ethical framework, all contact with clients will be bound by those terms. It is important therefore to consider whether what you are communicating is consistent with the requirements of your ethical framework. It is often helpful, particularly in the early stages of practice, to discuss with a supervisor or colleague any correspondence before it is sent. It is not uncommon for another perspective to pick up on a particular tone or phrase that might inadvertently communicate something that was not originally intended.

In summary, all contact with clients, whether it be within the therapeutic relationship or outside of the therapy 'hour', forms part of the therapeutic process. Even though the contact might have an administrative aspect, it is appropriate to consider such communication as a therapeutic intervention rather than merely an administrative action. As a consequence, the same level of care and attention is required when considering all aspects of how you communicate yourself as a practitioner generally, and with clients specifically, as you would provide when working face to face.

DISCUSSION QUESTIONS

1 What does your pre-therapy publicity (your website, leaflets etc.) say about you as a practitioner?
2 How carefully do you consider 'out of therapy' communication with clients?
3 How might you incorporate the matter of 'out of therapy' communications more specifically when you contract clients?
4 How might you bridge 'out of therapy' communications with the face-to-face therapeutic process?

10.3 KEEPING RELATIONSHIPS APPROPRIATE

SECTION OUTLINE

Counsellors and psychotherapists can easily be drawn into inappropriate relationships with clients. This section considers what is meant here by 'inappropriate' relationships, how such relationships might develop, and what steps can be taken to minimise their likelihood.

When I think of the dangers of inappropriate relationships with clients, a particular situation immediately comes to mind. It wasn't harmful or abusive, but it was potentially seductive, centring on the difference between a therapy relationship and friendship. There are clear boundaries that few would argue with – for example, allowing a therapeutic relationship to become a sexual relationship (at any stage during therapy or thereafter) or perhaps engaging in a financial venture with a client. Like many situations in therapy, we can be aware of the more extreme ones and hold appropriate boundaries clearly and unambiguously. The situation I think of, however, was more subtle than that, and therefore equally dangerous. Consider the scenario in Box 10.6.

CASE STUDY 10.6
Sam

Sam referred himself to counselling because of high levels of anxiety. He was mid-way through his course at university when he began to experience panic attacks and intrusive negative thoughts (of wanting to hurt people). Sam had never threatened anyone previously and he knew his thoughts to be irrational. He understood them to be an aspect of his anxiety and, additionally, part of a mild form of obsessive-compulsive disorder (OCD) he had been aware of for several years. His father had left many years before; a major trauma in his early years. I met with Sam for several months, and then less frequently during the rest of his undergraduate course. He returned to counselling on beginning his postgraduate studies and attended regularly, though not frequently, throughout that time. I came to know Sam very well and liked him very much. During one session he remarked, 'You know more about me than even my closest friends; it is like we're best friends, but I also know we're not – I don't know very much about you at all.' After he left university he emailed regularly for a while, inviting me to his wedding (which I did not accept) and keeping me updated on how things were going.

Sam was someone with whom, if we had met in any other circumstance, I would probably have become good friends with. We got on very well, liked each other and worked together very effectively. We had, however, met as counsellor–client when he had referred himself to therapy. Our capacity to get on well had facilitated the therapeutic process and, as such, much had been achieved. Sam's panic attacks had stopped, his anxiety reduced, he had explored his feelings in relation to his father (it is worth noting the possible transferential dynamics additionally at play in our relationship), and he had, over time, learnt to cope with his OCD and manage his intrusive negative thoughts. The latter stages of our work had become more supportive contact, enabling him to finish his degree successfully. The ending of our work had marked a turning point for Sam, with him leaving university and moving on with his own life.

(Continued)

(Continued)

While receiving his emails had been enjoyable, I was also aware of the dangers of losing the important boundaries of our work and drifting into friendship. I discussed this at length in supervision and we agreed for me to write to Sam and to thank him for his emails but to suggest that we needed to end our contact. Prior to me doing this I received his wedding invitation. I was clear that it would not be appropriate for me to accept, yet the temptation was there for me to do so. We had talked a great deal about his relationship with his partner and I was aware of the significance of his wedding. Attending however, would have stepped across an important line in blurring boundaries and undermining the potency of the relationship we had had. The difficulty here was not of managing sexual attraction or financial exploitation, both of which would have been easier to identify and work against, but rather of friendship. The compulsion for contact beyond the terms of a therapeutic relationship, moving it instead into something very different, was powerful, seductive and insidious.

I am also reminded of a client who wrote to me after a series of sessions wondering whether we could meet for coffee occasionally to 'catch up'. I replied to the client by letter saying that this would not be appropriate, outlining why this was the case. That is, I explained that what she had achieved in therapy was because of the boundaries that had contained it and that moving beyond those boundaries would potentially undermine that achievement. Two years later the same client returned for a further series of counselling, but began by thanking me for respecting and holding on to the boundaries. Had I broken them, she said, she would not have been able to return to me and all the previous benefits would have been lost. With Sam, stepping out of the way of a potential friendship, no matter how tempting stepping into a friendship might have been, was clearly the right thing to do.

The wolf in sheep's clothing

The point I wish to illustrate with the example of Sam is that all therapeutic relationships have the potential to become something they were not meant to be – more often through a process of incremental slippage rather than an apparent immediacy. Counsellors and psychotherapists often engage in a relationship the intimacy and depth of which many clients will never have experienced before. As we discussed in the chapter on dependency, there can be something incredibly powerful about the process of two people meeting and exploring intimate and often very private aspects of experience. There have been countless occasions during the years I have worked as a counsellor when clients have said, 'I have never told anyone about this before'. It is imperative for therapists to be aware of potential pitfalls and to recognise that they can be very easy to fall into. They might include the following.

- A client becoming unhelpfully dependent on a therapist, or on therapy (see the section on Dependency)
- A therapist becoming dependent on a client
- Erotic transference (i.e., where a client becomes sexually attracted to the therapist, or vice versa)
- Where therapy slowly moves into friendship
- Where the client possesses particular skills and knowledge relevant to the therapist and this is – overtly or covertly – sought (e.g. a client who is a financial adviser being asked by the therapist for financial advice)
- Any transferential or countertransferential dynamic that is acted on (e.g. the therapist reacting angrily to the client because they are reminded of an unloving mother)
- A client who offers praise and compliments to the therapist as a means of seeking approval.

There may be countless variations on the above examples – and other kinds of example not included here. The idea of the wolf in sheep's clothing, however, is to reiterate the point that crossing the line between appropriate to inappropriate rarely happens quickly or apparently, but rather slowly and incrementally. The therapist can find themselves in a difficult situation without ever realising they were in danger (similar to swimming in the sea, not realising the tide is carrying you further out of your depth).

Dual relationships

There are times when counsellors and psychotherapists can find they have potentially two or more roles in a client's life. This circumstance is referred to as a dual relationship. BACP's Ethical Framework defines a dual relationship, 'when the practitioner has two or more kinds of relationship concurrently with a client, for example client and trainee, acquaintance and client, colleague and supervisee' (p. 5). For example, in a mental health setting in which I worked I occasionally found myself offering therapy to a person whose mental health was deteriorating. Within the same setting I also worked as a worker approved under the Mental Health Act to undertake statutory mental health assessments with people in crisis. It would have been inappropriate for me to be someone's therapist but also assess their mental health state following a deterioration. It might be argued that as their therapist I might have a particular insight into why their mental health was deteriorating and thus offer a more informed assessment. However, as with all dual relationships, the danger is that the boundaries of therapy become confused, client confidentiality potentially compromised, and ultimately the therapy no longer becomes a safe space for the client to explore their distress.

Other dual relationships might include a line manager also offering therapy supervision, for example, or a counsellor or psychotherapist becoming a client's advocate or support worker. BACP's Ethical Framework warns against entering into a dual relationship:

> The existence of a dual relationship with a client is seldom neutral and can have a powerful beneficial or detrimental impact that may not always be easily fore-seeable. For these reasons practitioners are required to consider the implications of entering into dual relationships with clients, to avoid entering into relation-ships that are likely to be detrimental to clients, and to be readily accountable to clients and colleagues for any dual relationships that occur. (p. 5)

Safeguards and benchmarks

Supervision provides the best opportunity to explore the potential dangers of any therapeutic relationship and ways of keeping within safe waters. However, supervision is not foolproof: ultimately we can select which clients we take and which others cannot be discussed and will remain unexplored. As therapists we pass all our work through a filter prior to supervision, consciously or unconsciously paying attention to those that might be difficult, exposing or potentially shameful. The answer to this is perhaps not entirely straightforward. In my own experience I often discuss in supervision clients with whom I experience some difficulty: perhaps I feel stuck, or they feel stuck; maybe we have had a difficult session; or perhaps the client provokes strong feelings in me I wish to explore further. The clients that I feel are 'going well' can easily get overlooked. It is useful when preparing for supervision to reflect on those passed-over clients and consider whether there are any potential dynamics that are wolves in sheep's clothing. Perhaps the sessions are going well simply because they are going well, but additionally perhaps because we like the client, feel comfortable, and thus are running the danger of finding ourselves suddenly out of our depth.

Personal therapy provides an important space to explore our own needs and to consider how we might sometimes look for our needs to be met by clients or in our therapeutic relationships. It provides us with our own safe space to contemplate our own process, and work very effectively alongside a challenging and supportive supervisorsy relationship. Additionally, discussing more general processes with colleagues or peers while respecting client confidentiality, thus without necessarily going into the level of detail we would in supervision, can be invaluable in helping us to reconsider aspects of our work that might need further thought and attention.

In summary, we clearly need to pay attention not only to the obvious dangers of therapeutic work in relational terms – such as sexual attraction or other behaviours that might be exploitative of the client – we also need to keep a close eye on those dynamics that can spread slowly into a relationship – those that might have gone undetected in the early stages and on the surface seem to be benign, but have the potential to cause great harm to client and therapist alike. Paying attention to these dynamics in our own reflections, in supervision, personal therapy and in discussion with colleagues and peers can help ensure our therapeutic relationships remain ethically grounded and appropriate at all times.

DISCUSSION QUESTIONS

1   What time do you create to reflect on your therapeutic relationships beyond supervision?
2   Which dangers do you think you are most susceptible to in your therapeutic relationships?
3   Consider a time when you were aware of dangers in a relationship? How did you manage the situation and what did you learn?
4   What issues concerning therapeutic relationships might you be less willing to talk about in supervision? Which might have the potential to be wolves in sheep's clothing?

10.4 THE PROFESSIONAL SELF

SECTION OUTLINE

Being a counsellor or psychotherapist goes beyond the immediate role of client work. Increasingly, counsellors and psychotherapists are being asked to be involved in multi-disciplinary meetings and case conferences. They thus need to communicate effectively with other professionals. This section considers the benefits and dangers of working with other professionals and how counsellors and psychotherapists can achieve the right balance between working within and beyond therapeutic boundaries.

Whether counsellors and psychotherapists have ever worked truly in isolation, concentrating solely on the face-to-face work with clients, is a moot point. Certainly the majority of counsellors and psychotherapists, regardless of their working context, are very likely to face a request at some point for liaison with another professional, or to be involved with some activity related to their work outside of face-to-face client contact. This poses a number of important challenges for therapists in being able to liaise with others in a way that is appropriate, while at the same time respecting the confidentiality of their client work.

There are many reasons why therapists' work might take them beyond the confines of their therapy room. These can include non-client-related reasons. For example:

- Contact with a team or other colleague about the general work of counsellors and psychotherapists
- Undertaking presentations about counselling or psychotherapy or particular aspects of the work
- Offering training workshops around particular presenting issues, such as anxiety, depression or trauma
- Attending conferences and seminars about counselling and psychotherapy
- Being a member of a committee or organisation to do with counselling or psychotherapy
- Presenting information – written or verbal – for external sources (e.g. offering a perspective on a particular issue for the media).

Client-specific liaison might include:

- Needing to refer a client to their GP or for a specific service
- Consulting others about a client's problem
- Providing a report for a third party about a client (e.g. an employer, if working for an EAP)
- Providing evidence to a court
- Writing reports or letters about clients (e.g. a letter outlining mitigating circumstances in an education setting)
- Contacting a client's family to answer questions or provide information
- Being asked to attend a case conference or case discussion meeting.

These two lists include many of the typical instances where therapists are required to act in a capacity beyond direct work with clients. The distinction between non-client activities and client-related activities is quite clear: one requires acting on behalf of the profession, while the other requires acting on behalf of, or about, the client.

Non-client activities

In relation to non-client activities, BACP's Ethical Framework notes the importance of practitioners acting in a way that is consistent with, and respectful of, the fundamental values of counselling and psychotherapy. A practitioner may be deemed to bring the profession into disrepute if 'the practitioner has acted in such an infamous or disgraceful way that the public's trust in the profession might reasonably be undermined, or might reasonably be undermined if they were accurately informed about all the circumstances of the case' (p. 18). At first this statement implies that the practitioner's actions must be widely known so as to undermine the 'public's trust' in the profession; this is not the whole story, however. The second part of the statement, 'might reasonably be undermined if they were accurately informed about all the circumstances of the case', is important here in that if a practitioner acts in a way that undermines the profession (e.g. makes disrespectful and unfounded comments about others in a public forum), this would lead to a potential case of misconduct. It is therefore essential that all actions, while undertaken in the capacity of a counsellor and psychotherapist, should be conducted in line with the principles of ethically sound practice.

There is also a danger that the behaviour of an individual, when not acting in their capacity as a counsellor or psychotherapist, might be so concerning that they would be liable for a case of professional misconduct, even though their actions took place within a personal capacity. Such situations may include a proven case of abuse or harm or where the association between the actions in a personal capacity and the individual's role in a professional one were very obvious. Ultimately, if the public's perception of the integrity of counselling or psychotherapy was potentially undermined through the actions of an individual, that individual might ultimately be held accountable for that if they were additionally a member of a professional organisation. (It is worth noting here that, in the UK at least, unless an individual was a member of a professional organisation there would be no route for pursuing a case for professional misconduct other than through civil court proceedings given that there is no statutory regulation of therapists. However, the development of voluntary registers, as discussed previously, may provide for greater public protection.)

Client-related activities

In all client-related activities that fall beyond the direct work with clients, two considerations need to be kept in mind. First, all the points made above in relation to non-client activities still apply. The counsellor or psychotherapist is still representing the profession even though their actions are not client-specific. Second, all third-party contact should take place only with the expressed and written consent of the client, unless the counsellor or psychotherapist is duty bound to act without consent (e.g. risk, or where there is a statutory requirement to break confidentiality, such as anti-terrorism). By 'written consent' I mean that there should be a clear and accurate record that consent was obtained in a free and non-coercive manner, appropriate to the client's ability to provide it. This may take the form of a written and signed consent form, but can include other forms appropriate to the client's needs. A good-practice benchmark here is that spoken consent is not, in and of itself, sufficient and it is wise not to rely on it as such.

While discussing the need to consult with a third party about the client (which might be initiated by the third party, or might come as a request directly from the client), one needs to discuss the scope and limitations of any potential disclosure. By this I mean that you should be very clear with clients what information is to be shared and what is to be kept confidential. These agreements can then be clearly recorded in any notes from the session. You can only really act in good faith, and with the consent of the client, if you are clear what the client has actually consented to. It is often the case that clients are happy for information A to be disclosed to a third party, yet not information B. Or, that person 1 may know about A but not B, but person 2 may be told A and B. You can quickly find yourself in a difficult situation, and a client's confidentiality inadvertently transgressed, without proper care and attention to detail.

In summary, counsellors and psychotherapists are often required to act in a professional capacity in situations that involve non-related client activities, or client-related activities. Whatever such situations, if a therapist is a member of a professional organisation, all of their work – not just the client-specific work – will be underpinned by the ethical and practice requirements of that organisation. Practitioners who are not members of professional bodies should still act in a way that respects the values and integrity of the profession. When acting on behalf of clients, or about clients, it is imperative that informed and written consent is obtained and that the boundaries of disclosure have been clearly agreed with the client beforehand. By keeping these simple principles in mind, you can retain the potential to make a varied and important contribution both to the experience of the client and to the wider profession.

DISCUSSION QUESTIONS

1   Think of a time when you were asked to do something in your role as a counsellor or psychotherapist that was not directly related to client work. What considerations did you keep in mind?

2   When acting on behalf of a client, or about a client, what steps do you take to demonstrate that informed consent was fully obtained?

3   What steps do you take to clarify the limitations of client disclosure before making contact with a third party?

4   Consider a client with whom there are communication difficulties: how can you (a) ensure you obtain informed consent and (b) demonstrate that you have done so?

10.5 THE USE OF TOUCH

SECTION OUTLINE

Many counsellors and psychotherapists are anxious about how to manage touch – for example, holding a hand of a distressed client or a client asking for a hug at the end of a session. This section explores the complexities of managing physical contact with clients and how to ensure that ethical practice is maintained.

The use of touch is an issue that I am often asked about in supervision, particularly by trainees, and is one that still perplexes even the most experienced practitioner. The question of whether to have physical contact with clients during a therapy session is understandably loaded with a number of ethical and moral complexities and there is no simple or straightforward answer. For many counsellors and psycho-therapists the question doesn't arise at all: the use of touch as a therapeutic interven-tion would not be consistent with, and in some cases would be very opposed to, the fundamental philosophical and theoretical constructs of therapy. For example, in psychodynamic therapy (for more detail see Chapter 3) the therapist's abstinence is an essential feature, allowing a blank screen onto which transferential dynamics can be projected. Likewise, in cognitive-behavioural therapy the focus of work is on the client's thoughts and behaviour; touching the client as a means of supporting them with their distress would not have a natural place. For humanistic therapies, where the focus of work is the relational quality between therapist and client based on certain personal qualities of the therapist (e.g. positive regard, empathy and con-gruence, for example), touch is seen to be more relevant. What is clear is the need for greater discussion about the use of touch to bring about a greater degree of clarity and debate. Orbach states (2004, p. 36):

> Leave the discourse and theorising about touch to body-orientated therapists, and keep quiet about those hugs, the touch on the shoulder, the hand that needs holding, the kiss that got planted on us. In so doing we short-circuit an attempt to think about when and why we should or should not touch.

Touch might be initiated by you, or your client, and can come in a variety of forms. For example:

1   The client/therapist shaking hands at the beginning and end of sessions as a greeting or farewell ritual
2   The therapist holding the hand of a client who has become very distressed
3   The therapist holding the hand of a client during a period of particularly difficult or disorientating exploration in therapy

4   The therapist touching the client on the shoulder/arm/knee as a means of either offering reassurance or communicating intimacy

5   Client and therapist hugging each other at the beginning and end of therapy as a greeting or farewell ritual

6   Client and therapist kissing each other at the beginning and end of therapy as a greeting or farewell ritual.

While we can agree that there are forms of touch that would never be sanctioned (e.g. flirtatious or sexual touch), it is difficult to ensure that a hand innocently placed on a client's knee at a time of their distress is not misinterpreted as an unwanted sexual advance. Or, a ritualistic hug at the end of therapy develops, over time, a greater meaning for therapist or client than was originally intended. It is interesting to note that BACP's Ethical Framework makes no mention of touch, as is the case with the majority of UK counselling and psychotherapy organisations (Tune, 2008). This leaves counsellors and psychotherapists in an uncertain and confusing arena, and many, because of the lack of guidance, decide that touch is best avoided altogether.

Guidelines for the use of touch

It is possible to outline some basic guidelines to keep in mind when reflecting on the use of touch. Hunter and Stuve (1998, cited in Tune, 2008) suggested a number of areas for practitioners to consider, which I will briefly discuss here.

The client wants to be touched: Therapist-initiated touch is always a high-risk strategy because you cannot easily gauge how clients will receive it. Wherever touch occurs, the client should initiate it. This can create space and time for the therapist to reflect on the client's request and explore it further, if appropriate.

Touch is intended for the client's benefit: You must reflect carefully on your motivation to make physical contact with the client. It can be challenging to sit alongside a very distressed client, and the compulsion to reach out to them for comfort – as one might do in more personal relationships – can be strong. It is very easy to assume the client wishes to be touched, or that touch will be of benefit to the client, whereas in fact the need belongs more to you than the client themselves.

The client understands concepts of empowerment (and they can say no): It is important to keep in mind that, however equal the therapeutic relationship appears to be, there is always the potential for a power imbalance in favour of the therapist. You must therefore be clear that the client has the wherewithal and confidence to say 'no' to touch if they do not wish it to take place – otherwise the potential to disempower the client and lead to further distress can be very high.

The therapist has a solid knowledge base about touch: Before you consider physical contact with clients, it is essential you have already considered the use of touch in training and/or supervision. Any use of touch within therapy should be fully and frankly discussed with supervisors, preferably beforehand. If you do not feel sufficiently comfortable to disclose your use of touch in supervision, that might be a good indicator that you should not be making physical contact with your clients.

Boundaries are clearly understood by both client and therapist: You need to have ensured that the contracting process is thorough so that both you and the client are entirely clear about the boundaries and limitations of therapy. Specifically, if you see touch as a potential therapeutic intervention it is important for you to have discussed this with the client at the beginning so that you and they can take time to fully explore feelings and responses. Asking a client a simple question, such as 'Sometimes when people are very distressed they find it comforting for me to hold their hand, or to put a hand on their shoulder. What are your thoughts about this?' can provide an opportunity to gauge the client's response and reaction.

There is enough time in the session to process touch: If touch has taken place in a session it is important for both you and the client to have the time to discuss the implications of this, how it was experienced and whether it was helpful. Touching a client, particularly if initiated by you, towards the end of the session may leave a client feeling confused, hurt and potentially silenced, unable to express how they genuinely felt about it.

The therapeutic relationship has developed sufficiently: It is highly unlikely that touch will be appropriate early on in a therapeutic relationship, as there will have been insufficient time for you and the client to get to know and understand each other. As such, touch will be less likely to have a relational context in which it can be safely understood and experienced. A more established relationship allows for this contextual understanding to develop.

Touch is offered to all types of clients (there is no differentiation on the basis of gender, age, sexual orientation, for instance): If used, touch needs to be viewed as a therapeutic intervention and not a relational communication. As such, touch needs to be used as a response to certain situations or presentations, rather than particular people or demographics. If you feel more comfortable touching a young female, but less so a young male, or a gay client but not a straight client, you need to carefully explore your motivations for touch in supervision to be clear as to how and why you are making such differentiations.

Supervision is available and used: Therapists who use touch need to discuss this openly and fully in supervision, preferably before making any physical contact with clients, but certainly following it. It is important you not only understand your own motivations for the use of physical contact with clients, but know and understand your supervisor's views.

The therapist is personally comfortable with touch: If you do not feel comfortable with being touched yourself, you should feel very wary about using touch with clients. Fundamentally, if touch is to be used you need to feel entirely comfortable with it for yourself so that this is communicated to your clients. Similarly, if you feel uncomfortable with the idea of being touched yourself, you will quickly communicate this lack of comfort to clients, leading to a greater potential for misunderstanding and discomfort by both parties.

Tune (2008, p. 267) has suggested the following as questions that therapists might ask themselves about using touch in a session:

1 Is the touch consensual? If it was not (because it was spontaneous, for instance) have you checked afterwards that it was all right with the client?
2 Do you feel the same about touching this client as you do about them touching you? If not, why not?
3 Have you reflected on what touch meant to you and the client in this session?
4 What opportunities have you created for you to process your feelings about touch in counselling with peers, supervisor or trainer?
5 Have you taken the opportunity to enquire how the client felt about touch in the session?
6 Have you explored what touch might mean to this client in the context of his/her culture, gender and history?
7 Have you sought to develop your own awareness of your bodily sensations and personal space in your personal development?

In summary, while some counsellors and psychotherapists use touch in sessions, it is inconsistent with several approaches to therapy. Therapists need to take particular care before using touch and, if at all possible, should discuss touch with their clients fully and openly to gauge their client's feelings and attitudes. It is better to have had this discussion with clients, preferably at the contracting stage, than to respond awkwardly in a session when a client tries to initiate touch, perhaps hugging the therapist at the end of the session, for example.

10.6 WORKING WITHIN ONE'S OWN COMPETENCE

SECTION OUTLINE

Working within one's capability is an ethical requirement for good practice. Knowing the point at which a client's need or presenting problem goes beyond one's competence is essential for the safety of client and therapist alike. This section provides guidance on how to self-monitor, respond accordingly and, if appropriate, manage a referral on.

What is competence?

Competence is not some static entity based on a given level of knowledge at any particular time. It is too easy to assume that whether I am competent to work with a particular client, or with particular issues, is based on what I know about those issues. There are many instances when I have supported people with problems of which I have known little, or indeed have never experienced personally. I will never know first-hand the anguish that can accompany the decision whether to have a termination, or the trauma of miscarriage from a woman's perspective. I have worked with many clients facing both of these situations; was I competent to do so, given my lack of personal experience?

Clearly we regularly work with clients whose experience and difficulties fall beyond our own personal knowledge. We might therefore assume that sharing a personal experience with a client isn't a prerequisite for competent therapy. Thus, rather than take personal experience as a defining factor for competence, we might look towards discrete knowledge: understanding and knowing about something at a theoretical and/or intellectual level. Let's consider the three scenarios in Boxes 10.7 to 10.9:

CASE STUDY 10.7
Judith

Judith is a 43-year-old woman with myalgic encephalomyelitis (ME). She attends counselling because of the devastating impact that ME is having on her life – on her relationships, her job, and her day-to-day experience of herself. She describes excruciating physical pain and a terrible and overwhelming sense of fatigue for even the things she loves the most.

CASE STUDY 10.8
Salsi

Salsi is a 17-year-old man with drug-related problems. He does not get on with his family and has very low self-esteem. He has been using drugs since he was 13 years old and now feels that his life is spiralling out of control. He has recently started a new relationship that is important to him, but he fears that it won't be sustainable because of his drug use.

CASE STUDY 10.9
Eddie

Eddie is 74 years old and has recently been diagnosed with prostate cancer. He is soon to have surgery and is fearful about his future. He is the main carer for his partner, who has Alzheimer's disease, and worries about who will look after him should his cancer progress or not be treatable.

A number of factors in these three scenarios may separate the client from our own demographic or personal experience. We have already suggested that this is not, necessarily, a problem. To be competent to work with Judith, Salsi or Eddie, therefore, how much do I need to know about their particular circumstances? For example, what might I need to know about ME, or the particular types of drugs Salsi takes or how drugs affect someone's relational capacity, or how much might I need to know about cancer or Alzheimer's disease, or the demands of being a carer? There is no doubt that understanding more about these particular situations on a theoretical or intellectual level might enhance my capacity as their therapist to support these clients with their difficulties. Such knowledge might mean I have to ask fewer questions, or enable me to achieve a more facilitative level of empathy earlier in the relationship, or perhaps identify which aspects of their thinking or behaviour might most usefully be worked on for change. I might instead argue, however, that having shared experiences can lead to a great chance of identification (rather than empathy), and that I do not necessarily need to know anything about these aspects, but instead be available for psychological contact and be able to develop a therapeutic relationship in which Judith, Salsi and Eddie feel understood and heard. I have certainly worked very successfully with many people when I have not necessarily known very much about the complexity of their problem.

If we accept these points, the definition of competence becomes more problematic. That is, if we don't necessarily need to have experienced the same or similar experience as the client, and don't necessarily need to fully understand the complexities of their problem at a theoretical or intellectual level, then what is left to define competence? The Oxford English Dictionary defines competence as 'the ability to do something successfully or efficiently' (OED, 2012). The imperative therefore is to know what factors must be in place to do something 'successfully' or 'efficiently'. This raises the question of how, in counselling and psychotherapy terms, might we define 'successful' or 'efficient'? For 'successful' we might assume that the client's problems have been solved; yet we all know that some problems are not solvable (Eddie's cancer might not be treatable). Perhaps they will feel better – though clients sometimes do not necessarily feel better but instead understand their problems more: they might then define this as a 'successful' outcome of therapy. Likewise, what would 'efficient' counselling or psychotherapy mean? Am I a more efficient therapist because I can achieve a 'successful' outcome in four rather than eight sessions (whatever 'successful' means anyway)?

BACP's Ethical Framework (2010) defines competence as 'the effective deployment of the skills and knowledge needed to do what is required' (p. 4). This definition helps us understand competence in terms of counselling and psychotherapy a little more clearly. First, it talks about the 'deployment' of skills and knowledge; second it talks of 'what is required'. Deployment suggests skills and knowledge that belong to the therapist, but are not necessarily related to the specific problem of the client. That is, the therapist must be competent in the knowledge and skills they possess as a therapist, such as an ability to listen effectively, to communicate understanding of another's problem, to empathise with another, to formulate and interpret another's words or meaning, to identify problematic thinking, to assess and identify mental health distress, to assess risk, and so on (dependent on the training and theoretical orientation of the therapist). Similarly, the therapist must be able to do 'what is required'. That will be defined by the client's goals or hopes for therapy, their particular situation, and the context of the employing agency (if employed by an agency). With these concepts in mind it is therefore helpful to revisit the three earlier case scenarios, in Boxes 10.10 to 10.12.

CASE STUDY 10.10
Judith

The task here is to be able to connect with Judith's sense of loss at a physical, emotional and relational level – to enable her to verbalise her experience of living with ME and to explore the ramifications of that experience for her at all levels, to facilitate her feelings – whatever they might be – and to provide her with a confidential space to consider ways in which she might be able to move forward. Research that has explored counselling people with ME indicates it is helpful for counsellors to understand what ME is and how it affects individuals (Ward et al., 2008). There is no doubt about this; in the context of a mutually respectful, engaging and facilitative therapeutic relationship, however, it might not necessarily be essential given that one person's experience of ME may be very different to another's. This will be dependent on 'what is required' by Judith's definition.

CASE STUDY 10.11
Salsi

Salsi essentially appears quite disconnected in his life. The task here is to be able to connect with him in order to provide him with a safe space to explore his feelings about his family, the means of safely expressing those feelings, and to help him understand a little more how he actually feels about himself and what 'low self-esteem' in his experience might mean. Additionally, it is important to provide Salsi with an opportunity to talk about his hopes and fears regarding his new relationship, what the relationship means to him, and a chance to explore ways in which he might be able to make it work. There is no doubt that if Salsi is looking for a specific drug-rehabilitation programme, which might include medical input, he would need to be referred on to that. Salsi might be able to access such specialised support while the therapy continues.

CASE STUDY 10.12
Eddie

The task here is to provide a space for Eddie to voice his worst fears, both for himself and his partner. Having recently been diagnosed with cancer, Eddie is likely to have been thrust into an existential struggle about his own mortality and health, while at the same time grieving the slow and relentless loss of his partner to Alzheimer's. He may need a space in which to prioritise his questions and problems and to consider what he needs to do in the context of how he feels. He may have many questions about his diagnosis and prognosis, which will be best answered by his medical team. Likewise, he may need to consider respite care options for his partner during his surgery and recovery. Therapy may provide him with the best opportunity to engage with these challenges in a grounded and thought-through way.

I hope what is clear in my comments about Judith, Salsi and Eddie is that counsellors or psychotherapists do not necessarily need to have the answer to all the problems to be able to deploy their knowledge and skills effectively. Rather, 'what is required' might include other important aspects too. The therapist is not rendered incompetent simply because they cannot do it all.

The Ethical Framework makes a further assertion about competence when, under the heading of Beneficence (a commitment to promoting the client's well-being), it 'directs attention to working strictly within one's limits of competence and providing services on the basis of adequate training or experience' (BACP, 2010, p. 3). The point here is that you should not aim to provide a service to clients if you are not trained or sufficiently experienced to do so. Clearly, it would not be appropriate to see clients as a therapist if the level of training received was at a 'counselling skills' level. Beyond this, judgements are not so simple to make. A level of training does not necessarily equate to specific knowledge of every client's problem, but rather to having been trained to a level of competence to work as a therapist. Similarly, 'adequate experience' does not equate to having experienced everything a client has experienced. Rather, it refers to a body of experience as a therapist that allows for transferable learning and skills to meet a client's needs in a different situation or presentation: for example, a newly qualified counsellor with no previous experience might not necessarily be competent to work with a client presenting with complex mental health problems and high suicide risk.

Judging competence

At the point of qualification as a counsellor or psychotherapist, competence will have been judged by the training organisation through the student's performance in terms of academic work, skills, personal development and work on the practice placement. That measure of competence is clearly defined and apparent. The challenge for therapists is to judge their level of competence in an ongoing and less discrete way. This can be achieved through supervision, personal therapy, self-reflection and in dialogue with colleagues or peers. Competence will be strongly influenced by a therapist's capacity to cope with given problems at any given point. For example, following the death through suicide of one of my clients early in my career and the subsequent personal impact of that experience, I judged – in collaboration with my supervisor – that I temporarily lacked capacity to cope with (at an emotional and professional level) other clients at risk of suicide. As a consequence I temporarily lacked competence to work effectively with such clients. I monitored this closely with my supervisor and manager and, after a period of time, felt able to return to such work. This is an example of thinking ethically about my work, using the skills and knowledge of others to do 'what was required': to make decisions about my level of competence.

There are many reasons therefore why competence to work effectively might be diminished. They include the following and are additionally summarised in a **PowerPoint presentation** on the companion website:

- The therapist experiences a period of physical ill-health that undermines their capacity to be available to clients.
- The therapist's experience mirrors that of the client too closely to remain separate from the client's world.
- The therapist experiences a trauma or major life event that means they are not emotionally available to work with clients (or with a particular type of client presentation).
- The therapist is simply unable to work safely with clients and should consider discontinuing their practice.

Or there may be:

- A strong or powerful relational dynamic (transferential or countertransferential, for example) that undermines the therapist's capacity to engage with the client
- A client presentation that falls beyond any level of training or experience in practice (complex mental health problems)
- A lack of personal insight or an unwillingness or inability to engage in self-reflection
- A lack of appropriate supervision, or not using supervision effectively or appropriately.

Here we need to separate *being* incompetent from *feeling* incompetent, which is a much more common phenomenon. It is not unusual for therapists to think 'I really don't know what to say next', or 'I feel really stuck'. Thériault and Gazzola (2008) discuss therapist feelings of incompetence, and I would recommend reading their work for more detail – see further reading for details.

Continuing professional development

Most professional organisations expect their members to embark on continuing professional development (CPD): undertaking a range of activities specifically to enhance skills, knowledge, competency, self-reflection and self-care. Applications for accreditation by such bodies, and subsequent re-accreditation, usually require the applicant to evidence such CPD activities. A useful metaphor here might be flowing water, which is always regenerated and oxygenated, as opposed to still water, which always has the potential to become stagnant. The latter, in therapy terms, runs the risk of causing harm to both clients and therapists alike.

In summary, competence need not require us to know everything about a client's problem, nor to have experienced ourselves everything the client has been through. Instead, it is about deploying skills and knowledge in an appropriate way, respectful of the client, to do what is necessary. What is necessary for each individual client will vary considerably and the task of the therapist is to explore fully and openly with the client so there is a shared sense of the purpose of therapy. Therapists may sometimes experience feelings of incompetence with clients: they should use supervision carefully to explore these feelings further. However, there are times when therapists may move into periods of incompetence and should, in consultation with their supervisor, consider how they might adapt or suspend part of their practice to accommodate this and prevent harm.

FURTHER READING

Thériault, A. and Gazzola, N. (2008) 'Feelings of incompetence in therapy: causes, consequences and coping strategies', in W. Dryden and A. Reeves (eds), *Key Issues for Counselling in Action*, 2nd edn. London: Sage. pp. 228–43.

DISCUSSION QUESTIONS

1   What client presentations cause you the most anxiety? Why do you think this is the case?
2   How do you work effectively with clients when you have not been through what they have been through or do not understand the complexities of their problems?
3   What steps do you take to monitor your practice? How do you know these steps are effective?
4   What action might you take if you felt unable to work with particular client problems?

10.7 SELF-CARE

SECTION OUTLINE

Being a counsellor and psychotherapist can be immensely rewarding – but also draining. Developing good self-care strategies is central to ensuring safe and appropriate client work. This section explores what is meant by self-care and what strategies can be used to help maintain good mental health in therapists.

I suspect that the term 'self-care' is one of the most over-used – and either mis-understood or disregarded – terms in counselling and psychotherapy. Though as therapists we all like to think that we have good self-care strategies in place (and I say 'we' because I include myself very much in this), too few of us do (and I include myself very much in that category too). While there is always an important balance to be struck between looking after ourselves and meeting the commitments we make to clients and others, I have lost count of the number of times I have spoken with therapists who, through physical illness, emotional distress or trauma, really should be at home and not instead intending to see clients. I have lost count too of the number of times I have gone into work feeling utterly terrible, and attempted to carry on with therapy sessions. The reality is that while my intention was to not let my clients down, the level of attention and facilitative connection they received from me during those sessions was probably questionable. Clearly, though cancelling a session or suspending work as a counsellor or psychotherapist are decisions that should not be taken lightly, we also have to consider our own physical and emotional wellbeing and that of our clients.

Paying attention to self-care is not optional. It is enshrined within a number of professional codes of ethics. For example, BACP's Ethical Framework states that, 'Attending to the practitioner's wellbeing is essential to sustaining good practice' (p. 10). It goes on to say that, 'Practitioners have a responsibility to themselves to ensure that their work does not become detrimental to their health or wellbeing by ensuring that the way that they undertake their work is as safe as possible and that they seek appropriate professional support and services as the need arises' and that, 'Practitioners are entitled to be treated with proper consideration and respect that is consistent with this Guidance' (p. 10). Thus, everything the Ethical Framework says is as applicable to the wellbeing of practitioners as it is clients. It seems, however, that we can be very selective in how we interpret and apply such ethical considerations when thinking about ourselves. We would never act in such a way that was dismissive of, or potentially harmful to clients, and yet we often do that to ourselves.

The challenge of self-care

According to Hough (1996, p. 16), 'counsellors need to know how to take care of themselves before they can help others'. This is true for all theoretical orientations and particularly so for those where the use of 'self' is integral to the process, such as the humanistic approaches. You need to be acutely aware of how the work of counselling and psychotherapy can demand and drain our personal resources, as well as contribute to and replenish them. However, again regardless of theoretical orientation, we tend to be very 'client-focused' and can quickly lose a sense of our own wellbeing in the session-to-session, day-to-day and week-to-week rhythm of our work. Beyond the world of counselling and psychotherapy it might also be argued in the UK that the predominant culture is also not entirely encouraging of self-care. Certainly we can make the 'big gestures' (e.g. a gym membership for a while, or a two-week holiday), but paying attention to an incremental and insidious sapping of ourselves is much more challenging to keep a track of.

Self-care strategies

Larcombe (2008) helpfully distinguishes three aspects of self-care:

1 Care for the therapeutic self
2 Care for the managerial self
3 Care for the career self.

Let us explore each of these in turn.

Care for the therapeutic self

This aspect considers how we care for what we do as counsellors and psychotherapists and particularly our use of our 'self', as outlined earlier, in our work. Making an empathic connection with clients, and connecting in an intimate and sharing therapeutic relationship (dependent on theoretical orientation), makes significant demands on our personal and psychological resources. This is particularly true given the traumatic and sometimes profoundly shocking narratives we are sometimes witness to. Larcombe (2008) notes that the dangers of this for therapists are compassion fatigue and vicarious traumatisation.

Compassion fatigue

Figley (2002, p. 7) describes compassion fatigue (or secondary traumatic stress disorder) as 'the stress resulting from helping or wanting to help a traumatised or suffering person'. A useful metaphor here is to imagine a stick of plastic (our emotional responses might be said to have a degree of plasticity, i.e 'the quality of being easily shaped and moulded'). The stick of plastic is repeatedly shaped in one particular direction, with the result that it becomes weakened at that point and vulnerable to fracture. If the continual re-shaping is not mitigated with a compensatory movement (in this sense, self-care), then damage can occur. Larcombe (2008, p. 287) notes two compensatory strategies for mitigating against compassion fatigue: '(a) establishing a method for gaining a sense (of achievement; and (b) finding ways to disengage or create distance from clients between sessions'.

Vicarious traumatisation

Pearlman and Saakvitne (1995, p. 31) define vicarious traumatisation (VT) as 'a process through which the therapist's inner experience is negatively transformed through empathic engagement with the client's traumatic material'. The impact of working with traumatised clients can be great, with practitioners experiencing their own traumatic response if good self-care strategies are not put in place. Symptoms can include anger, lack of energy for otherwise important things, a lack of affect or a decreased capacity to experience joy or happiness.

Care for the managerial self

Larcombe (2008) states that as therapists we are all 'managers' of ourselves, regardless of working context and including independent practitioners. As such we have a responsibility – a duty of care if you will – to take care of ourselves in our work. While caring for the therapeutic self is focused on the direct contact with clients, the managerial self instead takes 'one step back' and looks towards the bigger view. Aspects of the managerial self to attend to include:

- Workload
- Deadlines
- Working environment
- Control over the work you are involved in
- Continuing professional development and training needs
- Professional relationships
- The specific nature and type of work you undertake
- The management of change.

Larcombe (2008, pp. 290–3) provides a table covering these types of issues with reflective questions for practitioners to consider in relation to the nature of their work.

Care for the career self

The third aspect of self-care is the career self, whereby therapists see their work in the context of a longer-term process. This helps them to think about how their previous work informs their current work and how they might manage and protect their future opportunities that might be influenced or shaped by a number of factors, such as ill-health, disability and certainly in the current climate, redundancy or the need to close down a practice due to financial difficulties. Consider Bill in Box 10.13.

CASE STUDY 10.13
Bill

Bill is a 38-year-old person-centred counsellor who works for a mental health service. He offers group work and individual counselling to people with severe and enduring mental health problems. Bill has a long waiting list. He is required to work shifts, which at times entails his working nights. As well as direct counselling, he supports people in crisis either by telephone or face to face. He finds the counselling enjoyable but very challenging, with many of his clients disclosing earlier abuse or trauma. He takes time to recover from his night shifts and often feels tired, listless and has very low-mood both before a night shift and for a few days afterwards. He has contemplated looking for another job but is not really sure what to do or where to go.

Bill's situation is not uncommon and there may be several aspects that resonate with your own situation. Using Larcombe's three aspects of self-care, Bill's needs might involve the components itemised in Box 10.14.

BOX 10.14   BILL'S COMPONENTS OF SELF-CARE

Therapeutic self

1   A challenging workload
2   A disproportionate number of clients with trauma
3   Higher risk of compassion fatigue or VT, with some evidence of compassion fatigue (for example, mood changes prior to and following working night shifts)
4   Little opportunity for emotional recovery or rejuvenation
5   Evidence of early emotional harm: 'tired, listless and low-mood'

Managerial self

1   Challenging working setting
2   Little control over the working environment
3   The demands of a waiting list
4   Physical and emotional demands of working changing hours
5   Work always involving meeting with or supporting highly distressed individuals
6   Lack of opportunity for recovery or rejuvenation

(Continued)

(Continued)

Career self

1 Given early evidence of compassion fatigue or VT, uncertainty over how long Bill could sustain the current level of work
2 Despite having developed a number of important and transferable skills, lack of confidence about the 'next step'
3 A changing job market
4 Lack of clarity about how to locate and apply for a new post
5 Difficulty in extricating the self from a situation once it becomes difficult (which can result in a feeling of helplessness).

Separating Bill's difficulties into the three areas, as we have done in Box 10.14, immediately helps to clarify his difficulties and so pave the way for potential solutions. Bill needs to take action to look after his physical and emotional wellbeing, but might find this more manageable by attending to each aspect at a time. Certainly when in a difficult situation, where self-care has not been adequately attended to, it can be difficult to identify a positive way forward. In taking care of his therapeutic self Bill might negotiate with his manager a temporary reduction in his caseload – or to introduce a greater level of variety in his work so as to reduce the high number of traumatised clients. He can pay immediate attention to how working nights affects his mood by putting in place strategies to look after himself. Such strategies might include discussing fully in supervision, meditation, physical exercise, ensuring he exposes himself to natural light when working nights, eating well, or paying attention to sleeping patterns.

For his managerial self he might identify and attend to those aspects he feels he might have control over – for example, discussing fully in supervision, seeing the waiting list as that of the service and not his own, negotiating the implementation of different referral or assessment procedures, or managing his shift as best as possible to allow for recovery time following night work.

Finally, for his career self, Bill might look at things he can do to facilitate change. These might include: discussing fully with his supervisor; compiling a skills audit to remind himself of what he knows and does well; beginning to register with online job websites; prioritising his continuing professional development; or getting involved in work-related activities that do not involve client work. Bill can begin to manoeuvre himself from a position of relative helplessness and the process of engagement with his situation can, in itself, form part of an important self-care strategy.

Always available?

I should add a note here about the wonders of technology. As a gadget nerd I know that having the Internet and email everywhere I go, to be always connected and in touch, can be a fabulous thing. However, in the context of self-care it can be an insidious process in which you are always connected, never allowing yourself really to have 'downtime'. As I have written elsewhere (Reeves, 2010b), it is important to remember to switch off smartphones, computers, tablet computers and so on. The 'always connected' lifestyle is a potent force for both good and harm. While at the right time it can expedite basic matters and simplify the complicated, at other times it has the potential to never really allow you to be in the 'here and now' and experience the moment. This is a threat to good self-care.

In summary, self-care is not an optional extra to the work of counsellors and psychotherapists: rather it as an essential component that should be integrated in all that we do. The dangers of not attending to self-care can include compassion fatigue, VT and an overall sense of loss of 'self' in our work and career. Considering our therapeutic, managerial and career selves can help us to develop useful self-care strategies. They can include a whole variety of activities including supervision, personal therapy, relaxation, meditation, a balanced caseload, a means of 'switching off' at the end of the day so that thoughts about clients don't invade personal space, and a clear demarcation between 'work' and 'play'.

DISCUSSION QUESTIONS

1 What does self-care mean to you?
2 Is self-care something you integrate into your day-to-day life or something you pay 'lip service' to?
3 Complete a self-care audit on yourself, similar to Bill's, using Therapeutic Self, Managerial Self and Career Self as headings. What do you notice and what can you change?
4 What are your 'next steps' as a counsellor or psychotherapist?

11

Supervision and Consultation

11.1 INTRODUCTION

CHAPTER OVERVIEW

In the UK, supervision is a professional requirement of counsellors and psychotherapists in practice. As such, from the beginning of training, into placement and then into qualified practice, regular supervision will be an important component of professional activity. This chapter considers a number of important areas in establishing, sustaining and ending a supervisory relationship. In establishing supervision it considers: what is supervision; finding the right supervisor; and contracting for supervision. In sustaining supervision we consider: making the most out of supervision; negotiating difficulties and reviewing. In ending supervision we explore: expected and unexpected endings; moving on; and the transferability of learning to a new supervisory relationship.

We discover early on in our training that supervision is an integral part of what we do as counsellors and psychotherapists. Though it is not the case in all countries, in the UK and many other areas supervision is a professional requirement of practice. For example, the BACP's Ethical Framework (BACP 2010, p. 3), under the section Beneficence (a commitment to promote the client's wellbeing), states that, 'There is an obligation to use regular and on-going supervision to enhance the quality of the services provided and to commit to updating practice by continuing professional development'. The same is true for most other professional codes of practice.

This requirement often takes trainees by surprise. There have been many occasions when trainees have come to supervision at the start of their training placement bemoaning the apparently escalating costs of their course – course fees, books, travel, residential weekends, personal therapy (for many courses) … and now this thing called supervision! Many are also unsure as to what supervision is and struggle with incredulity at having to pay for something that in most jobs comes free, namely line management supervision. Yet, as this chapter explains, counselling and psychotherapy supervision is very different from the line management type of supervision experienced elsewhere. As we progress through our careers as counsellors and psychotherapists, the joys and challenges of supervision continue unabated. We need to find and develop ways to embed supervision into our day-to-day work, transfer learning from it into our client work, expose our deficiencies, struggles and shame to another person (or worse, a group), and engage with all the intricacies that are inherent to a human relationship.

This chapter considers the issues pertinent to supervision from the beginning of the process through to the end. The section Defining Supervision and Finding the Right Supervisor outlines a number of definitions and draws them together to clarify exactly what is meant by supervision for counsellors and psychotherapists. The chapter then identifies the factors that need to be kept in mind when finding the right supervisor, as achieving this takes care and attention. In practice, finding the right person who can best support your professional development and ongoing work often means meeting several different people; we also need to know what to reflect on having met the person.

Making the Most of Supervision and Negotiating Difficulties takes us to the next stage. Here we will consider aspects such as contracting, identifying and agreeing mutual expectations, preparing for supervision sessions, managing competing demands, and how we might present client work in a way that best provides for what we need. In our early work as therapists the temptation is to recount clients' stories, sometimes verbatim to an apparently interested, but in fact increasingly weary, supervisor. Achieving a balance between retelling a client narrative and exploring the process of our work together can be particularly challenging. This section also considers differences in supervision when working individually or in a group, and how we can maximise our learning from either. There may also be aspects of supervision and supervisory relationships that can take our learning to the next level – or leave us feeling irritated, angry or unheard. The process of shame in supervision and the subsequent fear of exposure or of being 'found out' as not good enough all go into the mix here. What happens when we disagree, or when our views of therapy or of the client differ? All of these issues need to be negotiated in the supervisory relationship.

I spoke above of supervision being a lifelong commitment. However this does not mean you will be with the same person throughout. Reviewing Supervision and Changing Supervisor explores how we can ensure supervision remains fresh and relevant to our work. Questions of whether to review supervision and, if so, how and when, are considered and some prompt questions are provided to help both supervisor and supervisee reflect on that process. Finally, the section considers what to do when it is time to move on and, in particular, how to manage the ending of a supervisory relationship (whether planned or unplanned) so that we can find our next supervisor in the context of learning that is transferable and new opportunities identified.

11.2 DEFINING SUPERVISION AND FINDING THE RIGHT SUPERVISOR

SECTION OUTLINE

In the UK supervision is embedded in the day-to-day work of nearly all counsellors and psychotherapists as an ethical requirement. However, until you begin supervision it is difficult to really understand what it is and why finding the right supervisor for your work is so important. This chapter considers what is meant by supervision, explores different types of supervisory models and ideas, and reflects on what makes a good supervisor and how to find one.

Supervision and client work go hand in hand. Regular supervision becomes embedded within the day-to-day rhythms of practice: supervision almost becomes part of our very being. However, having worked with many supervisees over the years I recognise that it can still come as a surprise: one sees trainees arrive for their first supervision session wondering what all the fuss is about. Many see the prospect of supervision as just another thing they have to do and, more importantly, just another reason to extract money from them. While courses devote time to exploring what supervision means and how it fits into professional practice, it remains an unfamiliar and uncertain phenomenon until you find yourself sitting in your first supervision session. We can draw an analogy here with abseiling: we can talk through and imagine what it will be like to abseil for example, but until attached to the rope and stepping over the edge of the cliff, no amount of description and preparation will quite prepare us for the anxiety and apprehension. Not that supervision is necessarily like stepping over the edge of a cliff attached to nothing but an apparently flimsy rope – the point is that, once familiar with the process, we can also forget the anxiety and apprehension experienced when meeting a supervisor for the first time. It is important, therefore, that the first few sessions of supervision with someone new to practice are spent clarifying what supervision actually is. For an experienced counsellor or psychotherapist, it is easy

to take the nature of supervision for granted, but I find such assurance on the matter soon comes to a stuttering halt when asked that simple, appropriate and important question. Many books have been written explaining the intricacies of the
supervisory process.

So, what is supervision?

While supervision is 'something we do', in fact we do it for very good reasons.
However, we need first to think about some definitions. Consider the following:

1 Hess (1980, p. 25) states that supervision is a 'quintessential interpersonal interaction with the general goal that one person, the supervisor, meets with another,
   the supervisee, in an effort to make the latter more effective in helping people'.
2 Inskipp and Proctor (2001, p. 1) write that supervision is, 'A working alliance
   between the supervisor and the counsellor in which the counsellor can offer
   an account or recording of her work; reflect on it; receive feedback and, where
   appropriate, guidance. The object of this alliance is to enable the counsellor to
   gain in ethical competence, confidence, compassion and creativity in order to
   give her best possible service to the client.'
3 The BACP's Information Service Editorial Board (2008, p. 1) state that,
   'Supervision is a formal arrangement for therapists to discuss their work regularly with someone who is experienced in both therapy and supervision. The
   task is to work together to ensure and develop the efficacy of the therapist/
   client relationship. The agenda will be the therapy and feeling about that work,
   together with the supervisor's reactions, comments and challenges. Thus supervision is a process to maintain adequate standards of therapy and a method of
   consultancy to widen the horizons of an experienced practitioner.'
4 Carroll (1996, p. 6), while also noting there are no agreed definitions of counselling supervision, writes of there being seven generic tasks in supervision. These
   are: to set up a learning relationship; to teach; to evaluate; to monitor professional
   and ethical issues; to counsel; to consult; and to monitor administrative aspects.

As we can see, each definition offers a different level of complexity but covers
essentially similar ground. In focusing on the points of similarity in these definitions we can, perhaps, begin to distil the essential meaning of supervision. We are
told that supervision is:

- A relationship and a process
- A professional, formal working alliance
- A place where work with clients can be explored and discussed
- A relationship in which feedback can be given and received

- A space for personal and professional development and the development of efficacy as a 'helper'
- A time during which professional standards, ethics and care can be scrutinised.

Note that, in general terms, many of the above statements are similar to how we might describe a counselling or psychotherapy relationship: that is, something that is a relationship based on content and process, is professional and formal (we are not friends with our clients), a place for exploration where feedback can be given and received, and a space for personal development in which ethics and professional standards must be maintained.

The resemblances between the two forms of relationship might appear to be a coincidence, but it is, of course, not a coincidence. So much of what happens in supervision can parallel that of the therapist–client relationship – this is called parallel process (Mattinson, 1975). In this process 'aspects of the counselling relationship are expressed in the supervisory relationship' (Carroll, 1996, p. 103). More specifically, it is assumed that the therapist in supervision enacts conscious or unconscious processes of the client, again consciously or unconsciously in the supervisory relationship. An experienced supervisor works to identify these and bring them into the supervisee's awareness, thus helping to provide further insight and understanding into the therapeutic process. Some reject this as philosophically and theoretically incongruous with their understanding of therapeutic relationships, given its early origins in psychoanalytic literature. However, while this conception of parallel process might nod towards some acknowledgement of unconscious (or, at the very least, an unaware) process, it is often so apparent in a supervision session that to disregard it would be like ignoring an extremely large, elephant-like animal flicking through the books in the corner of the room. For an example of this see Box 11.1.

CASE STUDY 11.1
Salman

Salman has been working with his client Judi for several weeks now. Judi experiences her life and relationships as very complicated and rarely feels sufficient self-confidence to make decisions about what to do or where to go next. In her first session with Salman she explained that she hoped counselling would provide her with a space for clarity and an opportunity to make some important decisions about her future. Salman's experience of Judi since, however, has been of repeated expectations for Salman to make decisions for her, and of her exasperation when he fails to do so. After several weeks of this Salman feels stuck, frustrated and confused. Salman's supervisor, Ellie, has noted that during the last two sessions Salman has talked of his confusion in increasingly exasperated tones. During the current supervision session Salman says to Ellie, 'I just don't know what to do next and feel really stuck. I had hoped you might point a way forward for me so that I can help Judi but you just keep bouncing it back; it is really irritating.'

PAUSE FOR REFLECTION

1 What do you think is happening for Salman in his work with Judi?
2 What would you say is happening between Salman and Ellie in the supervision session?
3 How would you suggest Ellie could best support Salman in this process?
4 What opportunities can you see for Salman to transfer his learning from supervision back to his relationship with Judi?

Thinking again about the definitions of supervision discussed before, it is helpful to consider here in more detail each of the key components of supervision identified.

A relationship and a process

Counselling or psychotherapy supervision is very similar to the counselling and psychotherapy relationship it supports. The supervisor contracts for and enters into a relationship with the supervisee (or supervisees if it is a group). It is the content and process of the relationship that is the essence of supervision, together with the tasks embedded within the role of supervision. What is said, how it is said and the dynamics between members of the supervisory alliance all contribute to learning and insight.

A professional, formal working alliance

Like counselling and psychotherapy, supervision is not a friendship. It certainly helps for the supervisor and supervisee(s) to get on in a friendly alliance, but this is not essential. It is more important that the relationship is boundaried by a clearly nego-tiated and agreed contract, which attends to issues such as confidentiality, frequency, location, cost and accountability (to the agency, the client, the training programme, etc.). Again, as with counselling and psychotherapy, this is the cornerstone of creating a safe, respectful and facilitative supervisory alliance and space. What is arguably more important than friendliness is respect: the supervisor and supervisee(s) must respect each other so they can trust and hear each other's contributions to the process.

A place where work with clients can be explored and discussed

Supervision is about both us and our clients. Inskipp and Proctor (1993) summa-rise the 'tasks' of supervision as normative, formative and restorative. The norma-tive task is quality control, to ensure that our work is safe, ethical and appropriate. The formative task is to facilitate our professional skills and insight and to identify ways in which we may continue our personal and professional development. The restorative task of supervision is to provide a space for us to reflect on our capac-ity to work with clients at any given point, to consider strategies for self-care, for support and to work against burnout or vicarious trauma. When these three tasks are all fully attended to, supervision becomes an invaluable resource in the professional and personal development for us and our clients.

A relationship in which feedback can be given and received

Regardless of our own level of experience or competency, there is always scope for learning. In supervision we can reflect on our work with clients, the impact the work has on our emotional and professional capacity and responsiveness, as well as flagging areas for continuing professional development. The role of the supervisor in this process is to highlight potential areas for development that we might not immediately be aware of, challenge our professional self-perceptions and notice areas that might limit our capacity to work effectively with clients.

A space for personal and professional development and the development of efficacy as a 'helper'

Though supervision can sometimes be similar to counselling and psychotherapy, it is not in fact counselling or psychotherapy. Consequently, any contract for supervision should consider how those boundaries would be managed for both the supervisor and supervisee(s). This is a difficult matter, as often issues will arise in supervision that emanate from our own personal experiences. There is general acknowledgement that it is not helpful for a counsellor or psychotherapist to bring personal material into a session with a client (other than through a carefully managed self-disclosure, if theoretically acceptable), yet unexplored personal struggles, or feelings that fall outside of awareness can powerfully undermine our efficacy as a 'helper'. Supervision is a vital opportunity for these to be sensitively 'flagged', but not necessarily explored in any depth. We might be advised by our supervisors to seek out personal therapy, if that is considered a helpful next step.

A time during which professional standards, ethics and care can be scrutinised

At all times counselling and psychotherapy need to be rooted within clear professional and organisational standards, while professional relationships and therapeutic interventions must be ethically grounded. Supervision provides an opportunity to maintain an 'overview' of our work to ensure that such standards are maintained. Where they are not, we can, through the normative, formative and restorative tasks, be supported and guided in addressing these concerns – for example, through additional supervision, role play, attending further training or beginning personal therapy. From the points above we can see that a number of important tasks are undertaken during the process of supervision. It seems that some important principles centre on the formal nature of supervision: supervision is not an informal process that we can dip in and out of. Rather, time and other boundaries need to be discussed and agreed so that a 'professional, formal working alliance' may be achieved; the process of contracting is important in this respect (a point to which we will return later in the chapter).

Supervision in context

There are, of course, many different contexts in which supervision can take place. It is often in the transferring of understanding from one context to another that confusion can occur. For example, if supervision in other forms of work has been experienced as something 'hands on' (i.e., overseeing a practical task, or perhaps something more akin to caseload management, such as maintaining an overview of workload or time management), the different focus of counselling and psychotherapy supervision can be experienced as a little more abstract, or perhaps less relevant to the task in hand. My own experience in counsellor training is a case in point. As a qualified social worker I was used to the concept of social work supervision. That is, I would regularly meet with my line manager and talk through the clients I was seeing, agreeing tasks and reviewing my time commitment with each. I struggled in the early stages of my counsellor placement to adapt to a new idea of what supervision required from me. I was now being asked what I felt about my work, as opposed to whether I could fit it all in within the next day or two and whether I had space for several more clients. I felt irritated by my supervisor's (in fact, quite appropriate) insistence on exploring my part in my working relationships, as opposed to caseload management, which it later dawned on me I had been more used to as a social worker. Neither approach to supervision was wrong, but was instead appropriate to the context in which I was working, and the nature of the work I was undertaking. We therefore need to appreciate the context of supervision to ensure we get the most out of it. This is the case not only where the contexts are obviously very different: it is also true for different working situations as a therapist. For example, supervision I might need for my work in a primary care mental health team might be very different from that needed when working in higher or further education, or in a bereavement service, or in independent practice, for example. We need to be context-aware in enabling us to 'locate' supervision appropriately and thus make it as relevant as possible for our personal and professional requirements.

Group and individual supervision

Like counselling or psychotherapy, supervision can happen individually, in pairs, or in groups. Many training courses require that supervision of their trainees takes place within a group setting, or perhaps a combination of individual or group supervision. My own first experience of supervision was in a group setting, which felt both containing and supportive, and a little exposing (knowing that others would be listening to my mistakes). Proctor (2008) characterises group supervision using an interesting analogy of performers and a stage. She states, 'Group supervision is an enactment. For the most part, supervisor and group supervisees are on stage. However, off stage, there are at least two powerfully silent participants, and possibly one or two other influential players who may appear in the opening scene or closing acts, or at times of crisis' (2008, p. 3) It is worth paying some attention here to what Proctor refers to as 'silent participants'. Diagrammatically she presents these as 'stakeholders', as in Figure 11.1.

Proctor highlights the point that, while on the face of it supervision can appear to be a process between supervisor and supervisee, in fact there are several others who participate, in some form, in the process – the 'stakeholders'. The same can be said for work with clients: while individual work appears to take place only between the client and their therapist, a systemic view would see the importance of the therapist's 'system' (e.g. agency, professional organisation, team) and the client's 'system' (e.g. family, friends, employer, education institution etc), all exerting influence over the process. Of course, the stakeholders may include other group members for group-based supervision. The idea of being supervised in a group can be exciting and anxiety-provoking in equal measure. Having the opportunity to learn from others, receiving and offering feedback with other people, sharing the experience of a supervisory process, having a sense of relief when hearing of others' mistakes, receiving and

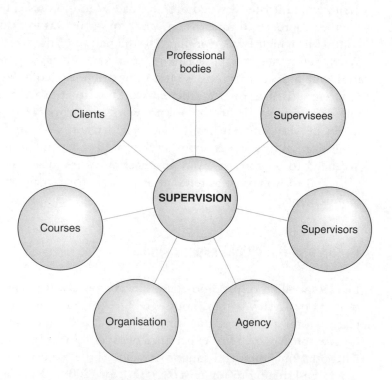

FIGURE 11.1   The supervisory stakeholders (Proctor, 2008, p. 3)

offering affirmation of success – all provide a multi-dimensional opportunity. Of course, the dark clouds of anxiety may also loom large: fearing other people's judgements of ourselves, becoming competitive with other group members, secretly (or openly) seeking approval from the parental figure of the supervisor, or experiencing a sense of shame in our own struggles. These all need to be negotiated and talked about openly in working towards a safe supervisory environment.

Models of supervision

As with counselling and psychotherapy, there is not one fixed model of supervision. A number of models have developed over recent years, each bringing a particular perspective to how the supervisory process might be negotiated and understood. Though there is insufficient space to explore all of them in detail, a selected few are highlighted here.

Hawkins and Shohet process model

Hawkins and Shohet (2007) presume that at a minimum there are four elements to supervision: a supervisor, a supervisee, a client and a work context. The supervisor and supervisee will be present in supervision, thus representing two systems or 'matrices': the therapy matrix and supervision matrix. The authors suggest that supervision styles can be divided into two main categories as follows:

> 'Supervision that pays attention directly to the supervisee/client matrix, by reflecting on the reports, written notes or tape recordings of the client sessions;
>
> Supervision that pays attention to the supervisee/client matrix through how that system is reflected in the here-and-now experiences of the supervision process.'

> (Hawkins and Shohet, 2007, p. 82)

In subdividing these two main categories, Hawkins and Shohet create a process model with seven modes of supervision. They represent this model diagrammatically, as reproduced in Figure 11.2.

The levels can be understood as follows:

1 Reflection on the content of the therapy session. Focus is on the actual content of the therapy session – how the client presented, what they said, their goals, etc.
2 Exploration of the strategies and interventions used by the therapist. Focus is on what the therapist did, why they decided to use particular interventions and when, and what others might also be used.

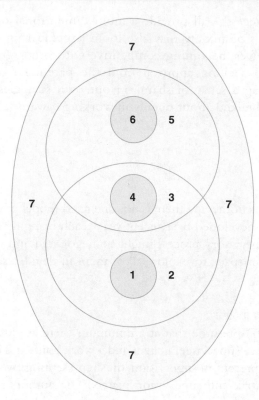

1 = The client (and reflection on the therapy session)
2 = Strategies/interventions used by the therapist
3 = Therapy relationship (and exploration of it)
4 = The therapist (and reflection on countertransferential dynamics)
5 = Here-and-now process paralleling the 'there-and-then' process of therapy
6 = The supervisor
7 = Organisational context

FIGURE 11.2   Hawkins and Shohet seven-eyed model of supervision (Hawkins and Shohet, 2007, p. 82)

3 Exploration of the therapy process and relationship. The focus here is on the process of therapy, the metaphors that were used, and changes in voice and posture.

4 Focus on the therapist's countertransference. Focus is on the therapist's personal material that might have been triggered, projections and other transferential issues.

5 Focus on the here-and-now process as a mirror or parallel of the there-and-then process. Focus is on the supervisory session as an insight into the therapy session.

6 Focus on the supervisor's countertransference. The supervisor focuses on their own here-and-now experience of the supervision session to provide further insight for the therapist.

7 The organisational context. The supervisor and therapist consider the organisational context and its relevance for the processes discussed.

Hawkins and Shohet characterise a 'good' supervisory session as one in which the supervisor moves between these different modes, as opposed to remaining in one predominantly. This will, however, also be influenced by the experience of the supervisee to make best use of such supervisor interventions. For example, locating and working with countertransferential dynamics may be an area of development for those new to supervision. Where the concept of countertransference is not necessarily explicitly worked with as a theoretical concept, the supervisor and supervisee can instead focus on the therapist's responses to the client and their presentation within the concept of congruence.

Page and Woskett cyclical model

Page and Woskett (1994) outline a cyclical model of supervision containing five distinct stages, namely: contract, focus, space, bridge and review. We can understand these stages as follows:

1   Focus. The focus consists of the material brought by the supervisee, e.g. specific client material.
2   Contract. This is the process by which the supervisor and supervisee negotiate and agree a contract for their supervisory relationship.
3   Space. The space forms what Page and Woskett call the 'heart' of the supervisory process. 'It is the place where the counsellor is held, supported, challenged, and affirmed in his or her work' (p. 35).
4   Bridge. The bridge represents the way in which the supervisor facilitates the supervisee to consider transferring learning from supervision back into the work with the client.
5   Review. The review operates on two levels, the micro and the macro. Taken at a micro level, the review stage allows for the supervisor and supervisee to consider the exploration and review the process of it. At a macro level, review also allows for feedback on the supervisee's work, as well as the wider process of supervision.

Stoltenberg and Delworth's developmental model of supervision

Stoltenberg and Delworth (1987) present a four-stage model of supervisee development, which tracks the counsellor or psychotherapist from inexperience through to greater levels of competency.

Level 1: The beginning of the journey

At this level the supervisee is highly motivated to learn but is generally more focused on the development of micro skills and particular ways of working with clients. The supervisee's self-awareness and awareness of their client's process is limited. The role of the supervisor at this level is to create a structured supervisory relationship, which the supervisee experiences as supportive. The educative, or formative, role is perhaps more prominent, guiding the supervisee through the development of skills and knowledge.

Level 2: Trial and tribulation

Moving on to level 2, the supervisee moves between feeling dependent on their supervisor, to periods of greater autonomy. Understanding of the client's process increases and there may be a shift between self-confidence and feeling incompetent. The supervisee will begin to have a greater sense of their own 'self' as a counsellor or psychotherapist and will be self-reviewing interventions with a view to increasing their repertoire. The role of the supervisor at this level is to enable supervision to become less structured, encouraging a balance between self-reflection and client focus.

Level 3: Challenge and growth

The supervisee's level of confidence and sense of identity will be much more evident, with an enhanced capacity to review particular strengths and areas for development. The supervisee's willingness to use 'self' as a therapeutic tool will also be much more evident. The supervisor will make greater use of more implicit processes, e.g. parallel process, and will challenge the supervisee on a personal and professional level more effectively.

Level 4: Challenge and growth (integrated)

According to Stoltenberg and Delworth, level 4 (integrated) will not see a change to the structures, but instead a greater degree of integration of learning and development. Typically at this stage supervisees have a greater sense of their own 'internal supervisor', are highly motivated and aware and highly insightful into

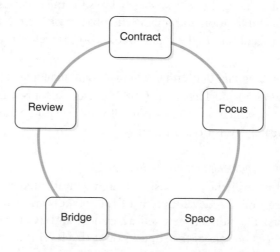

FIGURE 11.3 Cyclical Model of Supervision (Page and Woskett, 1994, p. 34)

Source: Page, S. and Woskett, V. (1994) *Supervising the Counsellor: A Cyclical Model*. Abingdon: Routledge. p. 34. Reproduced with permission.

both their own and their client's process. Not all counsellors and psychotherapists will necessarily reach this level, even though many may suspect they are there already.

In truth these three models (while not an exhaustive list of supervisory models available) are not necessarily stand-alone. It is pretty easy to see how each complements the other and can be used interchangeably. For example, during the focusing stage in Page and Woskett's model the supervisor may be working at different levels of Hawkins and Shohet's process model, while at the same time being contextually aware of the supervisee's level of development (Stoltenberg and Delworth). Using models together arguably provides the best opportunity for the supervisor and supervisee to have a rich experience characterised by depth, intimacy and insight.

Frankland's person-centred model of supervision

Frankland (2001) holds the view that there are two important strands in working as a supervisor: that work as a supervisor needs to be consistent with the 'way of being' (p. 26) as a therapist; and a willingness to be open to personal history and its myriad of meaning remains central to a person-centred position. Frankland states that, 'Person-centred supervision like person-centred therapy is not merely a supportive relationship (in this case facilitating and ensuring the safety of another supportive relationship), but a significant meeting between committed participants which is capable of sustaining and developing ... "relational depth"' (p. 28). A seven-step approach to supervision is offered:

1   The supervisee raises in supervision what it important for them. The supervisor pays attention to the 'way of telling' and the content.
2   Empathy is both communicated and received.
3   Respect and acceptance is both communicated and received.
4   The supervisor is congruent.
5   An exploration is undertaken of symbolic/metaphorical material.
6   Best practice and ethical issues are regularly explored.
7   After 4, 5 or 6, there is clarification of what has been gained, valued work is undertaken and there is offering of 'congruent affirmation' (p. 28).

Frankland's model of supervision is very consistent with a person-centred approach to therapy, bringing the same qualities and philosophical structures to the process.

Finding the right supervisor

With all these factors to consider, finding a supervisor might seem a case of 'here's a haystack, now find the needle'. I have been lucky in my own career to have worked with a number of skilful and engaging supervisors. However, locating them has not always been easy. Finding the right person to share your successes, but also to explore those things that have gone wrong is not always a straightforward process. Other requirements, e.g. theoretical orientation, specific demographic requirements, such as age, gender and qualifications, can make the process seem even more cumbersome.

It is possible to have individual supervision (where an individual person meets with a supervisor), group supervision (where two or more people meet with one supervisor), large group supervision (where a larger number of people meet for supervision, as sometimes happens on training courses) and peer supervision. (Where there is no recognised 'supervisor', but instead a group of therapists meet as peers to supervise each other. Such peer groups will agree the same level of contract around confidentiality and accountability as in other supervision, but will all share supervisory responsibility at different points of the discussion. Peer supervision usually supplements other, more 'formal', supervision arrangements rather than replaces them).

Often training programmes will have a list of supervisors they have 'approved': they have copies of the supervisor's CV and believe that supervisor to be well placed to supervise trainees from the programme. Such approval requirements will often be based on theoretical orientation, supervisor qualifications and experience, and cost. If, as a trainee, your programme maintains such a list it will almost certainly be a requirement that you work with one of the approved supervisors. It is still important though to consider whether there are factors important to you, e.g. gender, culture, physical location. You will be working closely with the supervisor and exploring unknown areas with them, so it is important to feel comfortable. Additionally, supervisors of trainees will also often have an assessment role, providing the course with a placement report detailing progress. You need to trust that the person you are working with is able to provide a fair and honest account of your development. Beyond the parameters of training, finding the 'right' supervisor is not always so easy. Word-of-mouth recommendations are a good start, as is referring to professional organisations' lists of supervisors (e.g. BACP, BABCP, COSCA, UKCP), particularly if you are looking for a supervisor working from a particular orientation. Several professional bodies accredit supervisors in the same way that individual therapists are accredited. Such accreditation will demonstrate that the supervisor has submitted their practice to particular scrutiny and has been assessed as meeting particular good practice benchmarks. Despite such accreditation schemes having been established for some time, the numbers of accredited supervisors (for individuals or groups) is not as widespread as that for individual therapists. A potential supervisor not being accredited will not necessarily mean they are not an excellent supervisor, but simply that they have chosen not to apply for accreditation. Sometimes people will also advertise themselves as supervisors on websites or in professional journals and magazines (e.g. BACP's *Therapy Today*). The checklist in Box 11.2 is useful to keep in mind when looking for a new supervisor.

> ### BOX 11.2 CHECKLIST FOR FINDING THE RIGHT SUPERVISOR
>
> - Particular characteristics or demographics, e.g. gender, age, sexuality, culture
> - Theoretical orientation, similar or different
> - Experience of working in a particular setting or context
> - Qualification and experience as a supervisor
> - Supervisor's working style
> - Days and times available
> - Geographical location of supervision
> - Venue for supervision
> - Frequency
> - Cost
> - Structure of supervision, e.g. individual, group, peer group, etc.

It is reasonable to expect an introductory meeting with a new supervisor before making a commitment to work together. Some supervisors will make a charge for this meeting, while others will not. During that meeting it is important to ask any questions you have, and expect that the supervisor will ask questions of you. If you feel unable to ask questions, even if you consider them to be 'stupid' questions (which almost certainly they won't be), perhaps that is an indication to reflect carefully on whether that person is the right supervisor for you. While confidence in challenge is likely to develop over time, it is important to feel sufficiently confident to ask appropriate questions of your prospective supervisor, and for them to be fully and honestly answered.

Final thoughts

We might begin by knowing very little about supervision or what it means, but we will quickly develop an appreciation of its essential place in our work as a counsellor or supervisor. Likewise, we might not always know what we want or need from supervision, but this again will quickly emerge as the supervisory alliance becomes more established. It must be acknowledged, however, that even in a well-established, facilitative supervisory relationship, knowing what we want and need can still ebb and flow from moment to moment. What is not disputed is the value in positioning supervision as a central tenet to our work as counsellors and psychotherapists, creating the opportunity to ensure that, at all times, we remain ethically and professionally grounded and accountable for what we do.

DISCUSSION QUESTIONS

1   What do you consider to be the advantages and disadvantages of working with a supervisor from the same theoretical orientation as yourself?
2   What is the most important thing you would look for in a prospective supervisor, and why?
3   How might/do you work differently in group and individual supervision?
4   How might working with a supervisor who is very different from ourselves (in terms of, for example, gender, age, or sexuality) facilitate or hinder the supervisory process for you?

11.3 MAKING THE MOST OF SUPERVISION AND NEGOTIATING DIFFICULTIES

SECTION OUTLINE

Merely ensuring that a supervision arrangement is in place does not necessarily mean that the supervisory time will be used to the greatest effect. Getting the most out of supervision requires preparation and attention to detail. This section considers the factors that need to be addressed in setting up a supervision contract and how supervisees might best prepare for their supervision time to maximise its potential. There are also factors that might challenge the value of supervision: these are considered here along with ways in which they might be successfully negotiated.

We established in the previous section what we mean by supervision, and how integral it can be to successful and ethical counselling practice. However, most counsellors and psychotherapists would, I imagine, acknowledge that successful supervision is not simply a matter of turning up on the right day, at the right place and at the right time (though this itself can be a challenge on occasions). Simply being there when you should be there is not in itself sufficient for purposeful and facilitative supervision, though it is a good start. Likewise, a client simply turning up for a counselling or psychotherapy session is unlikely, in itself, to lead to a successful therapy outcome. The question therefore is, having turned up, what else needs to be in place to maximise the benefit from time spent with a supervisor? As I will explore in the next section, Reviewing Supervision and Changing Your Supervisor, there are important ingredients that need to be present for supervision to contribute to your personal and professional development. Too often these may not be present, or have disappeared over time, with the result that the supervisory process is experienced as stale or stagnant. It is pertinent, before considering reviewing and ending supervision, to explore how we can make it go well.

Contracting for supervision

Like counselling and psychotherapy, thorough contracting, in which both or all parties can state their needs and agree a means of achieving them, is an important first step. Skipping over the contracting process, or rushing it through, has the potential to overlook or miss important aspects, at best potentially undermining the future credibility of supervision, or at worst contributing to the potential for harm. Time and care need to be given to contracting so that practicalities, fears and hopes can be fully aired and explored. How supervisors facilitate the process of contracting will be dependent on how they like to work, and as such can give a good indication of supervisory style. The process of engagement and thus contracting begins with the first contact. Consider the examples in Box 11.3.

CASE STUDY 11.3
Contracting

- **John** prefers not to contract formally but instead will talk things through at the first point of enquiry, usually over the telephone.
- **Sahid** will arrange a face-to-face meeting as soon as possible, which will not be charged for, but prefers for agreements to be verbal. He dislikes the formality of written contracts, feeling that they bring an unhelpful dynamic into the relationship.
- **Kelly** prefers a face-to-face meeting, which she will charge for if the supervisee decides to begin supervision with her, and develops a written 'agreement' based on discussions with the supervisee.
- **Khalida** begins with a face-to-face meeting, for which she makes a small charge, and talks through a pre-set contract for supervision while making no changes (other than for the cost and frequency).

PAUSE FOR REFLECTION

1   Which approach to contracting do you prefer? Why?
2   Which approaches do you dislike? Why?
3   If you prefer a combination of different approaches, what are they and why do
    they appeal to you?

The process of contracting should provide you with ample opportunity to talk through a number of things that will inform your supervisory experience. Your supervisor may have specific aspects of how they work that they wish to point out to you, such as: venue and time of arrival (if working at home); preparation they expect; use of audio-tapes for evaluation; or any assessment role they have. These factors need to be highlighted and discussed early on. There is little point in moving into a deeper exploration of your own relational styles if there isn't a mutually convenient time to meet. Proctor and Sills (2006) describe the contracting process as important in creating a supervisory frame. King (2008, pp. 217-18) outlines the following points that need to be included in a supervisory contract.

Practicalities

These include: time; place; frequency; length of sessions; fee and review date; methods of payment; time payable; agreement about holidays and cancelled sessions; contact between sessions; emergency contact; telephone supervision; online supervision; reports; the process of terminating the supervision contract (how, by whom, with how much notice?).

Accountability

This covers: responsibilities for client work; clinical responsibility; monitoring and feedback requirements for employers or courses; professional accountability; professional insurance; membership of professional organisations; professional and organisational codes of ethics; complaints procedure; duty of care; management of complaints; specific legislative requirements; information about supervisee's caseload; emotional intensity or complexity and number of clients on which to be supervised.

Confidentiality

This covers: limits with respect to clients and supervisee; specific issues regarding limitations, boundaries, contract between client and counsellor, contact with GP; status of client notes; supervisor and supervisee notes.

Practice arrangements

These include: physical setting; health and safety; formal client-counsellor/psychotherapist contract; long-term or time-limited counselling; psychiatric and medical back-up; contact with other agencies and GPs; arrangements for serious illness; professional will in the event of the unexpected death of the therapist or supervisor, including the management of supervision and/or therapy notes, for example.

Presentation in supervision

This covers the use of: verbatim or process notes; transcripts; audio-visual recordings; number of clients presented; how feedback is given; use of creative feedback.

Professional development

This deals with: the amount of support and/or personal therapy; training requirements; continuing professional development; other supervisory relationships; providing references.

Review and assessment

This covers: frequency and format of supervision review; duration of supervisory relationship; joint review and evaluation process; evaluation of client work. While there are a number of things to consider, all of them are important in creating the frame for supervision. Depending on the context of supervision, the level to which all these points will need to be discussed will inevitably vary. However, there are many 'givens' here that will need to be included in any supervisory contract.

Making the most of supervision

If we know where we are to meet, when we are to meet, how much it will cost and how we both like to work, and if the contract is in place, we're ready to go.

Preparation is an important factor in taking the right steps in making the most out of supervision. We need to know what we are going to do next, and why. In the context of a busy life – a full caseload of clients, or lots of professional or personal commitments – it is very easy to arrive at supervision with little thought for which client(s) will be discussed and why. What can result is the supervisee floundering around trying to think of something to say, then launching into a long-winded, content-orientated discussion about the client they can remember best, with the supervisor struggling to help the supervisee make any meaningful sense of their work. Then, as the supervisee leaves the room – usually within an hour or two – they remember the really important client issues they had meant to discuss. All in all it leads to an unsatisfactory and frustrating experience for all concerned. You need to have thought about the whole of your current work as a therapist (including non-client contact aspects), reflected on the personal and professional impact of these issues, prioritised between them and created an 'agenda' (albeit a flexible one) to explore with your supervisor. The following checklist of questions may help preparation:

1   What are the issues currently presenting in my client work?
2   What themes or recurring presentations do I notice?
3   Which clients are causing concern?
4   Are there any specific clients who have experienced particular breakthroughs or successes?
5   Do I have new clients to introduce, or clients that are ending/ended?
6   Which clients do I regularly discuss or avoid? Why?
7   What issues currently present in my wider work as a counsellor or psychotherapist?
8   What organisational issues are helping or hindering my work?
9   What are the issues currently presenting on a personal level that are relevant or impacting my work as a counsellor or psychotherapist?
10 Which areas of continuing professional development could I helpfully explore?
11 Are there any issues in supervision, either facilitative or inhibiting, that I need to name?

This is not an exhaustive list of questions, but if worked through it does help to structure your thinking about how best you might use the supervision time available. It is also helpful to think of your wider work in this way. A second key ingredient, after preparation, is prioritisation. Certainly for those new to counselling and psychotherapy supervision, and sometimes those more familiar with it, there can be the 'quart in a pint pot' anxiety: how can I talk about all of my clients in such a short space of time? I have supervised counsellors who have tried to manage this extraordinary feat, offering a snapshot view of many clients in one supervision session. While there may be occasions where it is useful for the supervisee to summarise their current caseload so that the supervisor is better able to understand their work in context, doing so more than occasionally is probably unhelpful and unproductive. It is more productive to consider the questions above and consider how best to use the time and how to prioritise your needs as a supervisee to ensure that some are met. Of course, it is important too to pay attention in this prioritising process to whether there are issues or clients we are regularly leaving out, otherwise prioritising can become an effective smokescreen for avoidance. The final ingredients are precision and process. This is not to say we necessarily need to fully understand what we need when we go into a supervision session – often the 'outcome' from supervision can be a very different beast to the one we imagined when we began. It is helpful, however, at least to have a clear starting point. Vagueness will often mean that we draw on content rather than process to engage in our exploration, which is usually a cul-de-sac. This is not, of course, to say that content (i.e., the client's story) has no place in supervision. It is essential that both you and your supervisor have a shared understanding of the client's problems and what has brought them to therapy. However, the narrative – the story and how it was told: the intonation; expression; bodily expression; what was not said and so on – is much more helpful in giving insight into process and thus the opportunities for change. Consider the example of Kirsten in Box 11.4.

CASE STUDY 11.4
Kirsten

Kirsten is an experienced counsellor who brings her work with Adrian, her client, to supervision. Her supervision session lasts one hour and Kirsten spends the first 25 minutes telling her supervisor about who Adrian is: age; relationship status; employment; family history; and the nature of the problems he brings (depression and anxiety). The supervisor tries to encourage Kirsten to move on to the process of the work, rather than staying with the content, on a couple of occasions but Kirsten is resistant to do so. The supervisor gently challenges Kirsten about her continued focus on content and asks her how she is feeling as she tells his story. Kirsten becomes tearful and replies 'overwhelmed' and 'angry'. She tells her supervisor that Adrian was angry in the session, and reported feeling helpless about his future.

PAUSE FOR REFLECTION

1 Why do you imagine Kirsten focused for so long on Adrian's story?
2 What might this tell us about how Kirsten is feeling in sessions with Adrian, and how Adrian is feeling?
3 What is the task of the supervisor in this instance?
4 What do you consider to be the relative importance of content and process in this example?

In summary, then, we are most likely to benefit from supervision if we pay attention to a number of important factors:

- Contract thoroughly and carefully
- Prepare carefully for each session (as we would for a counselling or psychotherapy session with a client)

- Prioritise what to take to each session
- Have a clear starting point and focus on process rather than simply being content-driven (this, of course, being heavily influenced by our developmental level as a supervisee – see the Stoltenberg and Delworth developmental stages above).

Negotiating difficulties

Despite our best efforts in preparing for success there will, of course, be difficulties in supervision to negotiate. Difficulties are not necessarily insurmountable and, if negotiated with care and trust, can even facilitate a deeper supervisory process. The parallel here with counselling and psychotherapy is again very evident: difficulties encountered in therapy can be vital in helping the therapeutic relationship move to new depths, and can facilitate trust. Potential difficulties include:

- Failure to manage boundaries between supervision and therapy
- Dual relationships and the assessment role
- Mismanagement of power dynamics
- Ineffective or over-zealous challenge leading to a 'silenced supervisee'
- Lack of experience on the part of the supervisor
- Concerns regarding potential unprofessional practice.

The brief scenarios in Boxes 11.5 to 11.10 illustrate these difficulties in action.

BOX 11.5   FAILING TO MANAGE BOUNDARIES BETWEEN SUPERVISION AND THERAPY

Angela has been seeing her supervisor, Julie, for some time, and they get on well. Julie has been increasingly aware of Angela's physical health problems and how it is becoming harder for Angela to manage the pain she experiences. During one session Angela is quite tearful, and Julie begins to ask in more detail about the impact of Angela's physical health problems. Angela begins to explain that it is causing problems at home, with tensions between her and her partner. This discussion continues until Angela realises she has disclosed a number of highly personal issues about her relationship. She feels angry and exposed.

BOX 11.6   DUAL RELATIONSHIPS AND THE ASSESSMENT ROLE

Jacques is a trainee counsellor on placement. His supervisor, Susie, is also the head of service in which the placement takes place (as she is the only qualified supervisor). Susie is additionally required to complete a report for Jacques's course as part of his training requirement. During the placement Jacques becomes irritated that he is not always allocated clients, thus wasting time. He raises this in supervision and finds himself in a difficult discussion with Susie, who hears his comments as criticism of the service, and therefore of her as head of the service.

BOX 11.7   MISMANAGEMENT OF POWER DYNAMICS

Rochelle is a black counsellor working with a white supervisor, Karl. Their relationship is generally good. Rochelle is struggling with a client whom she experiences as angry and critical. She has tried to explore this with her client, but he is very resistant to her challenges. In supervision she feels that she is again struggling, believing that Karl is not really listening to her. When she raises this, Karl challenges her by suggesting that culture or gender is maybe the issue here, with her struggling with two white men. She feels angry and powerless to challenge.

BOX 11.8   INEFFECTIVE OR OVER-ZEALOUS CHALLENGE LEADING TO A 'SILENCED SUPERVISEE'

Tara is an experienced psychotherapist who works in an agency where she is expected to work briefly with clients. She regularly talks with her supervisor about how she doesn't agree with a brief model as it doesn't 'match her model of working'. Her supervisor, Alex, is aware that the agency is quite strict on brief working as a means of managing high demand for therapy, and tries to challenge Tara on this. When she rebuffs his challenge he capitulates and agrees with her.

BOX 11.9   AN INEXPERIENCED SUPERVISOR

Andrew has been qualified for two years and establishes a private practice in which he offers supervision. He has taken on a new trainee supervision group and manages the group to the best of his ability. He is new to supervision and has never facilitated a group before (as a therapist). The group has several strong personalities who soon begin to quibble and argue over points. One member of the group states that they feel unsafe as he is not managing this dynamic, and Andrew is unsure of what to do.

BOX 11.10   CONCERNS REGARDING POTENTIAL UNPROFESSIONAL PRACTICE

Joy is a supervisor who works with Rebecca. She has been concerned about Rebecca's management of boundaries for some time, and has discussed her concerns on a number of occasions. Rebecca talks about having finished with a client recently – their relationship was very good and Rebecca and the client got on well personally. Rebecca states that she has given the client her phone number and said, after a few weeks has passed, it would be nice for them to meet up for a coffee or perhaps for a meal one evening. Rebecca is resistant to Joy's challenge about this unprofessional practice and says to Joy that perhaps it might be better if she found a new supervisor.

PAUSE FOR REFLECTION

1   How do you find you respond to the scenarios?
2   What similarities or common themes between these situations can you find?
3   If you were the supervisor in each situation, how might you manage?

Such scenarios make the argument for supervision of supervision compelling. In each one the supervisor is struggling with their role and authority – either failing to use their authority appropriately or using it as a means of attacking their supervisee by acting out some need or defence of their own. Supervision of supervision, like supervision of counselling or psychotherapy, provides a space for the supervisor to reflect on their work and their use of 'self' in the supervisory process. Careful contracting would have prevented several of these situations from developing – for example, not agreeing to supervise when managing a dual role, or being clear as to the boundaries between supervision and therapy. The need for potential supervisors to clearly reflect on their capacity to begin supervising at all or to take on new supervisees is essential. Such ruptures in the supervisory relationship need to be managed with care and attention; supervisors need continually to reflect on whether their supervisees take opportunities to challenge and disagree in supervision. This acts as a barometer for their perceived level of safety and trust. Supervisees need to take opportunities to reflect on whether they feel silenced or facilitated. Having a regular opportunity to review supervision can provide a forum in which such difficulties can be named and worked through. In the next section we will examine how to establish a good review routine and what to consider when reviewing. We will also consider how to recognise when it is time to move on to a new supervisor and begin the whole process all over again.

DISCUSSION QUESTIONS

1 If you are about to begin supervision, how might you ensure that you contract satisfactorily? If you are already seeing a supervisor, how many of the points made in this section are addressed in your existing contract (if you have one)?

2 How do you currently prepare for supervision? What works and what doesn't?

3 How could you prepare for supervision differently?

4 How do you and your supervisor manage difficulties when they arise?

5 When beginning supervision, how might you talk about managing difficult situations to help prepare for when they arise?

11.4 REVIEWING SUPERVISION AND CHANGING SUPERVISOR

SECTION OUTLINE

This section explains the importance of regularly reviewing supervisory arrangements. The review process needs to be collaborative and honest and to help: (a) restate or refine working goals; or (b) identify when a change of supervisor would be beneficial. This section outlines how this can be achieved and identifies the key factors involved in the process.

I would like to introduce here a bath metaphor to illustrate the way in which something can change over time. Imagine getting into a hot bath at the end of a tiring and stressful day. As you sink into the warm water, you can feel the tension, aches and pains just fade away as you drift into a state of stillness and relaxation. This metaphor came to me when I started to think about good supervision and, especially, the wonderful feeling of stillness and relaxation that can be experienced when a good supervisor really understands you, affirms your work and offers challenge to facilitate your learning and development. From my experience there comes a point during any bath time when you begin to notice that the water has gone just a little bit cold and the whole experience doesn't feel quite so good anymore. You have important choices to make: you can either top up with hot water in an attempt to re-create what you had, or recognise that it is time to get out. We look for supervision to be a safe and containing place (like a bath) where we can immerse ourselves in the process and support of supervision (the warm water).

This can work well for a while, but over time the focus or purpose of supervision can become a little lost in familiar ways of working or perhaps both parties (counsellor and supervisor) become a little too settled (the water getting cold). We might not easily notice the loss of focus, both caught in the routine of what we do one session after another. The supervision review (the equivalent of allowing ourselves to become aware of the temperature of the water) enables us to check whether what we are doing still works for us both and to make the necessary changes to get back on track (adding more hot water, as it were). However, a point might be reached when we realise that, whatever changes we might make or however we might refocus, the best step is to end supervision, having first identified what we next need (getting out of the bath).

Reviewing supervision

It is probably not possible to begin a discussion in a room full of counsellors and psychotherapists and reach a unanimous agreement of the place and purpose of reviewing in therapy. For some, the process of reviewing with a client sits naturally within the week-by-week process of therapy, whereas for others reviewing represents the imposition of one person's agenda (the counsellor or psychotherapist) on to another (the client). There are fundamental philosophical differences at work here. They are difficult to reconcile and they require reflection. The same is true when considering whether or how to review the supervisory relationship. This can be illustrated if we consider these two positions in practice in the examples in Boxes 11.11 and 11.12.

CASE STUDY 11.11
Frances

Frances is a counsellor who works in a voluntary agency. She attends hourly supervision fortnightly. She pays for supervision herself. She has been seeing the same supervisor for the last four years. When supervision started she and her supervisor agreed to review every three months. This initially worked well, with both Frances and her supervisor taking the review opportunity to explore successes and challenges, and making whatever changes were required to keep the supervision fresh. Over time, however, Frances has come to feel that the review process has become as formulaic as the supervision itself. She feels uncomfortable about raising this issue in the next review, as she feels that she should have mentioned something before now.

**CASE STUDY 11.12
Patir**

Patir is a counsellor working for a bereavement agency. He has been in supervision with the same supervisor for the last six years. When starting supervision, the supervisor stated that they preferred not to schedule 'formal' reviews of supervision, but instead thought that any issues or difficulties should naturally emerge during the supervision process. Patir got on well with his supervisor initially, and agreed with the idea that the supervisory discourse would allow for a more immediate expression of difficulties or challenges than would a structured review. Patir has been unhappy in supervision now for at least two years, but doesn't have the confidence to say so.

While both Frances and Patir are working to quite different supervisory contracts, their problems are essentially the same: both are unhappy with how supervision is progressing, yet neither feels able or comfortable to name their concerns – one because the review process has become too formulaic, the other because there is no specific process of review at all. It seems that regardless of philosophical differences underpinning our work, we can still end up in the same position (I can certainly relate here to my own professional experiences of being unhappy in a supervision arrangement, yet finding it difficult to say so). We can easily imagine that voicing these basic concerns would come with relative ease to personally aware and professionally trained individuals: however, the experience of feeling silenced, or the pull towards colluding with a process that no longer works can be compelling, despite our knowing better. Lawton (2000) notes that attachment can be an important consideration when reflecting on our willingness or otherwise to question or change supervision arrangements. Having a supervisor who we feel responds positively to our needs, creates a space in which we can feel heard and cared for, and takes an interest in our development and growth, can be seductive, perhaps replicating early childhood parental relationships (or putting in place such experiences that were absent from our early years).

Creating a review space in which these and other dynamics can be openly and honestly named is important for safeguarding ethical practice for both our clients and ourselves. If, how and when reviews are to be used in supervision must be clearly defined at the early contracting stage, where both parties can articulate their thoughts and ideas and an agreement reached. While making provision for a process of supervisory review is important, one eye needs to be kept on the nature of that process, ensuring that it continues to provide the opportunity to step back and re-consider how things are going compared to what was hoped for at the outset. Likewise, it is also important to review the process of reviewing too. Simple questions like 'Does this process still work for us?' or 'Does the review allow us to say difficult things?' might provide a starting point. I'm not here advocating a review of a review, which would then in itself need reviewing, and so on. As an aside, I've always wondered where that kind of regress would end: I have supervision for my clinical work, and my supervisor has supervision for their work in supervising me, and presumably their supervisor in turn has supervision for their work in supervising my supervisor's supervision of me, and … I can only imagine that somewhere, probably sitting in a remote but beautiful valley, sits the all-knowing supervisor who supervises everything!

Rather, the suggestion here is that supervision is best reviewed formally rather than simply allowing for issues to emerge. 'Formally' here means that time is put aside with the specific purpose of reviewing, to ask particular questions of each other and of the process. As we have discussed above, there are inherent power differences between supervisor and supervisee. Both have particular responsibilities – and the position can be further complicated by the fact that for trainee counsellors or psychotherapists the supervisor might also be an assessor. Factors that might contribute to a power imbalance, or add complications, include the following:

- The supervisor might be more experienced than the supervisee, bringing the authority of reputation, qualification and thus 'seniority'.
- The supervisor has primary functions to fulfil, such as normative functions (Inskipp and Proctor, 1993), which attend to issues of competence and ethical practice.
- The supervisor might additionally fulfil the role of assessor, writing reports for training courses etc.
- The supervisor often 'takes the lead', facilitating the supervisory process, depending on the supervisory model being worked with.
- The location, cost and format of supervision is often strongly influenced by supervisor preference.
- The supervisee might fear that naming the possibility of ending supervision might be seen by the supervisor as a criticism, leading to anger or disapproval; or the supervisor might fear that the supervisee might interpret the review process as a form of criticism or rejection.

Review: some suggestions

A planned and considered review thus provides a relatively safe opportunity for both parties to ask pertinent questions of themselves and the process. Suggestions as to what might be considered in the review are provided in Box 11.13.

BOX 11.13 REVIEWING SUPERVISION

For the supervisee

How do you experience supervision in relation to the expectations of each other we established at the beginning of our work? How do you prepare for supervision sessions? Has this changed, and if so how? Are you able and willing to bring all aspects of your client work (e.g. successes and difficulties)? How might you censor what you talk about, and why? Are you able to translate learning from supervision back into your client work? Who do you feel is in 'control' of sessions? Do you feel appropriately challenged? To what extent do the practicalities of supervision, e.g. timings, frequency, location, duration, cost, etc., continue to meet your needs? (How) do you prevent yourself from getting what you need? Is it time for you to move on?

For the supervisor

How do you experience supervision in relation to the expectations of each other we established at the beginning of our work? To what extent do you think the supervisee prepares for sessions? What evidence do you base this on? What is your experience of the work that is presented (e.g. a good range, all 'successes', all 'difficulties')? What evidence is there that the supervisee is applying learning from supervision to their client work? Who do you feel is in 'control' of sessions? To what extent do you feel able to be honest with the supervisee, particularly about areas of concern? Do you find yourself censoring what you say? Do you feel appropriately challenged by the nature of the work? To what extent do the practicalities of supervision, e.g. timings, frequency, location, duration, cost, etc., continue to meet your needs? Is it time for the supervisee to move on?

Perhaps the question about whether it is time to move on is central to the process of reviewing? The answer may well be 'no' – but asking the question keeps the possibility on the agenda.

The review process also allows for both supervisor and supervisee to become aware of when supervision is not working. Like counselling and psychotherapy, there are occasions when supervision is not only not working, but is potentially harmful or abusive. It can be extremely difficult as a supervisee to raise concerns about such situations. The power dynamics in supervision can be experienced as silencing and disempowering. A review might be a space to raise such concerns, or if these cannot be successfully resolved (and there is no intermediate employing agency where concerns could be taken) it might be necessary to raise them with the professional body of which the supervisor is a member. Clearly all relevant steps at seeking resolution should be taken first, but neither should anyone feel trapped into harmful or abusive experiences. Here the importance of ensuring that any potential supervisor is a member of an established professional body, subscribing to their ethical expectations, becomes apparent.

Sometimes as part of the reviewing process it is apparent that the relationship is reaching, or has reached, a useful end-point. That is, the time has come for you to begin to look for another supervisor. It is probably more helpful to allow a process of review to determine when the time is to move on than to follow mechanical or prescribed time-scales for supervision (i.e., changing supervisor after every three years, even if the supervisory relationship remains potent and helpful). The following sections consider in more detail what factors might lead to a planned ending for supervision, and circumstances in which supervision might end unexpectedly.

Planned endings

Planned endings in supervision can happen for a variety of reasons. For example:

- During review it is decided that it would be beneficial to end.
- The supervisor, supervisee or both consider that supervision has reached the end of its natural usefulness.
- The supervisor or supervisee need to end for practical reasons (e.g. change in availability, moving away, retirement).
- The supervisor or supervisee has health problems.
- Supervision has been provided as part of employment, which then changes.
- A training placement comes to an end.

If in the process of reviewing supervision the decision is that the time has come to end, it is important to prepare for ending carefully and respectfully. Many writers have highlighted the parallels between how we might terminate supervision and how we end our work with clients (Inskipp and Proctor, 1993; Lawton, 2000; Proctor, 2008; Stoltenberg and Delworth, 1987). With clients we would not consider an abrupt ending, without opportunity to reflect on the work undertaken or explore the 'next steps': the same should be true for supervision. If at all possible, it is desirable for a notice period to be agreed. This gives time for the supervisee to begin to look for a new supervisor, to discuss the relevance and impact of the work that has been undertaken, and for the supervisor to consider making arrangements to begin working with a new supervisee, if appropriate. I have found when changing supervisors that often my current supervisor, with whom I am ending, has been invaluable in helping me to consider the type of supervisor or supervision that might most effectively help me in my 'next steps'. For example, having worked for several years with female supervisors, my supervisor and I were able to consider the potential benefits for me as a male therapist in seeking out a suitable male supervisor. Also, as the nature of my counselling workload changed when I began working in different settings, I was able to consider whether a supervisor with different skills and experiences might be more able to meet my needs. The point here is that, while finishing with a good and respected supervisor might be difficult, the process can also present both parties with invaluable opportunities to move on and to develop and identify whole new aspects of themselves or their work.

Unplanned endings, or ending without agreement

Of course, not all endings are planned. As in client work, endings can be unpredictable, unforeseen and unavoidable. There again may be many reasons, including:

- Sudden loss of employment
- Sudden ill-health of the supervisor or supervisee
- Non-attendance or loss of contact
- Termination, by the supervisor or supervisee, of supervision in the event of a complaint or where there are unresolved ethical concerns
- Change in employment terms so that supervision is no longer funded.

One of the most difficult circumstances where an ending can take place is when there are concerns about ethical practice. The scenario in Box 11.14 illustrates one such situation.

CASE STUDY 11.14
Brandon

Brandon is an experienced supervisor working with Allan, a counsellor in independent practice. Brandon began to experience concerns quite early in the supervisory relationship about Allan's management of counselling boundaries. Allan talked of a client whom he had met for lunch, even though counselling was ongoing with this client. Brandon talked openly and honestly to Allan about this, explaining that he believed this was not respecting clear counselling boundaries, and thus was unethical. Allan disagreed and Brandon could not help Allan see the difficulties inherent in his behaviour. Allan then reported to Brandon that he had resigned from his professional body, as he believed the ethical requirements of membership did not reflect the 'real life work of counsellors'. Despite Brandon's best efforts to satisfactorily resolve these concerns, Allan did not respond to Brandon's suggestions or interventions. After thought, Brandon informed Allan that he would be terminating counselling supervision because he believed there had been a breakdown in trust, and that he was not willing to supervise what he believed to be unprofessional conduct.

As can be seen from Brandon's situation, there may be occasions when either the supervisor or supervisee feels ethically compromised by the actions of the other and, despite best efforts, these cannot be satisfactorily resolved.

Moving on

Having decided to change supervisor, or indeed having found yourself in a situation where you need to find a new supervisor, you embark on the next challenge. Finding a new supervisor who is able to appropriately supervise your work can be onerous. I have found on several occasions that finding the right person, who can meet me at the right time, with the right experience, is, as they say, a bit like plaiting sawdust. The temptation can be, therefore, to jump into any new supervisory relationship with the first person who might fit the bill. On the companion website there are two case examples of therapists seeking new supervision arrangements. However, caution must always be exercised: having the right supervisor is ultimately integral to safe and ethical practice. If you are working with a planned ending, begin making arrangements as soon as possible to research who might be available.

Where possible, ask colleagues and peers who might be able to recommend a suitable person. Consult professional websites where supervisors may advertise their details and qualifications and where accreditation status (either as a practitioner or supervisor) might be stated. When you have identified several names, go to meet them and talk honestly about what you need and how you work. It is a decision that demands consummate care and does not reward folly or haste. After all, not many people enjoy climbing into a bath that is already cold. As I have outlined here, the importance of supervision to the process of counselling and psychotherapy means that commensurate thought and attention needs to be given to beginning supervision, developing the nature of the supervisory relationship, reviewing the process and, when ready, moving on successfully. At the beginning of working as a therapist, when the concept of therapy supervision is new, it is difficult to appreciate the importance of taking time and care in setting up supervision, where there is a choice to be made (some therapists will not necessarily have much influence over their supervision contracts in virtue of their employment demands). However, having taken careful steps, the potency of good supervision in all aspects of our professional role will quickly become apparent.

DISCUSSION QUESTIONS

1   Does your supervisory contract include the process of review? How was this included (through negotiation or by imposition)?

2   How do you review your own supervision arrangements?

3   Reflecting on your previous and current experiences of supervision, what factors have facilitated or inhibited your willingness to take risks in talking about your work? What are the implications of this for your clinical work?

4   What factors proved helpful in finding your current supervisor?

12

Counselling, Psychotherapy and Research

12.1 INTRODUCTION

CHAPTER OVERVIEW

The purpose of this chapter is to consider the role of research in counselling and psychotherapy, which would include using research to examine the evidence for and against the efficacy of counselling and psychotherapy for potential clients. The chapter will begin by taking an overview of what is meant by research and highlighting some key methodological considerations. It then will consider how we might engage with research either as practitioner-researchers, or critical consumers of research, before looking at the next steps, including writing up research and disseminating research findings.

The arguments that I will offer throughout this chapter will be in support of the integration of good research practice into our day-to-day work as counsellors and psychotherapists. I hope to challenge the persistent and worryingly widespread idea that research has no place in counselling and psychotherapy practice: in contrast, I wish to suggest that developing research-awareness, if not necessarily actually becoming a practitioner-researcher, is an ethical requirement with the same imperative as supervision. My intention here is not to offer a blanket acceptance of all research, all of the time: I acknowledge that sometimes research is poor, misses the point, is used inappropriately to further spurious arguments often rooted in competition between modalities, and, frankly, can be very boring!

However, when the quality is good, the intentions clear and the rationale and method well argued and well presented, I would suggest that research sits alongside supervision, personal therapy and reflective practice as a means of supporting ethical practice.

My own journey to becoming a practitioner-researcher – i.e., someone who identifies themselves as a practitioner rather than an academic and who has embedded research philosophy, principles and approaches into their day-to-day work – is a case in point. I have told the story in much more detail elsewhere (Reeves, 2010a): here I summarise it as follows. As a new counsellor I was devastated following the death of my client (Isobel) through suicide. Isobel took a large overdose of prescribed medication the evening following a counselling session, abruptly ending our long-term therapeutic relationship. Working in a mental health setting, I was familiar with risk assessment principles and knowledge, but I had not foreseen her death, and therefore had not prevented it (whether or not that was my role).

I worked in a supportive team, received excellent supervision, and was helped to understand my own personal responses through personal therapy. However, I remember clearly a light being switched on when I came across a research article that talked of the experiences of counsellors and psychotherapists following the death of a client through suicide. Nothing previously had spoken more pertinently and eloquently of my experience than the writing in that article and the words of the participants in that research study. In other words, at that moment nothing was more relevant to my practice than research. My argument here isn't that this research paper on its own provided me with everything I needed, because clearly it formed part of a bigger picture. However, I am suggesting that in forming part of a bigger picture – including supervision, personal therapy, self-reflection and so on – the case for research in counselling and psychotherapy was for me made unequivocally.

However, since taking on the role of editor of a counselling and psychotherapy research journal, I have become very aware of the ambivalent relationship that seems to exist between practitioners and research. The perception seems to be that research is something that academics in universities or colleges 'do' because it is part of their job, whereas practitioners 'do' counselling and psychotherapy. It is an inaccurate demarcation that only contributes to false perceptions about the role of research in practice and the place of research findings in our understanding of counselling and psychotherapy.

As someone who supervises counsellor and psychotherapist trainees in the early stages of their research journey I am very aware of common themes: fear, anxiety, a sense of being deskilled, feigned (or actual) boredom, or a sense of being overwhelmed, for example. However, I am also fortunate to experience the 'other' side of these feelings when ideas and thoughts begin to fall into place: excitement, enlightenment, energy and engagement, to name a few. Whether or not the results or findings of the research study match the beginning speculations of the new researcher, the excitement that can emanate from a process of analysis, or insight that can be gained following a research interview, is hard to describe. It is at this point that research becomes alive and speaks an understandable language. Likewise, when accessible and well-written research is published or presented, a dynamic process of critical reflection, questioning, and further inter- and intra-personal exploration is unleashed. The cycle continues, fertilising new ideas and provoking new research questions.

This chapter explores different aspects of the place of research in counselling and psychotherapy. The first section, A Question of Methodology, will provide an overview of key philosophical positions in research and how ways of researching – method – have developed within those paradigms. This will include an exploration of what is meant by the term 'evidence-based practice', before offering a brief overview of some of the key methods counsellors and psychotherapists use when embarking on research for the first time, with links to more in-depth resources to help you explore the intricacies of method in more detail. Next, in Becoming a Researcher and Critically Evaluating Research I will consider how we might embark on our first steps as new researchers, including a consideration of what might help and hinder us in that journey. Here I will consider what is meant by the term 'practice-based evidence' and look at the emergence of practitioner research networks to help facilitate research across groups. Not all counsellors and psychotherapists will want to become active researchers themselves, however, but I will argue in Counsellors and Psychotherapists as Critical Consumers of Research that we all need to be able to locate, read, understand and critically evaluate research. This is increasingly necessary in the light of financial cuts and the need to present evidence in support of the provision of counselling and psycho-therapy, or for particular groups of clients. Finally, in The Next Steps … Disseminating Findings I will consider the various ways in which we can communicate research findings, and the importance of taking that final step. In short, the aim of this chapter is to present a case for counselling and psychotherapy research, and one built on evidence rather than gut-feeling.

DISCUSSION QUESTIONS

1 What are (a) the positive qualities and (b) the negative qualities that you might associate with research? Seek to identify up to six of each.

2 In question (1), which list did you find easiest to compile – the positive or the negative? Why might this be the case?

3 What previous experience of research have you had that influences your current thoughts about it?

4 To what extent do you agree with the proposition that research is as important to practitioners as supervision? Why?

12.2 A QUESTION OF METHODOLOGY

SECTION OUTLINE

In this section we will begin by defining what is meant by research and how research is conducted. The philosophical differences between different ways of approaching research will be considered, as well as how methods have been developed to help ask questions in particular ways. A list of key methods for counsellors and psychotherapists will be highlighted with links to additional resources for further enquiry.

Recently I attended a conference for students of counselling and psychotherapy. During an otherwise fascinating keynote talk, the speaker made the comment, 'but that is about research, which is thoroughly boring and not really relevant to us'. Many of the audience laughed in appreciation, while I was left feeling deeply concerned about the future of counselling and psychotherapy and how these views threaten to undermine the soul of what we do. The wording of my last assertion, 'threaten to undermine the soul of what we do' is, of course, similar to that of the claim typically made by those who take an anti-research position: that is, they argue that the process of evaluation, questioning, challenging and deconstructing will fundamentally undermine the human essence of counselling and psychotherapy as an inter- and intra-personal dynamic.

The irony here is that every modality and therapeutic approach has evolved over time precisely through a process of research. Here I make an assumption of the development of theory: that is, theory develops through the ongoing and systematic process of evaluation, questioning, challenge and deconstruction, and that those theories not subjected to this process fade into obscurity. Thus, people who fear that the process of research will of itself undermine the potency of therapy need only look toward their own theoretical orientation for evidence of the potency of research and its potential beauty in practice. A good example of this is person-centred therapy, which has evolved over many years through enquiry, writing, critique, challenge and development. I would argue the potency of the person-centred approach is that it has not allowed itself to remain stagnant, but rather continues to engage in a process of evolution.

What is research?

McLeod (2003) states that research is 'a systematic process of critical inquiry leading to valid propositions and conclusions that are communicated to interested others' (p. 4). Inherent in McLeod's definition are some key principles that distinguish research from simply asking questions: he talks of 'systematic', 'critical', 'propositions' and 'communicated'. At the most basic level, however, that is what research is intending to do: ask questions. As McLeod points out, in research this is done in a systematic way, by using specific methods of inquiry rooted in a philosophical and theoretical base. Research is a process of critical inquiry – that is, questions are asked to develop knowledge and to explore the assumptions already held; such inquiry leads to valid propositions, i.e., clear statements or conclusions that communicate the outcome of the study; these are, in turn, communicated to others.

Later sections of this chapter discuss in more detail how research is made systematic and critical through the use of methods, procedures and protocols that can all contribute to its validity, i.e., to supporting the claims made. This is an important concept in research: it provides the means for other people to judge the quality and validity of any claims or assertions made. Research can become dangerous if claiming something to be true, when perhaps that is merely the desired outcome of the researcher rather than the outcome of a rigorous research process. This is evident when applied to research by pharmaceutical companies, for example, where the issue of trustworthiness of evidence is essential in assessing the development of treatments for medical conditions. However, trustworthiness is equally essential in the development of counselling and psychotherapy, so that the development of models of practice is based on systematic and critical research findings to help ensure that the potential for harm is minimised. It is unethical to claim something works simply because we like it. In the same way it would be wrong to claim that chocolate bar X is better than Y, simply because X is my favourite. That would be an example of research bias. McLeod's definition communicates clear and useful parameters within which the term 'research' might be understood.

The parallel relationship of process and outcome in research and therapy

Therapy fundamentally is about process and outcome. When a client attends for counselling or psychotherapy they will present with intent – for example, a desire to address difficulties or distress, or to achieve understanding. The process will be facilitated on the part of the therapist by a number of counselling and psychotherapy skills and techniques. This might involve facilitating the client to tell their story, to reflect on the factors that have shaped their experience or created the problems, to think about what factors they might be able to change or decisions they could make, to reflect on what they would like to be different, and finally to work towards the client's goal or intention. We might loosely summarise this process by the following stages:

1   Awareness of problem or difficulty
2   Exploration of problem or difficulty, i.e., clarifying and defining

3   Investigation of other factors, i.e., family history, social circumstances

4   Implementation of specific skills and techniques, dependent on the therapeutic model

5   Review of progress and identification of change

6   The integration of learning and change.

The process itself may be more complex than these stages suggest, and they are not necessarily followed sequentially, but in summary they help to provide an outline of the journey of therapy. If we then consider the process of research, using the same structure as outlined above, we can see how in many ways the two activities follow parallel lines of development. The **stages of research** may be characterised as follows. On the comparion website this list is represented diagrammatically:

1   Awareness of the need for research in an area of inquiry, e.g. perhaps to argue for future funding, or to develop or test certain strategies or interventions

2   Exploration of the area of research, defining more specifically what questions are being asked and what methods might best be employed to find answers

3   Investigation of the wider subject, including searching the literature to discover previous research, allowing the process to be informed by a critical appraisal of it

4   Implementation of research methods and techniques to gather data and information

5   Review of the data through systematic analysis and the identification of results or findings

6   Integration of research knowledge through application into practice, or other dissemination of results or findings.

The point here is that while research and therapy are evidently tasked with a different function to each other, the process through which they are implemented is not so different. I suspect that we are often frightened of the research process, believing it to be alien to what we already know and believe, and to fall far beyond our value systems and structures of knowledge. Yet while the specifics of research might draw on different knowledge (of research methods, for example) the process is more familiar than might be imagined.

Research ethics

All research, whether conducted within a quantitative or qualitative paradigm, must attend to research ethics. This involves ensuring research is ethical and appropriate. Some previous research studies would now be regarded as unethical, even though they yielded useful results. Much has been learned from, for example, early studies on obedience, where participants were asked to give an 'electric shock' to others (they believed they were administering an electric shock, even though no shock was actually delivered) (Milgram, 1974). There is now a general acceptance that studies need to be ethically grounded and that harm should be minimised or avoided, wherever possible.

Many counselling and psychotherapy organisations now provide comprehensive guidance on conducting ethical research. Helpful documents include BACP's *Ethical Guidelines for Researching Counselling and Psychotherapy* (Bond, 2004), the ethical research code issued by the British Psychological Society and the draft ethics check-list of the UKCP (all available from the organisations' websites, which are listed below). Studies conducted within the context of a course based within a university or college, or within certain agencies (such as the NHS) will require approval from an Ethics Committee. Applications are made detailing all aspects of the proposed study and the Ethics Committee scrutinises the application to ensure it is ethical and safe.

Ethical thinking must cover all aspects of a research study, including the recruitment of participants, ensuring that participants are given full information so that they can give informed consent to participate, have the right to withdraw from the study without penalty, and are guaranteed confidentiality, and that appropriate post-research support is offered if required.

> ### WEBSITES
>
> BPS Human Research Ethics: www.bps.org.uk/sites/default/files/documents/code_of_human_research_ethics.pdf
> BACP Ethical Guidelines for Researching in Counselling and Psychotherapy: www.bacp.co.uk/admin/structure/files/pdf/e_g.pdf
> UKCP Research Ethics (Draft, 2011): www.psychotherapy.org.uk/thinking_about_ethics.html

Evidence-based practice

The term evidence-based practice has become commonplace over recent years, moving from the language of commissioning through to the mainstream. Many of you will be familiar with these terms now, particularly if working in centrally funded organisations such as the NHS where the move towards evidence-based treatments has been unceasing. Some therapists perhaps feel that the term 'evidence-based' has become a euphemism for having to justify everything one does, from dotting *i*s to crossing *t*s. In fact, however, the term is itself fairly benign, referring to the need for the acquisition and critical evaluation of evidence to support the development of treatments or approaches. In counselling and psychotherapy terms, evidence-based practice might be applied in different ways, for example: to support a particular way of working; to identify approaches that work for particular problems or difficulties, or what factors in a therapeutic relationship help to promote change for the client.

Sackett et al. (1996, p. 71) define evidence-based practice as 'the conscientious, explicit, and judicious use of current best evidence in making decisions about the care of individual patients'. Bower (2010) notes the potential incompatibility between some of the aspects of this definition and that of counselling and psychotherapy research; more specifically, whether 'current best evidence' (which is often seen as the randomised controlled trial) might sideline other good-quality counselling and psychotherapy research based within a qualitative paradigm. As Bower notes, 'Many practitioners are interested in questions relating to how their treatments work. However, the focus of evidence based practice is on whether treatments work' (2010, p. 1).

The outcome of evidence-based practice in the UK can be seen in treatment guidelines for specific mental health conditions, such as depression, anxiety, trauma, drug and alcohol use, schizophrenia and eating disorders. Treatment providers and referrers, e.g. GPs, psychologists, psychiatrists, will use such guidelines when referring their patients or clients on for specialist treatment. Essentially, if the psychotherapeutic approach isn't in the guidelines, it isn't really going to feature in the choices made by such clinicians. A case in point was the latest guidelines for the treatment of depression (NICE, 2010). Counselling had been removed as a treatment option due to what was claimed to be a lack of reliable evidence to support its inclusion. Only through extensive lobbying and reports citing such evidence made to the Department of Health was it included once again, albeit in a minimal form. While on one level this might not have a direct consequence for an independent counsellor or psychotherapist working with people who have depression, the longer-term consequences of an official exile of counselling as a choice of treatment would be far reaching, including a potential loss of faith in counselling amongst potential clients.

This focus of research on the efficacy of treatments is linked to the prevalence of one particular form of research, namely randomised controlled trials (RCTs) – seen by some as the 'gold standard' of research. They are discussed in more detail below. Many RCTs have examined the efficacy of CBT as a treatment approach and critics have argued that this lies behind CBT's dominance of UK government treatment guidelines. The assertion here isn't that CBT is not efficacious, but rather that the research evidence for CBT seems to shout louder than the rest.

The growth of the evidence-based approach is, of course, not just a UK phenomenon. In the United States the Institute of Medicine's report *Improving the Quality of Health Care for Mental and Substance-Use Conditions* (Board of Healthcare Studies, 2006, p. 180) stated, 'Measuring the quality of care provided by individuals, organisations, and health plans and reporting back the results is linked both conceptually and empirically to reductions in variations in care and increases in delivery of effective care'. Bower (2010) has outlined the advantages and disadvantages of evidence–based practice as shown in Table 12.1.

Probably the biggest criticism of the notion of evidence-based practice, alluded to in the introduction to this section, is that it is perceived to challenge the very nature and being of counselling and psychotherapy. As Bower (2010) points out in relation to medicine, the application of an evidence base does not challenge the very 'being' of medicine because one treatment can easily be changed for another.

TABLE 12.1   Advantages and disadvantages of evidence-based practice

Advantages	Disadvantages
Making use of available research evidence can help shift the profession away from dogma and an unthinking adherence to old ways of 'doing'	RCTs in particular by their nature are better at investigating certain treatments above others, e.g. short-term treatments where long-term options might be difficult to measure
Moving to an evidence-based practice helps shift counselling and psychotherapy into a 'scientist practitioner' context. For some this is seen as an advantage	Moving to an evidence-based practice helps shift counselling and psychotherapy into a 'scientist practitioner' context. For some this is seen as a disadvantage
Working from the principles of evidence-based practice can contribute to the development of new theories and interventions	A potential gap is created between 'evidence' and 'practice', as certain treatments and evidence are privileged over others
Clients may be protected through the identification of potentially harmful treatments or interventions	Reliance on an evidence base can lead to the development of 'brand name' therapies that have been tested. This does not account for the ability of the therapist to deliver the treatment effectively
Counsellors and psychotherapists can be more 'protected' against legal challenges if working within methods with a strong evidence base	
An evidence base can support treatments or interventions that might otherwise be under threat, or poorly funded	Difficult-to-measure scenarios tend not to be included in treatment guidelines, such as working with suicide potential
An evidence base helps develop guidelines of 'inclusion', thus making counselling and psychotherapy provision more transparent	The process of change often requires in-depth analysis of therapy. Methods such as case study approaches have not traditionally been incorporated into developing an evidence base
	RCTs are expensive and time-consuming to produce. Their 'evidence' might not reflect current developments in practice by the time results are published
	Research 'outcomes' are privileged over clinical judgement and 'wisdom' 'No evidence of effectiveness' does not mean 'evidence of no effectiveness'

Source: Developed from Bower, 2010, pp. 3–4

In counselling and psychotherapy, however, practitioners have often invested a great deal of time, energy and finance into developing competence in a particular model of practice, and it is not welcomed if this base is challenged by, what some people believe to be, selective research evidence.

> ### DISCUSSION QUESTIONS
>
> 1 In what ways do you think evidence-based practice influences your work?
> 2 Do you see evidence-based practice as being relevant for counselling and psychotherapy? Why?
> 3 How aware are you about treatment guidelines that either inform your practice setting or your work with particular client groups?
> 4 How could you contribute to the debate about the role of evidence in counselling and psychotherapy?

Research paradigms

McLeod (2003, p. 5) states, 'counselling research is conducted in the context of a massive ongoing philosophical debate about the nature of knowledge'. More specifically, this debate may be summarised as 'quantity versus quality' (Sanders and Wilkins, 2010). Sanders and Wilkins state that, 'newcomers to the world of social sciences research would be forgiven for thinking they had stumbled into an ideological war zone when people start debating the pros and cons of quantitative verses qualitative research methods' (2010, p. 9). At times the discussions do appear very polarised, with one group arguing not only for the benefits of their own preferred approach of research, but also dismissing the validity of others. Mischievously, one might suggest that this is not necessarily unfamiliar territory for counsellors and psychotherapists who, for many decades, have diverted much energy into a 'my approach is better than yours' discourse. Many have argued that counselling and psychotherapy would be much better placed in accepting a shared wisdom and moving towards unity rather than separation: the same is true for research approaches.

Taking Sanders and Wilkins (2010) 'quantity vs quality' position, research is broadly split between two dominant philosophical positions: quantitative methods and qualitative methods. Cooper (2008) states that quantitative research is, 'number-based research, generally incorporating statistical analysis' (p. 186), while qualitative research is, 'language-based research, in which experiences, perceptions, observations etc. are not reduced to numerical form' (p. 186). As was briefly outlined in the section on evidence-based practice, the application of quantitative methods to a particular research enquiry seems to hold greater importance as it is seen as more 'scientific' (measurable, precise and deductive), as opposed to qualitative methods, which are deemed more interpretive, less precise and more based on inductive analysis. In reality, however, different questions will require different approaches to research.

Few would argue with an assertion that there are many research questions best approached using quantitative methods and statistical analysis. For example, the development of CORE-OM (Clinical Outcomes in Routine Evaluation Outcome Measure; Evans et al., 2002), the benchmarking tool designed to measure clinical change before and after counselling and psychotherapy, provides an excellent example of the use of quantitative methods to design and develop a tool of benefit to counselling and psychotherapy provision. I have worked in an agency that has continued to support its counselling provision because of CORE-OM benchmark evidence: we were able to demonstrate efficacious clinical outcomes (i.e., what we were doing had benefit to our clients). While not everyone likes the idea of 'number crunching', it has its indisputable place as a valid approach to research.

Likewise, there are many research questions that are best approached using qualitative research methods. For example, one of my own research projects consisted of investigating counsellors' and psychotherapists' experience of working with suicidal clients. While I could have achieved this through the use of a well-designed questionnaire, analysed using a statistical approach, I was more interested in their accounts and how they conceptualised their experience. For me, their stories in the form of transcript data were more relevant for the questions I was asking (which were about experience and application of knowledge). This approach tends to have greater appeal for many counsellors and psychotherapists because it is more consistent with the work of therapy. That is, using research methods that are akin to counselling and psychotherapy approaches, such as interviewing skills, understanding and interpreting individual accounts of events and extrapolating meaning, for example, will always be philosophically closely aligned to the experience of counselling and psychotherapy practice. It is important, however, not to dismiss other approaches to asking questions simply because they are unfamiliar.

It is therefore helpful to understand key philosophical differences between quantitative and qualitative approaches. Sanders and Wilkins (2010) provide a helpful overview of these differences, as shown in Table 12.2. The table helps to demonstrate how quantitative and qualitative ways of asking questions are informed by different philosophical positions.

There remains a philosophical challenge in bringing the study of human experience into a scientific frame. As McLeod (2003, p. 7) states, 'The very aims of traditional science, centring on the prediction and control of events, are seen as philosophically and politically inappropriate when applied to the study of human action, which can be regarded as intentional and reflexive'.

The main message here, therefore, is that no one approach is better than another; each approach has something particular to offer to each area of inquiry; and indeed there is much to be said for a mixed-methods approach (i.e., using both quantitative and qualitative methods) for different parts of the same study. It is ultimately

TABLE 12.2 Philosophical differences between quantitative and qualitative approaches to research

Quantitative approaches	Qualitative approaches
Structure	Structureless or 'chaos'
Outcome	Process
Objective	Subjective
External frame of reference	Internal frame of reference
Neutral and detached	Involved
Science-centred	Person-centred
Analysis	Synthesis
Taking apart	Putting together
Variables are identified and measured	Complex variables that interact and are difficult to measure
Numbers	Thoughts, feelings, words, patterns
Reduction to simple units	Complexity and pluralism
People as objects	People as persons
Measurable and observable	Experiential
Abstraction of facts	Description of experiences
Deduced from facts	Elaborated from intuition
Technology	Nature
Quantity	Quality

Source: Sanders and Wilkins, 2010, p. 10; reproduced with permission

unhelpful to take a position 'for' or 'against' a method on the grounds of dogma. The researcher in counselling and psychotherapy instead needs to reflect on the questions they are asking, how those questions are best framed, and which approach is philosophically consistent with that process.

PAUSE FOR REFLECTION

Numbers or words – which are you most drawn to and what factors influence your choice?

Quantitative approaches

The philosophical underpinning of quantitative research is that it is objective: it seeks to search for certainties and propose truths that have universal applicability.

There is no room here for subjectivity – that just isn't 'science': indeed research is designed specifically to eliminate it. Instead, this form of research provides the measurement of defined concepts. The challenge for counsellors and psychotherapists, then, is to find a way of measuring terms and concepts that we understand. By attributing numbers to these concepts, we open up the scope of statistical analysis, which in turn, provides an opportunity to explore patterns and trends between variables. For example, while we can ask clients to talk about their anxiety or depression, if we attribute numerical values to a scale of intensity of feelings, such as an anxiety scale, we are then able to explore relationships between anxiety and a whole range of factors, such as age, gender, culture, socioeconomic status.

It is not within the scope of this book to provide a sufficiently clear overview of statistical analysis used to interpret data (and indeed it is beyond the scope of the author to do so): for this, there are some excellent texts cited at the end of this section that I recommend. Additionally, if contemplating developing a research study that draws heavily on quantitative methods, it is advisable to consult a statistician in the early stages to ensure the questions asked provide the best opportunity to reap the answers sought. Clearly a statistician might not be available, or might be too expensive, but if research is located within a college or university setting it is certainly useful to enquire about the possibility.

In published research papers, the statistical calculations are sometimes shown in full. However, if they are lengthy they might be available instead via a download from the journal website or via personal communication with the corresponding author (the author listed in the paper as being available for subsequent correspondence). Many counselling and psychotherapy journals that publish quantitative studies encourage authors to focus in writing their papers less on the detail of the statistical analysis and more on the meaning of the study and its potential implications for practice. Using this strategy journal editors are able to ensure good quality quantitative studies are published and important results disseminated, while at the same time acknowledging that many counsellors and psychotherapists, particularly in the UK, may not have received any training in the implementation or interpretation of statistical data.

FURTHER READING

Joseph, S., Dyer, C. and Coolican, H. (2010) *Statistics in Counselling and Psychotherapy.* BACP Information Sheet R13. Lutterworth: BACP.

Rowntree, D (2000) *Statistics without Tears: An Introduction for Non-Mathematicians.* London: Penguin.

Hand, D.J. (2008) *Statistics: A Very Short Introduction.* Oxford: Oxford University Press.

Roth, A. and Fonagy, P. (2005) *What Works for Whom? A Critical Review of Psychotherapy Research.* New York: The Guildford Press.

Types of quantitative research

The randomised controlled trial (RCT) is 'an experimental study in which participants are randomly assigned to two or more groups, such that the efficacy of the different interventions can be identified' (Cooper, 2008, p. 186). Such studies are often seen as the 'gold standard' of research and they involve large samples (often many thousands of participants). The results of an RCT are generally viewed as providing the safest and most reliable evidence: however, they are very expensive to design and implement. It would be almost impossible for an individual counsellor or psychotherapist to design an RCT due to the sheer scope and cost of such a method. Some key RCTs undertaken in counselling and psychotherapy have contributed to our increased understanding of a number of phenomena. Roth and Fonagy (2005) offer a comprehensive overview of key outcomes in counselling and psychotherapy research – see Further Reading above for details. Increasingly, RCTs are incorporating qualitative components into the research process to investigate in more detail particular aspects of the study.

Qualitative approaches

Qualitative research has developed in reaction to quantitative, positivist inquiry, which it has tended to regard as reductionist or even fundamentally incompatible with the human experience. As Mintz (2010, p. 1) points out: 'Qualitative research therefore has emerged from a range of philosophical positions such as phenomenology and social constructionism that have been in opposition to the positivist movement and have challenged traditional and accepted views of understanding the nature of "truth"'. From a qualitative position, the aim is not to present universal truths, but rather to gain insights into experience, perspective, thoughts, feelings and interaction. Nevertheless, to return to McLeod's

(2003) definition of research, qualitative inquiry is still conducted in a systematic and critical way, and rigour and validity remain central to the authority of any research outcome.

While quantitative studies rely on the analysis and interpretation of numerical patterns, qualitative research draws instead on narrative, stories, words and images. It would be a mistake to think of qualitative analysis as merely a research method: rather it is a philosophical position for research that encompasses a number of linked and separate approaches. There are some excellent texts available for the budding qualitative researcher: see the Further reading and Resources lists at the end of this section. I offer here a brief pen picture of some key qualitative approaches often used in counselling and psychotherapy research:

- Grounded theory (Box 12.1)
- Discourse analysis (Box 12.2)
- Narrative analysis (Box 12.3)
- Heuristic inquiry (Box 12.4)
- Single-case design case studies (Box 12.5).

BOX 12.1   GROUNDED THEORY

Developed by Glaser and Strauss (1967), grounded theory is a method of developing theory, or theory generation, and is based on the development of categories through a process of several rounds of analysis. Data collection and data analysis take place concurrently, in that the analysis of data informs further collection. This is described well by Rennie (2012), who states that, 'initially two or three sets of data drawn from reasonably homogeneous sources are acquired and analyzed resulting in an initial set of categories, which in turn guides the selection of new data, and so on. This concurrent collection and analysis of data continues until, in the researcher's judgment, the meanings of additional data are accounted for by the categories already developed'. At this point saturation is said to have occurred, i.e., new data will not add to the development of new, meaningful categories.

Grounded theory is a popular method amongst counselling and psychotherapy researchers in that it is rigorous, well-developed and historically has been used successfully in counselling and psychotherapy research. It is probably also fair to say that novice researchers are drawn to it because of the clear procedural steps that exist. Not all research that claims to be grounded theory necessarily is that, however: the term is sometimes used to describe a less rigorous approach to category building than would be demanded by following a grounded theory approach.

BOX 12.2   DISCOURSE ANALYSIS

Discourse analysis provides the researcher with an opportunity to explore how discourse – monologue or dialogue – is constructed and the influence that has on the participants. Additionally, it can also explore and consider the wider political dimensions and the role of power in social interaction. There are two primary approaches to discourse analysis: critical discourse analysis, consisting of the interpretation at a micro level of the nature, form and implications of social interactions, and Foucauldian discourse analysis, consisting of the exploration of the micro and macro implications of social interactions, particularly in the context of social construction and power. Again, there have been some interesting examples of discourse analysis. One of my own studies was a critical discourse analysis of how suicide risk assessment took place between therapist and suicidal client. I discovered amongst other things that in these cases 'suicide' was rarely mentioned by suicidal clients – rather it was alluded to or implied in metaphor – and that therapists, in response to suicidal thoughts, used predominantly reflective, rather than exploratory, responses. In the context of the research question this had implications for the assessment of suicide potential (Reeves et al., 2004).

BOX 12.3   NARRATIVE ANALYSIS

Similar to discourse analysis, a narrative analysis makes use of naturally occurring talk, but instead in the form of people's accounts of their lives. This analysis is more concerned with the meaning people attribute to their lives and experiences, how they tell their stories, and how they therefore interpret their world and experience. It can produce some powerful accounts that have contributed profoundly to our understanding of certain experiences or situations.

BOX 12.4   HEURISTIC INQUIRY

Moustakas, one of the founders of heuristic inquiry along with Douglass, wrote that, 'Heuristic investigation involves self-search, self-dialogue and self-discovery. The research question and methodology flow out of inner awareness, meaning and inspiration. It involves a subjective process of reflecting, exploring, sifting and elucidating the nature of the phenomenon under investigation ...' (1990, p. 9). While a heuristic study can be undertaken alone, it can also include co-researchers (rather than participants) who engage in a concurrent process of reflexivity with the main researcher. Moustakas provides a clear six-stage step in conducting a heuristic study, which can be as demanding as it is thorough. As with grounded theory, there is sometimes a temptation to present unstructured thoughts and musings as a heuristic inquiry, which does not do the method justice.

BOX 12.5   SINGLE-CASE DESIGN OR CASE STUDIES

While there is a re-emergence of literature extolling the virtues of case study approaches to counselling and psychotherapy research, this is probably where we started. After all, Freud and the other early analysts drew heavily on case study approaches to research, providing detailed descriptions and interpretations of casework. While the method has developed considerably over the intervening years, the main principle remains intact: that it is possible to learn a great deal about theory and process through the systematic and critical application of case study methods. McLeod (2010b) provides a compelling and engaging account of case study methods. Additionally, McLeod and Elliott (2011, p. 7) argue a strong case for case study approaches when they state, 'Many case studies ... offer detailed accounts of how particular therapists make sense of, and respond to, the needs of specific clients. This kind of learning makes it possible for practitioners to expand their repertoire of what is possible in therapy'. There are a number of other important qualitative approaches, including thematic analysis, interpretative phenomenology and autoethnographic studies.

FURTHER READING

Etherington, K. (2004) *Becoming a Reflexive Researcher: Using Our Selves in Research.* London: Jessica Kingsley.

McLeod, J. (2010) *Case Study Research in Counselling and Psychotherapy.* London: Sage.

Mintz, R. (2011) *Introduction to Conducting Qualitative Research.* BACP Information Sheet R14. Lutterworth: BACP.

Silverman, D. (2009) *Doing Qualitative Research*, 3rd edn. London: Sage.

Willing, C. (2001) *Introducing Qualitative Research in Psychology: Adventures in Theory and Method.* Buckingham: Open University Press.

RESOURCES

Two journals that publish relevant case study material are:
Clinical Case Studies: http://ccs.sagepub.com/
Pragmatic Case Studies in Psychotherapy: http://pcsp.libraries.rutgers.edu/index. php/pcsp

Collecting qualitative data

'Data' can come in a variety of forms. Most commonly associated with qualitative approaches is transcript data, i.e., the data produced from an interview with a research participant that is audio-recorded and then transcribed verbatim, or recordings of therapy sessions for use in a case study design. The process of transcription is an important part of the analytic process, where the researcher can immerse themselves in the quality of the data and begin noting patterns and meanings. Some researchers prefer to hand the process of transcription to a specialist agency or person with those skills (keeping in mind boundaries of confidentiality). My own preference is to undertake transcription myself, even though this is a lengthy process.

Interviews can take a number of forms. They may be: structured (i.e., where participants are asked a number of predetermined questions), semi-structured (where there are some questions to follow but the researcher allows for flexibility in the dialogue), or unstructured (where there is usually a 'starting point', but thereafter the interview follows its own natural course). The choice of interview type will depend on the research question, but often counselling and psychotherapy researchers opt for a semi-structured approach, which helps ensure certain key points are addressed.

However, data does not necessarily have to be transcribed data: other data sources might include reports in newspapers or magazines, films, TV programmes or advertisements.

Reflexivity in qualitative research

Etherington (2004, p. 19) talks of reflexivity as:

> a skill that we develop as counsellors: an ability to notice our responses to the world around us, other people and events, and to use that knowledge to inform our actions, communications and understandings. To be reflexive we need to be aware of our personal responses and to be able to make choices about how to use them. We also need to be aware of the personal, social and cultural contexts in which we live and work and to understand how these impact on the ways we interpret the world.

Taking a reflexive position in qualitative counselling and psychotherapy research helps you to place yourself as a researcher and thus address potential biases and influences that might be at play in your study. It is still important that biases are made transparent and addressed. We need, therefore, to note how the motivations to undertake a research study might have hindered, or indeed facilitated, the process. Increasingly, qualitative research papers will include a section on reflexivity, arguably bringing the paper alive and making it three-dimensional.

DISCUSSION QUESTIONS

1   Which are you more drawn to – qualitative or quantitative approaches? Why?
2   Think of a research question that would interest you: how could (a) qualitative, (b) quantitative or (c) mixed-method approaches help to tackle it?
3   How might your orientation of counselling or psychotherapy influence your choice of research methods?
4   Reflect on the quotation from Etherington concerning reflexivity: how would you describe your own 'personal, social and cultural contexts'? How might they shape your own research journey?

12.3 BECOMING A RESEARCHER AND CRITICALLY EVALUATING RESEARCH

SECTION OUTLINE

The purpose of this section is to explore who currently undertakes research in counselling and psychotherapy and then to consider how to become a practitioner-researcher and why that might be worthwhile. More specifically, it explores how counsellors and psychotherapists can integrate research thinking into their practice, undertake a research project, and what they would need to consider when undertaking a research project.

Who are the researchers?

There are various types of researchers. Some are academics based in education settings that undertake research as an integral part of their job. Some of these academics also maintain a private practice as counsellors or psychotherapists, or perhaps have a 'research clinic' offering free or reduced-fee counselling and psychotherapy for clients willing to participate in a research process. Some are experienced practitioners who, through the demands of evidencing their work to seek funding, undertake research, while others are motivated to research aspects of their practice simply out of interest and curiosity. Others again have decided to undertake further academic training at masters or doctoral level where conducting some research is a course requirement. Indeed, latterly there has been a move to introduce research training as a core part of counselling and psychotherapy training. This profile of researchers demonstrates the variety of motivations behind undertaking a research study, but also perhaps signals a sea change in the profile of the profession.

Research evidence has been informing counselling and psychotherapy for many decades. However, during my own training as a counsellor in the 1980s research did not feature on my course in any explicit way. Though we certainly made extensive use of theories and ideas, they were never presented as being informed by research outcome. We weren't encouraged to read research, still less to critically reflect on what research might be saying, and we were certainly never asked to undertake any form of research activity. For us, research was a separate, unrelated activity and, as the conference keynote speaker above so eloquently put it, research was thought of as 'thoroughly boring and not really relevant to us'. My own transition to becoming a research-practitioner was therefore a welcome surprise, as if I had wandered late into a party that, without my knowing it, had been going on for quite some time.

There is no doubt that counsellors and psychotherapists need to find their way of engaging with research, either as practitioner-researchers, or as critical consumers of research. Counsellors and psychotherapists have an important role in this respect, in manoeuvring themselves into a critically evaluative position with respect to research, articulating strengths and weaknesses in respective arguments, while also undertaking and disseminating good quality research to further enhance our understanding of counselling and psychotherapy provision. Clients can then access an evidence base from which to make informed decisions about how they would like to be helped.

```
PAUSE FOR REFLECTION

1  Reflect on your counsellor or psychotherapist training: to what extent was
   research embedded within your curriculum?
2  How much do you know about how your theoretical orientation has been
   influenced by research?
3  How can practice and research (a) support or (b) impair each other?
4  To what extent do you see yourself as a practitioner-researcher? What accounts
   for your answer?
```

Fears, anxieties and myths

Many counsellor and psychotherapist training programmes, at all educational levels, are beginning to introduce research into the curriculum. In some instances this is a requirement to locate and critically evaluate research papers pertinent to a particular question or area of practice. In other instances, it is a requirement to undertake a research methods module and produce a research proposal – i.e., a structured document that outlines a research question and a proposed approach of investigation, while also considering ethical and logistical aspects of implementing the plan.

Some courses also require their students to undertake a small-scale research project, following the successful submission of a research proposal, as part of a counsellor or psychotherapy qualifying route. This is an important opportunity for trainee counsellors and psychotherapists to dip their toes into the research waters, under supervision, and practise research theory and skills in action. It is also an opportunity for trainees to explore in much more detail a particular aspect of practice that interests them, from a critically evaluative position.

A training programme provides an ideal structure within which the trainee can make their first foray into research. For qualified counsellors and psychotherapists, the thought of beginning a research journey without such guidance can be much more daunting. This is particularly true when the future of a service is dependent on the ability to demonstrate efficacy. For trainee and qualified counsellors or psychotherapist alike, the first important step when beginning research concerns perspective rather than practicality. By this I mean reflecting on our own preconceptions, fears, anxieties and prejudices about research and, with a colleague or friend, challenging them. Attitudinal hurdles we might need to address include the following:

- 'Research has nothing to do with the practice of counselling or psychotherapy'
- 'Research only takes place in colleges and universities and is undertaken by academics'
- 'Research is something that happens in a laboratory under special conditions'
- 'I have no research skills applicable for what I want to do'
- 'I am not clever/skilled/competent (and so on) enough to undertake a research project'
- 'Research is something that usually takes several years'
- 'Research is always expensive and I can't afford to do it'
- 'Research is about analysing numbers, and I don't "do" numbers'
- 'I could never get a piece of research published'
- 'No one would be interested in what my research might say'
- 'Research is always a BIG activity, i.e., involving lots of people'.

Each of these statements is discussed briefly in turn below.

Research has nothing to do with the practice of counselling or psychotherapy

I hope this chapter has told a different story – that research has everything to do with counselling and psychotherapy. Research informs every aspect of counselling and psychotherapy practice and has the potential to continue to push barriers and challenge inhibiting assumptions. Likewise, the skills of counselling and psychotherapy have a great deal to offer the research process.

Research only takes place in colleges and universities and is undertaken by academics

Research does take place in colleges and universities and is undertaken by academics. The above statement is true, once the word 'only' is removed. It is fair to say that academic researchers have made a considerable contribution to our understanding of counselling and psychotherapy process and outcome. However, it is not an exclusive club. There are a number of journals keen to receive submissions from new researchers, keen to encourage the developing field. There is a great deal of counselling and psychotherapy research, particularly in the UK, undertaken by individual trainees or therapists, self-funded and small-scale.

Research is something that happens in a laboratory under special conditions

As for this statement, a proportion of research does take place in a laboratory under special conditions. This occurs where there is a necessity to manage circumstances so that variables, i.e., other aspects that might influence or change the results, are carefully managed. The overwhelming majority of counselling and psychotherapy research takes place in the counselling and psychotherapy relationship, which is rarely located in a laboratory!

I have no research skills applicable for what I want to do

As a counsellor or psychotherapist you already possess skills pertinent to research. You are familiar with investigation, asking questions, you are likely to be curious, you are committed to ethical practice and not causing harm, and with certain research methods, e.g. interviewing, you have many skills that facilitate narrative and discourse. What you may not have is an understanding of specific research methods or access to readily available research supervision. As stated previously, there are some excellent texts to support the novice researcher, and those already enrolled in a specific programme of study have a number of additional resources at their disposal.

I am not clever/skilled/competent (and so on) enough to undertake a research project

While good quality research does require a level of competence in approach, it is not an activity exclusively for only certain 'types' of people. There is no prerequisite for being 'clever' (whatever that might mean), but rather a need for commitment to integrity, honesty, transparency and a determination to see it through.

Research is something that usually takes several years

Some research takes many years, most notably longitudinal studies (where the focus of the study requires attention over a long period of time, e.g. studies in child/adolescent/adult development). Some studies take several months, while others might last a few weeks. The duration depends on the requirement of the research method that, in turn, is dependent on the question(s) being asked.

Research is always expensive and I can't afford to do it

Many counsellors and psychotherapists who are involved in independent research, i.e., not funded by an external body, are self-funding. Where research is related to a particular programme of study, e.g. at doctoral level, there is no doubt it can be an expensive process. However, there are increasing opportunities for you to become involved in research, discussed later in this chapter.

Research is about analysing numbers, and I don't 'do' numbers

As was discussed in the earlier section, research is about many things – numbers, words, stories, people, experiences and so on. Quantitative approaches to data analysis have perhaps dominated the research world and, as such, are naturally associated with research. However, the development of qualitative methods, drawing much more on textual sources, opens the door to other choices.

I could never get a piece of research published

As will be discussed later, publishing research is only one research 'outcome' – there are many other valid ways of disseminating your findings and ideas to the right audience. The important point is to ensure that dissemination does take place, in whatever form, so that good quality research does not disappear, never to be seen by the wider world. Publishing research remains, of course, a highly relevant way of telling your professional peers about your work.

No one would be interested in what my research might say

It would perhaps be fairer to say that not everyone will be interested in what your research has to say – but many people will. As soon as you move your work out of your private world into the public domain there is inevitably an aspect of exposure to narcissistic injury! This applies to any 'public' activity where your work comes under scrutiny, whether that be showing an exhibition of art, public speaking or singing, writing research for publication, or writing a book. Some will like it, some won't. It certainly can be tough to nurture your research project over a period of time and give birth to the final results, only for someone to say that your baby is ugly. However, it is my experience that the net outcome is likely to be gain, with further insight and ideas emanating from your work, and your research benefiting from the wider perspective.

Research is always a BIG activity, i.e., involving lots of people

A quantitative study (say, an RCT) might indeed involve many thousands of people, with a large research team involved in the process. However, at the other end of the continuum some excellent studies have emerged from single-case design, or a case study. McLeod (2010b) provides an excellent description of the effective use of case-study methodology in research. The point is that much excellent and engaging research in counselling and psychotherapy is undertaken by a single researcher, perhaps with the support of a research supervisor, with a handful of willing participants.

The relationship between research and practice

While research can be an important academic endeavour in its own right, the key question for many counsellors and psychotherapists is its position in relation to practice. Perhaps because for many years research has been separated from practice during early training experiences, it is often assumed that research can make no contribution to practice. Conversely, as research training and awareness becomes more embedded within core training, a new cohort of counsellors and psychotherapists will simply know that practice and research go hand in hand, rather than having to be persuaded this is the case. Cooper (2008, p. 1) makes this point eloquently when he writes that 'research findings can be like good friends: something that can encourage, advise, stimulate and help us, but also something that we are not afraid to challenge and argue against'.

Practice-based evidence

We discussed earlier the term evidence-based practice and its implications for the development of counselling and psychotherapy. However, there has been a philosophical shift in counselling and psychotherapy research, partly motivated by an evidence-based practice agenda, to complement the evidence-base with evidence that is derived from practice settings. There has been recognition of the perceived deficit between evidence-based research and its relevance for practice given its 'top-down' approach to practice (Barkham and Mellor-Clark, 2003). The practice-based evidence paradigm therefore describes the evaluation of data as it is routinely collected in usual practice settings – a 'bottom-up' approach to the development of evidence. As this routinely collected data accumulates and is analysed, evidence is developed. This evidence is then said to have emerged from routine practice first, as opposed to practice being shaped by evidence in the first instance. Thus, practice is based on evidence generated from within practice, as opposed to externally generated evidence shaping practice. In truth there is probably a cyclical relationship between evidence-based practice and practice-based evidence: where practice-based evidence informs RCTs and other research studies, thus generating an evidence-base for practice, which, in turn, is located back in practice to generate evidence, and so on. If evidence-based practice informs the development of practice, practice can, in turn, inform the development of evidence.

An advantage of the evidence-based practice model is that there is an excellent body of research available to help inform thinking about counselling and psychotherapy. If read with a critical eye, such research is invaluable in throwing different perspectives on a range of counselling and psychotherapy scenarios. Likewise, the move toward practice-based evidence provides the practitioner with opportunities to engage with a research process, rooted in their own day-to-day practice. For example, the use of outcome measures can form an important adjunct to the process of review in counselling and psychotherapy (Whipple and Lambert, 2010).

Practice research networks

Practice-based evidence can be generated at a service level where data is routinely collected on clients. When this is undertaken, large data sets (collections of information that can later be systematically analysed) can be collected and used. If you are on placement or work in an organisation that makes use of routine outcome measures, such as CORE-OM for example, you are probably already making your contribution to a research process. The study by Barkham et al. (2012) is a good example of practice-based evidence.

However, many counsellors and psychotherapists wish to contribute to the development of evidence through research but, in virtue of not working in services where data is routinely collected for example, are unable to easily do so. Clearly many counsellors and psychotherapists will first experience a process of research through their training, or by studying for degrees where there is a research component. The last few years has seen the emergence of practice research networks (PRNs) as a means of developing practice-based evidence. Castonguay et al. (2010, p. 328) define PRNs as 'an active collaboration between researchers and clinicians in the development of clinically relevant studies that are at the same time scientifically rigorous'. They provide a coherent structure within which groups of therapists can come together to research common questions or interests, collecting data in a rigorous and systematic way, presenting critically evaluative findings and, therefore, making an important contribution to the development of practice-based evidence.

One example of an active and successful PRN in the UK is SuPReNet, a PRN looking at supervision. The aims of SuPReNet are:

1   To identify and prioritise important and topical research questions for counselling and psychotherapy supervision in the UK
2   To design and develop research protocols to take key aspects of the research agenda forward
3   To identify relevant funding bodies and submit research funding applications to them
4   To write funding proposals for the above research protocol and identify/engage academics to take them forward
5   To develop a sustainable expert research network.

In conjunction with these aims, the overarching hope of SuPReNet is that it will 'help secure the future of supervision research in the UK' (SuPReNet, 2012). Another example of an active PRN is the newly established network looking at counselling in schools: SCoPReNet (Schools-based Counselling Practice Research Network). Such networks can provide an excellent structure for counsellors and psychotherapists to participate in research and develop competence through working with others.

WEBSITES

SCoPReNet: www.bacp.co.uk/schools/
SuPReNet: www.bacp.co.uk/research/networks/SuPReNet.php

Key things to know in doing research

If you are about to undertake some research there are a number of key areas for you to consider:

- Think about what it is you wish to know or explore further – develop and refine your research question (in discussion with colleagues, peers, tutors and a research supervisor)
- Are you keeping a research journal (so that you can trace your own thinking and responses as the research journey unfolds: this is particularly relevant when undertaking qualitative research where research reflexivity is important)
- Find out if others have already researched your area of interest, and if they have, what they have found (by searching the available literature using academic search engines, such as PsychINFO and Web of Science, as well as other sources, such as Google Scholar, reference lists in key texts, Internet)
- Consider how you intend to ask your question(s) (read texts on methodology, considering whether qualitative or quantitative methods best suit your question)
- Consider ethics (what are the ethical implications for your study, e.g. if interviewing participants how will you ensure they give informed consent to be involved, how can they withdraw, how you protect their anonymity etc. Also, if you need to obtain ethics consent from an organisation [such as the NHS or a university/college], make sure that is successfully completed before you begin to collect data)
- Think about how you will collect data (questionnaires, interviews, tools and measures, other written information, such as newspaper reports etc. Do you need to 'pilot' your data collection methods before you use them, i.e., try them out first and refine them accordingly?

- Have you prepared suitable information for participants to fully and clearly explain the purpose and scope of your study (so that they can decide whether or not they wish to be involved)
- Are you clear about how you will analyse your data, ensuring you do this systematically and critically (keeping a clear 'audit trail' of how you developed your results/findings)
- Have you critically reflected on your results/findings in the light of existing literature (does your study say something new, or is it contradicting or affirming previous research?)
- Presenting your study (how will you disseminate your findings: in written form, as a poster or conference presentation, an academic article, an article for a professional magazine, a training DVD or web resource)
- Have you, at all times, consulted with your research supervisor, or another person you have identified to support and guide you through the process of research (this step needs to be embedded throughout your research process).

12.4 COUNSELLORS AND PSYCHOTHERAPISTS AS CRITICAL CONSUMERS OF RESEARCH

SECTION OUTLINE

Not all counsellors or psychotherapists will consider taking on a research project, or becoming involved in research at all. However, increasingly we are required to read research papers and understand their relevance for our work. This section considers the particular skills required in critically consuming research.

Not all counsellors or psychotherapists will undertake research. However, along with allied professions, such as social work, nursing, and psychology, there is an increasing requirement for practitioners to be able to locate, access and critically evaluate research. So many policy and funding decisions are based on research outcomes that the ability to bring a critical perspective to such documents can be immensely useful. Other professional groups have been exposed to critically reviewing research papers from their core training onwards for many years. Latterly, perhaps as a consequence of the potential for statutory regulation and development of core competences for counselling and psychotherapy, counsellors and psychotherapists are also being provided with opportunities to develop similar skills.

Table 12.3 provides some good pointers for critically evaluating a research study, according to whether a quantitative or qualitative approach is used. Like most things judging what is, and is not, good quality and relevant research comes with practice.

TABLE 12.3   A guide to critically evaluating a research paper

What is the purpose of the study? Does the purpose of the study relate to an important problem?

Qualitative	Quantitative
• Is the purpose translated into a clearly worded research question appropriate for a qualitative study? • Does the research question offer insight into and ask questions about social, emotional and experiential phenomena to determine the meaning of 'X' or about the attitudes, beliefs or behaviour of a group or individuals? • Is the purpose inductive from the experience? • How was theory considered?	• Is the purpose translated into a clearly worded hypothesis or (guiding) research question(s) appropriate for a quantitative study? • Does it describe or imply a relationship among phenomenon using systematic, objective and empirical methods? • Is the purpose deducted from an adequate review of the literature? • Is a theoretical perspective identified? • What problem or gap in our knowledge is being addressed by this research study? Has the problem been clearly stated in the article? • Is the problem important? Why? To Whom?

How was the purpose investigated? Was the question studied in a credible and rigorous manner?

Qualitative	Quantitative

• Was the sampling strategy appropriate to address the research question[s]?
   ○ Purposeful selection?
   ○ Flexibility in sampling process?
   ○ Ethics procedure?
   ○ Saturation of data?
 • Was the paradigm/research strategy (ethnography, phenomenology, grounded theory, PAR, other] appropriate for the research question?
 • Were the data collected in a way that addresses the research question(s]?
   ○ Is there a clear and complete description of site participants?
   ○ Is there a clear description of methods used (observation, interviews, focus groups, other]
   ○ Are the role of the researcher and relationship with participants clearly described?
   ○ Are the assumptions and biases of researcher identified?
   ○ Is the data representative of the 'whole' picture?
	• Was the sampling strategy appropriate to address the hypothesis or research question[s]?
	   ○ Informed consent obtained?
	   ○ Inclusion and exclusion criteria identified?
	   ○ Bias minimized?
	   ○ Sample size and power?
	 • Was the research design appropriate for addressing the hypothesis or research questions?
	   ○ Type of design?
	   ○ Subject assignment to groups?
	   ○ Randomization used?
	   ○ Control group used?
	   ○ Independent variable(s) identified?
	   ○ Dependent variable(s) identified?
	   ○ Variables operationally defined?
	 • Were data collection procedures designed to limit bias and address the stated hypothesis or research questions?
	   ○ Instrumentation used identified?
	   ○ Instrumentation described in detail for replication
	   ○ Instrument validity and reliability documented?
	   ○ Type of data collected identified (nominal, ordinal, ratio or interval)?
	   ○ Dependent variables are appropriate outcome
	   ○ Measures
	   ○ Internal and external validity

- Was the data analysis sufficiently rigorous
  - ○ Is it clear how the categories/ themes derived from the data?
  - ○ Were decision trails developed and rules reported?
  - ○ Have steps been taken to test the credibility of the findings (triangulation, member checking)?
  - ○ Are you confident that all data were taken into account? Can you follow what the authors did?

- Was the data analysis appropriate for the study design, question and type of data?
  - ○ Statistical tests identified?
  - ○ Alpha level identified?
  - ○ Sufficient rigour?
- Do the results and findings relate the data to the purpose of the study and its hypothesis or research question?
  - ○ Do results match methods?
  - ○ Are findings statistically significant
  - ○ Are tables and figures appropriate and clear?
  - ○ Hypothesis accepted or rejected?
  - ○ Are alternative explanations provided?
  - ○ Are results clinically important?
  - ○ Are limitations discussed?

What are the findings and conclusions? Do the findings and conclusions relate the data to the purpose?

Qualitative	**Quantitative**
<ul><li>Is there a clear statement of the findings?</li><li>Is there a sense of personally experiencing the event or phenomenon being studied?</li><li>What were the main limitations of the study?</li><li>Were the conclusions appropriate given the study findings?</li><li>Do the findings contribute to theory development and future practice/ research?</li></ul>	<ul><li>Were the conclusions appropriate given the study findings?<ul><li>○ Were conclusions based on results?</li><li>○ Do the findings contribute to theory development and future practice/research?</li><li>○ Are there recommendations for additional study?</li></ul></li></ul>

Are the findings of this study applicable to my practice?

Qualitative	**Quantitative**
<ul><li>Does this study help me to understand the context of my practice?</li><li>Does this study help me understand my relationships with my clients and their families, community, or health care system?</li><li>Are the findings transferable to my practice?</li></ul>	<ul><li>Are the findings applicable to my patient/client?</li><li>Are the findings generalizable to the population?</li></ul>

Source: University of Southern California, 2012; reproduced with permission. © 2001, J.L. Forrest and National Center for Dental Hygiene Research Advisory Board

The pointers in Table 12.3 provide a structure within which to think carefully about research. However, a quick checklist to consider might include:

- Does the research provide a clear context and rationale for the study?
- Is there a review of existing literature and are you, as a reader, left with a good sense of what the existing literature does and doesn't say?
- Does the research clearly outline the research question?
- Does the research clearly indicate how the study was undertaken, including how data was collected, how participants were recruited (if participants were involved), what constituted 'data', how it was analysed?
- Are ethical considerations clearly described? Was ethics approval obtained (if not, why not)?
- For qualitative papers, is there evidence of reflexivity in the writing?
- Are the results clearly presented with evidence for how they were reached?
- Does the discussion critically reflect on the results in the context of what the existing literature had to say?
- Are limitations clearly outlined?
- Are implications for practice (if any) clearly outlined?
- Finally, if you reflect on the study taken as a whole, does is answer the 'so what' test (i.e., did you learn anything new)?

12.5 DISSEMINATING RESEARCH FINDINGS

SECTION OUTLINE

Having completed a research study it is important to consider how to disseminate the results. Many completed studies are never published: this denies the profession the opportunity to learn from outcomes, to challenge, discuss, replicate and develop further understanding. This section considers the importance of disseminating research findings.

Research outcomes

Research 'outcomes' come in all shapes and sizes. The stereotype of research outcome is of a dry and inaccessible research paper, full of heavy number-based equations and formulae, published in an obscure journal, housed in a dusty library, that no one reads; this picture is not entirely a myth. Research is sometimes undertaken simply for its own existence and the affirmation of the existence of the researcher. Of course, differentiating between this sort of 'outcome' and that which has the potential to inform and shape what we do in a positive way requires some critical awareness on behalf of the consumer – as I have outlined above.

Research outcomes that have the potential to shape the work of counsellors and psychotherapists can come packaged in a variety of ways. Box 12.6 provides examples, divided across three primary routes of dissemination: written, verbal and training/online.

BOX 12.6   A RANGE OF RESEARCH OUTCOMES: FORMS OF DISSEMINATION

- A dissertation or thesis prepared and presented for a course of study, e.g. undergraduate or postgraduate study
- A research paper published in a research journal
- A practice paper published in a practice journal
- A 'poster', i.e., a short summary of research findings or of research in progress, presented at a conference
- Research-based texts, i.e., texts about research
- Practice-based texts, i.e., theory texts about practice such as person-centred, psychodynamic, CBT etc.
- Verbal forms of dissemination
- A presentation of a research paper given at a conference (whether that be a research or practice-based conference)
- A keynote talk at a conference
- A short training workshop, e.g. of only a few days or single day duration
- Online forms of dissemination
- A training manual or training tools
- DVD, online or web-based or video training resources
- Symposiums or seminars.

Written forms of dissemination

Written forms of disseminating research are probably the ones most commonly considered and, if you are undertaking research for the purposes of a training programme or degree, the most likely way in which you will present your work. Undergraduate and Masters programmes usually require the submission of a dissertation (ranging from between 10,000 to 25,000 words typically), whereas a doctoral level programme will require the submission of a thesis (of anywhere between 50,000 to

80,000 words typically). This may vary depending on whether the doctoral level course is a traditional PhD, a professional doctorate or a taught doctorate, for example. Some programmes now require students to submit a paper ready for submission for publication as part of their requirement, as opposed to a traditional dissertation.

In the academic field in the UK and internationally the research paper, which is submitted to an academic journal, peer-reviewed (assessed for quality by another academic or practitioner, usually anonymously) prior to publication, is the most common means of disseminating academic research. There are a number of different journals related to counselling, psychotherapy and psychology that carry such papers. All journals will provide instructions for authors and some will provide accessible guidance for those new to writing. *Counselling and Psychotherapy Research*, BACP's international research journal, offers some additional, accessible guidance for those new to writing, written by Cooper (2012).

However, academic articles do not represent the only means through which research can be made available. Many conferences host 'posters', where researchers are invited to summarise research in the form of a large poster. Such posters can present finished research, but are also a good means of presenting research 'in progress'. Finally, most textbooks, whether about research specifically, or more general books about counselling and psychotherapy, will draw heavily on research. This book, as you will have noticed, has made many references to research and, as such, presents research 'in action'.

Buckroyd and Rother (2008, p.1) highlight some useful considerations when preparing a research paper for publication. Their guidance runs as follows:

- Ensure the paper is structured appropriately, according to academic and journal conventions. A typical structure of a research paper will be:

  o Title
  o Abstract
  o Key words
  o Introduction
  o Method
  o Results/Findings
  o Discussion
  o Conclusion
  o Acknowledgements
  o References
  o Author details

- Check for any specific requirements the journal might have regarding style of writing, structure or the presentation of references.
- Take time to find the right journal. Consider who the research was conducted for (e.g. other researchers or practitioners?) and whether the results are of interest to a specific audience.

- Consider whether the journal publishes papers based on the kind of methodology employed in the study.
- Consider whether the target readership is a national or international one.
- If required, consider whether the journal has an 'impact factor' (i.e., is it measured by the Social Science Citations Index for the number of times published articles have been cited elsewhere). Generally the higher the figure, the better the journal. It is worth noting, however, that many counselling and psychotherapy journals either don't have an impact factor at all or achieve only a low score. This is because counselling and psychotherapy research is still an emerging discipline – this limits the number of citations that papers in this discipline are likely to achieve.
- Ensure that papers meet word limits specified by the journal. Over-length papers are likely to be rejected.

Many journals make use of what is called a 'peer-review process'. Once a paper has been submitted to a journal and passed initial screening by the editor, an anonymised version will be sent out to one to three peer reviewers who will usually have expertise in the subject area or methodology used. Their feedback will inform the editor's decision, and will be given back to the authors, again in an anonymised form. While it is difficult to read critical reviews of your paper, often the comments made can be extremely useful in developing the paper specifically or your writing style more generally. Therefore, even if ultimately a paper is rejected, much can be gained from the process.

Verbal forms of dissemination

Not all research is presented in the written form. Attend any research conference and you will have opportunity to listen to a presentation of a study by the researchers themselves. This can make research really come alive as you have an opportunity not only to hear the enthusiasm and interest that motivated the researchers in the first instance, but also to ask questions and clarify particular points. A verbal presentation might accompany a paper of the research that has already been published, or is about to be published, but not necessarily.

Research can also be presented in an applied way through continuing professional development training workshops. In the world of counselling and psychotherapy there are many workshops advertised in magazines such as *Therapy Today* and online that are based within research. I have attended many over the years, including working with self-harm, addictions, brief therapy, mindfulness etc., all of which have drawn on research findings to inform content and delivery. My own teaching looking at work with suicidal clients is based on my own and others' research findings. This can be an informative and enjoyable way to find out more about research and really make the link between theory, research and practice.

Online forms of dissemination

Finally, an integration of written and verbal means of disseminating research can be achieved through online delivery in a multi-media experience. It is possible to provide articles with hyperlinks to other sites and articles, videos, audio-clips and interactive mechanisms of delivery. Additionally, many publishers are now developing apps for smartphones that deliver research findings, as well as social networks, including Facebook and Twitter. It is entirely possible that, in the not too distant future, the traditional printed journal will be replaced with online-only alternatives to deliver research content and training.

It is important to note that the three primary forms of dissemination of research are not mutually exclusive, in that there isn't one 'right' way to follow and, once followed, the others are no longer valid. In fact, it is better to find as many ways as possible to disseminate research findings, as that will ensure the widest audience is reached.

DISCUSSION QUESTIONS

1 Which areas of practice most interest you? What do you consider to be important research questions in that area?
2 How could you locate relevant research to help inform your thinking as a practitioner?
3 Select a research paper and work through the questions in Table 12.3. How do they help you engage with the research at a deeper level?
4 What are your next steps regarding research (for example, reading more research, participating in another person's research study, or developing your own ideas for research)? How will you implement your next steps?

13

Endings and the Next Steps

13.1 INTRODUCTION

CHAPTER OVERVIEW

This chapter revisits key aspects of working as a counsellor or psychotherapist, as explored through the previous pages. Rather than provide new information, the aim of this chapter is to provide a succinct overview of the work as seen from the counsellor or psychotherapist's own point of view. The chapter focuses on and reviews the key decision points, milestones and challenges arising from a career in this field.

To provide an overview of the work of a counsellor or psychotherapist, it is helpful to reflect on my own day-to-day work. My work regularly involves activities from various stages of the counselling cycle. For example, I assess written registration forms, make appointments for new clients, undertake initial interviews with those clients, identify (in collaboration with clients) the tasks and focus of counselling, commence counselling, work towards an ending (wherever possible), complete the final session with each client, and say goodbye (completing any outcome measure that may be required of me), and respond to all the unexpected things that inevitably and expectedly happen every day.

This work requires a number of supporting activities. For example, I send out emails with appointment times, respond to cancellations and DNAs, make appropriate notes of my work with clients in line with my organisation's policy, obtain consent as needed to speak with a third party about our counselling, attend supervision, ensure my insurance and accreditation are up to date, and attend and contribute to regular professional meetings. Furthermore, I continue my professional development through attendance at conferences, meetings and seminars, and sit on various committees. In particular, I monitor my competence and capacity to work with clients, take opportunities for self-reflection and self-care, and contribute to my profession in a variety of ways (such as writing, attending conferences, speaking to different audiences, and delivering training).

Such activities typify my work as a counsellor. As when learning to drive, in my early days of practice I would consciously consider each activity in detail, consult and be deliberate, and then act. As time has passed, much of this work has been integrated into a professional 'way of being': I now undertake many of these tasks without any discrete thought. Supervision helps to ensure that I remain on the right track, as does continuing professional development and regular contact with my peers. However, like driving, I turn the steering wheel and indicate my intentions with a familiarity and competence that hopefully makes me (as it were) a safe driver. There are even those occasions when I arrive at my destination without any clear recall of how I got there: these always act as flags to indicate that I need to reconnect and consider my actions more carefully. The same is true of counselling: those times when I might lose concentration or respond without sufficient thought indicate a need for more care or reflection.

My intention in writing this book has been to provide an overview drawing on my own experience as a practitioner and on others' writing and research. When I began the task, I wondered whether I would have enough to write to meet the nearly 200,000 words my publisher expected from me. However, as soon as I began drafting out the plan for this book I was struck, as I began to dismantle the work of a therapist into the constituent parts, just how much there was to it. The reality has been that the 200,000 words disappeared quickly – and there was so much else that could have been explored. It would, after all, be possible to take any one, single aspect of this book – one small section – and out of it another book in its own right could emerge. It is the juxtaposition of complexity and simplicity that seems to make counselling and psychotherapy what they are: a human relationship rooted within a particular way of being and informed by particular ideas and philosophy. This is true regardless of theoretical orientation, working context, political agenda or philosophical imperative, for essentially counselling and psychotherapy are about one person helping another. Yet the subtlety of human interaction, the application of theory and skills to it, and understanding how that interaction is informed by so many factors beyond it, can at times appear beyond understanding. As we move towards the ending, then, let me summarise some of the key areas covered.

13.2 DECIDING TO BE A COUNSELLOR OR PSYCHOTHERAPIST

Every journey begins with the first step. Motivations for becoming a counsellor or psychotherapist can be many and varied, from simply adding a skill set and knowledge to existing professional training, through to making a complete change in career path, or emerging from one's own distress and difficulty perhaps successfully supported by therapy. There is no 'right' or 'wrong' motivation, no one better than another: the important point is to think about what one's motivation is and how it might help and hinder personal and professional development. By this I mean how our motivation will energise us through the good times, and support us to continue through the more challenging ones. For example, we might have had a positive experience of personal therapy ourselves, but in beginning training are we looking for new professional skills, or instead seeking more personal therapy?

Having decided to embark on training, we need to consider a number of important factors. It is tempting to bypass this stage, but we do so at great risk. It is essential that we carefully reflect on a number of key issues when 'signing on the dotted line'. For example: do we have the time available to commit to training (and personal therapy ... and supervision ... and a placement ... and the writing of assignments ... and attending the course ... and attending residential weekends ... and so on)? Do we have (or can we secure) the financial resources required to pay the course fees (and the personal therapy ... and supervision ... and professional indemnity insurance ... and the fees of professional organisations ... and books ... and so on)? Have we thought about the personal change that we may well encounter, beyond the development of new skills and knowledge? Such change has the potential to affect not only ourselves, but also those around us.

If the answer to these questions is 'yes', we are well placed to begin counselling and psychotherapy training and might rightly be excited about the prospect. But we should take an opportunity, as early as is possible, to consider what sort of practitioner we might want to become. A counsellor? Or a psychotherapist? Here it is important to grasp the debates about the differences and similarities between these two professional titles. In dipping into this debate you are likely to experience more heat than light, but at least you will gain sufficient familiarity with the issues to make more informed choices. Then you can consider whether there is a particular client group you want to work with: this will have informed your choice of course (for example, if you wish to focus on work with children and young people, find a course that equips you for that). If you want to work in a particular working context (e.g. the health service or education), read around to see what types of qualifications are required. Finally, consider who you are and how you see the world. This will help throw important light on what motivated you to embark on the particular type of training you have done. You won't necessarily have answers to all these questions, but asking yourself these questions will itself prove of value. Once this stage has been negotiated, and course selected, then you are really ready to begin.

PAUSE FOR REFLECTION

1   What were your expectations when beginning training?
2   How many of these have been met and what could you do to meet any that are remaining?

13.3 THE TRAINING JOURNEY

While the particular nature of the course will shape your experience, there are some features common to all counselling and psychotherapy training. There will be a tutor team whose job will be not only to teach theory and ideas, but also to facilitate your learning as an adult learner so that you can take responsibility for your own personal and professional development. They will be there to guide and support you, but also challenge you, through your own particular version of the process. They will also very likely have an assessment role: they won't be your friends, but will be an integral part of your process in developing competence and awareness as a therapist.

You will almost certainly learn as part of a training group, in addition to your own self-directed learning. This group will play an important role in your training experience: it will not only provide you with an opportunity to discuss new theory, debate different ideas and practise and develop skills, but also become your anchorage point at times of uncertainty and your benchmark when you need clarity. Whether you make friends for life with members of this group will depend on you and them, but it is likely that you will always remember them and their influence on you.

Into practice and supervision

From the relative safety of the training group and skills practice, a point will come when you will be expected to begin a placement within a counselling or psychotherapy agency to see 'real' people with 'real' issues. Sometimes training courses have developed links with partner organisations and therefore setting up a placement will be quite straightforward. More often however, the early challenge is to find a suitable training placement that: (a) is willing to take trainees; (b) has a qualified therapist already in place to facilitate the assessment of clients; (c) has sufficient clients attending the service to meet the needs of a trainee; and (d) is available when you need it to be.

Once in a placement, many trainees find that it becomes the key environment for learning – a place where you can begin to integrate theory with practice, develop skills and, perhaps most importantly, allow your own 'self' as a therapist to develop. This is often the biggest challenge: how to fundamentally be yourself while, at the same time, use the skills and knowledge you have acquired in a way that is consistent with your model of training. My own view is that the best therapists are those who achieve this. I believe that our clients quickly see beyond someone who is acting as a therapist in almost a robotic way: sitting in the 'right' position; saying the right things at the right time; using micro skills in a textbook type of way; and ultimately never really being truly present. However, the therapist who is able to be honest, open, transparent and comfortable with their mistakes is likely to be the one with whom the client most quickly responds. Or, at least, I know whom I would prefer to see. I always try to encourage trainees (and hope for the same myself) to be a person first, and integrate skills and knowledge into your way of being, rather than perfect skills and knowledge and then spend the remaining years trying to find yourself again.

Qualification and beyond

To return to the driving test metaphor: they say we really learn to drive when we take the 'Learner' plates off the car. Likewise, being awarded the qualification that allows you to practise as a counsellor or psychotherapist is the start of a process, and not the end. It is at this point that we need to make decisions about the type of therapist we wish to be, with whom, and where. It is sadly also the time when too many trainees realise that the employment market is limited and highly competitive. Until that point many assume that eager employers struggling with a shortage of qualified therapists will quickly snap them up. This is not the case (certainly in the UK today) and many trainees decide that they need to take further action to make themselves more employable: perhaps by taking their qualification to a higher level, or adding a whole new qualification to their CV, or offering their services in a voluntary capacity to increase their practice experience. Some will certainly quickly find employment, or be able to develop their existing job to incorporate their newly acquired skills, but for most the first step post-qualification is about finding ways of further enhancing their skills and experience to make them more visible in an over-crowded employment market.

Whether in employment or not, counsellors and psychotherapists are in the lucky position of having a wide range of continuing professional development opportunities available to them. These can include:

1   Half- or full-day workshops
2   Seminars
3   Peer group forums
4   Professional networks
5   Shorter courses over a few days or couple of weeks
6   Longer-term specific training opportunities, typically related to particular client groups or working environments
7   Conferences.

While some of these can be financially demanding, others may be offered locally and at only minimal cost. I recommend making the most of such opportunities for a number of reasons: they contribute to the development of skills and knowledge; they contribute to an application for professional accreditation or registration with a professional body; they provide an opportunity to experience counselling or psychotherapy in different settings and with different client groups; they provide an opportunity to enhance job applications; they offer an opportunity to keep abreast of national or international developments at a professional level; and they offer unparalleled networking opportunities and a chance to meet key people in the field. They certainly provide a structure through which newly qualified counsellors and psychotherapists can develop and enhance their competence and sense of themselves as practitioners.

PAUSE FOR REFLECTION

1 If you have finished your training, or when you do, what do you intend to do to ensure a process of continuing professional development?
2 How will you monitor the effectiveness of what you do?

The client and context

As we have seen, much of our work as counsellors and psychotherapists is defined by the client group with which we work and our working context. Working for the health service or other statutory organisation will be very different to working in further or higher education, or in a school, or voluntary agency, or independent practice. How much we have control over our working day, and particular aspects of how we like to practise, will be shaped by the context in which we are based. Likewise, each will offer different opportunities for training and development and present different challenges to negotiate and manage.

The same applies to the clients we work with: some of us will work in a generic setting (i.e., one in which all clients will be seen regardless of their presenting problem), while others will work with particular issues (e.g. abuse, trauma, alcohol or drugs). My own setting has its specific qualities in that it is based within a university counselling service and therefore sees either students or staff who work in that setting. However, beyond that it is a generic service in that it will meet with anyone who registers regardless of their difficulty (as long as it is within the competency of the service to respond appropriately). In my previous working setting (secondary mental health care) I worked specifically with people who had long-term, enduring, mental health difficulties. Each setting presents different challenges and experiences. It is important that, having decided to work within a particular environment or specific client group, you take responsibility to educate yourself on the specific issues you might need to be aware of in offering an appropriate service. Each setting will require a discrete set of skills and knowledge, without which your capacity to work effectively as a counsellor or psychotherapist will be severely undermined.

PAUSE FOR REFLECTION

What aspects of working with clients do you feel skilled at? What areas do you find a struggle? What factors might inform your answers to these two questions?

Professional obligations and responsibilities

Being a counsellor or psychotherapist isn't just about seeing clients. As we saw at the beginning of this chapter, the levels of responsibilities and actions required go well beyond those that take place within the therapeutic space. Some of these may fall into what is sometimes called 'case management' (managing a caseload, managing beginnings–middles–ends, and so on), while others fall beyond the specific tasks that emerge from seeing clients.

Being a counsellor or psychotherapist can involve making a contribution to the wider professional field. It will also involve, on a smaller scale, being in contact with other professionals who, rightly or wrongly, may base their perception of the whole profession on our conduct and competence. Most importantly, the public's perception and therefore trust in counselling and psychotherapy will be shaped by the conduct of those who work as therapists. For counselling and psychotherapy to be viable and positive choices for people, often at the most difficult times in their lives, the profession must be seen to be responsive, ethical, respectful, self-questioning and evolving. As therapists, we need to find our own ways of making such a contribution.

PAUSE FOR REFLECTION

1 What steps might you want to take to become involved in the wider roles of being a counsellor or psychotherapist?
2 How might you make this happen, and what might get in the way?

Snakes and ladders

There will be good times, and bad. This will happen at a micro level where, say, our work with particular clients is going well with much change achieved or when either the client or we feel stuck and nothing seems to be working. Likewise, sometimes supervision will prove helpful and enlightening and at other times difficult and challenging. Sometimes professional relationships will be experienced as facilitative and energetic, while at other times we will realise that we need to move on. On a macro level, there will be times we feel happy and respected in our work, while at other times we feel as if we have reached the point where we have given all we can and need to find new challenges. Likewise, often we might feel happy, content, fulfilled, while at others we feel depleted, tired and drained.

The work of counselling and psychotherapy, with its unknowns and uncertainties, can feel like a game of snakes and ladders: sometimes much progress is made and ground covered, while at other times it can feel as if all we have worked for slips away too easily, leaving us back at square one. My own experience has taught me that it is too easy to lose perspective at these times and not see beyond the immediacy of our disappointment. Good supervision, professional relationships with colleagues, personal therapy, personal reflection and taking a break can provide a different view of our position and make available options that we did not imagine existed. It is important to develop the awareness as therapist of when we are climbing the ladder or when we are slipping down the snake, and to respond accordingly.

PAUSE FOR REFLECTION

Professionally, what have been your ladders, and your snakes so far?

The importance of 'self' in being a therapist

I want to return here to 'self-care', as it is too easily overlooked. Some jobs make no real demands on the 'self' of the person undertaking the job: rather a mere succession of tasks or activities is delivered and an outcome achieved. There are other jobs, however, where the very essence of what we do is bound in the 'self' of the person; I would include counselling and psychotherapy in this latter group. By 'self' here, I am referring to our physical, emotional, psychological and spiritual resources, all of which come into play during our work with clients, and beyond. We don't become counsellor or psychotherapist *tabula rasa*: that is, we are not blank slates onto which nothing has been previously written. Instead, we bring our own joys, passions, hurts and traumas that can positively and powerfully shape our life philosophy. While we can take steps to ensure we do not 'act out' in our therapy work, the very process of connecting with another person at a time of crisis or profound personal pain makes a demand of us stepping into their world and experiencing a little of it. I would argue this is the case for all counselling and psychotherapy approaches, whether or not the relationship is central to the focus of work.

As such, we can quickly become depleted, often without even realising it. In the busy-ness of our working and personal lives and in the commitments we make to others, we continually give little bits of ourselves away. Without noticing, we can find ourselves in a position where we have nothing left to give – we feel empty and drained and begin to blame others for our own condition. The importance of self-care therefore, cannot be overstated. Creating space, time and opportunity with the specific intention of replenishing our 'selves' is an essential task in working as a counsellor and psychotherapist. My experience is that we are very good at talking the talk, but not always so good at walking the walk.

Next steps

Finally, where next? Counselling and psychotherapy are developing in a number of areas in which your contribution will be important. Current or recent debates about statutory or voluntary regulation have brought many aspects of counselling and psychotherapy into sharp focus. At the time of writing the move is towards the voluntary regulation of the profession, at least in the UK. This will require the further development of training standards, consultation of key competences, parameters for accreditation and registration, ethical principles and the education of policy-makers and commissioners about what counselling and psychotherapy have to offer.

There is a need to underpin these developments with an evidence base for what we do. Too many counsellors and psychotherapists remain switched off from research, believing (at best) it is what others do and (at worst) that it has nothing to do with counselling and psychotherapy practice. It is the same people who bemoan the fact that national treatment guidelines seem to privilege one form of therapy over another. Other than in independent practice, all agencies work in an environment where the delivery of service is benchmarked against the efficacy of that service, in terms of outcome and cost. There is an important role for the practitioner-researcher in helping to contribute to the preservation of the profession in the face of frugality and cost-cutting. In the final event, research skills – developed either as a practitioner-researcher or a critical consumer of research – might prove to be the most important skills you will acquire as a counsellor or psychotherapist.

We can only speculate on what might lie ahead for the future of counselling and psychotherapy. Some will hope for the coming together of approaches through a unified set of core competences that are not modality-based, but rather rooted in philosophical and ideological principles common to all therapies. Others believe that difference in counselling and psychotherapy – between models, ideas and approaches – is its strength and the biggest threat to the profession would be a homogenised, manualised way of practice where we all do essentially the same thing.

13.4 FINAL WORDS

I sincerely hope this book has been of value to you. I suspect it has been 20 years in the making, drawing on my successes and mistakes; wisdom and folly. As stated at the beginning of this chapter, the writing of it has reinforced to me that counselling and psychotherapy are simultaneously exquisitely simple and befuddling complex tasks. They demand honour, wit, warmth, empathy, integrity and an ability to be humble, all in equal measure. In practice we will be transported to incredible heights, and accompany people to apparently unfathomable depths. Is it worth it? Oh yes, absolutely.

References

Abbas, A., Hancock, J., Henderson, J. and Kisley, S. (2006) 'Short term psychodynamic psychotherapies for common mental disorders', *Cochrane Database of Systemic Reviews*, (4).

ACA (American Counseling Association) (2005) *ACA Code of Ethics*. www.counseling. org/Resources/CodeOfEthics (accessed 29 May 2012).

Adams, D. (1979) *The Hitchhiker's Guide to the Galaxy*. London: Pan Macmillan.

Ainsworth, M.S., Blehar, M.C., Waters, E. and Wall, S. (1978) *Patterns of Attachment: A Psychological Study of the Strange Situation*. Hillsdale, NJ: Erlbaum.

AIP (Association of Independent Practitioners) (2012) Mission Statement. www.aiponline. org.uk/mission.php (accessed 30 June 2012).

Alderson, K.G. (2004) 'A different kind of outing: training counsellors to work with sexual minority clients', *Canadian Journal of Counselling*, 83 (3): 193–210.

American Psychiatric Association (2000) *Diagnostic and Statistical Manual of Mental Disorders*, 4th Edition (Text Revision) (DSM-IV-TR). Arlington, VA: American Psychiatric Association.

American Psychological Association (2012) Sexual orientation and homosexuality. www. apa.org/helpcenter/sexual-orientation.aspx (accessed 6 June 2012).

Amis, K. (2008) 'Working with client dependency', in W. Dryden and A. Reeves (eds), *Key Issues for Counselling in Action*, 2nd edn. London: Sage. pp. 172–82.

Amis, K. (2011) *Becoming a Counsellor: A Student Companion*. London: Sage.

Anthony, K. and Goss, S. (2009) *Guidelines for Online Counselling and Psychotherapy*, 3rd edn (including Guidelines for Online Supervision). Lutterworth: BACP.

Babiker, G. and Arnold, L. (1997) *The Language of Injury: Comprehending Self-Mutilation*. Leicester: BPS Books.

BACP (British Association for Counselling and Psychotherapy) (2010) *Ethical Framework for Good Practice in Counselling and Psychotherapy*, rev edn. Lutterworth: BACP. Available at www.bacp.co.uk/admin/structure/files/pdf/566_ethical_framework_ feb2010.pdf

BACP (British Association for Counselling and Psychotherapy) (2012) *What are counselling and psychotherapy?* www.bacp.co.uk/crs/education/whatiscounselling.php (accessed 29 May 2012).

Baker, K.D. and Ray, M. (2011) 'Online counselling: the good, the bad, and the possibilities', *Counselling Psychology Quarterly*, 24 (1): 341–6.

Bandura, A. (1969) *Principles of Behavior Modification*. New York: Holt, Rinehart & Winston.

Barkham, M. and Mellor-Clark, J. (2003) 'Bridging evidence-based practice and practice-based evidence: developing a rigorous and relevant knowledge for the psychological therapies', *Clinical Psychology and Psychotherapy*, 10: 319–27.

Barkham, M., Stiles, W.B., Connell, J. and Mellor-Clark, J. (2012) 'Psychological treatment outcomes in routine NHS services: what do we mean by treatment effectiveness?', *Psychology and Psychotherapy: Theory, Research and Practice*, 85 (1): 1–16.

Barnett, J.E. and Johnson, W.B. (2011) 'Integrating spirituality and religion into psychotherapy: persistent dilemmas, ethical issues, and a proposed decision-making process', *Ethics and Behavior*, 21 (2): 147–64.

Beck, A. T., Rush, A. J., Shaw, B. F. and Emery, G. (1979) *Cognitive Therapy of Depression*. New York: The Guildford Press.

Beisser, A. (1970) 'The paradoxical theory of change', in J. Fagan and I. Shepherd (eds), *Gestalt Therapy Now*. New York: Harper Collins, pp. 77–80.

Bell, M.E. (1961) *The Story of Hospital Almoners: The Birth of a Profession*. London: Faber and Faber.

Berne, E. (1966) *Principles of Group Treatment*. New York: Grove Press.

Bhui, K. and Morgan, N. (2007) 'Effective psychotherapy in a racially and culturally diverse society', *Advances in Psychiatric Treatment*, 13: 187–93.

Blazina, C. and Watkins, C.E. (1996) 'Masculine gender role conflict: effects on college men's psychological well-being, chemical substance usage, and attitudes towards help-seeking', *Journal of Counseling Psychology*, 43: 461–5.

Board of Healthcare Studies (2006) *Improving the Quality of Health Care for Mental and Substance-Use Conditions: Quality Chasm Series*. Washington DC: National Academies Press.

Bond, T. (2003) 'Future developments in ethical standards for counselling', in R. Bayne, I. Horton and J. Bimrose (eds), *New Directions in Counselling*. London: Routledge. pp 50–64.

Bond, T. (2004) *Ethical Guidelines for Researching in Counselling and Psychotherapy*. Lutterworth: BACP.

Bond, T. and Mitchels, B. (2008) *Confidentiality and Record Keeping in Counselling and Psychotherapy: Recording Confidences (Legal Resources for Counsellors and Psychotherapists)*. London: Sage/Lutterworth: BACP.

Bordin, E. (1979) 'The generalizability of the psychoanalytic concept of the working alliance', *Psychotherapy: Theory, Research and Practice*, 16: 252–60.

Bower, P. (2010) *Evidence-Based Practice in Counselling and Psychotherapy*. BACP Information Sheet R2. Lutterworth: BACP.

BPS (British Psychological Society) (2005) *Guidelines for Professional Practice in Counselling Psychology*. Leicester: BPS. www.bps.org.uk/sites/default/files/documents/professional_practice_guidelines_-_division_of_counselling_psychology.pdf (accessed 29 May 2012).

Buckroyd, J. and Rother, S. (2008) *How to Write a Research Paper and get it Published*. BACP Information Sheet R10. Lutterworth: BACP.

Burch, N. and Miller, K. (1977) *Teacher Effectiveness Training: An Instructor Guide*. Solana Beach CA: Gordon Training International.

Carroll, M. (1996) *Counselling Supervision: Theory, Skills and Practice*. London: Sage.

Casemore, R. (2011) *Person-Centred Counselling in a Nutshell*, 2nd edn. London: Sage.

Castonguay, L.G., Boswell, J.F., Zack, S.E., Baker, S., Boutselis, M.A., Chiswick, N.R., Damer, D.D., Hemmelstein, N.A., Jackson, J.S., Morford, M., Ragusea, S.A., Roper, J.G., Spayd, C., Weiszer, T., Borkovec, T.D. and Holtforth, M.G. (2010) 'Helpful and hindering events in psychotherapy: a practice research network study', *Psychotherapy: Theory, Research, Practice, Training*, 47 (3): 327–44.

Cavender, A., Trewin, S. and Hanson, V. (2009) General writing guidelines for technology and people with disabilities. Special Interest Group on Accessible Computing. www.sigaccess.org/community/writing_guidelines/ (accessed 6 June 2012).

Claringbull, N. (2010) *What is Counselling and Psychotherapy?* London: Sage.

Clark, D. (2011) 'Implementing NICE guidelines for the psychological treatment of depression and anxiety disorders: the IAPT experience', *International Review of Psychiatry*, 23: 318–27.

Clarkson, P., Gilbert, M. and Tudor, K. (1996) 'Transactional analysis', in W Dryden (ed.), *Handbook of Individual Therapy*. London: Sage. pp. 219–53.

Clarkson, P. (1999) *Gestalt Counselling in Action*, 2nd edn. London: Sage.

Cohen, M.H., Shi, Q., Fabri, M., Mukanyonga, H., Cai, X., Hoover, D.R., Binagwaho, A. and Anastos, K. (2011) 'Improvement in posttraumatic stress disorder in postconflict Rwandan women', *Journal of Women's Health*, 20 (9): 1325–32.

Coles, A. (2003) *Counselling in the Workplace*. Milton Keynes: Open University Press.

Cooper, M. (2008) *Essential Research Findings in Counselling and Psychotherapy: The Facts are Friendly*. London: Sage.

Cooper, M. (2009) 'Counselling in UK secondary schools: s comprehensive review of audit and evaluation data', *Counselling and Psychotherapy Research*, 9 (3): 137–50.

Cooper, M. (2011) 'Meeting the demand for evidence-based practice', *Therapy Today*, 22 (4): 10–16.

Cooper, M. (2012) 'Counselling and psychotherapy research: writing a paper for publication in CPR', www.cprjournal.com/authors/writingpublications.asp (accessed 7 June 2012).

Cooper, M. and McLeod, J. (2010) *Pluralistic Counselling and Psychotherapy.* London: Sage.

Cooper, M., Rowland, N., McArthur, K., Pattison, S., Cromarty, K. and Richards, K. (2010) 'Randomised controlled trial of school-based humanistic counselling for emotional distress in young people: feasibility study and preliminary indications of efficacy', *Child and Adolescent Psychiatry and Mental Health*, 4 (1): 1–12.

Cooper, M., Pybis, J., Hill, A., Jones, S. and Cromarty, K. (2012) 'Therapeutic outcomes in the Welsh Government's school-based counselling strategy: an evaluation', *Counselling and Psychotherapy Research* (in press).

COSCA (Counselling and Psychotherapy in Scotland) (2011a) Counselling and psychotherapy: COSCA's description. www.cosca.org.uk/docs/COSCA%20description%20of%20counselling11-29-11.doc (accessed 29 May 2012).

COSCA (Counselling and Psychotherapy in Scotland) (2011b) *Statement of Ethics and Code of Practice*. Edinburgh: COSCA. Available at www.cosca.org.uk/docs/Statement%20of%20Ethics%20nov%2007(july%2008)11-29-11.pdf.

Courtenay, W.H. (2000) 'Constructions of masculinity and their influence on men's well-being: a theory of gender and health', *Social Science and Medicine*, 50 (10): 1385–401.

CRUSE Bereavement Care (2012) About grief. www.crusebereavementcare.org.uk/ (accessed 29 May 2012).

Cuijpers, P., Geraedts, A.S., van Oppen, P., Andersson, G., Markowitz, G. and van Straten, A. (2011) 'Interpersonal psychotherapy for depression: a meta-analysis', *American Journal of Psychiatry*, 168: 581–92.

Davies, D. and Neale, C. (1996) *Pink Therapy*. Buckingham: Open University Press.

Davies, D. and Neale, C. (eds) (2000) *Therapeutic Perspectives on Working with Gay, Lesbian and Bisexual Clients*. Buckingham: Open University Press.

de Shazer, S. (1988) *Clues: Investigating Solutions in Brief Therapy*. New York: Norton & Co.

Dean, H. (2005) *Social Policy*. London: Wiley.

Department of Health (2002) *Requirements for Social Work Training*. London: Department of Health.

Dewan, M.J., Steenbarger, B.N. and Greenberg, R.P. (2012) *The Art and Science of Brief Psychotherapies: An Illustrated Guide*. Arlington, VA: American Psychiatric Publishing.

Di Loreto, A.O. (2009) *Comparative Psychotherapy: An Experimental Analysis*. New Brunswick, NJ: Transaction Publishers.

Dictionary.com (2012) http://dictionary.reference.com/browse/ (accessed 29 May 2012).

Donati, M. and Watts, M. (2000) 'Personal development groups in counselling psychology training: the case for further research', *Counselling Psychology Review*, 15 (1): 12–21.

Dryden, W. (ed.) (2007) *Handbook of Individual Therapy*. London: Sage.

Dryden, W. (2008) 'The therapeutic alliance as an integrating framework', in W. Dryden and A. Reeves (eds), *Key Issues for Counselling in Action*, 2nd edn. London: Sage. pp. 1–18.

Dryden, W. (2012) 'Rational emotive behaviour therapy (Albert Ellis, 1913–2007)', in C. Feltham and I. Horton (eds), *The Sage Handbook of Counselling and Psychotherapy*, 3rd edn. London: Sage

Dryden, W. and Neenan, M. (2006) *Rational Emotive Behaviour Therapy: 101 Key Points and Techniques*. Hove: Routledge.

Ellerby, M. (2007) *On Anti-Psychiatry*. Brentwood: Chipmunkapublishing.

Elliott, E. and Freire, B. (2008) 'Person-centred and experiential therapies are highly effective: summary of the 2008 meta-analysis', *Person-Centred Quarterly*, November: 1–3.

Ellis, M. and Leary-Joyce, J. (2000) 'Gestalt therapy (Frederick Perls 1893–1970)', in C. Feltham and I. Horton (eds), *Sage Handbook of Counselling and Psychotherapy*. London: Sage. pp. 337–40.

Erikson, E.H. (1950) *Childhood and Society*. New York: W.W. Norton.

Errington, M. and Murdin, L. (2006) 'Psychoanalytic therapy (Sigmund Freud, 1856–1939)', in C. Feltham and I. Horton (eds), *The Sage Handbook of Counselling and Psychotherapy*, 2nd edn. London: Sage. pp. 250–2.

Etherington, K. (2004) *Becoming a Reflexive Researcher: Using Our Selves in Research*. London: Jessica Kingsley.

Evans, C., Connell, J., Barkham, M., Margison, F., McGrath, G., Mellor-Clark, J. and Audin, K. (2002) 'Towards a standardised brief outcome measure: psychometric properties and utility of the CORE-OM', *British Journal of Psychiatry*, 180: 51–60.

Fairburn, C.G. (2008) *Cognitive Behavior Therapy and Eating Disorders*. London: Guilford Press.

Fallon, P., Katzman, M.A. and Wooley, S.C. (1996) *Feminist Perspectives on Eating Disorders*. London: Guilford Press.

Farber, B.A. (2006) *Self-Disclosure in Psychotherapy*. London: Guilford Press.

Fellman, J.D., Getis, A. and Getis, J. (2007) *Human Geography: Landscapes of Human Activities*. Maidenhead: McGraw-Hill.

Feltham, C. (2010) *Critical Thinking in Counselling and Psychotherapy*. London: Sage.

Feltham, C. (2012) 'Brief/time-limited therapy', in C. Feltham and I. Horton (eds), *The Sage Handbook of Counselling and Psychotherapy*, 3rd edn. London: Sage. pp. 559–63.

Feltham, C. and Horton, I. (eds) (2012) *The SAGE Handbook of Counselling and Psychotherapy*, 3rd edn. London: Sage.

Fernandes, F. (2008) 'Working with the concept of stuckness', in W. Dryden and A. Reeves (eds), *Key Issues for Counselling in Action*, 2nd edn. London: Sage. pp 160–71.

Field, N.P., Gao, B. and Paderna, L. (2005). 'Continuing bonds in bereavement: an attachment theory based perspective', *Death Studies*, 29: 1–23.

Figley, C.R. (2002) 'Compassion fatigue: psychotherapists' chronic lack of self care', *Journal of Clinical Psychology*, 58: 1433–41.

Fonagy, P. (ed.) (2002) *An Open Door Review of Outcome Studies in Psychoanalysis*, 2nd edn. London: International Psychoanalytical Association.

Forrest, J.L. and National Center for Dental Hygiene Research Advisory Board (2012) *Guide to Reading Research Articles*. University of California. Available at: www.usc.edu/hsc/ebnet/res/Guide%20to%20Reading%20Research.pdf (accessed September 2012).

Freud, S. (2004) *Civilisation and Its Discontents*. London: Penguin.

Freud, S. (2009) *Beyond the Pleasure Principle*. London: Martino Publishing.

Freud, S. (2010) *A General Introduction to Psychoanalysis*. London: Forgotten Books (Classic Reprint).

Frankland, A. (2001) 'A person-centred model of supervision', *Counselling Psychology Review*, 16 (4): 26-31.

Geldard, K. and Geldard, D. (2005) *Practical Counselling Skills: An Integrative Approach*. London: Palgrave.

Gersons, B.P.R., Carlier, I.V.E., Lamberts, R.D. and van der Kolk, B.A. (2000) 'Randomized clinic trial of brief eclectic psychotherapy for police officers with post-traumatic stress disorder', *Journal of Traumatic Stress*, 13: 333–47.

Gibbard, I. and Hanley, T. (2008) 'A five-year evaluation of the effectiveness of person-centred counselling in routine clinical practice in primary care', *Counselling and Psychotherapy Research*, 8 (4): 215–22.

Gilbert, P.R. (2007) *Psychotherapy and Counselling for Depression*, 3rd edn. London: Sage.

Gilbert, P.R. (2010) *Compassion Focused Therapy: Distinctive Features*. Hove: Routledge.

Gilbert, P., McKewan, K., Mitra, R., Franks, L., Richter, L. and Rockliff, H. (2008) 'Feeling safe and content: a specific affect regulation system? Relationship to depression, anxiety, stress, and self-criticism good practice', *The Journal of Positive Psychology*, 3 (3): 182–91.

Glaser, B.G. and Strauss, A.L. (1967) *The Discovery of Grounded Theory: Strategies for Qualitative Research*. Chicago: Aldine Publishing Company.

Grove, J. (2009) 'How competent are trainee and newly qualified counsellors to work with Lesbian, Gay, and Bisexual clients and what do they perceive as their most effective learning experiences?', *Counselling and Psychotherapy Research*, 9 (2): 78–85.

Gubi, P.M. (2002) 'Practice behind closed doors: challenging the taboo of prayer in mainstream counselling culture', *The Journal of Critical Psychology, Counselling and Psychotherapy*, 2 (2): 97–104.

Gubi, P. (2009) 'A qualitative exploration into how the use of prayer in counselling and psychotherapy might be ethically problematic', *Counselling and Psychotherapy Research*, 9 (2): 115–21.

Hallam, R. (1992) *Counselling for Anxiety Problems*. London: Sage.

Hanley, T. (2012) 'Understanding the online therapeutic alliance through the eyes of adolescent service users', *Counselling and Psychotherapy Research*, 12 (1): 35–43.

Hansen, N.B., Lambert, M.J. and Forman E.M. (2002) 'The psychotherapy dose–response effect and its implications for treatment delivery services', *Clinical Psychology: Science and Practice*, 9 (3): 329–43.

Hawkins, P. and Shohet, R. (2007) *Supervision in the Helping Professions*. Buckingham: Open University Press.

Hayes, S.C., Strosahl, K.D. and Wilson, K.G. (1999) *Acceptance and Commitment Therapy: An Experiential Approach to Behavior Change*. New York: Guilford.

Henretty, J.R. and Levitt, H.M. (2009) 'The role of therapist self-disclosure in psychotherapy: a qualitative review', *Clinical Psychology Review*, 30 (1): 63–77.

Henry, S.L. (2007) 'Interacting with people with disabilities', *Just Ask: Integrating Accessibility Throughout Design.* Madison, WI: ET\Lawton. Retrieved from www.uiaccess.com/accessucd/interact.html (accessed 6 June 2012).

Hess, A.K. (ed.) (1980) *Psychotherapy Supervision: Theory, Research and Practice*. London: Wiley.

Hill, A. (2011) *Curriculum for Counselling for Depression: Continuing Professional Development for Qualified Therapists Delivering High Intensity Interventions*. Lutterworth: BACP/London: National IAPT Programme Team.

Horvath, A.O. and Bedi, R.P. (2002) 'The alliance', in J.C. Norcross (ed.), *Psychotherapy Relationships that Work: Therapist Contributions and Responsiveness to Patients*. New York: Oxford University Press. pp. 37–69.

Hough, M. (1996) *Counselling Skills*. London: Longman

House, R. and Loewenthal, D. (eds) (2008) *Against and for CBT: Toward a Constructive Dialogue*. Ross-on-Wye: PCCS Books.

HSE (Health and Safety Executive) (2012) Stress and its impact. www.hse.gov.uk/stress/faqs.htm (accessed 29 May 2012).

Hunter, S. and Hickerson, J. (2003) *Affirmative Practice: Understanding and Working with Lesbian, Gay, Bisexual and Transgender Persons.* Washington, DC: NASW Press.

Information Service Editorial Board (2008) *What Is Supervision?* Lutterworth: BACP.

Inskipp, F. (2012) 'Generic skills', in C. Feltham and I. Horton (eds), *The Sage Handbook of Counselling and Psychotherapy.* London: Sage. pp 78–91.

Inskipp, F. and Proctor, B. (1993) *Making the Most of Supervision.* Twickenham: Cascade.

Inskipp, F. and Proctor, B. (2001) *Becoming a Supervisor.* Twickenham: Cascade.

Israel, T., Gorcheva, R., Walther, W.A., Sulzner, J.M. and Cohen, J. (2008) 'Therapists' helpful and unhelpful experiences with LGBT clients: an exploratory study', *Professional Psychology: Research and Practice*, 39: 361–8.

Ivey, E.E. (1971) *Microcounseling: Innovations in Interviewing Training.* Springfield: Thomas.

Iwi, D., Watson, J., Barber, P., Kimber, N. and Sharman, G. (1998) 'The self-reported well-being of employees facing organisational change: effects of an intervention', *Occupational Medicine*, 48 (6): 361–9.

Jeffers, F. (2012) Setting up in independent practice. www.aiponline.org.uk/independent. php (accessed 30 June 2012).

Jenkins, P. (2007) *Counselling, Psychotherapy and the Law.* London: Sage.

Jenkins, P. (2008) 'Organisational duty of care: workplace counselling as a shield against litigation?', in A. Kinder, R. Hughes and C.L. Cooper (eds), *Employee Well-Being Support: A Workplace Resource.* Chichester: John Wiley and Sons. pp. 99–110.

Johns, H. (1996) *Personal Development in Counsellor Training.* London: Cassell.

Johnson, S., Needle, J., Bindman, J.P. and Thornicroft, G. (2008) *Crisis Resolution and Home Treatment in Mental Health.* Cambridge: Cambridge University Press.

Jonas, S., Bebbington, P., McManus, S., Meltzer, H., Jenkins, R., Kuipers, E., Cooper, C., King, M. and Brugha, T. (2011) 'Sexual abuse and psychiatric disorder in England: results from the 2007 Adult Psychiatric Morbidity Survey', *Psychological Medicine*, 41: 709–19.

Jones, M.C. (1925) 'A laboratory study of fear: the case of Peter', *Pedagogical Seminary*, 31: 308–15.

Joseph, S. (2007) 'Agents of social control?', *The Psychologist*, July: 429–31.

Joseph, S. (2010) *Theories of Counselling and Psychotherapy: An Introduction to the Different Approaches.* Basingstoke: Palgrave Macmillan.

Joyce, P. and Sills, C. (2001) *Skills in Gestalt Counselling and Psychotherapy.* London: Sage.

Kadera, S.W., Lambert, M.J. and Andrews, A.A. (1996) 'How much therapy is really enough? A session-by-session analysis of the psychotherapy dose–effect relationship', *Journal of Psychotherapy Practice and Research*, 5 (2): 132–51.

Kanellakis, P. and D'Aubyn, J. (2010) 'Public perceptions of the professional titles used within psychological services', *Counselling and Psychotherapy Research*, 10 (4): 258–67.

Khele, S., Symons, C. and Wheeler, S. (2008) 'An analysis of complaints to the British Association for Counselling and Psychotherapy, 1996–2006', *Counselling and Psychotherapy Research*, 8 (2): 124–32.

Kilbourne, B.K. and Richardson, J.T. (1984) 'Psychotherapy and new religions in a pluralistic society', *American Psychologist*, 39 (3): 37–251.

King, G. (2008) 'Using counsellor supervision', in W. Dryden and A. Reeves (eds), *Key Issues for Counselling in Action*, 2nd edn. London: Sage. pp. 213–27.

King, M., Sibbald, B., Ward, E., Bower, P., Lloyd, M., Gabbay, M. et al. (2000) 'Randomised controlled trials of non-directive counselling, cognitive-behavioural therapy and usual general practitioner care in the management of depression as well as mixed anxiety and depression in primary care', *Health Technology Assessment*, 4 (9).

King, R., Spooner, D.M. and Reid, W. (2003) 'Online counselling and psychotherapy', in R. Wootton, P. Yellowlees and P. McLaren (eds), *Telepsychiatry and E-mental Health.* London: The Royal Society of Medicine Press. pp. 245–63.

Kingdon, D. and Finn, M. (2006) *Tackling Mental Health Crises.* London: Routledge.

Kinsella, P. and Garland, A. (2008) *Cognitive Behavioural Therapy for Mental Health Workers: A Beginner's Guide.* London: Routledge.

Klass, D., Silverman, P.R. and Nickman, S.L. (1984) *Continuing Bonds: New Understandings of Grief.* London: Taylor and Francis.

Kovel, J. (1976) *A Complete Guide to Therapy: From Psychotherapy to Behavior Modification.* New York: Pantheon Books.

Kubler-Ross, E. (1973) *On Death and Dying.* London: Routledge.

Lambert, P. (2008) 'Initiating counselling', in W. Dryden and A. Reeves (eds), *Key Issues for Counselling in Action*, 2nd edn. London: Sage. pp. 49–60.

Larcombe, A. (2008) 'Self-care in counselling', in W. Dryden and A. Reeves (eds), *Key Issues for Counselling in Action*, 2nd edn. London: Sage. pp. 283–97.

Launer, M. and Foster, S. (2005) *Severe Mental Illness (Psychosis)* Royal College of Psychiatrists Information Leaflet http://static.carers.org/files/psychosis-16.pdf (accessed 1 July 2012).

Lawton, B. (2000) '"A very exposing affair": explorations in counsellors' supervisory relationships', in B. Lawton and C. Feltham, *Taking Supervision Forward: Enquiries and Trends in Counselling and Psychotherapy.* London: Sage. pp. 25–41.

Lawton, B., Bradley, A-M., Collins, J., Holt, C. and Kelly, F. (2010) *AUCC Guidelines for University and College Counselling Services*, 2nd edn. Lutterworth: BACP.

Layard, R. (2003) *Happiness: Has Social Science a Clue?* Lionel Robbins Memorial Lectures 2002/3.

Leavitt, H.J. (2004) *Top Down: Why Hierarchies Are Here to Stay and How to Manage Them More Effectively.* Cambridge, MA: Harvard Business School.

Leenaars, A.A. (1994) *Psychotherapy with Suicidal People: A Person Centred Approach.* London: Wiley.

Lemma, A. (1996) *Introduction to Psychopathology.* London: Sage.

Lennie, C. (2007) 'The role of personal development groups in counsellor training: understanding factors contributing to self-awareness in the personal development group', *British Journal of Guidance and Counselling*, 35 (1): 115–29.

LeSurf, A. and Lynch, G. (1999) 'Exploring young people's perceptions relevant to counselling: a qualitative survey', *British Journal of Guidance and Counselling*, 27 (2): 231–43.

Levant, R.F. (1998) 'Desperately seeking language: understanding, assessing, and treating normative male alexithymia', in W.S. Pollack and R.F. Levant (eds), *New Psychotherapy for Men.* New York: Wiley. pp. 35–56.

Levi, D. (2010) *Group Dynamics for Teams.* London: Sage.

Lewin, K. (1952) *Field Theory in Social Science.* London: Tavistock.

Liddle, B.J. (1996) 'Therapist sexual orientation, gender, and counseling practices as they relate to ratings of helpfulness by gay and lesbian clients', *Journal of Counseling Psychology*, 43 (4): 394–401.

Lipsedge, M. and Littlewood, R. (1997) *Aliens and Alienists: Ethnic Minorities and Psychiatry.* London: Routledge.

Lister-Ford, C. (2002) *Skills in Transactional Analysis Counselling and Psychotherapy.* London: Sage.

Macaskie, J. (2008) 'Working with transference in counselling', in W. Dryden and A. Reeves (eds), *Key Issues for Counselling in Action*, 2nd edn. London: Sage. pp. 147–59.

MacDonald, J. (1995) *Representing Women: Myths of Femininity in the Popular Media.* London: Bloomsbury Academic.

Mackewn, J. (1997) *Developing Gestalt Counselling.* London: Sage.

Mahalik, J.R., Good, G.E. and Englar-Carlson, M. (2003) 'Masculinity scripts, presenting concerns, and help seeking: Implications for practice and training', *Professional Psychology: Research and Practice*, 34: 123–31.

Malan, D. (1979) *Individual Psychotherapy and the Science of Psychodynamics*. London: Butterworths.

Malyon, A.K. (1982) 'Psychotherapeutic implications of internalised homophobia in gay men', in J. Gonsiorek (ed.), *Homosexuality and Psychotherapy: A Practitioner's Handbook of Affirmative Models*. New York: Haworth Press. pp. 59–69.

Martin, D.J., Garske, J.P. and Davis, M.K. (2000) 'Relation of the therapeutic alliance with outcome and other variables: a meta-analytic review', *Journal of Consulting and Clinical Psychology*, 68 (3): 438–50.

Maslow, A. (1968) *Toward a Psychology of Being*. New York: Van Nostrand.

Matthews, C., Selvidge, M. and Fisher, K. (2005) 'Addictions counselors' attitudes and behaviors toward gay, lesbian, and bisexual clients', *Journal of Counseling and Development*, 83 (Winter): 57–65.

Mattinson, J. (1975) *The Reflection Process in Casework Supervision*. London: Institute of Marital Studies.

McCann, I.L. and Pearlman, L.A. (1990) 'Vicarious traumatization: a framework for understanding the psychological effects of working with victims', *Journal of Traumatic Stress*, 3: 131–49.

McLeod, J. (2003) *Doing Counselling Research*, 2nd edn. London: Sage.

McLeod, J. (2008) *An Introduction to Counselling*, 3rd edn. Maidenhead: Open University Press.

McLeod, J. (2009) *An Introduction to Counselling*, 4th edn. Maidenhead: Open University Press.

McLeod, J. (2010a) 'The effectiveness of workplace counselling: a systematic review', *Counselling and Psychotherapy Research*, 10 (4): 238–48.

McLeod, J. (2010b) *Case Study Research in Counselling and Psychotherapy*. London: Sage.

McLeod, J. and Elliott, R. (2011) 'Systematic case study research: a practice-orientated introduction to building an evidence-base for counselling and psychotherapy', *Counselling and Psychotherapy Research*, 11 (1): 1–10.

McMahon, G. (2000) 'Integrative counselling', in S. Palmer (ed.), *Introduction to Counselling and Psychotherapy: The Essential Guide*. London: Sage. pp.113–25.

Mearns, D. and Thorne, B. (2000) *Person-Centred Therapy Today: New Frontiers in Theory and Practice*. London: Sage.

Mellor, N., Mackay, C., Packham, C., Jones, R., Palferman, D., Webster, S. and Kelly, P. (2011) '"Management Standards" and work-related stress in Great Britain: progress on their implementation', *Safety Science*, 49 (7): 1040–6.

Mental Health Foundation (2012) *Mental Health Problems: The Most Common Mental Health Problems*. www.mentalhealth.org.uk/help-information/mental-health-statistics/common-mental-health-problems/ (accessed 1 July 2012).

Merkel, L. (2003) *The History of Psychiatry*. www.scribd.com/doc/41930822/History-of-Psychiatry (accessed 27 June 2012).

Merry, T. (1996) 'Client centred therapy: trends and troubles', in S. Palmer, S. Dainow and P. Milner, *Counselling. The BAC Counselling Reader Volume 1*. London: Sage.

Merry, T. (2002) *Learning and Being in Person-Centred Counselling*, 2nd edn. Ross-on-Wye: PCCS Books.

Milgram, S. (1974) *Obedience to Authority: An Experimental View*. New York: Harper and Row.

Mintz, R. (2010) *Introduction to Conducting Qualitative Research.* BACP Information Sheet R14. Lutterworth: BACP.

Mitchels, B. and Bond, T. (2010) *Essential Law for Counsellors and Psychotherapists.* London: Sage.

Mohamed, C. (2006) 'Race, culture and ethnicity', in C. Feltham and I. Horton (eds), *The Sage Hangbook of Counselling and Psychotherapy,* 2nd edn. London: Sage. pp. 50–60.

Morris, J. (ed.) (2008) *ABC of Eating Disorders.* Oxford: Wiley–Blackwell.

Moore, J. and Jenkins, P. (2012) '"Coming out" in therapy? Perceived risks and benefits of self-disclosure of sexual orientation by gay and lesbian therapists to straight clients', *Counselling and Psychotherapy Research,* iFirst: 1–8 (DOI:10.1080/14733145.2012.660973).

Moustakas, C.E. (1990) *Heuristic Research: Design, Methodology, and Applications.* London: Sage.

Mowrer, O.H. (1947) 'On the dual nature of learning – a reinterpretation of conditioning and problem solving', *Harvard Educational Review,* 17: 102–48.

Mytton, J. (2012) 'Cognitive therapy', in C. Feltham and I. Horton (eds), *The Sage Handbook of Counseling and Psychotherapy.* London: Sage. pp. 286–92.

National Audit Office (2012) Glossary of Terms: The Third Sector. www.nao.org.uk/sectors/third_sector/successful_commissioning/successful_commissioning/glossary.aspx (accessed 6 June 2012).

Nelson, A.A. and Wilson, W.P. (1984) 'The ethics of sharing religious faith in psychotherapy', *Journal of Psychology and Theology,* 12 (1): 15–23.

Newnes, C., Cailzie, D. and Holmes, G. (1999) *This Is Madness: A Critical Look at Psychiatry and the Future of Mental Health Services.* Ross-on-Wye: PCCS Books.

NHS (2011) Post-traumatic stress disorder. www.nhs.uk/Conditions/Post-traumatic-stress-disorder/Pages/Symptoms.aspx (accessed 29 May 2012).

NHS (2012) Clinical Knowledge Summaries: Depression – Background Information. http://www.cks.nhs.uk/depression/background_information/prevalence (accessed 1 July 2012).

NICE (National Institute for Clinical Excellence) (2004a) *Eating Disorders: Core Interventions in the Treatment and Management of Anorexia Nervosa, Bulimia Nervosa and Related Eating Disorders.* Clinical Guideline 9. London: NICE.

NICE (National Institute for Clinical Excellence) (2004b) *Self Harm: The Short-Term Physical and Psychological Management and Secondary Prevention of Self-Harm in Primary and Secondary Care.* Clinical Guideline 16. London: NICE.

NICE (National Institute for Clinical Excellence) (2005) *The Management of PTSD in Children and Adults in Primary and Secondary Care.* Clinical Guideline 26. London: NICE.

NICE (National Institute for Health and Clinical Excellence) (2009) *Depression: The NICE Guideline on the Treatment and Management of Depression in Adults.* Clinical Guideline 90. London: NICE.

Nieuwsma, J.A., Trivedi, R.B., McDuffie, J., Kronish, I., Benjamin, D. and Williams, J.W. (2011) *Brief Psychotherapy for Depression in Primary Care: A Systematic Review of the Evidence.* Washington, DC: Department of Veterans Affairs Health Services Research and Development Services.

Norcross, J.C. and Goldfried, M.R. (2005) *Handbook of Psychotherapy Integration,* 2nd edn. Oxford: Oxford University Press.

OED (Oxford English Dictionary) (2012) Oxford Dictionaries online http://oxforddictionar-ies.com (accessed 29 May 2012).

O'Carroll, P. (2008) 'Getting SOMEWHERE: goals and problems for counselling', in W. Dryden and A. Reeves (eds), *Key Issues for Counselling in Action*, 2nd edn. London: Sage. pp. 104–16.

O'Connell, B. (2012) 'Solution-focused therapy', in C. Feltham and I. Horton (eds), *The Sage Handbook of Counselling and Psychotherapy*, 3rd edn. London: Sage. pp. 392–5.

Ogunfowora, B. and Drapeau, M. (2008) 'A study of the relationship between personality traits and theoretical orientation preferences', *Counselling and Psychotherapy Research*, 8 (3): 151–9.

Oliver, J. (1995) 'Counselling disabled people: a counsellor's perspective', *Disability and Society*, 10 (3): 261–79.

Olney, S.H. (2010) 'Practicing under the influence: the medicalization of psychotherapy'. Unpublished PhD thesis, University of Minnesota.

Orbach, S. (2004) 'The body in clinical practice part one & two', cited in K. White (ed.), *Touch Attachment and the Body*. London: Karnac. pp. 17–48.

Owens, P. (2007) 'Benign revelation: writing about work with clients', *Self and Society*, 35 (1): 20–9.

Padesky, C. (2004a) *Guided Discovery: Leading and Following* (Clinical Workshop Audiotape). Newport Beach, CA: Center for Cognitive Therapy.

Padesky, C. (2004b) *Constructing New Underlying Assumptions and Behavioral Experiments* (Video). Newport Beach, CA: Center for Cognitive Therapy.

Page, S. and Woskett, V. (1994) *Supervising the Counsellor: A Cyclical Model*. Abingdon: Routledge.

Papadopoulos, L. (2010) *The Sexualisation of Young People: Review*. London: Home Office.

Parlett, M. and Hemming, J. (1996) 'Developments in gestalt therapy', in W. Dryden (ed.), *Developments in Psychotherapy: Historical Perspectives*. London: Sage. pp. 91–110.

Payne, H. (2004) 'Becoming a client, becoming a practitioner: student narratives from a dance movement therapy group', *British Journal of Guidance and Counselling*, 32 (4): 512–32.

Pearlman, L.A. and Saakvitne, K.W. (1995) 'Treating therapists with vicarious traumatisa-tion and secondary traumatic stress disorders', in C.R. Figley (ed.), *Compassion Fatigue: Coping with Secondary Traumatic Stress Disorders in Those Who Treat the Traumatised*. New York: Brunner/Mazel. p. 31.

Perls, F. (1969) *Gestalt Therapy Verbatim*. Moab, UT: Real People Press.

Phillips, J. and Fischer, A. (1998) 'Graduate students' training experiences with lesbian, gay and bisexual issues', *The Counseling Psychologist*, 26 (5): 712–34.

Pilgrim, D. (2001) 'Disordered personalities and disordered concepts', *Journal of Mental Health*, 10: 253–65.

Pipes, R., Schwartz, R. and Crouch, P. (1995) 'Measuring client fears', *Journal of Consulting and Clinical Psychology*, 27 (2): 933–4.

Pixton, S. (2003) 'Experiencing gay affirmative therapy: an exploration of clients' views of what is helpful', *Counselling and Psychotherapy Research*, 3 (3): 211–15.

Proctor, B. (2008) *Group Supervision: A Guide to Creative Practice*, 2nd edn. London: Sage.

Proctor, B. and Sills, C. (2006) 'Therapy contracts with trainee practitioners', in C. Sills (ed.), *Contracts in Counselling and Psychotherapy*. London: Sage. pp. 152–60.

Proctor, G. (2007) 'Disordered boundaries? A critique of borderline personality disorder', in H. Spandler and S. Warner (eds), *Beyond Fear and Control: Working with Young People Who Self-Harm*. Ross-on-Wye: PCCS Books. pp 105–20.

Proctor, G. (2010) 'BPD: mental illness or misogyny?', *Therapy Today*, 21 (2): 17–21.

Purton, C. (2004) *Person-centred Therapy: The Focusing-Oriented Approach*. Basingstoke: Palgrave Macmillan.

Rafaeli, E., Bernstein, D.P. and Young, G. (2010) *Schema Therapy: Distinctive Features*. London: Routledge.

Rankin, B. (2004) 'Transexual vs. transgender: explaining the intricacies', *Fusion Magazine*. Spring 2004. Retrieved from http://transwoman.webs.com/transawareness. htm (7 June 2012).

Reeve, D. (2002) 'Oppression within the counselling room', *Counselling and Psychotherapy Research*, 2 (1): 11–19.

Reeves, A. (2004) 'Suicide risk assessment and the ethical framework', *Counselling and Psychotherapy Journal*, May: 25–8.

Reeves, A. (2008) 'Client assessment', in W. Dryden and A. Reeves (eds), *Key Issues for Counselling in Action*, 2nd edn. London: Sage. pp. 61–76.

Reeves, A. (2010a) *Counselling Suicidal Clients*. London: Sage.

Reeves, A. (2010b) 'Log on, drop out', *Therapy Today*, 20 (2): 6.

Reeves, A. (2012) 'Counselling students', in C. Feltham and I. Horton (eds), *The Sage Handbook of Counselling and Psychotherapy*. London: Sage. pp. 653–8.

Reeves, A. and Mintz, R. (2001) 'Counsellors' experiences of working with suicidal clients: an exploratory study', *Counselling and Psychotherapy Research*, 1 (3): 172–6.

Reeves, A., Bowl, R., Wheeler, S. and Guthrie, E. (2004) 'The hardest words: exploring the dialogue of suicide in the counselling process – a discourse analysis', *Counselling and Psychotherapy Research*, 4 (1): 62–71.

Rennie, D.L. (1998) *Person-Centred Counselling: an Experiential Approach*. London: Sage.

Rennie, D.L. (2012) *The Grounded Theory Method of Qualitative Research*. cprjournal. com: www.cprjournal.com/documents/groundedTheory.pdf (accessed 2 July 2012)

Resnick, J. (2004) 'The clinical implications of dependency and counter-dependency', *Psychotherapy in Australia*, 10 (3): 52–9.

Rethink (2007) How is psychosis treated? www.rethink.org/about_mental_illness/early_ intervention/understanding_psychosis/how_is_psychosis.html (accessed 6 June 2012).

Rethink (2011) What is psychosis? www.rethink.org/about_mental_illness/early_intervention/ understanding_psychosis/what_is_psychosis.html (accessed 6 June 2012).

Ringer, M.T. (2002) *Group Action: The Dynamics of Groups in Therapeutic, Educational and Corporate Settings* (International Library of Group Analysis). London: Jessica Kingsley.

Rizq, R. (2011) 'IAPT, anxiety and envy: a psychoanalytical view of NHS primary care mental health services today', *British Journal of Psychotherapy*, 27 (1): 37–55.

Robinson, L., Perren, S. and Seber, P. (2012) 'Counselling in primary care', in C. Feltham and I. Horton (eds), *The Sage Handbook of Counselling and Psychotherapy*. London: Sage. pp. 636–40.

Robson, M. (2008) 'Anticipating and working with unplanned endings', in W. Dryden and A. Reeves (eds), *Key Issues for Counselling in Action*, 2nd edn. London: Sage. pp. 199–210.

Rogers, C. (1959) 'A theory of therapy, personality and interpersonal relationships as developed in the client-centered framework', in S. Koch (ed.), *Psychology: A Study of a Science*, vol. 3: Formulations of the Person and the Social Context. New York: McGraw Hill.

Rogers, C. (1962) 'Some learnings from a study of psychotherapy with schizophrenics', *Pennsylvania Psychiatric Quarterly*, Summer: 3–15.

Rogers, E. (2009) 'The need for reappraising psychological therapies in the light of IAPT', *Journal of Mental Health Training, Education and Practice*, 4 (1): 19–26.

Roosen, K. (2009) 'From tragedy to "crip" to human: the need for multiple understandings of disability in psychotherapy'. pi.library.yorku.ca/ojs/index.php/cdd/article/view/23382/21578 (accessed 2 July 2012).

Rost, K., Fortney, J. and Coyne, J. (2005) 'The relationship of depression treatment quality indicators to employee absenteeism', *Mental Health Services Research*, 7: 161–8.

Rowan, J. and Jacobs, M. (2002) *The Therapist's Use of Self*. Buckingham: Open University Press.

Royal College of Psychiatrists (2010) *Self-harm, Suicide and Risk: Helping People who Self-harm – Final Report of a Working Group*. Royal College of Psychiatrists College Report CR158. www.rcpsych.ac.uk/files/pdfversion/CR158xx.pdf (accessed 1 July 2012).

Ryle, A. (1990) *Cognitive Analytic Therapy: Active Participation in Change*. Chichester: John Wiley and Sons.

Ryle, A. and Kerr, I.B. (2002) *Introducing Cognitive Analytic Therapy: Principles and Practice*. Oxford: Wiley-Blackwell.

Sackett, D., Rosenberg, W., Gray, J., Haynes, B. and Richardson, W. (1996) 'Evidence-based medicine: what it is and what it is not', *British Medical Journal*, 312: 71–2.

Sakai, C.E., Connolly, S.M. and Oas, P. (2010) 'Treatment of PTSD in Rwandan child genocide survivors using thought field therapy', *International Journal of Emergency Mental Health*, 12 (1): 41–50.

Sanders, P. and Wilkins, P (2010) *First Steps in Practitioner Research: A Guide to Understanding and Doing Research in Counselling and Health and Social Care*. Ross-on-Wye: PCCS Books.

Sanders, D. and Wills, F. (2005) *Cognitive Therapy: An Introduction*, 2nd edn. London: Sage.

Saroja, K.I., Ramphal, K.G., Kasmini K., Ainsah, O. and Baker, O.C. (1999) 'Trends in absenteeism rates following psychological intervention – preliminary results', *Singapore Medical Journal*, 40 (5): 349–51.

Segal, J. (2012) 'Psychodynamic therapy (Melanie Klein, 1882–1960)', in C. Feltham and I. Horton (eds), *The Sage Handbook of Counselling and Psychotherapy*, 3rd edn. London: Sage. pp. 273–7.

Shapiro, F. (1989) 'Eye movement desensitization: a new treatment for post-traumatic stress disorder', *Journal of Behavior Therapy and Experimental Psychiatry*, 20: 211–17.

Sills, C. (ed.) (1997) *Contracts in Counselling*. London: Sage.

Smail, D. (1996) *How to Survive without Psychotherapy*. London: Constable.

Sommerbeck, L. (2003) *The Client-Centred Therapist in Psychiatric Contexts: A Therapist's Guide to the Psychiatric Landscape and Its Inhabitants*. Ross-on-Wye: PCCS Books.

Spinelli, E. (2006) *Demystifying Therapy*. Ross-on-Wye: PCCS Books.

Stein, M. (2011) 'Faith and the practising analyst', *Journal of Analytical Psychology*, 56 (3): 397–406.

Stiles, W.B., Barkham, M., Mellor-Clark, J. and Connell, J. (2008) 'Effectiveness of cognitive-behavioural, person-centred, and psychodynamic therapies in UK primary-care routine practice: replication in a larger sample', *Psychological Medicine*, 38 (5): 677–88.

Stonewall (2012) What is sexual orientation? www.stonewall.org.uk/at_home/sexual_orientation_faqs/2695.asp (accessed 6 June 2012).

Strümpfel, U. and Goldman, R. (2002) 'Contacting gestalt therapy', in D.J. Cain and J. Seeman (eds), *Humanistic Psychotherapies: Handbook of Research and Practice*. Washington, DC: American Psychological Association. pp. 189–219.

Stoltenberg, D. and Delworth, U. (1987) *Supervising Counselors and Therapists: A Developmental Approach*. London: Jossey–Bass Publishers.

SuPReNet (Supervision Practitioner Research Network) Homepage. www.bacp.co.uk/research/SuPReNet/ (accessed 7 June 2012).

Symons, C. (2008) 'Countertransference', in W. Dryden and A. Reeves (eds), *Key Issues for Counselling in Action*, 2nd edn. London: Sage. pp. 244–56.

Symons, C., Khele, S., Rogers, J., Turner, J. and Wheeler, S. (2011) 'Allegations of serious professional misconduct: an analysis of the British Association for Counselling and Psychotherapy's Article 4.6 cases, 1998–2007', *Counselling and Psychotherapy Research*, 11 (4): 257–65.

Tan, S. (1994) 'Ethical considerations in religious psychotherapy: potential pitfalls and unique resources', *Journal of Psychology and Theology*, 22 (4): 389–94.

Taylor, J. (2010) 'Psychotherapy for people with learning disabilities: creating possibilities and opportunities. A review of the literature', *Journal of Learning Disabilities and Offending Behaviour*, 1 (3): 15–25.

Thavasothy, R. (2009) *Mental Health in a Multi-Ethnic Society: A Multidisciplinary Handbook*. 2nd edn. London: Routledge.

Thompson-Brenner, H., Weingeroff, J. and Westen, D. (2009) 'Empirical support for psychodynamic psychotherapy for eating disorders', *Current Clinical Psychiatry*, Part I: 67–92.

Tseng, W. (1999) 'Culture and psychotherapy: review and practical guidelines', *Transcultural Psychiatry*, 36: 131.

Tudor, K. and Sills, C. (2012) 'Transactional analysis (Eric Berne, 1910–1970)', in C. Feltham and I. Horton (eds), *The Sage Handbook of Counselling and Psychotherapy*, 3rd edn. London: Sage. pp. 335–40.

Tudor, L.E., Keemar, K., Tudor, K., Valentine, J. and Worrall, M. (2004) *The Person-Centred Approach: A Contemporary Introduction*. Basingstoke: Palgrave Macmillan.

Tune, D. (2008) 'How close do I get to my clients?', in W. Dryden and A. Reeves (eds), *Key Issues for Counselling in Action*, 2nd edn. London: Sage. pp. 257–69.

UK Parliament (2012) Making laws. www.parliament.uk/about/how/laws/ (accessed 29 May 2012).

UKCP (United Kingdom Council of Psychotherapy) (2009) *Ethical Principles and Code of Professional Conduct*. London: UKCP. Available at www.psychotherapy.org.uk/code_of_ethics.html.

UKCP (United Kingdom Council of Psychotherapy) (2012) About psychotherapy. www.psychotherapy.org.uk/article140.html (accessed 29 May 2012).

University of Bristol School for Policy Studies (2011) What is social policy or public policy? www.bristol.ac.uk/sps/aboutus/socialpolicy (accessed 29 May 2012).

Vicarious Trauma Institute (2012) What is vicarious trauma?www.vicarioustrauma.com/whatis.html (accessed April 2012).

Walton, M. (2008) 'In consideration of a toxic workplace: a suitable place for treatment', in A. Kinder, R. Hughes and C. Cooper (eds), *Employee Well-Being Support: A Workplace Resource*. Chichester: John Wiley and Sons. pp. 9–24.

Ward, T., Hogan, K., Stuart, V. and Singleton, E. (2008) 'The exprinces of counselling for persons with ME', *Counselling and Psychotherapy Research*, 8 (2): 73–9.

Weinberg, A., Sutherland, V.J. and Cooper, C. (2010) *Organizational Stress Management*. London: Palgrave.

Wheeler, S. (2002) 'Nature or nurture: are therapists born or trained?', *Psychodynamic Practice*, 8 (4): 427–42.

White, J. (2000) 'Cognitive therapy: what is left when you remove the hype?', *Proceedings of the British Psychological Society*, 8: 16.

Wills, F. (2008) *Skills in Cognitive Behaviour Counselling and Psychotherapy*. London: Sage

WHO (World Health Organisation) (1992) *The ICD-10 Classification of Mental and Behavioural Disorders: Clinical Descriptions and Diagnostic Guidelines*. Geneva: WHO.

WHO (World Health Organisation) (2012a) Gender and Women's Mental Health. www.who.int/mental_health/prevention/genderwomen/en/ (accessed April 2012).

WHO (World Health Organisation) (2012b) Suicide Prevention. www.who.int/mental_health/prevention/suicide/suicideprevent/en/ (accessed April 2012).

Whipple, J.L. and Lambert, M.J. (2010) 'Outcome measures for practice', *Annual Review of Clinical Psychology*, 7: 87–111.

Winnicott, D.W. (1965) *The Maturational Processes and the Facilitating Environment*. London: Hogarth Press.

Worden, J.W. (2009) *Grief Counselling and Grief Therapy: A Handbook for the Mental Health Practitioner*, 4th edn. London: Routledge.

Yontef, G.M. (1991) 'Recent trends in Gestalt therapy in the United States and what we need to learn from them', *British Gestalt Journal*, 1 (1): 5–20.

Zimring, F.M. and Raskin, N.J. (1992) 'Carl Rogers and client/person-centred therapy', in D.K. Freedhaim (ed.), *History of Psychotherapy: A Century of Change*. Washington, DC: American Psychological Association. pp. 629–56.

Index